YUPIK

CHUKCHI SEA

Icy Cape

Wainwright

IÑUPIAT

Cape Schmidt

Point
Hope

Noatak River

Kobuk River

Kolyuchin
Bay

Kotzebue

Kotzebue
Sound

YUPIK

Uelen

Cape
Dezhnev

Cape Prince
of Wales

SEWARD
PENINSULA

INUPIAT

YUPIK

Dezhnevo

CHUKCHI PENINSULA

Bering Strait

Diomede
Islands

Port Clarence

Teller

Nome

Kresta Bay

Lavrentiya Bay

Sledge
Island

Safety
Sound

NORTON SOUND

St. Michael

Providemiya Bay

Plover Bay

Cape Chaplin

GULF OF
ANADYR

YUPIK

Emma
Harbor

Gambell

St. Lawrence
Island

Yukon River

YUPIK

BERING SEA

YUP'IK

Nunivak Island

0   100   200 mi
0   100   200   300 km

WHITE FOX AND ICY SEAS IN THE WESTERN ARCTIC

RECENT TITLES

Sovereignty for Survival: American Energy Development and Indian Self-Determination,
    by James Robert Allison III
George I. Sánchez: The Long Fight for Mexican American Integration,
    by Carlos K. Blanton
*White Fox and Icy Seas in the Western Arctic: The Fur Trade, Transportation, and Change
    in the Early Twentieth Century,* by John R. Bockstoce
Growing Up with the Country: Family, Race, and Nation after the Civil War,
    by Kendra Taira Field
*Grounds for Dreaming: Mexican Americans, Mexican Immigrants, and the California
    Farmworker Movement,* by Lori A. Flores
*The Yaquis and the Empire: Violence, Spanish Imperial Power, and Native Resilience in
    Colonial Mexico,* by Raphael Brewster Folsom
The American West: A New Interpretive History, Second Edition, by Robert V. Hine,
    John Mack Faragher, and Jon T. Coleman
*Legal Codes and Talking Trees: Indigenous Women's Sovereignty in the Sonoran and
    Puget Sound Borderlands, 1854–1946,* by Katrina Jagodinsky
Gathering Together: The Shawnee People through Diaspora and Nationhood, 1600–1870,
    by Sami Lakomäki
*An American Genocide: The United States and the California Indian Catastrophe,
    1846–1873,* by Benjamin Madley
*Home Rule: Households, Manhood, and National Expansion on the Eighteenth-Century
    Kentucky Frontier,* by Honor Sachs
The Cherokee Diaspora: An Indigenous History of Migration, Resettlement, and Identity,
    by Gregory D. Smithers
Wanted: The Outlaw Lives of Billy the Kid and Ned Kelly, by Robert M. Utley
First Impressions: A Reader's Journey to Iconic Places of the American Southwest,
    by David J. Weber and William deBuys

WHITE FOX AND ICY SEAS IN THE WESTERN ARCTIC

The Fur Trade, Transportation, and
Change in the Early Twentieth Century

John R. Bockstoce
Foreword by William Barr

Yale
UNIVERSITY
PRESS
New Haven & London

Published with assistance from the income of the
Frederick John Kingsbury Memorial Fund.

Published with assistance from the foundation established in memory of
Philip Hamilton McMillan of the Class of 1894, Yale College.

Yale University Press books may be purchased in quantity for educational, business, or
promotional use. For information, please e-mail sales.press@yale.edu (U.S. office) or
sales@yaleup.co.uk (U.K. office).

Original maps by Bill Nelson.
Set in Electra type by Integrated Publishing Solutions.
Printed in the United States of America.
Library of Congress Control Number: 2017951820
ISBN 978-0-300-22179-4 (hardcover : alk. paper)

A catalogue record for this book is available from the British Library.

This paper meets the requirements of ANSI/NISO Z39.48-1992 (Permanence of Paper).

10 9 8 7 6 5 4 3 2 1

To John J. Burns and John C. George,
friends and colleagues of fifty years

OTHER PUBLICATIONS BY
JOHN R. BOCKSTOCE

Furs and Frontiers in the Far North: The Contest among Native and Foreign Nations for the Bering Strait Fur Trade (2009)

High Latitude, North Atlantic: 30,000 Miles through Cold Seas and History (2003)

Arctic Discoveries: Images from Voyages of Four Decades in the North (2000)

Arctic Passages: A Unique Small Boat Voyage through the Great Northern Waterway (1991, 1992)

The Journal of Rochfort Maguire, 1852–1854. Two Years at Point Barrow, Alaska, aboard H.M.S. Plover *in the Search for Sir John Franklin* (editor) (1988)

Whales, Ice, and Men: The History of Whaling in the Western Arctic (1986, 1995)

American Whalers in the Western Arctic (with William Gilkerson) (1983)

The Voyage of the Schooner Polar Bear: *Whaling and Trading in the North Pacific and Arctic, 1913–1914 by Bernhard Kilian* (editor) (1983)

The Archaeology of Cape Nome, Alaska (1979)

Steam Whaling in the Western Arctic (1977)

Eskimos of Northwest Alaska in the Early Nineteenth Century: Based . . . on the Voyage of HMS Blossom *. . . in 1826 and 1827* (1977)

CONTENTS

FOREWORD

Soon after the establishment of Soviet (Bolshevik) control of Kamchatka and Chukotka in 1923, the international boundary between the Soviet Union and the United States (Alaska), running between Big and Little Diomede islands in Bering Strait, became a total barrier between two worlds—politically, socially, and commercially. But prior to that date the entire immense area from the Kolyma River in the west to Boothia Peninsula in the east possessed a remarkable degree of unity in economic terms, initially through Native trade networks and later through the American-European fur trade. As with his earlier work *Furs and Frontiers in the Far North* (2009), which deals with that trade until 1900, Bockstoce's present work embraces this enormous area.

The fur trade's supply routes reached their farthest extent to the east—that is, from Bering Strait or the Mackenzie River—in 1937, with the establishment of the Hudson's Bay Company's Fort Ross at the east end of Bellot Strait. It is therefore entirely appropriate that the opening chapter in Bockstoce's book deals with the establishment (and short life) of that trading post.

The white fox, which features in Bockstoce's title, had long been trapped earlier, but it became the mainstay of the fur trade in the Arctic following the collapse of the whaling industry in 1908, which had resulted in turn from a drastic change in women's fashions which saw the end of the boned corset. It is therefore equally appropriate that the second chapter in the book presents a remarkably detailed study of the species, followed by an equally detailed account of trapping; of skinning and preparing the pelts; of fur auctions; of grading, cleaning, and dyeing the fur; and of fur fashions in the early twentieth century. Rarely, if ever, has the topic been handled so comprehensively. This chapter provides an excellent introduction to the chapters that follow, detailing the evolution of the fur trade up until midcentury. These are divided into three parts, covering three periods—1899–1914, 1914–1929, and 1929–1950. Each of these parts consists of chapters dealing with the three major geographical regions involved: Chukotka, northern Alaska, and the Western Canadian Arctic.

The scholarship displayed is of an extremely high order, and the amount of time and effort invested in the research quite staggering. The bibliography of works consulted contains nearly four hundred titles. In addition, Bockstoce has studied manuscripts and other materials held in a large number of archives and institutions in the United Kingdom and North America, in many cases involving several collections in a particular repository (very few of them are online). He also cites twelve newspapers and periodicals that he consulted throughout. Even more impressive is the fact that he lists interviews or conversations with numerous individuals, including residents of settlements in northern Alaska and Arctic Canada, ranging in time from 1969 to the present. This represents the epitome of thorough scholarly historical research.

The high caliber of Bockstoce's research is matched by an engaging, readable style. The reader is introduced to a remarkable range of intriguing characters (even a possible/probable murderer). The text also contains details of many little-known and interesting aspects. For example, Bockstoce discusses the Hudson's Bay Company's "Siberian Venture," whereby the company expanded its activities into Chukotka and Kamchatka in 1919, and in 1923 negotiated a trading monopoly for that area with the Provisional Government. The reader is also introduced to two cases of abandoned ships that drifted around with the ice, as derelicts, for several years.

John Bockstoce is uniquely qualified to tackle his topic. In the 1970s he was privileged to be invited to be a member of an Eskimo whaling crew, hunting bowhead whales from an umiaq out of Point Hope, Alaska. Subsequently he has twice made transits of the Northwest Passage under his own command, once by umiaq and once in a steel-hulled sailboat, and is thus familiar with much of the area with which his book deals. No other historian can match these credentials for handling the topics of this book.

William Barr

PREFACE

For many centuries the peoples of the Western Arctic have adapted to and exploited external challenges and opportunities, one of which was a trade in furs that evolved from the Indigenous exchange systems that had existed among Native societies; however, their close embrace of a global fur trade began late in the eighteenth century, in 1789, when Russians established a trade fair in Chukotka, 4,000 miles east of European Russia and 800 miles west of Bering Strait, a fair that ultimately drew furs and other products via intra-Native trade networks from as far away as Alaska and Western Arctic Canada. Not long after this, in 1804, the Hudson's Bay Company (HBC) established a trading post at Fort Good Hope on the lower Mackenzie River. Three decades later the Russian-American Company built a fortified post in Alaska near the mouth of the Yukon River, and in 1840 the HBC advanced farther north on the Mackenzie with a post on the Peel River, where it traded with both Siglit and Gwich'in (see glossary).

By the middle of the nineteenth century a greater abundance of foreign goods became available to them with the arrival of whaling and trading fleets of the United States, France, Hawaii, and Australia. Native middlemen filled the gaps between the coastal trade and the trading posts, and throughout the region manufactured goods changed hands many times in return for furs, whalebone, and walrus ivory—commodities that ultimately were carried to markets in Asia, North America, and Europe.

But the inhabitants of the Western Arctic suddenly gained vastly increased access to manufactured supplies in 1899, when the gold rush city of Nome sprang up near Bering Strait on Alaska's Seward Peninsula and its resident fleet of small trading vessels spread throughout the region. Further access came when merchants of San Francisco and Seattle established posts in northern Alaska, while simultaneously the Hudson's Bay Company and its competitors commenced operations in the Mackenzie River delta and on the arctic coast.

This book focuses on the pursuit of white fox pelts by both Indigenous peoples and foreign trappers and traders, activities that took place during the early twentieth century in lands and waters that span 2,500 miles from eastern Chukotka in today's Russian Federation to the Boothia Peninsula in the Canadian Arctic. Oddly enough, this rugged and demanding enterprise was ultimately governed by tastes in fur fashion in the metropolitan centers of Europe and North America. The fur trade was a global business that involved many persons in the acquisition, transportation, manufacture, finance, and marketing of furs. Native peoples for the most part served as the primary producers in the acquisition of the furs throughout the Arctic, and they were joined in this pursuit by non-Native trappers, traders, and fur farmers from many nations. Yet the huge area that they exploited possessed a measure of uniformity. Until 1923, when the Soviets finally gained control of Chukotka, it was a vast, loosely integrated economic zone within which trappers and traders sought profits and adapted to the challenges of survival in an extreme climate, wherever they found themselves from year to year, whether by planning or by chance.

Unfortunately it is an undefined geographic region that offers no conveniently encompassing designation, and in this absence and for the purposes of this book, I have chosen to use the broad term "Western Arctic" as an economic and transportation area comprising the lands and waters of the greater Bering Strait region (including the Chukchi Peninsula of Russia), northern Alaska, the Arctic Slope of the Yukon, the Mackenzie River delta, Canada's continental arctic coast, its Western Arctic islands, and its Western Arctic Waterway. Within this district the participants in the fur trade included Chukchi, Siberian Yupik, Alaskan Eskimos, Alaskan and Canadian Gwich'in, Canadian Inuvialuit, Inuinnait, Inuit, persons of European descent, Russians, and many other foreign nationalities. All of these peoples—and there was much intermarriage among them—acquired knowledge and skills from the others, and their interrelations were in general remarkably amicable, resulting in the development of a unique trapping way of life, a hybrid melding of cultures that was relatively similar across the region.

It should be noted that the ethnonym "Inuit" (which in the 1990s superseded "Eskimo" in Canada) is awkward if it is broadly applied to those speakers of the Eskimo-Aleut language group. "Inuit" is correctly employed to describe the Natives of Canada's Central and Eastern Arctic (which in this volume include the Inuinnait of Coronation Gulf and Victoria Island), but today in the Mackenzie

River delta and on the Yukon's Arctic Slope the people refer to themselves as "Inuvialuit." In Alaska, however, "Eskimo" is commonly used as a general reference to include the Iñupiat of northern Alaska, the Inupiat and Yup'ik of western Alaska, and the Yupik who live on St. Lawrence Island. There is also a small Yupik population on the Chukchi Peninsula and on Wrangel Island. (For further discussions of the ethnonym "Eskimo" see Krupnik 2016: xvii; Goddard 1984: 5–7 and 1999; Kaplan 1999; and Carpenter 1997: 310.)

The book follows my two earlier histories, *Whales, Ice, and Men* (1986, 1995) and *Furs and Frontiers in the Far North* (2009). Like the two preceding volumes, it draws on research and fieldwork that I began in 1969 during my first visit to the Bering Strait region when I was an assistant on an archaeological survey on St. Lawrence Island. I was immediately struck by the severe beauty of the Bering Strait region and by the Natives' robust whaling and hunting societies. In the following years I continued my archaeological investigations in the region, and as an adjunct to those studies, for a decade I served as a member of an Eskimo whaling crew, hunting bowhead whales in spring on the ice of the Chukchi Sea at Point Hope, Alaska. There I saw firsthand that the Eskimos were participating in a hunt that had been ongoing for at least a thousand years, yet they were using whaling equipment, some of which had been manufactured in the United States in the nineteenth century. I became fascinated by how this mix of cultures had occurred and by the people of Point Hope and their rich history. This in turn led me to ask the elders of the community about their lives in the early twentieth century and the developments they had witnessed. In summers for the next twenty years I worked in boats, traveling along the coasts and among the islands of the North, from the lower Yukon River to Greenland. During those voyages, described in my book *Arctic Passages* (1991, 1992), I began to perceive how the lives of these "Northerners" (a phrase within which I aggregate both Natives and non-Natives) had changed because of their participation in the whaling industry and the fur trade—and in the opinion of most of them, mainly for the better.

As my understanding grew about the trade I was fortunate to be able to interview many elders throughout the region. These Northerners lived and trapped in one of the world's harshest environments and endured isolation in their pursuit of fox furs; but because of their energy, training, discipline, and skills, they mostly thrived at it, and for a time they were able to take advantage of the fur trade and use it for their own material gain, which they perceived as a betterment of their condition in an era when government services and social support were minimal or nonexistent. Their quiet competence and humorous descriptions of the hardships they endured impressed me immensely and made me want to know more. In my interviews I usually asked them if they felt that they had been exploited by the fur trade; they often laughed and shook their heads, saying no, adding that, on the contrary, *they* were the ones who were exploiting the fur trade for their own profit. The narratives of their lives during the fur trade decades became the basis of my studies, investigations that I expanded via examinations of written and oral archival collections and research in newspapers and periodicals, such as *Fur Trade Review*, the *Nome Nugget*, the *Edmonton Bulletin*, the *Seattle Post-Intelligencer*, and the Hudson's Bay Company's archives and its magazine, *The Beaver*.

It is an unfortunate but indisputable fact that the literature of the Western Arctic fur trade is dominated by non-Native observers. Natives' accounts of their own history, both written and oral, are far fewer. The result is that there are gaps within the records of Natives' descriptions of their own participation in the trade. I have tried to use as many of their reports as possible, but there are places in my narrative where Natives' observations about the fur trade would, no doubt, have enriched it.

The belief that the Native peoples were grossly exploited by fur traders has long been current, yet the Northerners willingly participated in these exchanges, and on both sides of the exchanges the trappers and traders usually thought they were receiving a favorable reward. As my investigations progressed it became clear to me that while, on one hand, northern trappers and traders, Natives and non-Natives alike, had been engaged in a relationship wherein each needed and depended upon the other, on the other hand, the traders, both large and small, were engaged in a sometimes bitter rivalry among themselves.

My glimpses of that era led me onward, to learn about the equally important activities of those who supplied the trade goods to the Northerners. Those traders were, for the most part, just as resilient and competent, and, in general, they were held in high regard by their customers. Persons such as Angulalik of Queen Maud Gulf, John Backland (senior and junior), Joe Bernard, Charlie Brower, Fred Carpenter of Banks Island, Charlie Klengenberg, Natkusiak ("Billy Banksland"), C. T. Pedersen, George Porter Sr., Ira Rank, Taaqpak of Point Barrow, and their families were proficient mariners and traders. They carried out their trade quietly and efficiently, year after year, and mostly without fanfare, in an environment where stories of shipwrecks and incompetence often drew the headlines. In the 1970s and 1980s, as I traversed thousands of miles in boats in the Western Arctic, I was forced to deal with some of the challenges that they routinely overcame, and as I began to understand something of the magnitude of their achievements, my admiration for the trappers and the traders only grew.

At every level, from the trapper to the retail furrier, the fur trade was a hard-nosed, extremely competitive, unforgiving business. Trapping and skinning foxes was messy and unpleasant, competition was fierce, and logistics were challenging. In fact, in those distant regions, thousands of miles from the sources of supplies, the fur trade was an enterprise that was concerned as much with solving the logistical challenges of transportation as it was about trade. In the arctic fur trade the furs were, of course, in remote, inaccessible places, but the trade goods originated in the South. The problem for the traders was how to swap them. The traders were forced to cope with the difficulties of transport in those waters—a very short shipping season, rudimentary charting, a lack of navigational aids, the dangers of ice floes, extreme cold, and violent weather—in their struggle to carry their supplies to the North and to return to the South with their furs; consequently the practicum of arctic marine navigation and ice-piloting constitutes an important element of this narrative.

It is difficult to overstate my admiration for those participants of the fur trade era in the Western Arctic, and this book is my attempt to shed light on a complex, quickly changing, and largely forgotten era.

Part 1

INTRODUCTION

This narrative begins in the last years of the nineteenth century and continues toward the midpoint of the twentieth, but one of the final acts in the expansion of the arctic fur trade took place in 1937, when the Hudson's Bay Company established its Fort Ross post on Somerset Island, at the nexus of the Western Arctic and Eastern Arctic shipping routes. Before addressing the history of the early twentieth-century fur trade in the Western Arctic, by way of introduction it is necessary to review the short-lived Fort Ross post as a paradigm for the larger story of the arctic fur trade (chapter 1) and then to examine the practical matters involved in the capture, manufacture, and marketing of arctic fox pelts, all of which affected the lives of the northern trapping families (chapter 2).

1

———————◆•◆———————

FORT ROSS: FOUNDING AND ABANDONMENT, 1937 TO 1948

FOUNDING THE POST

One of the last events in the expansion of the arctic fur trade took place only two years before the outbreak of the Second World War. Although the Hudson's Bay Company (HBC) had been trading for furs in northern Canada since receiving its royal charter in 1670, it was not until the beginning of the twentieth century that it began to operate on the arctic coast. At that time prices for arctic fox pelts had begun to rise, the result of furriers and couturiers in Europe and the United States appreciating the fashion potential for the arctic fox's dense, silky fur, which could be dyed to imitate more expensive fox pelts. In 1909 the company established a post on the Quebec shore of Hudson Strait, and for the next fifteen years it expanded throughout the Eastern Arctic. In the Western Arctic, in response to the advances of independent traders and competing trading houses in the Arctic, its advance began in 1912 with posts in the Mackenzie River delta and then in 1915 on the arctic coast at Herschel Island, not far from the Alaska border. The company aggressively continued this expansion with more new posts, and by 1923 it had moved its trading perimeter eastward 600 miles, as far as King William Island.

But the company's more remote Western Arctic posts had proved expensive to restock via the HBC supply route that ran north from Edmonton, Alberta, then down the Mackenzie River watershed (a distance of nearly 2,000 miles), and then through the Western Arctic Waterway. Occasionally, when heavy concentrations of ice had impeded shipping, these posts had proved difficult to reach at all. Consequently a new post at Bellot Strait seemed to offer the opportunity of supplying the stations on and near King William Island via the Eastern Arctic. There, it was thought, a boat from the west might rendezvous with a ship from the east and return west with cargo for the King William Island area.

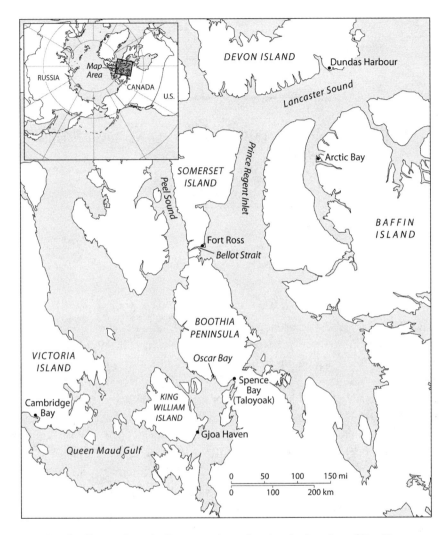

Boothia Peninsula and adjacent regions, showing the location of Fort Ross.

In late August 1937, the Hudson's Bay Company's 285-foot icebreaker *Nascopie* steamed south out of Lancaster Sound in the Canadian Arctic. Moving through seas that were nearly ice free, the ship headed down Prince Regent Inlet, slipping slowly past Somerset Island's steep limestone cliffs. The 2,500-ton *Nascopie* was headed to Bellot Strait, the fifteen-mile east-west gash that separates Somerset Island from the Boothia Peninsula, which itself is the northernmost projection of continental North America. Lying just above the seventy-second parallel of latitude, the strait is nearly 400 miles north of the Arctic Circle, but more significantly, it is the southernmost meeting point of the waters of the Eastern and Western Arctic. The strait is one of several routes through the Northwest Passage, the waterway across the top of North America between the Atlantic and Pacific oceans. A little more than a mile wide at its narrowest, the result is a tidal millrace that at times can flow faster than nine miles per hour.

On the afternoon of September 1 the *Nascopie* anchored at the strait's eastern approaches while Captain Thomas Smellie, with Chief Trader William ("Paddy") Gibson and HBC District Manager J. W. Anderson, quickly departed in the ship's motor scow to take soundings and to scout the shore for the site of a new trading post, a post that would lie at the most distant range of the company's Eastern Arctic supply route. The next day the captain cautiously brought the *Nascopie* a mile closer to the coast and anchored in Depot Bay. "He had been fortunate in reaching Bellot Strait so easily," the young archaeologist Graham Rowley remembered, "and he was well aware of the danger of ice moving in and imprisoning his ship for the winter." In Depot Bay Gibson and Anderson found a suitable spot to erect the buildings: the bay offered reasonable protection from swells and moving ice, and it had a good landing beach, with fresh water nearby.

The *Nascopie* was the first foreign vessel to reach there since 1859, when the explorer Francis Leopold McClintock had discovered the fate of Sir John Franklin's missing expedition. The ship arrived, however, not on a voyage of discovery, but in a bold attempt to establish a foothold in one of the most remote regions of the Canadian Arctic. The Hudson's Bay Company's staff planned to inaugurate a shipping route between the company's Eastern and Western Arctic posts and, with this link, to establish a commercial use of part of the Northwest Passage.[1]

Aboard the *Nascopie* were three Inuit families who had joined the ship at the settlement of Arctic Bay on northern Baffin Island. Although a group of local Natsilingmiut hunted in the area, the Baffin Islanders would be the first Inuit residents to trap for furs near the Fort Ross post with the support of the Hudson's Bay Company. The Baffin Islanders' journey had actually begun three years before, in 1934, when Hudson's Bay Company men had persuaded a number of Inuit families from several regions of the island to accompany them to an experimental settlement for hunting and trapping on the north coast of Lancaster Sound at Dundas Harbour on Devon Island—with the proviso that they could return to their homelands after two years if they wished. The Inuit were disappointed to find poor hunting at Dundas Harbour, and most of the families returned home. A few of them had, however, spent the winter of 1936–1937 near the company's post at Arctic Bay on northern Baffin Island before moving, yet

The Hudson's Bay Company's schooner *Aklavik*,
which reached Fort Ross from the Western Arctic in
1937 to rendezvous with the *Nascopie* and establish
the first commercial use of the Northwest Passage.
Archives of Manitoba, Hudson's Bay Company
Archives (HBCA) 1987-258-93.

again, to Fort Ross. On arrival, the eighteen Inuit pioneers went ashore with
their baggage, sleds, and thirty-seven dogs to set up camp at the new site, and
the crew began discharging cargo and lumber for the buildings.

While anchoring in Depot Bay, the *Nascopie*'s men spotted a small vessel
approaching from the west in Bellot Strait. It was the company's fifty-eight-foot
wooden supply schooner *Aklavik*, inbound from Cambridge Bay on Victoria
Island. Ten minutes later the *Aklavik* was alongside the ship. The crew included
Captain E. J. ("Scotty") Gall, trader J. R. Ford, and Patsy Klengenberg, a son of

Scotty Gall, captain of the *Aklavik*, at Fort Ross,
1937. Archives of Manitoba, HBCA 2004-7-90.

the pioneering Western Arctic fur trading couple, Charlie Klengenberg and his
wife Qimniq, from Point Hope, Alaska. Patsy's family accompanied him aboard
the *Aklavik*.

The *Aklavik* had endured a difficult voyage—to say the least. Scotty Gall
had waited in Cambridge Bay until the HBC motor supply boat *Audrey B.* arrived with cargo. But, sadly, just before the *Audrey B.* reached Cambridge Bay,
Scotty's wife Anna Fagerstrom died suddenly of heart failure. She was buried at
Cambridge Bay. It is a measure of Scotty Gall's commitment to the company—
and perhaps his need to cope with his grief via hard work—that the next day
the crews of both vessels transferred the cargo, and he immediately set off for
the east aboard the *Aklavik* on a voyage of more than 500 miles. After delivering
freight to the HBC's post at Gjoa Haven on King William Island the schooner
continued up the west coast of the Boothia Peninsula toward Bellot Strait. Pack
ice closed in on the *Aklavik* several times, threatening to crush it, but worse,
as it approached the western entrance of the strait, the tidal race caught the
schooner and swept it toward the rocky shore just as a clogged fuel strainer shut

Patsy Klengenberg, who with his wife and son
were the crew of the *Aklavik* in 1937. Archives of
Manitoba, HBCA 1987-258-94.

down the engine. The crew scrambled to make repairs and managed to bring
the engine back to life in the nick of time. Although the *Aklavik*'s reverse gear
was also broken, it was able to motor east through the strait at half speed.

With the *Aklavik* secured alongside the *Nascopie*, the senior staff aboard the
ship noticed that the Gjoa Haven post manager Lorenz Alexander Learmonth
was not aboard the schooner as planned. L. A. Learmonth, a widely experienced arctic trader and rugged northern traveler, had been one of the principal
advocates for establishing the new post, and Learmonth was anxious to arrive
first at Bellot Strait to choose the site for Fort Ross. Accordingly, he and his
assistant Donald G. ("Jock") Sturrock had set out from Gjoa Haven before the
Aklavik arrived from Cambridge Bay. On July 30, towing a sixteen-foot canoe,
they departed in a motorized whaleboat in an attempt to cover the 275 miles by
water and to be first to reach the eastern entrance of the strait.

At 10:30 PM on September 3, bedraggled, weather-beaten, and nearly out of
fuel for their outboard motor, Learmonth and Sturrock arrived at the ship in

Building Fort Ross, 1937. With snow already on the ground, the
passengers and crew of the *Nascopie* scrambled to build the
post before hastily leaving for the South before freeze
up. Archives of Manitoba, HBCA 1987-363-F-56-10.

their small canoe. Ice and foul weather had forced them ashore on the mainland for a week, and then, when they were only about thirty miles from the
western end of the strait, pack ice had blocked them for a further ten days. In
the end, fed up, they cached their whaleboat, portaged the canoe across the
Boothia Peninsula to its eastern shore, and proceeded onward. On August 31,
fifteen miles from Fort Ross, they came upon an encampment of about thirty
Natsilingmiut, and there they were weather-bound yet again. "It was a hard and
grueling trip that few would have undertaken," J. W. Anderson wrote, "but for
Learmonth it was routine." Learmonth was bitterly disappointed at not having
reached the site before the *Nascopie* because he had located "an excellent site
for the post on the other side of the strait; it was now, however, too late to consider a change," Graham Rowley recalled.

That day the ship's crew, assisted by passengers, had raised the framework of
the post's staff house and began fastening the siding, and the next day the small
schooner *Seal*, which had been carried as deck cargo aboard the *Nascopie* to

serve as the post's tender, went south to the Inuit camp to alert its inhabitants that there soon would be a trading post much closer to their lands.

Ernie Lyall was another arctic veteran who was a member of the first group to winter at Fort Ross. He was impressed by the richness of the resources at Bellot Strait: "The hunting around Fort Ross was really good. You could get everything there," he remembered, "narwhals, white [beluga] whales, walrus, caribou, all sorts of seals. And trapping was really good." In fact, as an indication of the trapping potential of Fort Ross, when the HBC men had gone ashore on September 2, they were greeted by a number of arctic foxes that ran to the water's edge.

By September 6, while the work on the buildings proceeded at a frantic pace, the weather turned colder and snow now covered the land. The *Aklavik* was beached to allow the men to work on its shaft and propeller, while aboard the *Nascopie* the chief engineer had been toiling flat out to make a new reverse gear for the *Aklavik*. Two days later, as noted by Rowley, "the symbolic exchange of cargo [had been] made and recorded by every camera on the ship and, with due ceremony and a speech or two, a wreath was thrown into the sea in memory of Sir John Franklin." The buildings were now secure, all cargo had been stored, and L. A. Learmonth and his assistant were ashore at the new post. Just before going ashore Learmonth had fallen from the rigging and cracked several of his ribs, but he said nothing and continued on, a testament to his dedication. Ernie Lyall, who would serve as the post's interpreter, was also there with his family. At 6:30 PM on September 8, 1937, the *Aklavik*, with Paddy Gibson, Jock Sturrock, and Patsy Klengenberg and his family, started west through Bellot Strait, and the *Nascopie*, with Scotty Gall aboard, weighed anchor and proceeded toward home.

Several days later the *Nascopie* received the following radio message: "Gjoa Haven, King William Island. . . . The schooner *Aklavik* arrived safely here on the fourteenth of September, thus completing the first successful freighting of goods in via the North-west Passage. Chief Inspector W. Gibson sends his best regards to all the passengers on board the *Nascopie* and wishes them all the best of luck."[2]

The Hudson's Bay men were justifiably proud of what they had accomplished, having successfully founded a post at the most distant range of the company's Eastern Arctic supply route. They realized that it had been a historic achievement: the *Aklavik* had become the first foreign vessel to transit Bellot Strait, and part of the Northwest Passage had thereby become an experimental commercial transportation way. Their news was broadcast both by the Canadian Broadcasting Corporation and by the National Broadcasting Company in the United States. "Fort Ross was on the map," J. W. Anderson remembered, "and another pioneering job [was] done by the 'men of the Hudson's Bay.'"[3]

CLOSING FORT ROSS

At first the Fort Ross venture appeared to work, and for the next four years the *Nascopie* met the schooner from the Western Arctic at Bellot Strait. But in 1942 the ship ran into heavy ice in Prince Regent Inlet, ice that it could not break through, and the *Nascopie* was forced to return south with the Fort Ross supplies.

Many arctic trading posts were provisioned for more than a year in case the annual resupply mission should fail to reach them; consequently at first there was no great anxiety for the small settlement, nor for the local Inuit. According to Barbara Heslop, whose husband Bill had replaced L. A. Learmonth at Fort Ross in 1940, "By April [1943], a year and a half after we had received our last supplies, Darcy Munro, the post clerk, and three natives took two dog-teams to Arctic Bay for mess supplies, ammunition, and a few other essentials for the Eskimos. This was a round trip of five hundred miles, and it was not without its hazards, as part of the journey was made on moving ice in Prince Regent Inlet. With these supplies, supplemented by other food . . . we estimated we had sufficient to carry us through until ship time in September."

Even so, "About the middle of August 1943, we began to have doubts as to the possibility of the ship reaching us. Although the ice had broken up, it had moved very little, remaining solidly packed in all the bays and harbours. We could not even take our small boats out in the waters around the post. . . . One evening in September we sighted the *Nascopie* about fifteen miles off shore. We thought our worries were over," she wrote, "but it was not until later that we were to realize that they were just beginning." None of the participants ashore or aboard the *Nascopie* foresaw that the ship would once again be unable to deliver the supplies to Fort Ross.[4]

Aboard the *Nascopie* "all on board ship were in a happy mood," Lewis Robinson recalled. "Since the boat left Montreal the big question in everyone's mind was whether we would reach Fort Ross this year. . . . Our preparations to land the next day were premature, however. Towards evening we again met more scattered ice. Soon the masses were packed closer together and open water became less and less. Finally there was no open water ahead—nothing but a mass of broken blocks of ice, jammed together and wedged one over the other. . . . The following morning . . . the temperature was 28 degrees [Fahrenheit] above and new ice about one inch thick had formed in the cracks between the ice blocks. . . . After reversing engines the ship moved forward a distance of its own length and smashed into a solid field of ice, which stretched ahead to the horizon. We travelled about fifty yards, but were stopped again as the bow slid up on a sheet of ice which would not break."

At noon the ship was only about twenty miles from Fort Ross and started to make a little headway. The crew could see the eastern entrance to Bellot Strait, but once again the ice brought the *Nascopie* to a halt. The next day, September 18, the temperature dropped to 22 degrees, but worse, the wind shifted to the north, packing the ice in tighter. "For an hour the ship plunged into the ice," Robinson wrote. "Fourteen times we reversed and came grinding, crashing, pushing forward. Sometimes we made ten yards, but usually less."[5]

Captain Smellie then gave up icebreaking for the rest of the day, while the south-flowing current carried the ship, surrounded by ice, to a position off the entrance to Bellot Strait. The following day the *Nascopie* was only able to move half its length. "It was apparent that it was a hopeless task and a waste of coal to smash through when a storm or strong wind would break up the pack and give us a lead. Thus, strangely enough, amid the icy emptiness of the bleak Arctic, where storms were the fear of all navigators, about sixty men and two women prayed for a storm."

"Due to wartime restrictions on radio communications from ships, at no time were we in radio contact with the people at Fort Ross, although both parties were equipped for it." J. W. Anderson continued, "We often wondered how the three [Hudson's Bay Company] people felt about us being so close to them and yet so far away. We knew that our smoke was visible for several miles when the ship was breaking ice. We were told afterwards . . . that they saw us for two days before we drifted southward out of sight."[6]

On September 21, with the temperature hovering between 24 and 26 degrees, Captain Smellie again tried to make headway and again was able to cover only 100 yards, while the crew and passengers began to think about the possibility that they themselves might be trapped for the winter. But at noon the ship began to move a little, and it entered a narrow lead between the floes. The *Nascopie* began to grind ahead northward, moving into slightly larger leads until finally it reached relatively clear water. "Fort Ross was about thirty miles behind us," Lewis Robinson wrote. "Our problem was no longer to try to reach there; it was to bring the ship out safely. With no chance to land supplies at the post, it was with sad hearts that we realized that our failure meant that the post would have to be abandoned. The *Nascopie* had failed in her mission, but had won the fight for survival."[7]

Those ashore at Fort Ross were deeply despondent: "For three days we saw her or her smoke, on the horizon and it was evident she was having difficulty in the ice-pack," Barbara Heslop wrote. "That was an anxious three days, but we didn't give up until we finally saw her heading north with black smoke." Aboard the *Nascopie* Lewis Robinson was devastated: "How their hearts must have sunk as they prepared to begin a third year without supplies!"[8]

At Fort Ross "this called for a conference," Barbara continued, "and after taking stock of our dwindling supplies we recognized our position was definitely not good. Our foodstuffs were low, and our meals had little variation. For some time we had been without butter, milk, coffee, fruits and canned vegetables excepting beans. We all became very diligent hunters, always hoping to bag any wild game. Seals as a rule are plentiful at Fort Ross, but owing to the heavy ice-pack we were not able to get as many as we ordinarily would use."

Meanwhile, at the Canadian headquarters of the Hudson's Bay Company in Winnipeg, Manitoba, the senior staff was alarmed at the situation of Fort Ross. Robert Chesshire, the manager of the Fur Trade Department, kept the Heslops informed of rescue plans by radio. "We knew," noted Barbara, "that the Company would do all it could to get supplies to us by plane and to take us out if that was possible. We realized nothing could be done during the month of October as the weather then is not good for flying because of heavy fogs. But this condition usually clears with colder weather in November." However, she added, "We also knew we would see the last of the sun on November 17, and the days would soon grow short."

The U.S. Army Air Force (USAAF) was asked to undertake the mission to re-supply Fort Ross and positioned a Douglas C-47 "Skytrain" (the military version of a DC-3), fitted with special tires, skis, and long-range fuel tanks, to wait for suitable flying conditions. On the first attempt blowing snow forced the plane to turn back, but "November 4 turned out to be a perfect day for flying." Barbara Heslop continued, "They were to fly over the post and drop supplies by parachute." Leaving Bill Heslop and Darcy Munro to man the radio, she headed two miles away with a group of Inuit to Hazard Inlet, a small bay, which, unlike the bay in front of the post, was covered by smooth ice.

Captain J. F. Stanwell-Fletcher—who formerly had been an arctic trapper and a member of the Royal Canadian Mounted Police but now was with the USAAF—had been assigned to parachute in with the supplies. As soon as the supplies had been dropped Stanwell-Fletcher bailed out, landed, and rolled safely. Having had only one day's parachute instruction prior to the mission, not only was this his first parachute jump in the field, it was the first jump made in Arctic Canada and perhaps in the entire Arctic.

Stanwell-Fletcher's task was to locate a landing place for a plane where the

ice was smooth and thick. Guided by the Inuit, he chose a lake ten miles from
Fort Ross and staked out a 3,000-foot runway, marked with snow blocks covered
with coal sacks. On November 7 word arrived that a plane was on the way. "All
our baggage was loaded on dog-sleds and we took it to the selected spot, two and a
half hours journey away," Barbara Heslop remembered. A year's supplies were delivered to the Inuit and the Hudson's Bay Company's personnel were evacuated.[9]

At last, in 1944, the *Nascopie* managed to force its way through heavy pack
ice in Prince Regent Inlet and succeeded in reaching Fort Ross on September
1. With a crowd of enthusiastic Inuit greeting the ship, J. W. Stanners and his
assistant Ken Hunt reopened the post and raised the company flag. "Everything
about the post was spick and span," wrote J. W. Anderson. "So orderly and tidy
was the dwelling that one would hardly think Mrs. Heslop had left hurriedly . . .
in November 1943." For two days the crew ferried supplies ashore and set up the
radio station, while several government officials surveyed the Inuit population
to evaluate its well-being and health. Before the ship departed on September 3
one of the officials married Ernie Lyall and his Inuk wife Nipisha. Ernie was the
HBC interpreter who helped found Fort Ross and had stayed with the Inuit.

The *Nascopie* resupplied Fort Ross again in 1945 and 1946, but in July 1947, it
struck an uncharted reef in Hudson Strait and sank near Cape Dorset on Baffin
Island. By then, however, the company's senior staff had concluded that the
post could not be maintained—it was simply too difficult to reach. In March
1948, it was closed permanently. Ken Hunt, the clerk, went east by dog team to
Arctic Bay, and Post Manager Stanners headed west to Gjoa Haven and onward
to Cambridge Bay.

In late August 1948, the Hudson's Bay Company's motor vessel *Nigalik*, arriving from the west, delivered supplies for a new post, 150 miles south of Fort
Ross, at Spence Bay (today, Taloyoak, Nunavut) on the west side of the Boothia
Isthmus, where it would be easier to resupply from Tuktoyaktuk, via the Western Arctic Waterway.

The Fort Ross venture had been a daring experiment but a step too far. The
difficulties that the *Aklavik* and Learmonth had encountered in 1937 might
have been a warning to the company's planners, and it appears that they had
ignored—or were unaware of—the advice of Major L. T. Burwash, who from
1925 to 1930 had carried out exploratory surveys for the Canadian government
in the Central Arctic. Burwash wrote in 1931: "To sum up the possibilities of the
route it may be said that the possible season of navigation is very short and sub-
ject to serious complications due to ice floes at any time. . . . Much will depend
upon the summer ice conditions which vary from year to year and much upon
the prevailing winds."[10]

Fort Ross was established for several reasons, but central among them was the optimistic premise that a strong market would continue for arctic furs. But this event took place eight years after the price of white fox pelts had reached its peak. By 1937 the value of a good white fox skin had dropped to only a third of its 1929 price, when the arctic fur trade was in retreat, when many traders and trappers were abandoning the pursuit for northern furs, leaving the Hudson's Bay Company in monopoly control in the Canadian Arctic. At the same time only a handful of traders were still operating in northern Alaska, and the Soviet state had achieved complete control of the fur production of Chukotka.

2

WHITE FOX: FROM THE TRAPPER
TO THE RETAIL CUSTOMER

To understand the history of the arctic fur trade in the early twentieth century it is essential to recognize the practical techniques, skills, and business realities of acquiring, manufacturing, and marketing the pelts, that is, to examine the activities that drove the trade—in the field, in the auction houses, and in the workshops prior to their sale as finished garments.

In 1912 the pioneering arctic naturalist Dr. Rudolph Martin Anderson declared, "The white fox is the staple fur of the Arctic coast, and the common medium of exchange." His was an accurate evaluation of the state of the fur trade, acknowledging the realities and attraction of an endeavor that had once been peripheral to the Natives' lives. Trapping certainly became the primary source of income for many Northerners, both Native and non-Native, in the early twentieth century. For those in the subarctic Mackenzie River delta, muskrats and mink also provided reliable revenue, but apart from subsistence hunting and fishing, for those living farther north, throughout the Arctic their principal occupation would become the quest for white fox pelts for commercial trade.

Traders in the Arctic purchased a wide variety of furs, some of which had been taken far away, occasionally hundreds of miles south of the treeline, and then traded north. For example, from 1899 to 1938 at Barrow, Alaska (today, Utqiaġvik), Charlie Brower, the agent for H. Liebes and Company, furriers of San Francisco, bought seal, lynx, ermine, mink, otter, wolf, polar bear, grizzly bear, black bear, marten, beaver, and muskrat pelts, in addition to whalebone (baleen) and walrus ivory. He also acquired nearly 2,900 red fox skins in several color phases ("red," "cross," and, the most valuable of all, "silver"). But, most important, he bought more than 32,000 arctic fox pelts.[1]

An arctic fox in its full winter coat. North Slope Borough (Alaska),
Department of Wildlife Management, photographer: Kalyn MacIntyre.

ARCTIC FOX

The arctic fox, also commonly called the white fox (*Vulpes lagopus*), is among the most highly adapted of arctic mammals. Living primarily beyond the treeline on tundra and frozen oceans, it is found in northernmost Europe, Asia, North America, Iceland, Greenland, western Alaska (including the Pribilof Islands and St. Matthew Island), the Hudson Bay region, northern Quebec, and coastal Labrador.

Arctic foxes generally weigh from six to ten pounds, with a length of about forty-three inches including their bushy tail. An arctic fox has a small, compact body, with a short muzzle, legs, and ears, as well as a thick fur covering on its paws, and it has excellent circulation in its legs. Most important, however, is its heavy, luxurious winter coat comprised of long silky guard hairs and dense underfur. The guard hairs cover the underfur and protect it, while the underfur insulates the fox's core temperature, allowing it to live in extreme cold—well in excess of minus 40 degrees.

In winter, arctic foxes appear in two pelt colors, white and "blue," both of which may occur in the same litter. White-color foxes are pure white, with perhaps a few black-tipped guard hairs. They begin to shed their winter coat in early April, molting into a gray-to-dark-brown coat on their back and sides. In September and October they begin to grow their winter coat, which is complete by November. During the autumn molt the fox's back and tail are the last parts of the coat to become fully white. The "blue" foxes (which are the manifestation of a recessive gene) in winter vary in color from slate gray to dark blue-black: "more on the order of the blue seen in the fur of maltese cats," wrote the trapper and publisher A. R. Harding.[2]

In summer, blues are a uniform dark blue-black. The ratio of whites to blues varies among populations across the Arctic, with the white phase predominant in mainland Europe, North America, and Asia, in which blues represent only 1 to 2 percent of the population. Blues are found in greater proportion in Greenland. Depending on fashion's dictates, blue fox pelts have sold for several times—occasionally for *many* times—the price of white pelts, a fact which not only stimulated the development of fur farms specializing in ranch-breeding blues but also encouraged fur dyers to imitate blues by altering whites with dyes.

Arctic foxes are omnivorous. They consume a variety of foods, including lemmings, voles, ground squirrels, insects, snails, hares, fish, seabirds, ptarmigan, bird eggs, ringed seal pups, berries, and such wave-cast marine debris as fish, mollusks, invertebrates, and seaweed. They also scavenge from whale, caribou, and walrus carcasses and often range far offshore on sea ice, foraging on the carrion of seals killed by polar bears.

"In the fall of the year after the ice makes on the ocean they leave in droves, coming back in the spring if the ice lets them," Charlie Brower observed during his sixty years at Barrow, Alaska. "All winter they live on the ice following the polar bears, and living on what they leave from their kills, mostly seals. Then in the early spring [the foxes] catch the young seals that are born on top of the ice under the snow, smelling them out and digging until they reach where they lay. The young seals do not go in the water until they are over a month old and are just fine hunting for the foxes. If a dead whale drifts in near the shore and stays all winter[,] hundreds of foxes will be caught around it."[3]

Lemmings and voles are a primary terrestrial food resource for white foxes. The fox's exceptional hearing and sense of smell allow it to locate the rodents under the snow and to pounce on them by breaking through the snow cover. The populations of lemmings fluctuate widely, however, going through booms and crashes, causing the numbers of white foxes to fluctuate in similar cycles of about three to five years.

When food is plentiful foxes will bury surplus food in caches, and they will constantly move their hoarded stores, reburying them again and again. "All summer the white foxes are burying food that they seem to be able to find no matter how much snow is over it," wrote Charlie Brower, "I have watched them as they robbed a duck's nest[,] carry the eggs away and bury them in the moss[,] never putting more than one in the same place[.] If they have a bird[,] after eating what they want[,] the rest is put away in the ground for later use." John C. George, an arctic wildlife biologist who cared for a colony of captive arctic foxes in Barrow, Alaska, told me that the foxes "would stash most of the food we fed them. In spring 100s of (chicken) eggs, chicken wings, seal scraps etc that we had fed thru the winter thawed out of the snow drifts. In amazement, my thought at the time was, 'Did they eat anything at all last winter?'"[4]

White foxes form breeding pairs in March and April and often seek previously excavated dens in dry, sandy soil, some of which are used year after year. "A good den for raising young . . . has many entrances and a number of chambers, giving the foxes lots of options for quick escape underground and comfortable living," Donald Reid stated, adding, "However, good den sites are rare. They need relatively dry soil that is easy enough to dig out but not so coarse and soft that it will collapse, combined with a good vantage from which to search for danger, and southerly exposure to keep warm. Such sites are used repeatedly, and the foxes clean and fix them with extra digging most summers. Dens can last for decades."[5]

"At times in the spring while I have been whaling," Charlie Brower recalled, "I have seen fox after fox come from the pack [ice] on their way to ashore to where they will have their young. Generally they begin to come ashore along in April." He added, "White foxes are the most plentiful in the north. Seldom do they go far inland . . . where ever they find a suitable place to dig their homes in the banks." Litters average seven pups but may contain as many as fifteen. "Many young are killed by the white owls that hang around the dens[,] waiting till they come out playing," said Brower.[6]

Other than man, the arctic fox's predators are red foxes (which are larger than white foxes and overlap their southern range), wolves, wolverines, snowy owls, eagles, and perhaps lynx. When red foxes are plentiful, the catch of white foxes can decline markedly. Rabies and canine distemper also affect white fox numbers. Nevertheless, the International Union for the Conservation of Nature and Natural Resources lists the arctic fox as a species of "least concern" for its survival: "In most areas . . . population status is believed to be good. . . . Because of their large reproductive capacity, Arctic Foxes can maintain population levels under high hunting pressure. In some areas, up to 50% of the total population has been harvested on a sustainable basis."[7]

THE TRAPPER AND THE TRAPPER'S FAMILY

The family was central to an arctic trapper's work. Only in a very few instances was an arctic trapper able to operate on his own; rather, his work on
the trapline was a product of family support and a mutual effort by his wife and
children to enable him to operate. His wife was essential to his activities, and
they worked together in a shared division of labor. She maintained the camp,
prepared the food, assisted in skinning, fleshing, and drying the pelts, looked
after the children and sometimes the dogs—and often set some traps of her
own near the camp. Most important, she made the clothing and footwear that
allowed the family to live and work in the punishing cold of winter where 160
days of the year may average below zero degrees Fahrenheit and temperatures
can fall to minus fifty.[8]

Beyond the family unit, in northern Alaska it was common for two or three
trapping families to build camps together for mutual support. This web of cooperation provided a margin of safety for all and let the trapper concentrate his
energies on securing pelts.[9]

It required skill, study, and endurance to become a successful white fox
trapper. The human geographer Peter Usher observed that "although the rudi-
ments of trapping can be learned quickly, the refinement of its skills comes only
through years of experience. Even the best trappers feel they are still learning,
although some men in their late twenties and early thirties are already highly
skilled. To gain an intimate knowledge of fox behaviour is considered to take
even longer, however. The mastery of this aspect of trapping is generally agreed
to lie with a very few older trappers." He added, "There is no substitute for 30 or
40 years' experience."[10]

An important consideration was the type of trap to use. Before the advent
of the fur trade white foxes had been of relatively marginal use to the Natives
because they provided little food and their pelts were not large or durable; nevertheless, long before the arrival of metal traps in the Arctic, Natives had been
trapping a variety of fur bearers by using several devices and methods, but primarily they employed deadfall traps. A deadfall is in essence a heavy weight—such
as rocks, ice, or logs—propped up by a trigger device on which bait is set. It is
designed to collapse when an animal wrenches bait from the prop mechanism,
causing the weight to fall, pinning the quarry under the heavy fall weight, killing it quickly.

It was not until the 1860s or 1870s that metal foot-hold traps reached the
Bering Strait region. By the early 1880s Point Barrow Eskimos had acquired
them from whalers and trading ships and were using them in addition to dead-

An Oneida Victor number 1½ longspring trap. Author's collection.

fall traps. By one estimate, the use of steel traps increased the catch of foxes by northern Alaskan Natives tenfold. Metal traps were easier to set and maintain, and as a result, steel foot-hold traps had largely replaced most deadfall traps there by the end of the nineteenth century.[11]

Initially the northern Natives used a variety of types of foot-hold traps to capture white foxes, but by the beginning of the twentieth century two basic styles of traps were commonly employed: the longspring design, which contained a U-shaped spring that protruded from the side of the trap jaws, and the lighter and more compact underspring, or "jump trap," with a single arm of spring steel set directly beneath the trap jaws. When captured, the fox usually froze to death quickly.

The traps were made in various sizes, but one of the most popular for capturing arctic foxes was the number 1½ longspring, a trap that was manufactured by several companies. It had an open-jaw spread of a little less than five inches. "The number 1½ used to be the principal trap . . . for everything up to and including foxes," wrote the trapper Edward Finnerty.[12]

"How do you catch fur?" This rhetorical question was posed by A. R. Harding at the beginning of the twentieth century. His answer: "Remove all suspicion and lay a great temptation." Although white foxes are not as wary of traps and human beings as are red foxes, trap placement was important, and it was an artifact of the trapper's close study of fox behavior and his familiarity with his trapline and its landscape. "Trapping is not easy nor can the art be learned overnight," was the opinion of a reporter in *Fortune* magazine in 1936. He continued, "Raymond Spears, a literary woodcrafter, once followed an Adirondack trapper over 150 miles of trap line with a notebook in his hand and calculated that it required knowledge of 3,000 individual facts to place a single mink trap."[13]

"Over the years one gets to know how animals move around in relation to physiography of the area, specific features along the line such as shoreline, gulley, brush lines, knolls, ridges, exposures, etc.," the Alaskan biologist and trapper John J. Burns told me. "On arctic tundra," the *Alaska Trappers Manual* advises, "where there are few natural landmarks, the wind creates small mounds of snow around dead animals, grass tussocks and other small shrubs, which are attractors to the foxes and provide a lookout point for the foxes, which provides an excellent area for the trapper to make his set." According to William Van Valin, who lived at Barrow, Alaska, from 1912 to 1918 and studied trapping techniques, "A high point of ground is preferable in that it can be seen for some distance and does not get deeply covered with snow."[14]

If no natural high point was nearby, the trapper might simply build a mound from snow or earth. Such mounds attracted the fox's curiosity, and many trappers made "blind sets" by concealing their traps on or near them, using a snow knife (often a long-bladed butcher's knife) to excavate a shallow hole in firmly packed snow or by pounding a depression into the tundra with the butt of an axe. The trapper then carefully placed the trap in the depression he had created. He might secure the trap's chain by anchoring it with a spike or by putting a stick through the chain's terminal ring to form a toggle or "deadman," which was "stomped hard" into the snow, as David Greist put it, where it would freeze solid. If the trap was placed near an animal carcass, the trapper might wire it directly to the remains. He often then dug a shallow trench to cover the chain in the snow.

But the trap itself had to be protected from freezing to the surrounding snow. To prevent this the trapper often placed a thin tissue (for example, one-ply toilet paper, waxed paper, facial tissue, or similar materials) beneath the trap and folded it over at least one of the trap's jaws. The trap was then concealed by a wafer of snow. "You then carved a thin, pancake-like slice of snow," David Greist remembered. "Very carefully you placed this over the opened jaws of the trap and then, with the knife, you scraped back and forth until the snow pancake was very thin." The trapper had to be careful that this wafer of snow was set absolutely level because if it slanted to windward of the trap, the wind would gradually erode the snow covering and expose the trap, or if it slanted to leeward, it could become covered by drift snow.[15]

Other trappers concealed the trap with coarse snow, "what they call in Eskimo *pukak.*" "It's just like grain," said Waldo Bodfish, an Iñupiaq trapper from Wainwright, Alaska. Simon Paneak, another highly respected Iñupiaq elder, also described the technique: "Over along the Arctic coast, where there is a lot of wind, we know how to cover the trap with old granulated snow. Granulated snow is much better than snow from a new bank, as new snow is no good after it gets frozen hard. The granulated snow never gets spoiled for quite a while unless a [covering of] snow buries it." Some trappers in windy areas built a small "cubby" of snow blocks around the trap to keep it from being buried by blowing snow or exposed by the friction of the wind.[16]

If the trap had been set near an animal carcass there was no need to set bait, but if it was set elsewhere it had to be baited. Trappers used a variety of baits depending on what was available. These could be blubber, bits of seal, caribou entrails, rotten fish, or other meat scraps. Small pieces of bait were then scattered around the trap. In describing trapping the blue foxes that had been introduced to many islands in the Aleutians during the heyday of fur farming, the Aleut elder Henry Swanson recalled, "When you bait a trap, cut your bait up into tiny pieces and scatter it all around. He'll forget about the trap and be searching around there and, bang, he's caught. Whereas if you put a big hunk of bait right at the trap he might be scratching around there and spring the trap. Then he'll get the bait without getting caught. . . . I used almost anything for bait. Seals, ducks, whatever I could shoot on the island. I used duck mostly. One time I used bacon rind. That worked good."[17]

In northern Alaska, where winter winds usually blow from the northeast, the bait was often placed upwind of the trap so that the fox, approaching the scent from downwind, would step on the trap. If using a cubby, the bait was placed at the back of the cubby, behind the trap, so that the fox could not get at the bait without springing the trap. In some areas, such as on St. Lawrence Island, Alaska, where white fox trapping was especially productive, before the trapping season began trappers would scatter meat and blubber around the areas where they intended to set their traps, hoping to accustom the foxes to finding food there.

Some trappers also placed bits of snow upon which a fox or a dog had urinated or set an upright post of wood or caribou antler (a "pee post")—sometimes enhanced with human urine—near the trap to use as a visual and olfactory attractor, and some might tie a ptarmigan wing, or feather, or other moving object to it to

Adam Leavitt gathering his traps at the end of the trapping season near Barrow, Alaska, ca. 1940. A kayaq rests upside down on the rack behind him. North Slope Borough Collection, Archives, University of Alaska–Fairbanks, UAF-1977-0158-00421.

catch the fox's attention and curiosity. Today, even a broken piece of snowmobile metal protruding above the snow may have plenty of fox tracks around it.[18]

The trapper also had to be an experienced winter traveler. Prior to the arrival of motorized snowmobiles (which came into widespread use in the Arctic in the 1960s) it was essential to have a reliable dog team to maintain the trapline. Many trappers in the late nineteenth century in Alaska (and as late as the second or third decade of the twentieth century among Canada's Inuinnait) had only a few dogs to help pull their sleds, but with the rise in white fox prices in the early twentieth century, larger dog teams allowed trappers to put out many more traps—from 50 to 300, although 100 to 200 traps were more common in northern Alaska—and traplines became much longer, hence the need for pulling power and speed. In fact, on Banks Island in the mid-1960s—just before snowmobiles became generally used there—a few trappers put out 700 or 800 traps on lines that required two weeks on the trail and more than 400 miles of travel to work the line.

"The rule of thumb was that a dog could pull about 100 pounds," according to David Greist. Consequently, many trappers began using teams of about seven to nine dogs per sled, and sometimes more were added if the dogs were pulling heavy loads at the beginning of the trapping season when the land was not yet well covered with snow. The dogs were harnessed in pairs and pulled along a central line. While running the trapline, a trapper's dog team might therefore be hauling a load of much more than 500 pounds, including the trapper himself at times, the sled, and such things as extra clothes, a sleeping bag, a rifle and ammunition, an axe, a snow knife, a hand saw, a shovel, camping gear, a stove and fuel, a tent, extra traps, fox carcasses, dog feed, bait, and human food. And this in turn increased the requirement for dog feed.

In the early 1950s the geographer Joseph Sonnenfeld, who studied the residents of Barrow, Alaska, reported that "about 50 traps could be serviced in a good day." It might take an experienced trapper ten or fifteen minutes to remove a captured animal and reset a trap, and depending on the terrain and the snow and ice conditions, a dog team might travel at about five or six miles per hour, covering thirty, or at most, forty miles per day when on a long trip. "They are fed three times a day when they are working, once a day when they are tied up at home," David Greist recalled. "A normal meal on the trail consisted of a softball-size chunk of seal, walrus or whale meat."[19]

"According to trappers in interior Alaska, a working sled dog of 65 to 70 pounds is fed 3 to 4 pounds of food a day," writes the trapper and biologist John J. Burns. "It depends on how hard it is being worked, the fat content in the food and the ambient temperatures it is working and living in." Rather than feeding a dog team only frozen meat, when on the trail the trappers at times cooked a mixture of cornmeal, rice, or rolled oats with meat and fat in a large dog pot set over an open fire. For example, the Episcopal priest Archdeacon Hudson Stuck, on a winter journey from Fort Yukon around the entirety of northern Alaska, left Barrow village in 1918 with two teams, starting toward Herschel Island, more than 400 miles to the east. He carried his initial load of dog feed, which included 200 pounds of rice, 100 pounds of corn meal, 200 pounds of whale blubber, and he expected to quickly acquire another 150 to 200 pounds of walrus meat at Nuvuq, the Native settlement at Point Barrow. He expected this load "to last until we reach the region of drift wood [far to the east of Barrow] where we can cook our dog feed."[20]

"Every third day we cooked dog pot seal with corn meal during the winter months," said Thomas G. Smith, a wildlife biologist who worked a team of nine dogs along a trapline on Victoria Island in the 1960s. "Our days were long, about 15 hours, then we slept for about 12 hours. Our lines were about 400–450 miles long and we would be gone 10–12 days. In peak fox years . . . we would only stay home for 3–4 days, then go again."[21]

Thus, in winter a working team of nine dogs, if fully employed daily, might hypothetically require about thirty-six pounds of feed per day, although in reality the monthly requirement was considerably less, when accounting for rest days and forced idleness because of inclement weather. At Coppermine and Holman (today, Kugluktuk and Ulukhaktok, settlements on Canada's Coronation Gulf and Victoria Island), Peter Usher calculated that in the early 1960s each sled dog, if fed solely on ringed seals (with each seal averaging a little more than thirty-five pounds of usable dog feed), would need 19 seals per year, which would mean that a trapper with a team of nine dogs might have to acquire 171 seals for an entire year, just for dog feed.

This necessity, plus the food needed for the trapper and his family, made it crucial to obtain reliable food supplies. Many trapping camps were located on the coast near rivers, where seals and fish were seasonally available and where caribou hunting was good and—equally important—fuel sources were nearby. Beyond a trapping family's basic need for seals for their own food, as well as for dog feed and other domestic uses (such as for clothing and footwear), any surplus skins might also be sold to traders: for example, in forty years at his post at Barrow, Alaska, Charlie Brower bought more than 20,000 seal skins. Polar bears, which the trapper frequently encountered in camp or on the trapline, were another source of income: in the same span of years Brower bought 1,300.[22]

Housing, too, was essential, and the structures the trappers built varied from place to place. The anthropologist Diamond Jenness visited an Eskimo trapping camp at Cape Halkett on the north coast of Alaska in the winter of 1913–1914: "What one may call the standard cabin was a rectangular dwelling about 10 feet long by 12 feet wide, with a gabled roof 5 feet high at the front and back and 7 feet in the middle, where alone it was possible for a man to stand upright. It had walls of untrimmed driftwood logs set perpendicularly side by side, and a roof and flooring of similar logs flattened on one face. The door, 4 feet high and hinged with leather straps, faced southward, and the roof above it contained a skylight that was 'glazed' with a seal intestine slightly domed to catch more light. This intestine possessed the opaqueness of celluloid, and although very thin, was strong enough for the housewife to scrape off the frost and to stitch up any rents."

He added:

A layer of turf encased both roof and walls, and, with its mantle of snow, rendered the dwelling virtually air-proof. Indeed, if the door had fitted at all closely, the inmates would have suffocated whenever they lit their stove, for the temperatures at such times often exceeded 100°; but the door hung very loosely, as a rule, and the covered passage that led up to it, 15 feet or more long, about 3 feet wide, and 5 feet high formed a natural channel for an inflowing draft. The passage itself was built from snow blocks supported by a framework of timber; for the Alaskan Eskimos, unlike the Eskimos farther east, did not know how to make a domed roof from snow blocks alone. Its entrance was sometimes closed by a cloth or skin to keep out the drifting snow; more often it was left wide open, but pointed away from the prevailing wind. In summer the dwelling rose prominently above the bare ground; but in winter the snow that drifted over it reduced it to a low, almost imperceptible mound where only the dark, gaping hole of its passage entrance, and the tip of the black stovepipe protruding above the white snow, betrayed the presence of human habitation in the otherwise featureless landscape.

The inside of each cabin matched the primitiveness of its exterior. The walls were quite bare, with turf visible between the logs in many places. Caribou skins and sleeping bags littered more than half the floor, and two or three boxes containing tools and miscellaneous trifles generally lay secreted somewhere against the back wall. A log stretching right across the floor from one side wall to the other separated the back "bed-and-parlor" section of the room from the "kitchen," which held nothing but a stove to the right (or left) of the door, a light crib of sticks above the stove for drying damp footwear and mittens, and, in the corner, a few utensils for cooking and eating. When the sun was shining—from mid-November until mid-February the sun never rose above the horizon—the intestine window above the stove transmitted just enough light for the housewife to cook and sew; but the more prosperous families always possessed at least one kerosene-burning hurricane lantern, while many used homemade contraptions that burned seal oil or whale oil. Most of the household possessions were not brought inside at all, but were cached out of doors on a high wooden platform. It was there that the families kept their stores of food, their bags of spare clothing, their weapons, sleds, and dog harnesses. It mattered little that these objects should be fully exposed to the weather, or lie buried all winter beneath a mound of snow. What did matter was that they should be out of reach of the ravenous sled dogs, which habitually slept beneath the platform except when severe blizzards or extreme cold drove them for shelter into the passageway. . . . A chill draft that blew through the chinks in the walls made the interior rather uncomfortable; but the winter was still young, and the dwelling promised to be very snug later in the season after snow had drifted over it. I saw among its furniture a hand sewing machine and a primus stove.[23]

These camps could also be very crowded. In 1937 the Reverend Fred Klerekoper, on a circuit from Barrow along the north coast of Alaska, described Roy

A trapper's house on the sandspit at Baillie Island, 1925. Sod blocks insulate the house and gunny sacks are used to block drafts on the walls and roof of the entrance shed. Burwash [1927]: opposite p. 15.

Ahmaogak's camp near Cape Simpson: "Every available space is being used. Woolen socks, dog harnesses, a lantern . . . the foot high table, mittens, binocular case, sleeping bags . . . a hand-crank sewing machine, a bunk for sleeping, a cookstove, five gallon tin Coleman camp stove, a sack of flour, boots, liners, skins suspended from the ceiling, the necessary pot for the baby. . . . But the crowded condition of the room in no way inhibits the friendliness and warmth of this home."[24]

On long traplines the trapper also had to build small shelters, either at a day's travel apart or central to the line's radii. "I would travel by dog team inland for some 20 or 30 miles, one day's journey, and set up a base camp," wrote David Greist about trapping out of Barrow, Alaska, in the early 1930s. "My base camp was a large snow house where I stashed my sleeping bag, food and gear. From this camp I would start out in the morning, making a circle circuit via a loop. Returning to base camp that evening, I would place a trap every 100 yards or so on this circuit." In northern Alaska these snow houses were not the dome-shaped igloos of arctic fame; instead, they were rectangular, built from snow-block walls that were cut with a hand saw from dense, wind-compacted snow and covered with a gabled snow-block roof. Snow was then shoveled over the entire structure for added insulation. At other times a rectangular snow wall might be built without a roof to serve as a windbreak, and a wall tent would be

Froelich Rainey's drawing of the interior of a trapper's house at Point Hope, Alaska, ca. 1940. The cabin's frame is made from driftwood timbers. To the left of the low door is a sheet iron stove, with a traditional soapstone lamp resting on the rack above it. Above the door is a skylight made from translucent gut membranes. To the right hang two kerosene lanterns and the trapper's rifle. On one of the beds is a hand-crank sewing machine. The two beds are mounted on long legs to keep them in the warmer upper air of the cabin. Under the bed at the right is a hand-crank gramophone and to its left is a chamber pot. Courtesy of Froelich G. Rainey, author's collection.

put up inside the wall. On Banks Island trappers usually carried double-walled canvas tents to set up temporary camps each night. Inuit trappers from Tuktoyaktuk, NWT, who specialized in trapping marten in the wooded areas of the Anderson River to their south, built their own log cabins for camps.[25]

Peter Usher described how trappers, using dog teams, worked their lines on Banks Island in the early 1960s:

Having selected a route, the Bankslanders travel in a fairly direct line along it, setting traps periodically along the way. Sometimes they are set as frequently as 10 or 15 to the mile, although the average is three or four. Some trappers set traps in pairs, most prefer to use a single trap at each site. Very occasionally, if a trapper happens upon an animal carcase [sic] . . . or some other object likely to attract foxes, he will set out a number of traps around it. In the main traps are more or less evenly spaced, a quarter mile or so apart along the route.

The general preference for coast or valley routes is apparent, although some trappers have overland trails. More specifically, the trappers quite naturally prefer such easily followed terrain features as low coastal or river banks, valley terraces or small stream beds. Where a flat or gently undulating surface is to be traversed, large markers of snow may be erected, but frequently the trappers make their way without these. Small knolls, crests of river or coastal banks, or other small eminences in the terrain are sought for individual trap sites, again partly because of their visibility and partly because foxes tend to frequent such features.

Usher was amazed at the trappers' traveling skills. "To the uninitiated traveller, slowly sledging across this vast, almost featureless, snow covered landscape in the dull blue light of midwinter, it seems incredible that anyone could even approximately follow an unmarked route, let alone find every drifted over trap along it. A multitude of tiny visual clues escape this traveller, but the experienced trapper knows those of his own route well, and he also knows the little tricks of navigation by which he can orient himself, such as drift direction, snow consistency, stars, etc. His well trained team of dogs will also assist him in finding the way. In fact some trappers, even if they have set out 700 or 800 traps over 200 miles, can probably visualize the location and set of every single one of their traps."[26]

But even the most experienced trappers routinely encountered problems. First was the challenge of simply locating the trap. If it had been snowed over, it would have been difficult to spot; often the trapper's dogs helped the trapper to find the set. "A good trapline dog," writes the dog team trapper Julie Collins, "will not only remember the trail even in open areas but also remember the sets, glancing toward or even stopping at each one. He can show you natural scent posts, dens and kill sites, not to mention alert you to bears, thin ice and other hazards." At other times a trapper might discover that polar bears, caribou, snowy owls, or even lemmings had sprung his trap. He might have the bad luck to find that wolves, wolverines, lynx, arctic foxes, stray dogs, ravens, or, especially, red foxes had followed his trapline and had stolen his bait or, worse, had eaten any foxes that had been caught. "I hate those colored foxes," the veteran arctic trapper and trader Slim Semmler told me, remembering red foxes' depredations on his trapline in Coronation Gulf. Furthermore, foxes could escape, trap chains could break, and traps could be stolen or lost outright. On Banks Island in the 1960s trappers lost 10 to 15 percent of their annual fox catch.[27]

PELT PREPARATION IN CAMP

When a trapper found a fox in his trap, it was usually frozen, but if it had been caught very recently and was alive, the trapper would stun it by giving a sharp tap to its snout with the handle of his snow knife and then either step on the chest cavity to stop its heart or bend the head back hard to snap its neck.[28]

If the fox's fur was frozen to the trap it was necessary to bring it, trap and all, to the camp to allow it to thaw. Forcefully removing the fox from the trap while the hair was frozen to it would result in some hair being pulled from the pelt, reducing the pelt's value. Similarly, the trapper had to take care not to damage the fur when moving over rough trails on the way to the trapping camp. "The trapper's catch is usually found frozen at the trap site or, if not, it freezes during the trip back off the trapline," states the *Alaska Trappers Manual,* "Unless precautions are taken to prevent it, every mile of travel will reduce the value of the pelts. Frozen tails can and will break, and although they can be sewn back on and the damage may not devalue the pelt, the overall quality and appearance of the fur will be hurt."

Long-haired furbearers, such as foxes, are more vulnerable to "rubbing" in situations like this than are the more durable short-haired furbearers, such as mink. "When things in the sled are bouncing around, this can be a real problem with marten and white foxes," John J. Burns told me. "Pack them carefully and use whatever is available (canvas cover, burlap bags, extra clothing, etc.). A 'rub-line' on a prime pelt is a loss of 20% of its full value." If foxes had been found alive in the traps, it was important not to leave the still-warm bodies piled together on the sled, because the remaining internal heat would contribute to decomposition, which would cause the fur to become loose and fall out ("fur slip").[29]

Once the trapper had reached his camp and had tethered and fed his dogs, he usually began thawing the foxes in preparation for skinning. The thawing might take anywhere from twelve to twenty-four hours, and care had to be taken not to put the fox too close to a hot stove because excessive heat would cause the fur to "singe" and curl the tips of the guard hairs, reducing its value. When thawed, any blood and dirt had to be washed from the fox with soap and water.

There are four separate processes in preparing a pelt in camp: skinning, fleshing, stretching, and drying. Foxes are "case skinned"—that is, the pelt is removed in one piece. This is in contrast to animals that are skinned "open," which is done by slitting the hide down the anterior side of the animal, as is done for bears, wolves, wolverines, and beavers. Foxes could be skinned from the head or from the rear legs. The trapper might begin skinning a white fox by cutting around the mouth of the animal and peeling the skin back. "The old fashioned high-liners skin white foxes through the mouth. It's fast and clean— no blood or grease," writes John J. Burns.

> Some of the folks I watched kept the white foxes on their laps or occasionally on a work bench. Others, including myself, suspend them (hang them) using an "S" hook or some other type of hook on the lower jaw. The head is first skinned back to about the level of the eyes. Most other furbearers cannot be skinned in this manner because the mouth opening is too small to work the body through. . . . The beauty of skinning through the mouth is that you go 'with the grain' in that fat and underlying fascia stays on the carcass. If light scraping is required [to remove remaining bits of fat and other material] it is done when the pelt is first put on the stretcher, skin side out. . . . Scrapers are made out of all sorts of things including, among other things, caribou and moose leg bones, springs from old traps, thick plastic, or store-bought ones. All the home made ones I have seen and used are very slightly rounded, bev- eled (one side) and slightly serrated.

It was important not to scrape the skin too hard because over-scraping might cut the roots of the hair, causing them to fall out. Some trappers used a spoon or a dull butter knife to remove the fat, and if the trapper's wife was doing the work, she might carefully use her *ulu*, the Eskimo woman's crescent-shaped knife. The tailbone also had to be removed from the pelt. Any cuts in the pelts were then mended with needle and thread.

Unlike skins such as muskrats, which are sold "skin out," fox pelts are sold "fur out," which allowed the buyer or grader to assess their condition quickly. Before turning the skin fur out, however, the next step was to put the pelt skin- side out on a "stretcher," really a drying frame, shaped like an elongated letter A. The stretcher was not intended to increase the size of the skin; rather, it was to aid in drying it and to prevent the skin from shrinking and thus becoming wrinkled and crumpled, which would detract from its price. "Unfortunately the word 'stretching' is too often taken literally by trappers," stated Harry J. LaDue in his handbook on trapping. "Skins that are stretched out of proportion always result in misshapen pelts. They are an eyesore and are materially disqualified by the raw fur buyer. . . . They not only lack trimness but if over-stretched invar- iably show up natural thin spots that should be . . . covered with underfur and guard fur."[30]

The pelt on the frame was allowed to dry at room temperature; again, away from a hot stove. "When drying in a camp or shanty put your furs as far as pos- sible from the glare of the open fire or heat of the stove. Sudden drying grease

Fox skins bleaching in the rigging of the schooner *Polar Bear* in spring
1914. An overturned kayaq is in the foreground. Courtesy of the
New Bedford Whaling Museum, Bernhard Kilian Collection.

cooks them, and makes them brittle." Brittle pelts could easily be torn when
handling them, so after three to six hours—that is, before the pelt had become
too dry and stiff to turn it fur side out—the partially dried fox pelt was removed
from the frame, turned fur side out, and then placed back on the frame. The
total drying time varied from twelve to twenty-four hours before the pelt was
finally removed from the stretcher. Then the fur was cleaned with flour, cornmeal, Fels-Naptha soap—or even "white gas" (camp stove fuel)—to remove
any oil or grease that might cause discoloration or matting. Agnes Carpenter
described the method that the Banks Island families used: "We used cornmeal,
flour and white gas. . . . And mixed all that together and then used a hairbrush
or some kind of a brush and then just comb the fur, right into the cornmeal
mixture. It comes out very, very clean, takes all that oil stains, the yellow stains
on the fur. Also it brings the hair back to life and it makes it very clean."[31]

Apart from the time spent in thawing and drying, the time spent in skinning,
fleshing, and cleaning the pelt might add up to one hour of added labor per fox
for an experienced pelt handler. The clean pelt was then hung outside in the
cold and sunlight to bleach further. "Stains from the fat of sea mammals turn

the white fur pale yellow," the biologist David Chesemore wrote, "and badly stained fox pelts are often discounted by fur buyers up to 50 percent of their original value." He added, "Foxes taken on sea ice often have these fat stains on their fur."[32]

SELLING THE PELTS

When the trapping season ended, or when he judged that he had sufficient furs to sell, the trapper had several options for marketing his pelts. He might go to a nearby trading post, or the trapper might wait for an itinerant fur buyer to visit him either via dog team in winter or by boat in summer. (In the 1930s a few fur buyers made their rounds by aircraft.)

"The trapper would pull the first white fox out of a sack and lay it on the counter," wrote George Burnham, describing an exchange at the Hudson's Bay Company's post at Walker Bay on Victoria Island. "He would select some item, such as four pounds of tea, and [the trader] would indicate on the skin how much was used for the tea or how much was left. Another selection would be made and when goods had been purchased to the full value of the skin, [the trader] would pull the skin over to our side of the counter and drop it onto the floor. Out would come another pelt and the trading was resumed. The fox skins were not put in the sack 'willy nilly,' no indeed, the best skin was always at the bottom . . . so that the poorest skin was always the first one to be traded. Thus the trapper felt that the more he could squeeze on a poor skin, the more he would be able to get on the better skins."[33]

The posts were often operated by large trading companies, such as, in Canada's Western Arctic, the Hudson's Bay Company or C. T. Pedersen's and Albert Herskovits and Sons' Canalaska Company. In northern Alaska the largest operators were H. Liebes and Company of San Francisco, the John Backlands' (senior and junior) Midnight Sun Trading Company of Seattle, the Northern Whaling and Trading Company (C. T. Pedersen and Albert Herskovits and Sons of New York City), with smaller traders in Kotzebue and Nome. In Chukotka the largest operators were the Karaev family, Olaf Swenson, the Hudson's Bay Company (only briefly), and later, exclusively the Soviet trade monopoly. The smaller traders, and some of the larger ones, whose representatives often lived in a community for a number of years and had married a local woman, possessed an advantage based on mutual trust and respect and in advancing credit from the trader to the trapper.

Even in the years before the advent of radio receivers the auction prices of white fox pelts were usually fairly quickly known to trappers. The information was passed by word of mouth, and all traders, large and small, were forced to pay for the furs according to that scale. And consequently the traders usually made their profit margin on the price they charged for their trade goods. These prices were based on the wholesale cost of the goods, plus the cost of freight, which, for example, in 1923 was $60 per ton from San Francisco to Herschel Island and $100 per ton to Bernard Harbour at Dolphin and Union Strait. From 100 to 250 percent was added to the cost of the goods, depending on the remoteness of the posts, to cover the "turnover."

As large as these profits may appear, they were a direct reflection of the time the trader's capital was "tied up" between obtaining a loan, with interest, to purchase his trade goods and the receipt of payment for his furs, the so-called turnover time, which was frequently two years or more. For example, a trader might receive a loan and buy his goods in January and ship them to Seattle or San Francisco, carry them to the Arctic in summer and stock his post or posts for the winter, then return the following summer to collect the furs that had been purchased with his goods and carry them south to put them in an auction in December, from which he might receive his payment in January. Traders therefore "carried a heavy debt load," as the historian Timothy Mahoney put it. And the journalist D. A. Holmes stated, "[The trader] was always one year behind and made a turnover every two years. On such operations a large profit was justifiable."[34]

Smaller independent traders ran posts in competition with the larger companies—and frequently were more nimble than they were—and these traders were equally important to the widely dispersed trappers. Although the credit arrangements varied, some traders shared the risk and offered a winter's outfit to a trapper in return for half of his fur catch, although many only bought furs and sold goods with small credit advances to the trappers. Wilson Soplu, an Iñupiaq trapper on the north coast of Alaska, fondly remembered the elderly trader Jack Smith. "Even before the trapping season one could get as much supplies as one wants," he recalled. "One could buy on credit. And then when one gets some foxes one just goes and pays it off. He helped ease our struggle for existence."[35]

The ships that visited the coasts in summer were operated by the larger companies, but smaller trading schooners, often from Nome, also cruised along the coasts, trying to beat the bigger vessels to the furs. The schooners and the itinerant fur buyers—also called "trippers," "country buyers," or "country collectors"—were frequently the bane of the company trading posts and the larger ships, which often had loaned traps and advanced a winter's outfit of food and equipment to the trapper, and they, of course, wanted the debt retired. Instead, the tripper and the schooner captain might persuade the trapper to sell some pelts on the spot in return for trade goods that he needed quickly, and thus they would cut into the profits of the trading posts and the large ships. The tripper might also be an agent of a large city merchant or "city collector," who gathered furs into batches large enough to export, or to send directly to auction, or to sell directly to manufacturing furriers.

In 1929 the Canadian government, with the support of the Hudson's Bay Company, outlawed "tripping" in northern Canada, forcing traders to maintain fixed posts in those areas that were not off-limits to them, and considerable thought was invested in the placement of the posts so that the native trappers could stay on their traplines and not waste time traveling to and from distant posts. But in northern and western Alaska perhaps a dozen buyers ranged across the country, acquiring pelts for their own accounts or as agents of Albert Herskovits and Sons, Joseph Ullman and Company of New York, and several others.

One of the most widely known Alaskan buyers was "Muskrat Johnny" Schwegler, who arrived in Nome in 1908 and "spent the next 50 years crisscrossing the last frontier by dog sled, ship and plane, always in search of pelts—especially muskrat pelts," working primarily for the Seattle firm of Jacobsen and Goldberg. The journalist Michael Carey remembered, "If Muskrat Johnny Schwegler wasn't the king of Alaskan fur buyers, he was at least a ranking prince. . . . He wore the odor of fur like a cape. Before you saw Johnny walking the halls of his Fairbanks headquarters, the Nordale Hotel, you smelled him coming. . . . Buyers and trappers need each other but often have different ideas about what constitutes a fair price. . . . Johnny Schwegler enjoyed the reputation of a man who could be trusted."[36]

Many country collectors carried trade goods, but in certain areas where cash was widely accepted some offered the convenience of paying in cash or via a bank draft on the spot. Of course, if the purchase was made in trade goods, it allowed the tripper to make a profit on both sides of the exchange: profit on the sale of the goods and profit on the sale of the pelts. Many trappers viewed the country collectors with justifiable suspicion because of their perceived skinflint offers for the furs, and, as Mike Dederer of the Seattle Fur Exchange told me, "The country buyers always tried to get the furs for as little as possible."[37]

Still, the trippers did not succeed in making big profits on every purchase. The tripper at all times had to be on the lookout for damaged skins that had been artfully patched and perhaps stashed deep within a bundle of pelts. Charles Gillham remembered that hare skins could be disguised as white fox: "[arctic hare] skins are beautiful and silky, though they are almost valueless. They are fully as large as the foxes'. By skillfully sewing the fox tails onto the rabbit pelts, and clipping off the tips of the ears that are black, a fine substitute for a fox skin can be made." And because fur prices in the southern markets might have fluctuated while the country buyer was in the field and out of touch, he had to be careful not to overpay for a skin.[38]

Up-to-date information was crucial. As early as 1915 Charlie Brower at Barrow, Alaska, was paying for current price information from the operator at the end of the telegraph line in the town of Candle on the northern Seward Peninsula, about 400 miles south of Barrow. The operator regularly mailed the current fur prices to him via dog team mail. In 1917 H. Liebes and Company installed a wireless transmission and receiving set aboard its ship *Herman* to acquire the latest information on the state of the fur market.

Some of the trippers sent their skins directly to the fur exchanges, and, to keep their allegiance, the exchanges issued private code booklets to the trippers. During the 1920s and 1930s commercial wireless radio continually improved in coverage and signal strength, and in winter, when propagation was at its best, Northerners across the Arctic listened to many stations, among them KDKA in Pittsburgh, which had regular evening broadcasts to the Arctic as early as the winter of 1922–1923; WGN in Chicago; KMOX in St. Louis; and WBZ in Boston. The exchanges transmitted the current prices in code. The Seattle Fur Exchange aired this information via KSL in Salt Lake City, which seemed to have the best propagation to Alaska. The exchange had a radio show, and at the end of the program the price information was sent in a five-letter code, different for each type of fur. The code was changed every year, and each year a new booklet was produced for the trippers.

It could be a high-stakes game for the tripper. Occasionally news of the current fur prices reached the trapper before it reached the country buyer, who might have arrived in camp lacking the latest information. For the trapper there was much satisfaction in fleecing the tripper by getting higher prices than the current market. For example, Gary Schroeder, a former country collector, shared the tripper's angst: "Back when I traveled to all parts of Nevada buying fur," he wrote, "I never stopped at a casino nor did I ever drop a nickel in a slot machine. Buying fur was all the gambling I needed."[39]

The trapper also had other outlets to sell his furs. In areas where dog team (or in the 1930s, airmail) postal service was available he could mail them to a fur broker in the south who would then sell the pelts directly to a manufacturing furrier, but the disadvantage to this method was that the turnaround was slow and the trapper, if he did not like the broker's offer, had to pay the cost of the return shipment.

Winter mail service by dog team began at Barrow and Fort McPherson at the beginning of the century. The reindeer herder Chester Seveck remembered that

in 1910 "they take one month from Barrow to Kotzebue and went back one
month from Kotzebue to Barrow. They stopped and delivered mail [at] every
village—Pt. Hope, Kivalina, Icy Cape, Wainwright, and Pt. Lay. This total
miles about one way 560 [coastal] miles."[40]

The biologist Alfred Bailey described the situation in 1921.

> In the days immediately prior to the arrival of the airplane to Arctic areas all
> mail was carried to northern Alaskan settlements by dogsled three times each
> winter, a letter posted in New York reaching Barrow eighty to ninety days
> later, if it made it [on] through connections—and six months possibly if it
> did not. The mail was sent from Seattle by steamer to Seward, the terminus
> of the Government railroad, and then over the rails to Nenana or Fairbanks;
> then down the Yukon River by dogsled hundreds of miles to Unalakleet, and
> from there ten days or more by sled to Kotzebue, the distributing point for
> Arctic Alaska.
>
> The last leg of five hundred or more miles from Kotzebue to Barrow was
> probably the most difficult scheduled mail route in the world; the men were
> constantly gambling with their lives, but the Eskimos were so capable that
> few accidents happened. The mail man was supposed to transport a load,
> two hundred pounds—for which he received $350.00 round trip, but there
> was a special allowance of excess for which the driver received one dollar a
> pound. The route was along an uninhabited coast, except for an occasional
> occupied igloo which the carrier tried to reach for shelter from the constantly
> menacing storms; dog food was a serious problem—and yet the mails had to
> go through on time.[41]

Charlie Brower was one of the first to export furs from Barrow to the south via
dog team mail. And by being located at the beginning of the southbound mail
route Brower enjoyed a considerable advantage over those who lived farther
south. Hudson Stuck remarked in the winter of 1917–1918 that the missionary at
Point Hope, the Reverend W. A. Thomas, was "annoyed that the Point Barrow
post office has taken the whole limit of weight allowed to send out furs so that
he [the missionary] is unable to dispatch the 75 lbs or so of parcel post lying at
this office. The parcel post in Alaska in the winter is simply a means of getting
furs cheaply and quickly out of the country."

In Alaska, once mail service had become more widespread, trappers could
also post their pelts directly to Montgomery Ward or Sears, Roebuck and Company. These companies sold large quantities of traps and trapping supplies
via mail order catalogues, and to keep the trappers' business they offered free
trapping advice through their own booklets, such as Sears, Roebuck's "Tips
to Trappers by Johnny Muskrat" and Montgomery Ward's "Trails to Trapping

Profits." Montgomery Ward did not buy furs, but it served as an agent for the trapper with its "Free Nationwide Fur Marketing Service." Sears, Roebuck did the same, proclaiming: "We Handle Raw Furs—We do not buy these furs ourselves, but immediately upon receipt of them we notify a number of fur dealers who bid against each other, and we dispose of them to the highest bidder. The amount received is immediately sent to you, less the express charges we paid upon receipt of the goods. . . . We deduct no commission, as this department is solely for your accommodation."

To attract business Sears also advertised cash awards—which were dispensed in addition to the fur payments—in contests for the best-prepared pelts. As the trapping historian Tom Parr wrote, the content of "Sears *Tips To Trappers* . . . from 1931 to 1958 was much the same: testimonials from trappers, prize-winning photos, trapping tips, and a fur market outlook. Each *Tips To Trappers* included four shipping tags complete with the return address to one of the nine receiving depots." Sears continued its fur marketing service until 1959.[42]

"The principal competitor of the itinerant buyer . . . [was] the receiving house," David C. Mills stated. The advantage to the small trapper was that the receiving houses usually handled smaller shipments and paid more promptly than the auction companies or large buyers. There the furs would be graded, and "the shipper paid according to a published price list," wrote Victor Fuchs. "The shipper and buyer frequently disagree about the grading, but since the buyer is dependent upon further shipments, the results are usually fairly equitable."[43]

"Goodwill plays an important part in the matter," said Mills. "It costs a good deal to get a trapper to ship his furs to a distant receiving house and it hardly pays to treat him unfairly and lose his trade. It is customary to mail a check to each trapper on the same day that his shipment is received and this in itself is an important factor in satisfying him. Still there are differences and disappointments enough, for one's collection looks very much more valuable in one's own woodshed than it does on the floor of a warehouse, where it can be compared with thousands of similar collections."[44]

Before shipping the pelts south, if there were a large number of furs in the collection, they had to be "baled"—that is, packaged by compressing them as much as possible to reduce their volume, while simultaneously wrapping them to protect them from water or other damage during shipment. To do this the Hudson's Bay Company and other major shippers used fur presses. George H. Burnham described the process at the Hudson's Bay Company's post at Walker Bay. "Our post . . . was equipped with a fur press, a supply of twine, burlap and seals. When everything was ready, we laid the fox skins into the burlap which had been put into the press, after which the burlap was pulled tight along the sides and over the top, the press was turned to compress the bale as much as possible, the burlap tightened again[,] and when the sewing was finished, a metal Company seal was clamped wherever two threads joined each other, to ensure that there would be no tampering with the bales en route."[45]

Then the bales had to be marked. In 1939 Tahoe Washburn witnessed a Hudson's Bay Company press in operation in Tuktoyaktuk, NWT. "The job was finished by sewing a red label with the London destination on one end of the bale, and by painting on both ends in black paint: the Outfit number (270 = 1939), Post number, 'Hudson's Bay Company,' number of foxes (about 100), and weight." These bales were heavy: 100 baled white fox skins weigh about 130 pounds.[46]

THE FUR AUCTION

Although some brokers and large dealers sold directly to large manufacturing furriers and to small dealers, once the companies and buyers had acquired the furs, the most usual method of selling them was at auction. The advantage of selling furs at a major auction was that the auctions attracted large numbers of pelts for sale, which in turn attracted large numbers of buyers and brokers. Usually the purchasers were either representatives of large manufacturers or small buyers who tried to put together batches for small manufacturing furriers.

The Hudson's Bay Company, for instance, ran its own auctions in London (and later in Montreal as well) in competition with several other auction companies, and eventually it also sold the furs of many competing buyers. During the boom years of the fur trade in the early twentieth century, fur auction companies sprang up in many cities: New York, Chicago, Tacoma, Montreal, Edmonton, Winnipeg, and Vancouver, among others. One of the largest competitors of the Hudson's Bay Company for Western Arctic furs became the Seattle Fur Exchange, which sold many of the Alaskan and Siberian pelts. Its frequent sales were attended by fur dealers throughout the world. In spring 1929, for example, the exchange's monthly auction catalogue listed 5,000 red fox, 750 cross fox, 225 silver fox, 400 blue fox, 400 white fox, 2,750 lynx, 5,500 ermine, 175 wolverine, 15,000 muskrat, 50 fisher, 7,000 beaver, 1,200 marten, 800 otter, 3,500 wolf, 9,000 mink, and other furs.[47]

The auction companies usually charged 5 or 6 percent of the value of the consignment, plus the costs of storage and insurance. At the Seattle Fur Exchange, consignments valued at more than $1,000 were charged 4 percent. As early as 1911 some Alaskan Eskimos were sending their furs directly to Seattle auctions. The sellers always tried to play the market price cycles to their best advantage, and, if the seller requested it, the Seattle Fur Exchange would store the furs for a fee, sometimes for as long as two years, but the seller ran the risk of the raw furs becoming "stale"—dry and brittle—if stored too long.[48]

When "raw" (camp-prepared) furs of any kind reached an auction house they were first marked with a metal tag to identify the seller, and, if the seller requested it, a minimum sale price was assigned to protect the seller against "any possible collusion of buyers." If the minimum price was not met, their batch of furs would be withdrawn from the sale. "However, we suggest that shippers do not place a prohibitive limit," the Seattle Fur Exchange advised, "preferring for good business reasons, such as a sudden advance or decline in the market, that sale prices be left to our judgment, as we will take every precaution and do our utmost to obtain the highest prices possible."[49]

Then the furs were placed in large spinning drums with hardwood sawdust to clean the pelts by removing oils, thus fluffing the furs before they were sorted into batches. Some lots of fur were sold in bundles that would allow the manufacturing furrier to make up one garment from the lot; others were gathered in conveniently sized batches.

First, the pelts were segregated into groupings that had originated from a specific geographical area (often called a "section"): pelts taken in one region often exhibit uniquely similar characteristics, which eased the manufacturing furrier's job in assembling them for consistency in a fur garment. The pelts were then further separated into lots of uniform quality (the "grade," both of the fur itself and of the skillfulness of the preparation of the pelt), and color.

It required training and a keen eye to grade the skins into consistent lots, and it took four or five years to train a competent grader. To keep the grades consistent, at the Seattle Fur Exchange—which employed 100 graders out of a total of 200 employees—the windows in the grading rooms were blacked out and the room was illuminated by special lamps that approximated natural light, the intensity of which was always constant. Mike Dederer told me that without the invariably steady artificial light it would have been impossible to produce highly consistent grades of furs.[50]

The graders sorted the furs into batches comprising similar numbers of the various grades of the pelts. This process required a substantial amount of trust between the auction house and the fur buyers. For example, Joseph E. Agnew described how the lots were assembled at the Seattle Fur Exchange: "We make a business of finding out the percentage of ones and twos, the percentage of threes, the percentage of culls, the actual number, in fact. We prorate the same number of threes to each lot. If we have a thousand foxes . . . [containing] two hundred No. threes, and we would make five lots out of it, and put forty threes in one lot. If there happened to be one hundred lower grades, blue backs, we put twenty in each lot, so that each lot would be fairly equal."[51]

Once the furs had been aggregated into similar lots, they were assigned a lot number, and a brief written description was listed in the auction catalogue. The number of pelts in a lot could vary widely, and sometimes it was quite large, especially in lots of average or slightly defective skins. A representative number of them were then chosen from the batch. "As each selling lot is completed, a sample is withdrawn which fully represents the total quality," wrote the fur buyer Max Bachrach. "Several hundred or several thousand skins are very unwieldy and bulky for many buyers to examine simultaneously, so sample bundles of from 10 to 50 skins are sealed, tagged, and placed on convenient racks from which they are taken on request by sample men, who bring them to the tables where buyers are standing to examine them. The prospective buyer marks each lot in a catalogue that has spaces corresponding in number with those of the tags upon the sample bundles." A sample lot might represent 20,000 skins, stated the furrier J. G. Links: "Although it contains only 20 or 30; these 20 or 30 are all the buyers will see until they have paid their money and taken away their purchases. It says much for the technical skill of the sorters that a claim that a show bundle failed to represent the bulk fairly is almost unheard of."[52]

Describing the fur buyers as a group, a reporter for *Fortune* magazine declared: "All dealers have two things in common. They are as a class the best judges of fur in the world. They can tell by a cursory inspection whether a given sable pelt is a late-caught Amur or an unhealthy Baikal smoke-darkened by the trapper. And they exhibit, to a man that familiar combination of secrecy and disputatiousness that is known as trading instinct. . . . He is a jealous and demanding purchaser."[53]

As Terence Ruttle wrote:

> The way to examine a pelt is to put it on the table, take a quick glance at the belly to make sure that there is no damage or bare spot there, and then, holding it belly down with your left hand on the rump and your right hand holding the head, give it a couple of shakes by moving your right wrist. This shakes the fur up so that it can be seen more fully and also loosens any hairs that may have got out of place or that were clinging together. As you do this, you have to let your eyes travel all over the fur. . . . During this examination, you should stroke the whole of the back lightly downwards towards the tail, then shake it up and stroke again. If you keep your fingers together, slightly bent but not too stiff, you can judge the denseness of the fur with the sides of the fingers and the edge of your palm. The tips of the fingers are not used much when examining long-haired furs. . . . As you stroke the fur, you should

get an impression of a cushiony effect that keeps you from being aware of the skin underneath the fur; that is, unless you are handling an early flattish pelt. Furthermore, as your hand moves along, the displaced fur should spring up again immediately, showing that it is supported by a dense underfur. On a well-furred fox, the fur should flow over the tops of your fingers when it is stroked in the other direction—towards the head. . . . Although all this takes a long time to describe, an experienced grader will do the whole thing in a few seconds. After one glance, he will . . . nearly always make up his mind right away as to the correct grade. He can easily examine several hundred foxes in an hour.[54]

The fur buyer, examining each sample lot, took careful note of a pelt's size, color, and the density of the guard hairs and underfur. "The Fur should be dense. . . . The Fur should be bright. It should have lustre or sheen. . . . Finally, the fur must be silky. Generally speaking, lustre goes with silkiness and a coarse fur is nearly always dull," according to J. G. Links. "The essence of fur grading," wrote Terence Ruttle, "is knowing how to assess the qualities and defects [of] fur pelts in question." "The chief beauty in any long-haired fur," said Ruttle, "is its luxuriant growth, if this is rubbed off or damaged in any way that reduces complete coverage, the value of the pelt drops considerably." He was describing the length of the guard hairs, which protect the underfur. As the winter season progressed, some of an animal's fur might have been rubbed off from freezing to the snow when resting or from contact with its burrow's walls.[55]

The size of the pelt also influenced the value: the best white fox pelts measure between twenty-four and twenty-eight inches from the base of the tail to the nose. The pelts were segregated into four sizes: extra large, large, medium, and small. The smaller skins were sold at reduced prices.

"A pelt is at its very best at the moment the winter fur stops growing," Gary Schroeder stated. "From that point on, hairs can break, rub or otherwise be damaged, and new ones do not come in to replace them." For arctic foxes, "firsts" were perfect pelts, with a full coverage of guard hairs and dense underfur, white all the way to the skin, and thick enough to make the guard hairs stand erect. Because true firsts are so rare, the top class of furs was often listed as "firsts and best seconds" or "ones part twos." A "best second" was a good pelt with a small defect. Some of the guard hairs might have been missing, or the fur might be slightly yellow, or the underfur might be somewhat weak, or perhaps showing slightly blue underfur. "Twos" were early caught pelts (with blue leather) or late caught pelts (with hard leather). "As the hairs grow pigment accumulates at the bases of the follicles. This will color the fur as it grows. But before then, it gives the leather of not-yet-prime pelts a bluish color. . . . If a skin is harvested too far ahead of prime," said Gary Schroeder about early caught pelts, "the bases of the hairs are not yet set in the leather, and those hairs may be cut on the leather side when fleshing. If you pull on this fur after it is tanned, the hairs can come out."

According to Terence Ruttle, "Seconds represent the bottom end of the quality range an average good manufacturer would be likely to use. Anything below this is generally referred to as a 'low-grade' and is handled by manufacturers who specialize in cheaper garments and trimmings." "Low twos and threes" were furs that had definite defects resulting from having been caught very early in the season, showing bluish underfur ("blue backs"), or very late in the season ("very springy"), having rubbed areas. "Fourths and Kitts" exhibited more extreme defects than "thirds" and were often summer-caught before the fox had obtained its winter coat.

In addition to evaluating the quality of the fur, the buyers also assessed the degrees of damage to the pelts. These conditions might have occurred, for example, from trap-wear while in the trap, or from mice or shrews eating the carcass while in the trap, or from inexpert pelt handling. Those damaged pelts were graded as "light," "light damaged," and "damaged."

For a white fox pelt, the degree of staining was also an important factor in grading it because if it had been yellowed from contact with sea mammal fat, it created problems for the dyers who might have to bleach the pelt prior to dyeing it, which would weaken the leather. For any grade, the degree of yellow staining would reduce the price: clean skins usually sold for 100 percent of the grade price; slightly stained at 80 percent; stained at 60 percent; and badly stained at 40 percent of the grade price. At auction, "firsts" usually sold at 80 to 100 percent of the highest price for the best quality lot; "seconds" at 50 to 80 percent; "thirds" at 30 to 50 percent; and "fourths" at a maximum of 30 percent.[56]

The fur buyers were commission agents who acted on orders from skin merchants. They never purchased skins for their own account, and they often charged a commission of 3 percent on their purchases. "But he is a man to be trusted and he understands fur," stated J. G. Links. During the sales, "He will be at work from eight in the morning until late at night alternately examining show bundles in order to record his description and valuation in his catalogue and attending the salesroom to bid on those lots which he considers come closest to the orders he has received from his customers; in the evening he cables or telephones descriptions of what he has seen, what he has bought and what he considers will be the next day's market movements."[57]

Once the buyers had examined the sample lots, they assembled in the auction room and took seats at desks "much the same as in a classroom," said Max

Bachrach. "The auctioneer and his assistants are seated behind a large desk on a raised platform, so that, as they face the buyers, they can conveniently note bids in all parts of the room. The auction, in so far as the offering of prices by the buyers is concerned, is a silent one. The auctioneer is the one that maintains the price quotations, and these advance upon the raising of a pencil or a nod on the part of the buyer. The auctioneer's assistants each have their particular aisle to watch and a nod to them is followed by their crying 'Up' to the auctioneer in the center, who raises the bid according to a stipulated amount . . . for each different peltry, for these amounts vary according to the average value of the article. The conduct of the sale is otherwise much the same as any auction sale."

Mike Dederer, the general manager of the Seattle Fur Exchange, told me that the auctioneer's assistants had to recognize each buyer and remember the special private signal that each one used to indicate his bid. Because the buyer did not wish his competitors to know his degree of eagerness for the lot, his signal might be a flicked finger or a "bid" as long as his cigarette remained in his mouth. Others might look directly at the assistant as long as the signal was a "bid" or remove their glasses when retiring from bidding.[58]

The fur lots were usually sold in "strings," "a series of lots of identical type and value." J. G. Links described the procedure in London auctions:

> When the first lot has been sold the market price of all the others has been established; the problem that remains for those wishing to buy some of the others is to get them. The buyer of the first lot has the option of taking as many of the following as he wishes at the same price so long as no one is prepared to bid more. The hammer goes on falling, therefore, for as long as he keeps his eye on the auctioneer. If it looks as if he is going to absorb the entire string, or if other buyers think he has bought well, one of them will call out an overbid, which he must either better or drop out. In the absence of an overbid, though, he will continue until he has had his fill and then signal that he 'drops.' All other interested buyers now endeavour to catch the auctioneer's eye and so replace the first buyer at the price established by him and with his option to continue at the same price.[59]

Max Bachrach continued, "The buyer has to make a cash deposit for his purchases and pay the balance on or before *Prompt Day*, which is the final payment day, and usually is set a month or so after the sale. Peltries that are unpaid for at the time become the property of the auction company for further resale, and any losses incurred must be borne by the defaulting purchaser."[60]

The buyer then arranged for the pelts to be shipped to the skin merchant, who often financed "large purchases beyond a manufacturer's resources. His superior knowledge, moreover, of markets also enables him to procure goods which the manufacturer, busily occupied with his workroom problems, would otherwise miss."[61]

DRESSING AND DYEING THE PELTS

When the auction sale was complete the furs might have been acquired directly by large dealers or by brokers who were agents of other dealers. The dealers then arranged for the raw pelts to be processed, that is, to be "dressed" and, if so desired, to be dyed. The dressers and the dyers did not own the pelts; rather, they performed their services for a fee, as contractors to the fur dealers and the manufacturers.

"Dressing" is essentially the process of tanning the pelt and making it durable and supple. This work was performed at a fur dressing plant. When the batch of skins arrived at the plant the pelts were first "plugged," marked "in some inconspicuous place, such as the paw," by a needle punch or "skin stamp" to give them the owner's identification code. The skins were then placed fur-down on a rounded "scraping beam" where a worker used a dull knife on the leather side to remove any residual fat or material still adhering to the pelt. White fox skins were then usually softened in damp sawdust in preparation for "fleshing." The fleshing step was carried out by craftsmen with sharp knives who very carefully removed the "areolar tissue," the membrane of fibrous connective tissue on the leather. "Fleshers," according to the furrier Russel R. Taylor, "are classified as highly skilled labor because the material on which they work is so valuable that none but the well-trained can be allowed to handle such delicate work." The skins were then washed in water or a mild soap solution to clean the hair and remove any remaining particles.

Next, the pelts had to be tanned, or "converted," by soaking in a liquid, such as salt or alum or other chemicals, to prevent "putrefactive agents from attacking the tissues"—in other words, to prevent them from rotting. Various oils were then applied to the leather side of the skin to make it supple. When dry, the skins were cleaned again by "drumming" them in large spinning containers filled with hardwood sawdust to absorb any excess oil. After that step they were "combed" to remove any clumps and matting, "beaten" by leather strips attached to a rotary roller to soften the leather, and spun in a revolving wire cage or blown with compressed air to remove any remaining sawdust.[62]

"Fur dyeing . . . is one of the most difficult operations encountered in the application of dye to materials," wrote the chemical engineer William E. Austin.

"The successful progressive fur dyer must be somewhat of a scientist as well as an artist," he added.[63]

Until the 1880s white fox pelts had been of only marginal value to the fur trade, but the market for them began to change when furriers saw the potential for dyeing them to imitate more expensive furs. In 1904, according to *Fur Trade Review*, in Vladivostok a white fox skin worth $2.50 could be dyed to imitate a blue fox worth $30.00 to $50.00. Prior to the First World War, much white fox dyeing was carried out in Leipzig or by Leipzig dye manufacturers who sold proprietary dyes to others, but as *Fur Trade Review* reported in 1921, "The war cut off the supply, so American chemists undertook the manufacture of these products. And have eminently succeeded in furnishing all the needs of American fur dyers."[64]

Russel R. Taylor declared, "Practically every [type of] fur money can buy is dyed. There are probably not a dozen [types of] furs marketed entirely independent of dyes." "Dyeing, more than any other step in the preparation of furs, has processes which are of immense value. Formulas are guarded as invaluable secrets, and each dye of acknowledged superiority . . . is the result of patient study and repeated experiments. Their composition and manipulation cannot be obtained from the discoverers. In many cases, fur-dyeing firms remain in the hands of one family, and the business, with its secret formulae, is handed down from one generation to another."[65]

Some white fox skins also needed to be chemically bleached to remove yellow tinge that the fox acquired from contact with sea mammal fat. Then the pelts had, first, to be "killed" with an alkaline solution to remove the oily protective covering on the guard hairs and underfur. Next, the skins were rinsed and dried before "mordanting" them with solutions of metallic salts to allow the hairs to retain the dye permanently and, if so desired, to help create certain colors. The furs were rinsed and dried again before the dyes were applied with a brush or by dipping them in a vat.[66]

By the 1920s fur dyers had developed an increasingly wide range of colors. And the trend accelerated in 1922, when blue fox scarves became popular. Even though fur farms were established to meet this demand, the market was so strong that it temporarily far exceeded the supply of blue fox pelts, forcing furriers to turn to dyed white fox skins. "Up to several years ago the range of colors employed by the fur dyer consisted of such colors as were found only on natural furs, namely, black, brown and grey," William Austin stated in 1926. "Today," he added, "almost every conceivable color and every shade and tint has been produced on fur." For example, by 1928 he listed the following colors for dyed white fox pelts: "pearl gray, silver, platinum, blue platinum (silvertone), ashes of roses, taupe, beige, new beige, peach, sand, champagne, rose, orchid, and cocoa."[67]

Some white fox skins that had been dyed black were also "pointed" to imitate the very expensive silver fox skins:

> Pointed fox . . . is usually either red or white fox dyed black, to which white hairs have been added by a very tedious process. . . . The fur pointer sits before a good specimen of a silver fox skin, or a good example of her own work, and carefully copies it by inserting white badger hair into the inferior skin where her eye tells her it is needed.
>
> This is done in the following manner: namely, holding the skin with her left hand, she picks up a white badger hair with her right and dips one end of it into especially prepared cement. A tiny globule of cement sticks to it. She blows gently into the fur at the point where the white hair should be. The effect is to create a funnel-shaped pit in the fur and into this she puts the white hair with its globule of cement. The cement instantly connects with several other hairs growing naturally in the skin and, hardening, anchors the foreign hair firmly. The process is repeated until the desired silver effect is attained. As is not at all usual with imitations, the pointed fox is fully as durable as genuine silver fox and a good pointed fox is more beautiful than a poor silver fox.[68]

MANUFACTURING THE FUR GARMENTS

Once the dressing-and-dyeing process was complete, the dealers and brokers sold their furs to large and small manufacturing furriers. "The White Fox is used for trimmings and for scarfs [*sic*]," Max Bachrach stated in 1930. "As trimmings for evening wraps, it is used either natural or dyed pale shades of gray and brown to match the various light-colored materials used. It is also used for trimming fur coats and wraps made of the flatter varieties of fur."[69]

Prior to the Second World War, although some white fox pelts were made into entire garments, such as ladies' evening coats and wraps, most were made into scarves, fur neckpieces, collars, and trimming. "Nearly everything was fur-trimmed in the 1920s and 1930s," stated the fashion historian Elizabeth Ewing. "Even more widespread than fur coats were fur-trimmed coats. Almost every winter coat, and many a summer one, had its fur collar and fur cuffs too. Such collars were wide and large, sometimes immense and rising to the ears, and they were of every kind of fur. . . . Black fox and blue fox were used on day and evening wraps, the entire animal being used to form huge collars for evening wraps."[70]

Fur manufacturers usually specialized either in making coats and wraps or in making trimming ("trimming houses"). Neckpiece manufacturers, who created stoles comprising several complete skins, were a specialized subset of the latter. When the skins arrived at the manufacturer's premises the first task was to sort them into matched batches. This was always done by a highly experienced "sorter."

The next step in the process of turning a fox pelt into a garment was to match it to a pattern. Large manufacturers usually had an in-house designer to create new styles each season, but the smaller manufacturers used independent contractors for the designs or received them from wholesalers, who may have financed their purchase in the first place. Paper patterns were worked up from these designs. Then the skins were dampened with water and, with the patterns, were sent to the "cutter." The cutter was the most highly paid employee because of his skill in blending the skins and in conforming them to the pattern. If the pelts were destined to be used in full fur coats and wraps, the cutter might "let out," that is, "drop" the pelts by cutting diagonal strips to make the skin longer and narrower.

David Mills described the cutter's work:

The cutter examines the fur side of the skin carefully and makes a few tiny incisions through to the underside. Then he turns it over and deliberately slashes the skin this way and that until it is truly a wreck of its former self. Sometimes he first marks the skin, but often he cuts with a free hand. And all of the time he is slashing, a slip of the cutter's knife may reduce the value of a five hundred dollar sable skin to about five hundred cents.

He cuts away the short haired parts, shaping the skin somewhat in so doing. He pulls and stretches the skin while he works, with the purpose of increasing the surface area where the fur is naturally heavier and decreasing the area where the fur is thinner, thereby giving the whole skin an even distribution of fur.[71]

The cutter then passed the furs to another highly skilled craftsman, the "joiner," who used a fur sewing machine to join the skins together into sections. After this step the sections were soaked in water, and the "nailer" laid them flat over the pattern and pinned them around the edges to a wooden board. "As the nailer does this," wrote Russel R. Taylor, "he stretches the skin evenly outward[,] adjusting each piece to fit the pattern in order to guarantee that the finished product fits exactly to the designer's dimensions. The sections are then left to dry, whereupon they are removed from the nailing boards and joined with the sewing machine to form a garment."

When the garment had been furnished with a lining and had been "finished" with button holes, fasteners, or other details, the last step was to pass it to the "glazers," "who comb out the fur with fine wire brushes, dampen it and carefully run a warm iron over the entire surface of the garment to produce a lustre to the pelts."

A few manufacturers specialized solely in making neckpieces and stoles from the entire skin. It was a labor-intensive process that required packing the skin with wool wadding, forming the head on wooden molds, inserting glass eyes, and, if the skins had been damaged and were missing parts, adding paws or tails.

"It should be pointed out that in the fur industry, there is very little waste of raw material," Taylor added. "When skins go to the cutter's bench, the heads, paws, tails and portions of the flanks are removed but not thrown away[,] for even tiny scraps of fur have a commercial value."[72]

WHOLESALE AND RETAIL

When the fur garment was complete and ready for sale by the manufacturer, it might move in several ways to reach the consumer. Small manufacturers usually sold to wholesalers ("jobbers"), who might have supplied funding, guidance, and patterns to them. The wholesalers in turn sold mostly to small retail outlets at a markup of about 15 percent. Larger manufacturers sold directly to large retailers and to "resident buyers" who acted as agents for the retailers. The retailers fell into three categories: large department stores with fur departments, women's specialty stores, and custom furriers. The retailers made their purchases based upon trends in fashion and priced them according to their targeted customers.[73]

A purchaser typically paid bills from thirty to sixty days after receiving the goods. So, to increase the seller's cash flow, at any step in the process, from large fur lots to retail, the seller of the goods might turn to a factoring company to quickly obtain payment for the invoice. The factor would purchase the debt and—based on the creditworthiness of the billed customer—immediately pay the seller 70 to 90 percent of the invoice value and pay the remainder, less 2 to 6 percent, when the factor received payment of the debt.

Thus a fox pelt that had been collected in the Arctic in winter might have traveled thousands of miles and taken a year or more to reach the consumer. Before the customer acquired the fur garment it would have passed through many hands on the way, gaining value at each step and helping to provide a livelihood for many persons: the trapper, skinner, flesher, tripper, trader, baler, city collector, drummer, sorter, sample man, auctioneer, broker, dealer, grader, dresser, stamper, scraper, flesher, bleacher, dyer, pointer, manufacturer, designer, cutter, joiner, nailer, finisher, glazer, jobber, factor, resident buyer, and retailer.

Part 2

DEVELOPMENT OF THE WESTERN
ARCTIC FUR TRADE TO 1914

During the four decades preceding the outbreak of the First World War the Native inhabitants of the Western Arctic adapted to several profound challenges to their livelihood. They were forced to cope not only with the results of the whaling fleet's reduction of the bowhead whale and walrus populations but also with the severe reduction of the caribou herds of northern Alaska and the northern Yukon, all of which were central to their subsistence. The decline of the caribou herds was the result of several factors: among them, a probable natural cyclical fluctuation in herd numbers and changing migratory patterns, and also, perhaps, overharvesting through the widespread use of repeating rifles, and, after 1890, intense market hunting to provision the wintering whaling fleet on the arctic coast. In the same decades epidemic diseases heavily reduced the Indigenous population—in some northern societies by more than 80 percent. Other challenges assaulted them as well: the sudden arrival of large numbers of foreigners during the Klondike gold rush; the rise of Nome, Alaska, as a frontier city and market hub; and the equally sudden decline in the market value of whalebone (baleen). Simultaneously the value of northern furs, particularly fox furs, began a mostly steady increase, an event that many Northerners, both Native and non-Native, exploited to their advantage by turning to trapping and focusing their energies on acquiring marketable pelts.

The trend toward wearing furs as an ornamental article of fashion developed in the mid-nineteenth century. "To the couturier, Doucet of Paris, goes the credit for introducing to the mode the idea of handling fur as fabric with the texture to the outside," wrote the historian of fashion Ruth Turner Wilcox. There were several reasons for this change in dress, but one of them certainly was the beginning of the widespread use of central heating systems in northern areas of Europe and North America. Buildings became comfortably warm when fitted with circulating hot air, steam, or hot water systems. This in turn allowed lighter clothing to be worn indoors and stimulated the use of greatcoats and overcoats for outdoors wear over the lighter garments.[1]

At the same time the increasing wealth and prosperity of the growing middle classes led to displays of wealth in dress. The fashion historian Elizabeth Ewing declared, "The leisured, expensively and conspicuously dressed woman was, by a kind of unofficial revival of long past sumptuary laws, a social phenomenon, a status symbol by which not only she herself but her husband and family too were given their place in the stakes in a class-conscious society which, for the first time in modern history, equated class with money before anything else." Elsewhere Ewing wrote, "Victorian materialism and the rise of the great, increasingly numerous and prosperous middle classes . . . were part of an immense social revolution of which fashion would carry the imprint in its own ways. More and more of the populace were going to be involved in fashion as clothes manufacture and retailing grew and developed." An exemplar of this change in taste was that in 1851 in London the Hudson's Bay Company became one of the primary exhibitors at the Great Exhibition of the Works of Industry of All Nations, colloquially known as the "Crystal Palace Exhibition." The company's exhibit displayed its Canadian furs, among them: beaver, bear, fisher, red fox, white fox, cross fox, silver fox, marten, muskrat, otter, and wolf.

Throughout the latter half of the nineteenth century the market for fashionable furs increased on both sides of the Atlantic until, according to Elizabeth Ewing, "In 1900 a signal event was added to the story of fashion and of fur in fashion. For the first time fashion was featured in a major international exhibition; appropriately it was the Paris Exhibition Universelle. The fashion section, under the aegis of Madame Paquin, the first woman to achieve world-wide fame as a dress designer in the world of haute couture, was a spectacular display and it included not only day and evening ensembles but also newer fashion items, including fur coats and tea gowns. . . . From this time fur coats and fur accessories began to appear regularly in the collections of the leading French fashion houses." Madame Jeanne Paquin was renowned for the extensive fur department in her *maison de couture* and for her skill in advertising and marketing her creations.

Elizabeth Ewing continued, "All this was characteristic of the general trend of fashion in England as well as Paris. The trend grew through Edwardian times and probably never have fur stoles, wraps and coats been worn with such pride and bravura as in those golden years. The huge panoply of dress paraded by the wealthy and fashionable knew no bounds, and furs were one of the crowning glories of it. Photographs and catalogues galore record every detail of those strangely corseted, unnaturally curvaceous figures with their larger than life furs. . . . Stoles reached almost down to the ankles . . . muffs were contrived from two complete fox skins, and skins were used complete with heads, paws and tails. . . . The great age of fur display."[2]

Because of the growth of the middle class in North America, its domestic fur market was also developing swiftly. In 1870, for example, fewer than 200 fur manufacturers in the United States employed 2,900 persons, producing $8.9 million of gross product; thirty years later the number of furriers was five times as large, with 27,000 workers producing $55 million of gross product. The result was that the United States became a net importer of furs, whereas previously it had been a net exporter.[3]

Understandably, this surge in fur use was reflected in the price of white fox pelts. During the decade of the 1880s white fox pelts annually averaged $2.73 at the Hudson's Bay Company's London sales, but in the early 1890s dyed white fox began to come into vogue. "The fur until recent years was of little value," wrote Henry Poland in 1892, "but now it is much admired, and exceeds the price of red fox. It is dyed light brown, blue, dark brown, black, imitation silver fox, etc., and its tail makes excellent boas. In the natural state it also makes excellent wrappers or sleigh robes." By 1894 C. M. Lampson and Company, fur auctioneers of London, sold 7,000 white fox pelts from Alaska and Siberia, almost all of them going to the Leipzig fur dyeing trade. Eight years later Leipzig dyers were converting 30,000 white foxes, worth $500,000, which comprised "about the whole available product of the world's markets."

In the first decade of the twentieth century white fox was commonly used in wide stoles, and motoring coats, and, according to Ruth Turner Wilcox, "the flattering white fox neckpiece became fashionable summer wear." Consequently, from 1900 to 1909 the average price of a white fox pelt rose to $6.89 from $3.00 in the previous decade. The result was that although from 1870 to 1910 white fox pelts ranked between ninth and twelfth by volume in the Hudson's Bay Company's auctions, by price they now ranked third, after beaver and marten.[4]

Nevertheless, at the end of the Edwardian era—which may be said to have occurred roughly about 1910—fur fashions began to change again, and dramatically so. In 1908 a brilliant young Parisian couturier, the innovative Paul Poiret, introduced a slim, natural dress shape emphasizing "simple vertical lines" with a relaxed waist that did not require wearing a corset. The fashion spread quickly,

Edwardian actress Marie Studholme with
a white fox stole and trimming.
Getty Images 463966943.

and suddenly the market for whalebone corset stays collapsed, effectively ending the arctic whaling industry: the price of whalebone fell steadily from a high
of more than $5.00 per pound in 1907 to $1.35 in 1913, and in 1914, with the
outbreak of war in Europe, there was no demand. By then, however, some of
the resident arctic whalers, both Native and non-Native, had begun to turn to
trapping and trading for white foxes and other northern furs.

"The straight vertical line remains the basic principle of modern dress," Alison Gernsheim wrote in 1963. According to Elizabeth Ewing, Poiret's innova-
tion was nothing less than the start of modern fashion. "The costly fur coat,
made of finest sable or ermine, tapered into the Edwardian waist, was now
rivaled by the strait coat of less expensive fur and less expensive workmanship.
. . . Long, wide stoles of various furs, with matching pillow-shaped muffs of
huge size, also gave warmth and dignity to the simple up-and-down clothes that
fashion decreed. . . . Such furs became part of the ready-to-wear fashion scene

which was catering with increasing zeal and effectiveness for the many rather than for the few. Specialty fur shops of an inexpensive kind sprang into existence . . . and stores developed their fur departments with large stocks of popular priced fur coats and garments." This change in coat design was achieved because fur dressers had learned to produce pliable pelts that made it possible to treat fur as a lighter fabric.

A similar and contemporaneous development took place in fur trimming. It was used as an accessory and came into wide use after 1909, when, in Paris, the impresario Sergei Diaghilev introduced a vogue for exotic orientalism via his Ballets Russes. A wide variety of garments were suddenly fur trimmed—even lingerie and summer dresses—a trend that persisted for two decades or more. White fox fur was used to trim jackets and mantles, and white fox muffs and stoles were in vogue. Simultaneously French couturiers experimented with a wide variety of dyed furs, and white fox dyed to a champagne hue was a favorite.

Consequently the average price of white fox pelts jumped to four times what it had been in the decade of the 1890s: from 1910 to 1919 white fox prices at the Hudson's Bay Company sales in London averaged $12.07 a pelt, a figure that included a price slump during the war years. News of these prices was widely disseminated, both directly and indirectly, and this information did not take long to reach the traders and trappers in the Western Arctic. It set the stage for a vigorous expansion of the fur trade throughout the region.[5]

3

THE ADVANCE OF THE MARITIME TRADE IN THE BERING STRAIT REGION

THE CHUKCHI PENINSULA PRIOR TO 1899

In the late eighteenth and early nineteenth centuries Natives of the region—Chukchi, Yupik, and other groups—acquired manufactured goods primarily via an annual trade fair that took place in western Chukotka on a tributary of the Kolyma River, 800 miles west of Bering Strait. They received these trade goods in return for their whalebone, furs, walrus ivory, reindeer meat and skins, and other commodities, some of which had originated in Alaska and Western Arctic Canada. The manufactured goods were then traded hand-over-hand between Native traders in the same chain of exchange that carried the raw materials to Chukotka.[1]

The focus of this intra-Native trade changed dramatically in the second half of the nineteenth century. The Chukchi and Yupik of Chukotka and the Eskimos of western and northern Alaska suddenly received substantial amounts of manufactured goods via the whaling fleet, which had discovered the Bering Strait whaling grounds in 1848. Baleen ("whalebone") because of its flexibility and durability was a highly sought-after commodity: in the mid-1870s ladies' fashion began a thirty-year trend in accentuating women's waists, and this required flexible boning for ladies' corsets. The best corset stays and busks came from the baleen of the bowhead whale, a fact which drove the price of baleen steadily upward until about 1907.

The whaleships, of course, captured large numbers of bowhead whales at sea and steeply reduced the bowhead population, killing more than 18,000 by 1914 and perhaps as many as 150,000 walruses as well, but the whalers were also traders, and the coastal Natives likewise captured bowheads in spring and fall. The Native whalers hunted bowheads primarily for their meat and blubber; baleen was of secondary importance to them until its price shot up in the last decades of the nineteenth century. In addition to baleen, the Natives had other marketable commodities for trade: white and red foxes, wolverines, wolves, ground squirrels and marmots, walrus ivory, and reindeer hides.

The whaling captains traded for all of those products in return for manufactured goods. The Natives of the Bering Strait region had, in fact, long since passed the time when they could exist without foreign manufactured goods, goods which had become both necessary and a convenience to their livelihoods. One Native at Cape Chaplin understood how complete their reliance on trade from the ships had become and told the journalist Herbert Aldrich that the Yupik ("Masinkers" in the whalers' jargon) might perish, "I b'lieve no whale-ship, Masinker man all die."[2]

As an example of the size and variety of the whalers' trade, in 1887 the whaleship *Frances Palmer* of San Francisco sold the following goods at the Yupik settlement at Plover Bay: 5 boxes of tobacco, 2 packages of leaf tobacco, 1 Winchester rifle, 3 boxes of reloading tools, 2 dozen knives, 700 Winchester Center Fire cartridges, 300 fifty-grain loaded cartridges, 2 pieces of white drilling, 27 bags of flour, 300 pounds of bread, 12 packages of matches, 4 hatchets, 2 axes, 1 saw, 1 mechanical toy, 1 whaling bomb lance, 1 dozen thimbles, 1 dozen spools of thread, 1 dozen papers of needles, and 5 pounds of beads. In return the captain received 237 white fox skins, 10 red fox, 1 polar bear skin, 1 brown bear skin, 92 pounds of walrus ivory, 100 pounds of whalebone, 10 pairs of native boots, and 2 fur parkas. And this was the report of one transaction, at one settlement, by one ship out of a fleet of forty whalers and an unknown number of small trading vessels. In fact by 1901 the trade had become so pervasive that when the ethnographer Waldemar Bogoras visited the settlement of Ungaziq at Cape Chaplin he reported that within a population of 440 Yupik, there were 400 firearms.

These coastal Natives also bought American whaleboats, because a whaleboat's performance was in some aspects superior to their walrus-hide-covered skin boats. Eleven years after the *Francis Palmer*'s trade, Captain John A. Cook, master of the whaleship *Bowhead*, visited Plover Bay and wrote that the natives "have been very quick to grasp the big advantage a whaleboat is to them over their big skin canoe, and they will save for years articles sufficient to trade in for a whaleboat." By that year, 1898, Cook estimated that in the short stretch of about thirty miles of coast between Plover Bay and Cape Chaplin the Yupik owned about thirty American whaleboats. A decade later several trading vessels routinely carried two or three extra whaleboats to sell to the Natives. By 1915 the going rate to purchase an American whaleboat was $1,000.[3]

In turn, a number of Natives were able to amass substantial wealth and be-

A Yupik trader's storehouse (probably Quwaaren's) at
Cape Chaplin on the Chukchi Peninsula in 1901. The
materials for the storehouse were probably shipped
north from San Francisco aboard a whaling or trading
vessel. The man on the roof with the spyglass (possibly
Quwaaren) is apparently scanning the horizon for ships
or game. The woman in the foreground appears to be
scraping a walrus hide. In the distance on the far left
is a traditional Yupik house. American Museum of
Natural History Library, No. 1358.

come important traders on their own. One of the most successful Native traders was Quwaaren at Cape Chaplin. In 1891 Quwaaren owned 3 wooden store
houses that contained 200 sacks of flour, 80 boxes of tobacco, and ivory and
whalebone worth between $5,000 and $8,000. He also sold secondhand whaleboats, outfitted 4 whaling crews, and owned 100 reindeer. In fact, five years
earlier he had purchased the sixty-foot schooner *Henrietta* from Captain Benjamin Dexter in return for 2 heads of whalebone (approximately 4,000 pounds of

baleen worth almost $11,000), plus 800 to 1,000 pounds of walrus ivory, 500 fox skins, and 3 polar bear skins. Unfortunately for Quwaaren, however, the Russian patrol ship *Kreiser* confiscated the *Henrietta* because it was a foreign vessel operating in Russian waters, and Quwaaren had not obtained the necessary permit from the government.[4]

THE GOLD RUSHES

On the American side of Bering Strait large amounts of trade goods began flowing to Alaska in 1867, when the United States purchased Russian America. This ended the Russian-American Company's trade monopoly and opened the region to small traders, who quickly established many posts on the Yukon River. But the genesis of a vast invasion of foreigners took place in 1896, when prospectors discovered gold in tributary streams of the Yukon River near the Alaska-Canada border. The result for the Natives of the region was, as the historian Matthew Klingle put it, "the demographic equivalent of an earthquake." In 1897 the first ships carrying miners from the Yukon reached West Coast ports loaded with nearly $1,500,000 worth of gold—and the rush to the Klondike was on. Twenty steamers left for Alaska that summer, carrying 10,000 persons from Seattle alone. Others hiked over the Pacific mountains via the Chilkoot Pass to reach the upper Yukon drainage, and still others descended the Mackenzie River and crossed the mountains to reach the gold fields. Dawson City on the Yukon briefly became the largest city in the Pacific Northwest, and Seattle suddenly became a major point of supply for northern and western Alaska, and for the Chukchi Peninsula as well. Seattle merchants grubstaked many of the prospectors, who often turned to fur trapping to pay off their debts to the grocery and general merchandise businesses, sending them their furs, thus creating the beginning of Seattle as a major center in the fur trade.[5]

The whole Klondike region (and beyond) was soon staked for claims, and 800 of the miners, seeking new territory, spent the winter of 1898–1899 on the Kobuk River in northwestern Alaska, chasing a rumor in a fruitless search for non-existent pay dirt. But this spurious rush also coincided with the discovery of gold at Anvil Creek, thirteen miles west of Cape Nome on the Seward Peninsula. Many of the Kobuk prospectors heard the news and immediately headed to Nome, as did 8,000 from the Yukon. "The lucky ones found gold by washing it from the beach sands there, taking out $2 million that year alone. It was said that digging gold from Nome's beaches was easier than stealing it." The result was the founding of Nome, Alaska, in 1899, when 12,000 to 20,000 persons were reported to have immigrated to the region for the summer and about 5,000 were estimated to have overwintered.[6]

Nome, Alaska, 1900. In the center and on the left the Snake River winds toward the Bering Sea. A tent camp is on the sandspit. In the foreground, buildings are being hastily constructed. At the lower left is "Roscoe's Theatre Comique." Courtesy of Terrence Cole.

Suddenly on the sandy shores of Norton Sound, where only a handful of Eskimos had formerly lived, the brand-new town of Nome sprang up, with a brewery, twenty bars, four wholesale liquor stores, four hotels, six restaurants, two hospitals, one bank, thousands of tents and ramshackle houses, and—equally important—twelve general merchandise stores. It was raucous, disorganized, noisy, and occasionally lawless. Nome immediately became a frontier city, a transportation and communication center, an entrepôt that was the transshipment point for settlements throughout the greater Bering Strait region, and a point of cultural interaction and convergence for members of dozens of nations, Native and foreign.[7]

Immediately the Native inhabitants of the Bering Strait region—both Alaskan and Chukotkan—began visiting Nome for its opportunities for trade in skins, whalebone, ivory, carvings, native winter clothing and boots, and the possibility of wage labor. The King Island Eskimos sailed and paddled their skin boats (umiaqs) to Nome's east end and usually camped under them for

The Alaska Mercantile Company store in summer, Nome, ca. 1905.
Like all the general merchandise stores in Nome, the Alaska Mercantile
Company stocked fresh produce (lower left) that had been shipped from
Seattle. On the right are coal-fired stoves. Alaska State Library, ASL-P12-081.

the summer, while the Diomede islanders did the same at the west end. They
were joined by Native traders from St. Lawrence Island and the easternmost
settlements of Chukotka. Some Eskimos also arrived in Nome from as far south
as Nunivak Island, which lies offshore between the Yukon and Kuskokwim river
deltas.

In late May 1905, for example, Nome's *Daily Gold Digger* reported that
125 Natives had arrived, including two boats from the Diomede Islands and
two from "East Cape" (Cape Dezhnev): "Ok-to-yuk brought over much ivory
and furs which he traded for groceries and provisions. He says the natives are
very successful in whaling and he personally had in the neighborhood of 5,000
pounds of whalebone cached at home, which he will dispose of when the price
is high enough to meet his ideas. He left on the whaler Belvedere for his home
last night, taking with him about six tons of supplies."[8]

Beverly Dobbs's photograph of Yupik traders from Cape Dezhnev arriving in the Snake River at Nome, ca. 1905. These traders had traveled 150 miles from their homelands. Their skinboat is laden with hides and other trade goods. In the background are the hastily erected structures on Belmont Point in Nome. University of Washington Libraries, Special Collections, UW26276.

"Exorbitant prices were a classic marker of the frontier commercial outpost," the historian Timothy Mahoney wrote in his analysis of frontier cities of the American West. "A nascent frontier economy was initially supported by capital brought by settlers and merchants. This support could last for a season, several years, or in some cases for a decade or more. Whatever specie merchants received, they quickly transmitted it to the metropole to settle credit obligations. Because it took so long for orders to be received and for goods to be shipped from the metropole, merchants were compelled to order most of their inventory early so it would arrive before the start of the season. This forced them to tie up much of their capital in their inventories." And to balance their books, this debt load required high profit margins on the sale of their goods.

J. W. Anderson, a Hudson's Bay Company trader, had a similar view: "Rising or falling fur markets made it extremely difficult for the fur trader to estimate

Diomede Island Eskimos camped at Nome, 1905. These men use
their forty-foot walrus-hide-covered umiaq for shelter. Courtesy
of the University of Pennsylvania, Penn Museum, No. 11671.

his merchandise requirements, especially when the isolation of that day ne-
cessitated orders being placed months ahead of delivery dates." In fact, Anderson and Mahoney could well have been describing the dilemma of Nome's
merchants in coping with the four-to-five-month shipping season, which was
bracketed between "break up" and "freeze up" in the northern Bering Sea. The
payment for the furs they had bought in winter often was only received from
auctioneers the following year. Mahoney continued, "Town merchants, desir-
ous of developing trade, extended credit to farmers and then were often compelled, given the lack of specie, to accept produce for payment. In some ways,
merchants had no choice, as they needed something in remittance for the credit
extended that they could use to settle their rising debts back East. In an era of
slow communication and shipping, orders for goods for a coming season from
frontier merchants had to be out several months to a year ahead and shipped
weeks or months ahead to arrive at the beginning of the season. Thus almost all
a merchant's capital went into his stock of goods, the returns on which were at
most a guess, based on previous activity." And for those merchants who backed

long-distance trading expeditions in the Arctic, the payment might arrive only two or three years—occasionally four or even five—years later.[9]

In the first waves of arrivals at Nome were the soon-to-be-prominent merchants Antonio ("Tony") Polet, an Italian immigrant who established Polet's Store, and Ira Rank and his brother, who acquired the U.S. Mercantile Company. Polet and Rank, as well as several other merchants, including the Wittenberg and Seidenverg families, became a commercial force, supplying capital and commodities to miners and traders throughout the region.

Oddly enough, the evolution of the internal combustion engine was also an important element in the development of this trade. By the time of the Nome gold rush the gasoline engine had been well adapted for marine uses in smaller vessels ("gas boats"). Almost immediately a fleet sprang up in Nome, perhaps forty in all, many of which were thirty to sixty feet in length, with cargo capacities of ten to forty tons (measured by volume, not mass). The general merchandise stores of Nome often outfitted miners on credit, and they did the same for the group of maritime traders.

In 1910 John W. Kelly wrote in the *Nome Nugget* under the headline of "Nome's Mosquito Fleet":

> Looking at a chart of the routes covered by these vessels, the lines resemble a spread eagle whose feet rest on the Aleutian Islands and whose wings cover the Arctic Ocean from Cape North [today, Cape Schmidt] in Siberia, eastward over the north shore of Alaska to Mackenzie river. Some carry mining supplies and miners to various diggings, others take out cargoes of merchandise which is bartered for whalebone, ivory and various rare and valuable furs, such as the sable of Kamchatka and the rare black and silver gray fox from beyond the Mackenzie river in British North America. Others carry reindeer and school supplies for the United States Government. . . . All this commerce is strictly modern and consistent with the building of Nome [and] the development of the gas engine. . . . The modern Nome navigator has a little piece of machinery that does the work of 200 men, so he has more space for cargo and his store list of food and water is much less. Many of Nome's fleet have only three or four men on board. . . . A great future for the mosquito fleet is dawning.[10]

Rank and Polet and other merchants usually offered the maritime traders a deal that, if the trader supplied the schooner and the manpower to sail it, they would supply the trade goods, sell the furs and other cargo, and split the profits. At the same time transient fur buyers, acting as purchasing agents for fur companies in New York and elsewhere, simply chartered some vessels outright (including the services of the captain and crew in the fee), then outfitted the boats with trade goods and sailed aboard them while serving as the superintendent of cargo ("supercargo") in charge of trading and directing the movements of the vessel.

These small vessels fanned out from Nome, traveling throughout the Bering, Chukchi, and Beaufort seas on voyages that ranged as far south as the Kuskokwim River delta and the lower Yukon River, as far west as the Chukchi Peninsula, as far north as Point Barrow, and east into Canadian waters. A few merchants, such as the Rank family, the Rotmans, and the Magids, continued their practice of establishing outposts near centers of mining activity but also set up satellite stores at coastal and riverine Native settlements in western Alaska.

At the end of the navigation season in October the boats were hauled ashore via block-and-tackle at Nome or taken twenty miles east to Safety Sound, where they were allowed to freeze into its protected waters, safe from moving ice. As soon as the ice started to break up in spring, however, there was a mad dash to get the boats ready to leave as early as possible, so that they could work through the pack ice in advance of the rest of the trading fleet and thus "clean up" furs in remote settlements.

THE CHUKCHI PENINSULA, 1899 TO 1914

From the point of view of those Nome traders who were headed to the Chukchi Peninsula, "Siberia" began about 150 miles by water west of the city. Separating the Bering and Chukchi seas, the peninsula is the northeasternmost extremity of Asia. Its eastern tip, Cape Dezhnev ("East Cape"), lies only about 50 miles across Bering Strait from Cape Prince of Wales, which is itself both the westernmost point of the Seward Peninsula of Alaska and the westernmost projection of continental North America.

Perhaps a dozen Nome boats, carrying from 3 to 40 tons of cargo, visited the coastal settlements of St. Lawrence Island and the Chukchi Peninsula, ordinarily traveling as far west as Chaun Bay on the north coast, 800 miles by water from Nome, and to the town of Novo-Mariinsk (later renamed Anadyr) on the south, 500 miles from Nome. The Nome schooners often made voyages to the peninsula averaging between seventeen and forty-five days, and these vessels might make as many as five voyages per season.

In spring the urgency to launch the trading schooners as early as possible was particularly acute for the "Siberian" fleet, which hoped to beat the "outside ships" from Seattle and San Francisco to the Natives' winter accumulation of furs. But the Nome fleet worked at a disadvantage in the race to reach the western shore of Bering Strait. The outside ships usually were larger, more powerful, and better strengthened for bucking pack ice; furthermore, the sea ice on the west shore of the Bering Sea usually breaks up earlier, a fact that often allowed the outside fleet (which arrived from the southwest, sailing along the Kamchatka shore) the advantage of working through the opening water leads amid the pack ice, days or weeks before the Nome fleet could get across "the Straits." As the *Nome Nugget* reported in May 1912, "The gasoline trader Yorkey left last evening for Siberia with a full cargo of trading supplies . . . in hopes of cleaning up the furs and ivory ahead of the steam whalers, whose captains as a rule get the first crack at the Siberian trade in the spring."[11]

The anthropologist Waldemar Bogoras, who studied the Chukchi and Yupik at the turn of the twentieth century, summarized the foreign trade on the peninsula:

> At the present time [1901] the chief source of income of the natives are [reindeer] fawn-skins, which are much needed by the American natives and by the Alaskan [gold rush] miners for making fur garments; also skins of full-grown reindeer for sleeping bags, ready-made garments even of poor quality, and, most of all, various kinds of seal-skin boots, which are used both by the whaling crews and by the miners. Asiatic and American natives sell these boots by the thousand every summer; but the demand keeps increasing, and in 1901 the price at Indian Point [the settlement Ungazik at Cape Chaplin] was a sack of flour per pair.
>
> The chief places for trade continue to be East Cape [Cape Dezhnev], and especially Indian Point. . . . Two or three native traders in both places have acquired year by year a larger amount of native products, until finally they are able to obtain by exchange each summer a sufficient amount of European wares to last for the trade of the whole year. They have even bought wooden storehouses brought on purpose from San Francisco. At the present time the whole number of such storehouses on the Pacific shore is fourteen.

He added that in 1901 there were five wooden houses at Cape Chaplin (three owned by Quwaaren), three at Cape Dezhnev, and one at Uelen. "In trading with the whalers, a storehouse that is worth $100 in San Francisco, is sold for 100 slabs of whalebone (about 400 pounds), worth from $2.50 to $3.50 per pound; i.e. for $1,000 to $4,000."

Bogoras also noted that the American goods that were flooding the Chukchi Peninsula were of better quality and sold well below the prices asked by Russian merchants. "The American wares are generally twice as cheap as those brought from the interior of Siberia. Even those brought from Vladivostok by sea cannot compete with them, because most of them are of American origin."[12]

Nor did it take long for entrepreneurs and miners to conclude that if there was plenty of gold on the Seward Peninsula, then it must also be found across Bering Strait on the Chukchi Peninsula. In 1899, within a few months of the beginning of the Nome gold rush, investors organized companies and expeditions—"in search of a Siberian Klondike," as one promoter put it—to prospect for Chukotkan gold and minerals, as well as to trade for furs. And just as quickly word spread that an impoverished miner named Lipinski had borrowed $80 from the entrepreneur John Rosene in Nome and headed to the Asian coast, returning with a $1,500 profit from his trade.

And Rosene promptly headed to Russia to organize a company. In 1902, in association with a Russian partner, he secured a charter from the tsarist government and formed a joint-stock company, the Northeastern Siberian Company. Rosene set up an office in Nome and built three stations on the Chukchi Peninsula: near Cape Dezhnev, in Lavrentiya Bay, and at Emma Harbor in Provideniya Bay. According to the ethnohistorians Igor Krupnik and Michael Chlenov, "The stations . . . established in 1903–1904 were the first settlements built by outsiders on the Russian shore of Bering Strait. They consisted of a station house and store houses manned by a small permanent staff made up of the station chief and his assistants: prospectors, mining specialists, and guards. All of them were outsiders: foreigners, Russians, and locals of mixed origins called 'Kamchadals,' primarily from the Kamchatka Peninsula. These people were the first non-Natives to set up residence in local communities. They also facilitated the appearance of new actors from among the locals themselves: middlemen and traders with whom the later Soviet authorities would soon wage uncompromising war."[13]

By 1910 the Northeastern Siberian Company was bankrupt, but several of its employees remained on the peninsula, trapping and trading from a number of places on the coast. Among the newcomers: Julius Tomsen ("Billy Thompson"), a German from Latvia; August ("Gus") Masik from Estonia; Clarendon Coulson ("Charlie") Carpendale, an Australian; Bengt Vold ("Bender Wall"), a Norwegian; John Olson, a Dane; and Olaf Swenson, an American of Swedish descent. Swenson, as we shall see, stayed in the trade until 1931, forming his own companies and purchasing a number of large supply vessels for his operations. Several of these resident traders lived on the Chukchi Peninsula for many years, married Native women, and became part of the fabric of society there.

These traders were joined on the peninsula by some immigrants from surprisingly distant lands within Russia: from the North Caucasus came Fedor Karaev, his brothers Aleksandr and Moisei and his sister, and several others, including Sandro Malsagov ("Sam Malsago"), an Ossetian; Magometh Dobriev, a

Bengt Vold's ("Bender Wall's") house at Cape Serdtze
Kamen, 1913. The trader Vold married a Chukchi woman and
built a hybrid house similar to a Chukchi yaranga. Scull 1914: 149.

Chechen; and Bek-Sultan Galiev, a Dagestanian. They and other foreigners
set up posts at more than a dozen locations from Kresta Bay in the Gulf of
Anadyr to Cape Schmidt on the Chukchi Sea. Some also married local women,
and their ties of kinship within each community increased the volume of their
trade with the locals. The locally based traders immediately provided competition to the whaleships and the Nome schooners. The Yupik and Chukchi were
the beneficiaries of this newly reliable source of manufactured goods, which
they then distributed farther throughout the region via intra-Native trade exchanges.[14]

Simultaneously a handful of adventurous foreigners advanced the maritime
fur trading boundary along the north coast of Chukotka. Johan Koren, for example, a Norwegian naturalist and part-time trader, began his work in the area
in 1908. He was backed for trade by Ira Rank and later bought a small schooner,
the *Kittiwake*. In 1911 he sailed the *Kittiwake* as far west as the Kolyma River,
where he overwintered at the village of Nizhne Kolymsk, 1,000 miles by water
from Nome, becoming the first maritime trader to arrive there. On his way back
to Nome the following summer, pack ice trapped his schooner and crushed it
on the north coast of the peninsula in company with the motor vessel *Morris*,

A Chukchi house and trading posts at Dezhnevo, near Cape
Dezhnev, 1913. A yaranga, covered in walrus hides, is on the left.
On the right is a cluster of traders' buildings. Scull 1914: 157.

which was owned by the trader Max Gottschalk. Gottschalk, energetic and op-
portunistic, to say the least, was at that time wanted for murder by the Russian
authorities.

Koren was able to save his cargo and specimens and cached them safely on
shore. Then, with Gottschalk, he managed to sail a whaleboat to the Diomede
Islands in the middle of Bering Strait, where they were wrecked at freeze up.
Koren and Gottschalk were marooned on the Diomedes for several months and
then, in an amazing feat, crossed the dangerous moving ice floes of the strait
on foot in winter, reaching Nome in March 1913. Lawsuits and mutual recrim-
ination between Koren and Gottschalk concerning who owned the furs were
the result of this misadventure. In any case, in 1914 Koren bought the schooner
Eagle and again overwintered on the Kolyma, this time with the scientist Copley Amory. He continued his trading and collecting expeditions there until 1918,
when he became a victim of the influenza pandemic.[15]

Although there are a few anecdotal accounts of the barter with the peoples
of the Chukchi Peninsula, it is impossible to estimate its total volume because
there were multiple outlets for the Natives' fur, whalebone, and ivory: these
commodities could be traded not only to the schooners and whaleships but

also to local posts, to native traders, and to the occasional Russian trader who reached the peninsula overland. But it is certain that the volume of this trade was substantial, both inward and outward.

Nevertheless, fragmentary reports of four Nome trading voyages do offer a glimpse of this enterprise. In 1907, for example, Charlie Madsen headed west across Bering Strait. Outfitted by Ira Rank and sailing aboard the very small vessel *Immaculate*, which he had chartered from the Roman Catholic Church in Nome, Charlie carried three tons of trade goods, which included .45-70 and .44-40 Winchester rifles, barrels of flour, boxes of cube sugar, plug chewing tobacco, Black Bull leaf tobacco, knives, files, calico, spools of strong thread, colored beads, cups and saucers, and chewing gum. At the same time the small gasoline schooner *Hazel* was reported to have arrived at Nome from a trading voyage to "East Cape," but more likely it had also visited a number of coastal settlements on the Chukchi Peninsula. The *Hazel* returned with 600 pounds of whalebone, 220 white fox pelts, 266 red fox, 650 squirrel pelts, 18 sables, 150 reindeer skins, and 300 pounds of walrus ivory. And the *Duxbury* returned with 5,000 pounds of whalebone, 200 fox skins, 1,200 seal skins, "fur clothing of all sorts and a large amount of ivory." In 1909 the *Sea Wolf* reached Nome from "Siberia" with the pelts of 2 black foxes, 2 silver gray foxes, 2,320 white foxes, 60 brown bears, 23 polar bears, "and other furs of various kinds." In Nome in 1911, 26 arrivals and 31 departures were recorded for the Chukchi Peninsula, which exported $60,000 worth of goods and imported $115,637. In 1913 the *Nome Nugget* estimated that more than $1 million worth of furs had been exported from "Siberia" to Nome since its founding, and in that year alone $113,000 worth of furs had been exported.[16]

Natives proved to be quick learners in this trade, causing Charlie Carpendale, an agent of the Northeastern Siberian Company, to grumble that trading was becoming difficult and that the Natives were "growing too shrewd." Several Natives bought schooners on their own. The *Nome Nugget* stated in August 1910, "The natives are going into the trading business on a wholesale plan. Within the last two or three days they have purchased three of Nome's mosquito fleet of sailing boats, to engage in the trading business between this port and stations on the Siberian coast." The schooner *Hazel* was bought by "Charles Newvhakhah" (probably Nuuqaghaq), a Yupik of Plover Bay, where he "runs a trading post. The craft will compete with the white man in trading for bone and furs all along the Siberian coast." By 1915 "Kesunga" (probably Quzinga), an Eskimo from Diomede Island, had purchased part ownership in the schooner *Ram*. "Kesunga is a man of considerable substance and is a very progressive native," the *Nome Nugget* stated. At that time other "native schooners" were identified as the *New Jersey*, the *Spider*, the *Emily*, the *Belinda*—owned by natives from Little Diomede Island—and the *Chechaco*, owned by Itiahk of St. Lawrence Island.[17]

Initially at least, some of the Nome schooners and a few whaleships also carried alcohol, a contraband commodity that American and Russian laws forbade in trade with Natives. The *Nome Daily Gold Digger*, for example, stated in 1902 that Captain Edwin Newth (a notorious whiskey trader and pedophile) was reported to have sold whiskey at Cape Dezhnev. "The hootch was promptly taken to Cape Prince of Wales and as a consequence there was a spree and a murder."[18]

In the Territory of Alaska the U.S. Revenue Marine patrolled the coasts annually, and among its tasks was to control the illicit alcohol trade. By the 1890s it had suppressed that trade considerably. But on the Asian shore the Russian government's efforts to control the alcohol trade were modest and inconsistent, and consequently foreign vessels, flouting Russian laws, often operated with impunity. This problem developed in part because in the nineteenth century Russia's overland supply road between Yakutsk and the Sea of Okhotsk—its link with northeasternmost Asia—had been allowed to deteriorate. "With the road's dilapidation and other infrastructural shortcomings," wrote Ilya Vinkovetsky, "the entire region (including the Okhotsk Sea coast, Kamchatka, the Kurile Islands, the Commander Islands, the Chukotka Peninsula) became for much of the year essentially cut off from the rest of Russia."[19]

Although the Russian authorities wished to control the foreign trading activities in Chukotka, it was not until 1888 that they established "a special administrative unit" for the region, and its headquarters was not physically set up in Chukotka until 1895 at present-day Anadyr, which lies as many as 500 coastal miles from the settlements at Bering Strait. "It consisted of the local administrative headquarters, Cossack barracks, and a few wooden houses built for the Cossack families. For a full decade (1895–1905), the administrator of the Anadyr District, who had a few local troops called 'Anadyr Cossacks' in his command, was the sole resident Russian government officer between Kamchatka Peninsula and the Kolyma River. Prior to that there was none at all." The first resident Russian governor did not arrive on the Chukchi Peninsula until 1906, and only in 1912 was an officer stationed at the village of Uelen, near Cape Dezhnev.[20]

To make matters worse, the Russians' relations with the Chukotkan Natives were reported to be less than satisfactory. In 1897, for example, the governor of the Anadyr District, Nikolai Gondatti, stated, "When I was on Chukotsk Peninsula, the Chukchi asked me, 'Are the Russians our friends or enemies?' When

I answered, 'Friends,' they shook their heads doubtfully and said, 'When we are hungry . . . the Americans . . . give us flour and corned beef in exchange for our whale and walrus bone.'" And two years later Washington Vanderlip, a prospector and promoter, wrote that a group aboard a Russian ship near Cape Chaplin, wanting to trade with the Natives, "were set to work making [an American] flag, with which to decoy natives on board, for they can scarcely be induced to go on board a Russian ship, because of the rough treatment they frequently receive."[21]

"Language followed commerce," stated the historian John J. Stephan, noting that Russian bureaucrats "looked askance at English becoming a lingua franca among people who used the word 'Russian' to mean 'criminal.' Tsarist policies toward Americans oscillated between equally unsuccessful attempts at exclusion and regulation." To counter this the Russian government tried to enforce Russian sovereignty in the region through three means: by visits of ships from the Volunteer Fleet (vessels of the merchant marine that were subsidized to carry cargoes to Chukotka and the Kolyma River); by establishing government warehouses in the area to sell manufactured goods and foodstuffs to the Natives; and by increasing government patrol cruises. The Russian authorities unfortunately had been assigned a task that could not have been achieved with the limited resources at their disposal; they were attempting to patrol many thousands of miles on their Pacific coastline from Vladivostok to the Chukchi Sea.

In fact, in 1911, when the Russian icebreaker *Taymyr* reached Uelen, near Cape Dezhnev, one of the largest Chukchi coastal settlements on the peninsula, the ship's surgeon, L. M. Starokadomskiy, reported:

Uelen left us with the impression that this settlement was located on the American rather than the Russian shore. Nothing here was Russian, not even the language. The local inhabitants, Eskimos, knew more English words than Russian words. In the only store, kept by the Eskimo headman, all the goods—guns, harpoons, knives, axes, gramophone, dress coats, brick tea, sugar, flour, and assorted statuettes—were of American origin. The Vladivostok merchant Churin had attempted to open a store here, but had been unable to withstand the American competition. One should mention that the Americans had equipped the local inhabitants with good whaling boats with harpoon guns, and had supplied good hunting rifles, and a mass of essential domestic items. In one yaranga [a family house] I saw a sewing machine, on which they sewed overalls, which they wore over their normal fur clothing, from multi-coloured close-weave cotton cloth. One Eskimo had acquired a typewriter, on which he enthusiastically tapped out symbols that to him were quite unintelligible.[22]

But the Russian marine patrols were limited, and during the Russo-Japanese War of 1904–1905 they ceased entirely. And although Cossacks had been posted at a few settlements on the coast to prevent the alcohol trade, they often were more active as consumers of the traders' whiskey than in overseeing their trade with the Natives. By 1906 it seemed to Bill Jones—who reached the Chukchi Peninsula with trade goods but no alcohol—that "about all the natives seemed to want was tunga (whiskey) and we had none."[23]

In 1901, when Waldemar Bogoras visited coastal Chukotka, he reported on the scale of the trade. "Of ten ships which called at [Cape Chaplin] during my stay there . . . only two carried on a regular trade in rum. . . . However, quantities of rum, put into bladders and small gut bags, are carried inland far from [Cape Chaplin and Cape Dezhnev] . . . it even formed one of the most important items bartered by the Chukchee to the Russians. At present similar transactions take place at [Anadyr] every time the Chukchee and Eskimo traders come from the north."[24]

An anecdote describing the Russians' difficulties in suppressing the alcohol trade is a report of the behavior of Captain James McKenna, a flagrant bootlegger. Douglas S. Mackiernan, a sailor aboard McKenna's whaleship *Fearless*, recalled that in 1901 the ship left San Francisco bound for the Arctic, sailing via British Columbia to take on coal and cheap whiskey. McKenna cruised along the Chukchi Peninsula and traded the whiskey (in five-gallon coal oil tins), .45-70 Winchester rifles, reloading tools, gunpowder, candy, Bull Durham tobacco, flour, sugar, tea, and "fancy things" in return for furs, whalebone, ivory, and thousands of mukluks, which he intended to sell to miners in Nome. Unlike the common practice among whiskey traders in the late nineteenth century, McKenna never diluted his trade alcohol because the Natives by then had grown accustomed to that trick, and he never traded whiskey, solely because he knew that if he did he would have trouble with the Natives the following year.

When trading on the peninsula McKenna always kept a lookout to watch for smoke from the Russian cruiser that occasionally patrolled the coast. One day, at the settlement of Uelen, he spotted smoke on the horizon. Knowing that it would take too long to hoist the anchor to escape to American waters, McKenna immediately "slipped" the anchor chain (leaving it with a buoy on the chain) before hightailing it to Little Diomede Island, one mile on the U.S. side of the treaty line in the middle of Bering Strait. There McKenna dropped his other anchor. The Russian patrol ship arrived at Big Diomede, two miles away, on the Russian side of the treaty line, and sent a boat to the *Fearless* to inspect its cargo for contraband goods. But according to Mackiernan, McKenna, now in American waters, simply put his foot on the chest of the leader of the boarding party and shoved him back into the boat. Later, after McKenna had calculated that all was clear, he headed straight to Cape Serdtse Kamen, on the north coast of the peninsula, to continue trading, then returned to Uelen to collect his buoyed anchor.[25]

An account of the Bering Strait trade that was underway in 1905 appears in a report to the Imperial Russian Geographical Society. Describing Nome's trade with the Yupik and Chukchi, N. V. Kirillov listed the approximate yearly average trade goods of a family of ten:

> 20 pounds of whalebone, 100 pounds of walrus tusks, 250 seal skins, 10 arctic fox skins, 20 reindeer skins, 5 bearded seal skins, 5 pairs of native boots, and "other trifles," worth in total 273 rubles, 50 kopeks. In return, an average family received approximately: 2 Winchester rifles, 3½ gallons of alcohol, 120 pounds of sugar, 300 pounds of coarse flour, 36 bricks of tea, 1 shotgun, 600 cartridges, 24 pounds of shot, 12 pounds of gun powder, 24 pounds of lead, 500 percussion caps, 24 pounds [*sic*] of molasses, 12 pounds of leaf tobacco, 5 pounds of chewing tobacco, 10 pounds of kerosene, 60 yards of white drill (for a sail), 120 pounds of net fishing line, 50 yards of rope (for sail and anchor), 12 yards of calico, 50 needles, 5 spools of thread, 2,000 matches, 1 comb, 1 axe, 1 shovel, 2 large knives, ½ dozen teaspoons, 2 saucepans, 2 enamel teapots, 1 bucket, and others, including boards, biscuit, coal, and iron stove, canned food, clothing, etc., worth in total 273 rubles, 50 kopeks.[26]

In reality, the flood of inexpensive, high-quality goods from the United States into Chukotka in the late nineteenth and early twentieth centuries actually reversed the traditional flow of goods to Russian trade fairs in northeastern Asia. Previously furs from Alaska had been traded hand-over-hand by middlemen in return for Asian and Russian manufactured goods that were then carried east across Bering Strait. But the volume of the foreign maritime trade was such that by 1900–1901 it had completely distorted the values of the trade goods that were exchanged among the Natives. Waldemar Bogoras wrote, "American wares are bartered away by the Chukchee for commodities that, according to our scale of prices, are worth less than what is paid to the whalers for them. One rifle is sold for from 20 to 30 pieces of brick-tea, i.e., 8 to 12 rubles; one whale-boat, for 70 pieces of brick-tea, 30 pounds of sugar, 20 pounds of tobacco,—in all about 50 rubles. Smaller articles, such as [gun] powder, percussion-caps, cotton goods are bought by the Cossacks at still cheaper rates. The reason is that in former times the Russians did not accept whalebone, and set on their wares high prices in peltries; so that the Maritime natives who barter at present for American wares with whalebone are accustomed to regard them as of lesser value in comparison with Russian wares."[27]

In the years following the signing of the Treaty of Portsmouth in 1905 — which concluded the Russo-Japanese War — Russia resumed sending patrols along the coasts of Kamchatka and Chukotka, but the number of foreign vessels in those waters had also increased because Japan had received treaty rights to conduct fisheries on Russia's Asian coast, and the Japanese vessels also aggressively engaged in the alcohol trade.

Thus the volume of foreign goods that had entered the greater Bering Strait region surged after the gold rushes and the founding of Nome in 1899, when its resident fleet of small schooners saturated the area with trade goods, and this in turn encouraged the Natives to intensify their trapping and trading activities in both Chukotka and Alaska.

4

EXPANSION OF THE TRADE IN NORTHERN ALASKA AND WESTERN ARCTIC CANADA

NORTHERN ALASKA

In the early 1880s the price of whalebone (baleen) continued to rise, and in northern Alaska, where the Natives' access to manufactured goods had hitherto been largely from the summer visits of whaling and trading vessels, this seasonal availability quickly changed to year-round access when more than a dozen shore whaling stations were established between Point Hope and Point Barrow. These stations were built in an attempt to capture bowhead whales in spring, a season when pack ice prevented the ships from reaching that part of the dwindling bowhead population that swam near shore toward their summer feeding grounds in the Beaufort Sea. A few small schooners also overwintered in the same stretch of coast and also manned shore whaling crews in spring.

The stations and the schooners also served as trading posts, buying whalebone and furs in return for supplies and manufactured goods. The largest of the whaling station–trading posts was near the northernmost point of Alaska, at Barrow (today, Utkiaġvik), where, in 1893, Charlie Brower and two associates in the Cape Smythe Whaling and Trading Company entered into a partnership with H. Liebes and Company, furriers of San Francisco. Brower had arrived in northern Alaska in 1884 and thrived in the region, learning survival skills and marrying an Iñupiaq woman. He and his partners earned their living by shore whaling in spring and trading for furs throughout the year. For the winter of 1902–1903, for example, Brower sent to H. Liebes and Company 2,003 white fox skins, 18 blue fox, 27 polar bears, 53 red fox, 2 silver fox, 3 wolf, 166 pounds of walrus ivory, and 4,088 pounds of whalebone ("trade bone"), in addition to the company's own shore whaling catch of 1,486 pounds of whalebone ("catch bone").[1]

Left to right: Tom Gordon, Fred Hopson, and Charlie Brower at Barrow, 1898.
Five years earlier their Cape Smythe Whaling and Trading Company had become
an agent for H. Liebes and Company, furriers of San Francisco. Courtesy of
the New Bedford Whaling Museum, David Jarvis Collection.

View of the interior of H. Liebes and Company, San Francisco, 1893. Author's collection.

At its height, Brower's company outfitted ten to fifteen shore whaling crews, each of seven to eight men, paying them at the end of the spring whaling season with a year's supply of equipment, food, and firearms. The company kept the baleen from the whales they caught and traded for any that other shore whalers had taken on their own.[2]

The "trade bone" came mainly from several independent, entrepreneurial Iñupiat who outfitted their own whaling crews, sending out one or more boats in an evolution of their traditional whale hunt, and a number of them became wealthy. By 1910, for example, the famous whaling captain Taaqpak, from Point Barrow, was referred to as "a man of substance" by the Seattle *Post-Intelligencer*. "Takpuk's business with Seattle merchants this spring amounts to about $7,000, and next spring he hopes to double that amount. . . . Last fall when the schooner Volante, Capt. John Backlund [John Backland Sr.], arrived in from Point Barrow she carried Takpuk's whalebone and walrus ivory, and it sold for the sum mentioned. Acting on Takpuk's instructions, Capt. Backlund placed the money in a bank and this spring invested it in goods which he is taking north again on the Volante. . . . Takpuk has bought 400 sacks of flour, twenty cases of coal oil (for he uses a kerosene lamp and stove . . .), lots of groceries and other supplies,

The Cape Smythe Whaling and Trading Company buildings at Barrow.
The company's store is the large building facing front on the left. Courtesy
of the New Bedford Whaling Museum, Thomas Brower Collection.

and $1,500 worth of sporting goods, including rifles and ammunition. . . . Two
other Eskimo of Point Barrow, Apiow and Kungusuk, have freight aboard the
Volante aggregating $6,000."[3]

As more whaling stations were built, the competition for manpower increased, and so did the Natives' wages. At the height of the shore whaling boom
in the first decade of the twentieth century it required as much as $20,000 to
operate a large station for a year, which might approach approximately half a
million dollars in today's money. Because adequate manpower was essential,
and because the whaling fleet that was wintering in Canada's Western Arctic
had employed many of the local hunters, to retain their whaling crews for the
following year the stations had to pay the employees from $100 to $250 in trade
goods valued at San Francisco wholesale prices. For a while the profits were so
substantial for the shore whaling stations that in the Barrow area the Reverend
Sheldon Jackson reported that "supply and demand play upon each other in a
way not often seen on the outside. Last fall a man sold a good canoe [umiaq] for
a sack of sugar, sugar being a scarce commodity. The sugar originally cost about
$6 and a canoe costs $50. Mr. Brower values their canoes at about $75 each. . . .
Last year [1905] when Mr. [Fred] Hopson was manager during Mr. Brower's
absence, he paid many of his natives with guns—result, you could buy guns
cheaper for cash than you could in San Francisco." Describing this newly reliable access to manufactured goods, the geographer Joseph Sonnenfeld noted
in his study of Barrow village, "With increased supply came increased demand,
and in cases, increased dependence, in turn creating further demand."[4]

Little information exists describing the Iñupiat view of these circumstances, but in 1912 the explorer Vilhjalmur Stefansson observed of the Barrow Iñupiat: "The day has long gone when the Point Barrow people are economically independent. There was a time when they got from their own land and ice-covered sea all their food, clothing, fuel, and other necessities of life; but now they import tea, clothing, phonographs, jewelry, chewing gum, perfumeries, and a hundred other things of which they formerly knew no need. They must therefore have money to buy these things, and the money they get only from fox skins and whalebone."[5]

In summer Charlie Brower annually outfitted employees of the Cape Smythe Whaling and Trading Company with trade goods and sent them eastward by boat to the ancient trade rendezvous at Niġliq in the Colville River delta to buy furs from those few Natives that did not spend the spring whaling season working for the stations at Barrow. It was at Niġliq that coastal-dwelling Iñupiat had traditionally met interior dwellers to exchange products of the land and the sea. In conditions similar to the skewed intra-Native trade that took place on the Chukchi Peninsula at that time (chapter 3), this abundance of trade goods in turn stimulated and distorted the trade between coastal-dwelling and interior-dwelling Natives in northern Alaska. In July 1908—just before news of the collapse of the whalebone market had reached the north—Stefansson visited a group of Natives at Pitt Point, 100 miles east of Point Barrow, and described the strange economics that had developed because of their involvement with the shore whaling stations. These Eskimos, who were wealthy because of their participation in the shore whaling industry, were returning from visiting Niġliq, where they had traded for caribou, Dall sheep, and fox skins in return for

> ammunition, flour, tea, cloth, and other commodities—which they get cheaply at Point Barrow. . . . At Point Barrow these men work for the Cape Smythe Whaling & Trading Company, and for other white and Eskimo whalers. Some of the Eskimo at Point Barrow now carry on whaling on a large scale, maintaining as many as five or six boat crews. Irrespective of whether their employers are white or Eskimo, these men get each year as wages about two hundred dollars' worth of supplies. . . . The whaling season in the spring is six weeks. . . . For all the rest of the year the men have nothing to do . . . and can go wherever they like, while their employers must not only pay them a year's wage for only six weeks work, but also furnish them houses to live in, usually, and rations for the entire year. Of course the men are expected to get their own fresh meat, which they do by seal and walrus hunting, and by cutting in the whales, only the bone (baleen) of which goes to their employers. The employer supplies them with cloth for garments, and such suitable pro-

visions as flour, tea, beans, rice, and even condensed milk, canned meats and fruits. Each man each year gets, among other things, a new rifle with loading tools and ammunition. The result is that firearms are probably nowhere in the world cheaper than they are at Point Barrow. . . . When I first came to Point Barrow [in 1908] you could buy a new Winchester rifle of any type, with loading tools, five hundred rounds or so of smokeless powder ammunition, and a considerable quantity of powder, lead, and primers for five dollars in money; had you bought the same articles wholesale at the factory in New Haven, the price would have been in the neighborhood of twenty dollars.

Stefansson wrote later—and added prophetically—"but now [1912] that the price of whalebone has suddenly gone down . . . the Eskimo are facing a new era and the change will be hard on them." Stefansson was correct in his assessment, because, as we shall see, the second decade of the century proved to be a difficult one for the Iñupiat as they made the transition from whaling to trapping.[6]

Throughout the later nineteenth century a series of epidemic diseases entered the Arctic and steeply reduced the Native population of northwestern Alaska. The ethnohistorian Ernest S. Burch Jr. estimated that the Iñupiat population of northwestern Alaska fell from more than 5,000 persons in 1860 to about 1,000 in 1890. The decline was particularly acute at Barrow. In 1900 an interior-dwelling group of Eskimos had camped at Barrow to trade with the ships when a measles epidemic overtook them. According to the biologist Alfred Bailey, "one hundred seventy-six natives were buried at Barrow, while the river people were practically exterminated." Many died on their way back to their homelands, according to Charlie Brower. And measles struck again in 1902 when the whaling schooner *Altair*, under the command of Billy Mogg, stopped on its way back from Herschel Island. The schooner carried a woman who had been infected with measles. The disease had been carried down the Mackenzie River from the Yukon gold fields, and it quickly spread along the coast: the missionary John Driggs estimated that it killed 12 percent of the population at Point Hope and as many as half of the inhabitants in small settlements.[7]

At the same time, the collapse of the caribou herds in northern Alaska—the result of changing migratory patterns and a probable natural cyclical decline in the caribou herds' numbers, as well as possible overharvest by the Natives—had resulted in famine in the interior lands and the progressive depopulation of the North Slope of Alaska. One Native described the lean years to Captain Hartson Bodfish, who wrote, "They did have famines, when some great migration of game took place, and they suffered terribly at such times. One of my hunters told me of an experience that he had when the game left the section where he lived and he set out to find it. Leaving his hut, where his wife and children lay with nothing to eat, he travelled for five days until he found a deer [caribou] herd, of which he killed as many as he could. He first cut off the legs of a deer, cracked the bones, and ate the marrow. Then, taking a saddle on his back, he started for home. I don't know how long his family had been without food when he arrived, but they were all alive. After eating the meat he had brought, they hitched their dogs and brought in the rest. This was his toughest experience, he told me."[8]

In 1906 the geologist Ernest de Koven Leffingwell, who was based at Flaxman Island on the north coast of Alaska, reported that there were only two or three families living on the coast between Point Barrow and Herschel Island. And famine struck again: from 1907 to 1909 the caribou vanished almost entirely in the eastern Brooks Range, causing widespread starvation and some deaths and forcing many of the remaining interior-dwelling Eskimos to move to Barrow or to the North Slope of the Yukon. The Iñupiaq historian Simon Paneak remembered that there were very few caribou on the North Slope of Alaska in those years and that seven persons starved to death there. Charlie Brower at Barrow wrote that in 1908 "just at Christmas the Eskimo from inland began coming to the village[,] most of them hungry, no deer [caribou] had been seen for several years."[9]

At Barrow some of these deracinated persons found employment in the whaling crews or as reindeer herders in a government initiative that had been established to provide meat and hides to the Natives in the areas where the caribou had become scarce. By 1908, according to the Reverend S. R. Spriggs, who was the superintendent of government reindeer at Barrow, there were now 521 Eskimos living nearby in all walks of employment. In the winter of 1908–1909 Vilhjalmur Stefansson estimated that only about fifty families remained inland on the North Slope of Alaska between Point Barrow and the Canadian border: "Those who still live inland depend chiefly on river fish, though they get a few sheep in the mountains." Simon Paneak stated that in those hard times a few families turned to fox trapping.[10]

Of course, when the price of whalebone collapsed in 1908 everyone suffered, foreigner and Native alike. Couturiers in Paris embraced a new look that did not require boned corsets at all, and corset staying for the haute couture market had remained the last significant market for baleen. Most of those involved in whaling held on for a few years, hoping that the price would rebound. In 1904 the average price of whalebone had stood at $5.80 per pound, and it went higher still, but when the arctic whaling fleet reached San Francisco in autumn

1908 the men learned that the price had fallen well below the cost of acquiring it. That year, 1908, most of the few remaining whaling operators laid up their whaleships. In 1909 the market was so low that only three ships went north; in 1910 news reached Charlie Brower at Barrow that the price had dropped to $3.00 per pound. Of the 1911 whaling season Captain Hartson Bodfish wrote, "We had taken six whales and considerable trade bone, making a total of around 30,000 pounds for the voyage which was very good under normal conditions. But I didn't get a penny for my share. . . . The end of whaling had arrived, that was all, and I saw it plainly."

For a few years Charlie Brower and H. Liebes and Company continued to maintain their Iñupiat whaling crews at Barrow, which provided some support to the local Natives, but the company's profits from whaling were slim or non-existent, and Brower had the same view of the future of commercial whaling. He had spent the winter of 1910–1911 "outside," and in San Francisco he had attempted to convince Isaac Liebes to cease shore whaling, but "he thought the market for bone would come back and insisted we stay in the game. I wanted to quit then, while we were ahead," Brower wrote. "He told me if I quit they would wind up the business, so I stayed, and before long was broke. I wanted to cut out the whaleing [*sic*] [and] do nothing except a fur business."

In fact, so steep was the decline in the price of whalebone that in 1912 the steam bark *Belvedere*, commanded by Captain Steven Cottle, and the small schooner *Elvira*, commanded by Captain C. T. Pedersen, were the only whaleships to operate in the Beaufort Sea. That same year Cottle concluded that it cost him $3.00 or $4.00 per pound to take whalebone, for which he only received $1.50 to $2.00. He therefore planned to outfit the ship only for trade in the following season, and he calculated that he would require roughly half as many crew, perhaps twenty men.

Nevertheless, in the winter of 1909–1910 good news about the price of furs reached the Northerners. Seattle's *Post-Intelligencer* reported: "Record high prices for furs were obtained at yesterday's monthly sale of the Seattle Fur Sales Agency." Prime white foxes were now selling from $15 to $20 at auction, whereas in the early 1890s they had stood at $3 to $4. Three years later it was reported that the demand for wild furs had exceeded the supply.[11]

As a result of the rise in fur prices, in the winter of 1912–1913 Steven Cottle sold the *Belvedere* to the Hibbard-Stewart Company (fur and hide dealers of Seattle), retaining a share of the profits by running the ship. Hibbard-Stewart also formed a partnership with Olaf Swenson. Continuing its advance into the arctic fur trade, the company in 1912–1913 helped to finance Captain Louis L. Lane in building the motor schooner *Polar Bear*. Both vessels were intended to operate in the coastal trade throughout the Western Arctic, and simultaneously several small entrepreneurs began outfitting ships to concentrate on fur trading.

At the same time H. Liebes and Company and Charlie Brower reached an identical conclusion: although Brower continued to export "trade bone" until 1937, the final baleen exported by the shore whaling operation of the Cape Smythe Whaling and Trading Company took place in 1912. In 1914 Brower discharged his last Native shore whaling employees and encouraged them to concentrate on trapping.[12]

Thus the Natives of northern Alaska, who had migrated toward the whaling stations since the 1880s, began a slow dispersal, settling at points along the coast in groups of two or three families to trap for furs. In the winter of 1913–1914 the anthropologist Diamond Jenness reported that several Iñupiat trapping families were living on the coast between Point Barrow and Harrison Bay, and another six families were located between Flaxman Island and the Canadian border. "In winter," he wrote, "the families scatter by twos and threes for trapping. Frequently two families, generally but not necessarily connected by kinship, occupy a single hut. . . . In spring the families reassemble for sealing and whaling, but they are more or less unsettled throughout the summer and autumn."

Jenness noted that only one family was by then living on the Colville River and that a dozen Iñupiat families, the remnants of the former inland population, had moved south, over the Brooks Range, and were trapping below the tree line in the Endicott Mountains. Often those families traveled to the north coast in summer to trade with other Iñupiat, as well as with the handful of trading schooners that were beginning to visit the coast. He added, "Trade is producing a growing differentiation in the manner of wealth, but there is no distinction of class and no real poverty, for the needy are supported by their more prosperous neighbors."[13]

WESTERN ARCTIC CANADA

WHALERS AND IMMIGRANTS

In the four decades after about 1870, as we have seen, the decline of the caribou population in northern Alaska resulted in an existential disaster for the Natives and caused a diaspora that resulted in the gradual depopulation of the Brooks Range watersheds. In fact, in the mid-1880s the Iñupiat of the Upper Noatak River, facing starvation, had begun a migration northeastward to the North Slope of Alaska and the Yukon, where the Porcupine caribou herd was still fairly healthy, and where the Mackenzie delta Inuit had been reduced by scarlet fever, measles, and other epidemic diseases from approximately 2,000 persons in the mid-nineteenth century to 400 by 1910, according to some estimates.[14]

In the 1880s the rising price of whalebone and the declining number of bowhead whales had forced the commercial whalers to devise new strategies. First was the introduction of steam auxiliary whaleships to the fleet. With their greater maneuverability and range these ships immediately proved superior to the sailing vessels, and it in turn allowed them to expand their perimeter in search of the remaining bowheads. Each year the ships probed farther and farther east along the north coast of Alaska until, in 1888, one ship reached the Canadian border. In that year, too, the whaleship *Grampus* cruised near Barter Island. There, on August 7, the second mate, the young Hartson Bodfish, reported that he had traded for caribou meat, ducks, and two bearskins with "inland natives" who had never seen a ship before. These people were, in fact, the Nunatamiut emigrants from the Noatak River drainage who were moving eastward, scouting for new lands where caribou were plentiful.[15]

The other new strategy for the whaleships was to overwinter near the bowheads' summer feeding grounds. Of these wintering voyages (more than 100 in all) a few took place in northwestern Alaska, but the vast majority were in Western Arctic Canada: at Herschel Island, Baillie Island, and a few other sites. The whaleships also hired Natives (primarily from the Chukchi Peninsula, St. Lawrence Island, Point Hope, and Point Barrow) to serve as deck hands, boat crewmen, hunters, dog team drivers, and seamstresses. Entire families were often signed on for voyages of two years or more.

Once the ships had settled into their winter quarters a primary task became assembling food supplies for the winter, and the ships' officers and Native hunters set out to acquire caribou meat to feed the crew. They did this by hunting on their own and by buying meat from the Inuit and Gwich'in. The Nunatamiut were considered to be the best hunters, but Gwich'in from south of the mountains also hauled meat to Herschel. In summer the Natives, particularly the local Inuit (Siglit), whom the whalers and Nunatamiut referred to as "Kogmulit" ("people to the east"), also supplied fish and ducks to the ships.[16]

In the 1890s the whalemen bought meat for about six or seven cents per pound in trade, which they priced at San Francisco wholesale cost. In return, the whaling captains sold gunpowder, rifles, shotguns reloading tools, primers, lead, cartridges, pots and pans, carpentry tools, cloth drilling, calico, traps, needles, thread, thimbles, coffee, tobacco, pipes, sugar, flour, hardtack, bread, baking powder, molasses, raisins, knives, files, small stoves, coal oil, matches, soap, sunglasses, manufactured clothing, playing cards, and harmonicas, to name just a few of the items.

The whalemen, mainly the captains, also traded for furs: white fox, blue fox, red fox, polar bear, seal, marten, wolverine, caribou, and other pelts. And because they did not include the cost of transportation in the prices they paid, the whalers sold their trade goods at only about 20 to 30 percent of the prices charged at the Hudson's Bay Company's Fort McPherson post. In fact, in 1892 a group of enterprising Inuit traders arrived at the fort with a whaleboat full of trade goods and bartered with locals before returning to Herschel with their furs. John Firth, the company's factor at Fort McPherson, had seen his fur returns decline since the arrival of the whaleships at Herschel, and he sent word to the island that unless the whalers ceased trading for furs, he would no longer forward mail to the whaling fleet. Because they valued news from home, the whalemen may have reduced their trading activities somewhat, but some also trapped on their own. Captain Hartson Bodfish, for example, ran a trapline ten or fifteen miles long with "Fritz Wolki" (Franz Woeke), one of his harpooners.[17]

But sometimes these hunting and trapping arrangements between the whalemen and the Natives could go awry. The explorer Vilhjalmur Stefansson wrote in 1909: "The Man Kumaslik was hired on these terms: he was furnished fifteen (or twenty) sacks flour, besides rice, beans, tea, coal oil, etc., a new rifle, and a thousand cartridges, tent material, etc., and promised certain things at the end of the year, if he would do as follows: trap energetically with (fifteen) traps furnished for the purpose, and deliver all foxskins, half his deerskins and sheepskins, and the saddles of all deer and sheep killed to his employer. Kumaslik trapped six foxes and sold the skins, ate the saddles of all deer killed, and used all the deer and sheepskins, in fact willfully and openly broke every item of his agreement. Now he expects to receive . . . the things promised to him at the end of the year."[18]

The Nunatamiut immigrants from Alaska particularly ran long traplines and gained a reputation for entrepreneurial energy in contrast to the Siglit, the local Mackenzie Inuit, who less aggressively adopted the fur trade. In fact, by the winter of 1906–1907 the explorer Alfred Harrison reported that "the natives of this region do not consider that they have done well unless their traps have yielded them at least 300 dollars' worth of fur." With the proceeds from their furs and their sales of caribou meat, many bought wooden whaleboats, which allowed them to travel to Fort McPherson in July and to Herschel Island in August. In the same winter Alfred Harrison reported that although the Siglit had only "one or two" whaleboats among them, the Alaskan immigrants (Nunatamiut) had one per family. In 1909, for example, the *Edmonton Bulletin* reported that thirty Inuit-owned whaleboats had visited Fort McPherson.

Their whaleboats also enabled the Alaskan immigrants to hunt bowheads on

A group of Natives in their whaleboats sailing up the Mackenzie River toward the Hudson's Bay Company's post, Fort McPherson, 1906. Harrison 1908: 260.

their own. One group of them was so successful that in 1899 they paid Hartson Bodfish with enough whalebone to purchase a schooner for them in San Francisco. The following summer, 1900, Bodfish returned with the former sealing schooner *Sophia Sutherland*, aboard which the author Jack London had served in the Pacific. And in 1902 four Nunatamiut bought the small schooner *Penelope* for 1,200 white fox skins and wintered it for several years at Herschel Island, while using it in summer for trading and whale hunting.[19]

THE EASTWARD EXPANSION: FRITZ WOLKI, CHARLIE KLENGENBERG, AND BILLY MOGG

As fur trapping became increasingly rewarding in the early decades of the twentieth century it stimulated an eastward advance by trappers and traders. One of the first of these expansions of the trade perimeter took place when Hartson Bodfish outfitted Fritz Wolki to set up a post at the Horton River delta in Franklin Bay, southeast of Baillie Island. In 1905 Wolki delivered 1,400 white fox skins and 4 bear skins to Bodfish. In 1906 he salvaged several thousand pounds of whalebone from the wreck of the whaleship *Alexander* at Cape Parry.

An Eskimo family in their whaleboat, trading with the
schooner *Polar Bear* on the north coast of Alaska, 1913. Courtesy of the
New Bedford Whaling Museum, Dunbar Lockwood Collection.

The following summer he headed outside and quietly sold the whalebone in
San Francisco (without notifying the owner, H. Liebes and Company) and
bought the small whaling schooner *Rosie H.* He headed back to the Western
Arctic, but unfortunately for him that year turned out to be very icy, and he
could only get as far east as Flaxman Island on the north coast of Alaska before freeze up. Like most Northerners, he made the best of the situation and
wintered there, but the following winter, 1909–1910, he took the schooner to
the Booth Islands near Cape Parry, about 350 miles east of Herschel. After that
Wolki wintered the schooner behind the sandspit at Baillie Island and worked
from his Horton River camp about fifty miles south of there. In summer Wolki
used the schooner for whaling and trading.

Elsewhere, the movement east of Baillie Island began by accident and mal-
feasance. During the summer of 1894 or 1895 "Charlie Klengenberg" (Christian Klengenberg Jørgensen), a Danish cook turned sailor and shore-based
whaler, served as a ship's hunter aboard the steam whaler *Mary D. Hume*,
which cruised east of Herschel Island to the coast of Banks Island. Klengenberg
claimed to have landed there briefly and to have spotted human footprints on
the shore, despite the fact that the island was thought to be uninhabited. "If a

trader could get into their country with a good supply of trade goods," Klengenberg concluded, "he might have a chance to get furs cheaper than elsewhere in the Arctic, and could become wealthy."[20]

Klengenberg put his plan into motion in the exceptionally cold and icy summer of 1905. That summer, pack ice trapped most of the shrinking arctic whaling fleet east of Point Barrow, preventing it from returning south and forcing it to overwinter on short rations. Six ships wintered at Herschel and another four at Baillie Island. At the same time Roald Amundsen's exploration ship *Gjøa*— en route to completing the first ship's traverse of the Northwest Passage—was trapped offshore at King Point, about forty miles southeast of Herschel, and Captain James McKenna's *Charles Hanson* was frozen in on the coast a few miles east of the Mackenzie delta.

In the meantime no one knew the whereabouts of McKenna's other ship, the small schooner *Olga*. McKenna was in the twilight of a long and undistinguished career as a whaler, trader, and whiskey smuggler. At one time McKenna had owned a fleet of whaling vessels, but "his fortunes had gradually dwindled," wrote Vilhjalmur Stefansson, "until in 1905 [McKenna] had left of his whole fleet only the schooners *Charles Hanson* and *Olga*. . . . The *Olga* was commanded by an officer whom McKenna did not trust, so he decided to promote to the command Charlie Klinkenberg [*sic*], a Dane who had come to the country originally as a cook. Before this time Klinkenberg had acquired two kinds of reputation; one for enterprise, energy, and fearlessness, and the other for a character not very different from that of the buccaneers of old or the Sea Wolf of Jack London's story. McKenna, accordingly, did not trust Klinkenberg much better than he did the deposed officer. In that connection he got the bright idea of removing from the *Olga* all provisions except food enough for about two weeks, thinking that Klinkenberg would not try to run away with the ship if he had no food on it."

"That showed how little he knew of Klinkenberg," Stefansson added. Although McKenna had ordered the *Olga* to stay close to the *Charles Hanson* while they cruised for whales in the eastern Beaufort Sea, soon one of the Arctic's dense summer fogs enveloped both ships, and when it lifted the *Olga* was nowhere to be seen. Klengenberg had vanished.

During the winter of 1905–1906 speculation ran high, focusing on three possible scenarios: that Klengenberg was dead, that he had sailed the *Olga* outside to sell it in a foreign port, or that he had gone east in search of "Eskimos who did not know the present high price of fox skins."

The last supposition was the correct one. Klengenberg used the fog to cover his escape toward Langton Bay, where he knew that a whaleship had left a cache of provisions. He burglarized the ship's warehouse of its stores, tore it down, and put it aboard the *Olga*. He then headed to what he thought was the coast of Banks Island and overwintered there, trading with Inuinnait, who indeed were ignorant of the market value of their furs. Later, Joseph Bernard discovered that Klengenberg had, in fact, wintered on the southwest coast of Victoria Island, more than 150 miles from Banks Island.

Klengenberg returned to Herschel on August 10, 1906. But when the *Olga* had vanished in the fog in 1905, in addition to his Native crew, Klengenberg had nine sailors aboard, and when he returned he had only five. Klengenberg went immediately to the police and admitted to stealing McKenna's schooner. He claimed that during the winter two of the crew had fallen through the ice and drowned, another had died of natural causes, and the fourth man he had been forced to shoot to defend himself after the man began distilling alcohol against Klengenberg's orders.

"McKenna's ship was at this time not at Herschel although expected momentarily from a whaling cruise," Stefansson remembered. "Some of the other captains wanted the police to arrest Klinkenberg [Klengenberg] for having stolen the *Olga* . . . but they told the captains that they would restrain Klinkenberg if he tried to take the *Olga* away from Herschel Island before Captain McKenna arrived." Klengenberg agreed to this, and true to his word, then loaded his family into a whaleboat and headed west into United States waters, bound for Point Barrow.

As soon as Klengenberg left the island, his crew described an entirely different series of events. They claimed that Klengenberg had capriciously murdered one man, that the man who had died of "natural causes" had frozen or starved to death in chains, and that the men who were lost on the ice were the only witnesses to the murder of the first man. The Inuit who had been aboard as crew confirmed the sailors' report. According to Stefansson, "when the *Olga* had come in sight of Herschel Island, Klinkenberg had called all hands on deck and had made them a brief speech to this effect: 'Boys, you know the penalty for killing five men is the same as for killing four.' Then he outlined to them briefly what his own testimony to the police would be, and advised them to make their testimony similar."

Klengenberg eventually surrendered to authorities in Alaska, where a warrant had been issued for his arrest because although the alleged killings had occurred in Canadian waters, they had taken place aboard an American ship. Klengenberg was tried in San Francisco and, with few or no witnesses available, was acquitted on grounds of self-defense (see endnote).[21]

But most important for the Western Arctic fur trade and for its inhabitants was the fact that in spring 1906, Klengenberg had gone up the coast from the *Olga*

The whaleship *Olga* at Herschel Island, 1906. Charlie Klengenberg
wintered it on the southwest coast of Victoria Island and became the first
trader to visit the Inuinnait. RCMP fonds, e010869400. © Government of
Canada. Reproduced with the permission of Library and Archives Canada.

with a dog team and trade goods. In Prince Albert Sound he had met a group of
Inuinnait, people who had last encountered Europeans in the mid-nineteenth
century during the British search for Sir John Franklin's missing expedition.
Klengenberg traded with them and was disappointed by the fact that they had
few furs—the reason being, of course, that the perimeter of the fur trade had not
yet reached them. White foxes had little value to these Inuit because they were
entirely reliant on subsistence from the resources of their lands and waters, and
foxes provided them little food or warmth.[22]

Although Klengenberg claimed to have seen human tracks on Banks Island
in 1894 or 1895, it is more likely that he learned about the human tracks from
James McKenna or from one of McKenna's employees, because on August 3,
1902, McKenna's small whaling schooner *Altair,* under the command of Billy
Mogg, had landed a crew on the southwest coast of Banks Island. Mogg re-

ported seeing human footprints there, as well as musk oxen and caribou. Mogg was considered to be "a very low type of Englishman," according to Lieutenant David Jarvis of the U.S. Revenue Marine, who suspected him—as well as Klengenberg—of illicitly trading alcohol to the Natives. Jarvis added that Mogg had "been a number of years in the United States, acquiring the American manner and conceit."[23]

In any case, in 1907–1908 Mogg overwintered the *Olga* in Fish Bay in Minto Inlet on the west coast of Victoria Island and had traded with the Inuinnait of Prince Albert Sound, thus probably becoming the fourth foreign party (after the British explorers and Klengenberg) to trade with these people. When the *Olga* reached Baillie Island in 1908 the news of his encounter began to spread: suddenly it was believed that there were trading opportunities to the east, at a time when the profits from whaling were shrinking. Vilhjalmur Stefansson talked with Mogg and his crew in September 1908 when he visited the *Olga* near Cape Halkett, east of Point Barrow, where Mogg had unintentionally run it aground and it had been frozen in for the winter. Stefansson's field notes state: "The people of Prince Albert [Sound] Capt. Mogg estimates at 800, 250 of whom he saw. They are in the estimation of himself (and crew, including natives) a very superior class of people in honesty, resourcefulness and intelligence. Extremely hospitable. In winter they live on the ice. Seal are so abundant that at most abandoned winter camps one finds 'tons' of blubber either cached or left lying around. They have no fish nets, kill bears with spears, every man and dog turns out, and deer [caribou] with bow and arrow. . . . Spears and arrows copper and bone tipped."[24]

JOE BERNARD AND THE MOVEMENT EASTWARD

Among the pioneers who worked their way eastward into Canada's Western Arctic, without doubt the most adventurous was Joseph-Fidèle Bernard, an extraordinary man who was not only a trader but also an explorer and a self-taught naturalist and ethnographer. Modest and laconic, he summed up his arctic voyages fifty years later, writing, "I was a trader uninterested in fortune; an explorer uninterested in fame; but consumed with a great curiosity about things of science and nature."

Bernard, a native of Prince Edward Island, Canada, arrived in Nome in 1900 to join his uncle Peter Bernard in what turned out to be an unsuccessful mining venture. Trying another project, in 1903 Joe helped Peter build a small schooner, the *Augusta C*, which they used in the coastal trade in western Alaska and the Chukchi Peninsula. In 1906 Joe decided to enter the "Siberian" trade on his own, renting another small schooner, the *New York*, from Ira Rank. But in this endeavor Joe's results were disappointing.

Nevertheless, in Nome the following year he began studying navigation in preparation for a new undertaking and persuaded Rank to back him in a pioneering trading venture. It was to be an audacious multiyear voyage to rarely visited lands in Western Arctic Canada "to trade and explore," he wrote. "But I needed just the right kind of vessel: small and very strong in order to resist the severe ice conditions I knew I would find." He added, "I was broke but my friend Ira Rank agreed to stake me."

Bernard headed to Seattle, and during the winter of 1907–1908 he oversaw the construction of a fifteen-ton schooner, the *Teddy Bear*, built to his specifications for arctic wintering voyages. The schooner was fifty-four feet overall and was outfitted with a twenty-horsepower gasoline engine. But to ensure the *Teddy Bear's* survival in the ice, Bernard made the boat extremely sturdy: the ribs were six-inch-by-six-inch timbers set eight inches apart. The hull was composed of two-inch planks covered with one inch of Australian ironbark—one of the densest and most durable woods—to protect the hull from abrasion by the ice. Bernard added a heavy suit of sails, "as I would be depending more on sails than on power."

In 1908 Bernard departed Seattle with a load of merchandise for the Chukchi Peninsula. This time, however, his trade on the peninsula improved markedly, and by 1909 he was able to repay Rank $4,000 to own the schooner outright. Rank then agreed to stake him for his next voyage. Bernard stocked up with "old Army rifles, ammunition, kettles, knives, bright colored cloth and beads, candy, chewing gum etc."[25]

After another brief trading cruise to the Chukchi Peninsula, Bernard set off for the Canadian Arctic in late August, aided only by a miner named Gus Sandstrom. When the schooner reached Barrow, Joe encountered Charlie Klengenberg. Klengenberg had returned to the Arctic in 1908 after his acquittal on murder charges and had bought the wreck of H. Liebes and Company's chartered schooner *Ivy*, which had resupplied Charlie Brower's station before being "nipped" by the ice and shoved onto the beach. Klengenberg bought the hulk for $50 (which he borrowed from Brower) and did makeshift repairs to the hull. He and his family lived aboard the *Ivy* in Elson Lagoon for the winter. Klengenberg had planned to take the *Ivy* eastward in the summer of 1909, but he ran the ship aground near the entrance to the lagoon. It lay exposed on the coast without protection, where it was frozen in and carried away by pack ice in December 1909. He tried to blame Brower for the loss, claiming, with tortuous logic, that Brower had not allowed him sufficient crew to keep the ship from being taken by the ice.[26]

Most important, Klengenberg told Joe Bernard about his winter aboard the *Olga*. He mentioned "that he had to spend the winter of 1905–6 somewhere on the west coast of Victoria Land. He does not know where but he thinks he was probably in Minto inlet. He did not know how to determine his exact location in that part of the country." If Bernard's memory was correct, by then Klengenberg had changed his story about wintering on Banks Island. Minto Inlet is in fact about 120 miles from Klengenberg's actual wintering site on southwest Victoria Island (see endnote).[27]

By September 13, 1909, Bernard had moved onward to a position less than seventy miles from the Canadian border. But with young ice thickening around the *Teddy Bear*, he anchored in the lagoon at Barter Island. Accepting the situation, he wrote, "Even if we were able to continue we could easily find ourselves frozen in on the open coast where there is also danger of being crushed. So we will stay here for the winter; it is not safe to go on. Besides, I am all in. I have to rest for I have had no real sleep since leaving Nome."[28]

Joe and Sandstrom put up a driftwood cabin on the sandspit next to the *Teddy Bear*. They prepared for the winter of 1909–1910 by building a sled, collecting driftwood, hunting for birds and caribou, and putting out fox and bear traps. In November Joe decided to travel to Herschel Island, more than 100 miles to the east, where the whaleship *Karluk* was wintering under the command of Captain Steven Cottle. That winter Cottle did $10,000 in trade. The *Karluk's* winter presence at Herschel was "almost providential" for the Natives, according to the Mounted Police. The previous winter, 1908–1909, the combination of low prices for whalebone and extremely heavy ice conditions throughout the Western Arctic had prevented any ships from reaching the island. The 50 Mackenzie Inuit and the 250 Nunatamiut immigrants who lived nearby had come to rely on the presence of whaler-traders for goods that they could no longer do without. To obtain supplies during the winter of 1908–1909 some were forced to travel south, all the way to Dan Cadzow's trading post at Rampart House on the Porcupine River, a one-way journey of more than 200 miles. The only alternative was the Hudson's Bay Company's post at Fort McPherson on the Peel River.[29]

In fact, it would be a hit-or-miss situation for trading opportunities at Herschel Island until 1915, when the Hudson's Bay Company established a post there. In 1910–1911, however, again because of the low price for whalebone, no ships wintered at Herschel, repeating the hardship for the Natives. But in 1911–1912 the *Belvedere*, by then under the command of Steven Cottle, wintered at the island. "If it was not for the steamer wintering there," wrote Constable W. J. Beyts to his commanding officer, "a good many [Natives] would be good and hungry this winter."

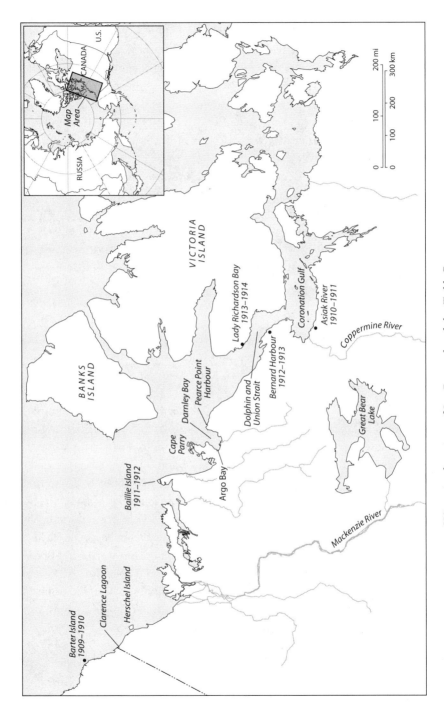

Wintering locations of Joe Bernard and the *Teddy Bear*, 1909–1914.

For the next winter, 1912–1913, only the decrepit forty-foot schooner *Alice Stoffen* was at the island, and it almost certainly lacked any significant amount of trade goods. In the icy summer of 1913 a number of vessels were forced to winter at several spots along the coast between Camden Bay in Alaska and Baillie Island in Canada, and C. T. Pedersen's *Elvira* was crushed by the ice and sank. But apart from the *Belvedere* and the *Polar Bear*, which were frozen in offshore east of Barter Island, none was well provisioned.[30]

On his return to Barter Island in 1909 Bernard was surprised to find that an Iñupiat family had set up camp "next door." They must have been among the few Iñupiat still living on the depopulated Arctic Slope of northeastern Alaska, where caribou had become extremely sparse, a scarcity that compelled the people either to rely on hunting Dall sheep in the interior or to move to the coast for seal hunting and fishing. "I have never seen such a fine, healthy family of Eskimos," Bernard wrote. "The man is Tulugak, about 35 years old and his wife Saijak is about the same age." They were accompanied by four children, aged 14 years to 18 months. "They have been living at the Jago River doing some sheep hunting; they ran out of supplies and came over here. Tulugak . . . impresses me as a very energetic sort of man. I would like him and his family to stay as we do need help. I will make him a proposition: to supply him with traps for half of his fur."

Tulugak and Saijak's arrival was indeed fortunate for Bernard: in later years he would become skilled in arctic survival, but at the time he lacked experience in living and trapping in the North. "During the past week," he wrote on December 14, 1909, "I set 12 fox traps from Manning Point to the mainland but I have caught only one fox so far in them. They are plentiful I know. . . . And they are getting into my traps and springing them but they are not getting caught. I cannot understand why so many of them are sprung every day. I guess trapping is a trade we all must learn." He added: "It took me almost 2 years to learn how to set a fox trap in the snow in the proper manner. I was a new hand at the game."[31]

In January Gus Sandstrom made the fatal decision to travel west alone to visit a nearby camp. He departed despite Bernard's advice that he should wait for a Native to accompany him. Several days later one of Sandstrom's dogs returned to Bernard's camp. They searched for Gus for several weeks but succeeded only in discovering pieces of his sled and some camping gear.[32]

On July 20, 1910, with Tulugak and his family aboard, the *Teddy Bear* set sail for the east. After a stop at Herschel Island they headed toward Shingle Point to take on fresh water. At Shingle Point Tulugak discovered that his mother and little brother were there, so they too joined Bernard's crew. They reached

The wreck of the steam whaler *Alexander* at Cape Parry,
1910. Joe Bernard salvaged supplies from the remains of the ship.
American Museum of Natural History Library, No. 15214.

the settlement of Baillie Island just as Fritz Wolki with his schooner *Rosie H.* arrived from having wintered in the Booth Islands, near Cape Parry. Wolki reported no ice to the east, so Bernard set off at once to cross Franklin Bay for the Parry Peninsula to visit the wreck of the steam whaler *Alexander*, which in 1906 had been driven hard ashore in a fog.

Bernard found that the *Alexander* was "pretty well stripped but the boatswain's locker I found full of rope and whale line — the very finest 1-inch manila; I took several coils. I also took off a lot of brass which I will use for trade." (In a footnote he added, "The Eskimos I traded with in Coronation Gulf went crazy for one piece, a piece of brass tubing about 12 feet long. . . . They used it for making spear handles.") Joe also discovered heaps of oak barrel staves that were saturated with whale oil. "There are piles of oak around which had been used for storing oil. I loaded up the Teddy Bear with as many stays as could find room for. They are so soaked in oil they will be fine for fuel."[33]

Bernard and Tulugak and family then pushed on, sailing through Dolphin and Union Strait into Coronation Gulf, waters that had last been visited by foreigners six decades earlier during the search for Sir John Franklin's missing expedition. Four hundred miles east of Baillie Island, and fifteen miles east of the mouth of the Coppermine River, they found a secure wintering site in the mouth of the Asiak River and started to unload the *Teddy Bear*'s cargo. At once Tulugak began building a winter house on the river bank. Bernard had become the first foreign trader to enter the region.

On August 29, 1910, Joe wrote, "We could not have picked a better place to stay . . . water in the river is fresh as the current is strong enough to keep out the salt water and squirrels are plentiful." Later he added, "The ponds and lakes around here are filled with loons, ducks, snow geese and other water birds. And bear, wolf, wolverine and caribou tracks are all along the banks, but so far we have seen no recent signs of Eskimos" (see endnote).[34]

As soon as the river froze Tulugak and his family began setting fish nets under the ice, and on shore he built a storehouse using ice blocks. It was "12 feet by 15 feet by 7 feet high," and he had it filled with fish by September 13. Despite the fact that the hunting in the area was at first disappointing, the group knew that they now had sufficient food to last them through the winter.[35]

At the end of October, with four dogs hauling a sled loaded with trade goods, Bernard and Tulugak headed west in search of Inuit. At the mouth of the Coppermine River they found a village of twenty-seven snow houses.

> It was a happy moment for us. Most of them were out fishing on the ice but soon the word was sent out and they all flocked over to see us. Quite a reception it was. There were about 200 Eskimos and at least 150 dogs. At first they did not come near us but sent two of their bravest men to meet us. They carried their spears and we carried our guns. As we drew near we put our guns behind us to show them we meant no harm. Then Tulugak spoke to them for a while. Soon the whole village flocked around while we pitched our tent. They were very friendly and brought us some wood for our fire and a good supply of fish.
>
> Our first night in the village was the most restless one I have ever spent. All night long they came to our tents. Whether they thought we should be watched I do not know but perhaps we should have watched them instead because when we started to leave we found our cups, a plate, ax and a hatchet gone. I asked them for them but they said they did not know anything about them. So I pretended to call their "spirit" to help me find the articles; soon one of them suddenly found the ax. Then I did some trading. I gave a snow knife, file and dish for which I got a deer [caribou], a wolf skin, wolverine skin, ice pick and spear! They got a good trade and so did I. I also traded a file for a dog. Tulugak said the file about matched for size but with a little good food he will make a good dog.[36]

When Bernard and Tulugak returned to their camp they met two Inuit families who had been hunting on the Asiak River. Their leader was Okomea. "Okomea later became my greatest friend," Bernard wrote. "He was a leader among his people—a sort of village wise man to whom other Eskimos came for advice. He was very much respected everywhere in the Coronation Gulf country. It was to Okomea I credit for establishing such friendly relations with them all. And it was not long before I had many visiting me for trade."[37]

Bernard was astonished to discover that some things that he viewed as value-less, such as old metal cans, were highly regarded by these visitors. "Now I wish I had saved all of the cans I threw away at Barter Island last winter." Tulugak, too, was a canny trader; one day he received seven fox skins for a piece of iron pipe.[38]

On April 19, 1911, Bernard learned that he and Tulugak's family were not the only foreigners in the region. He was surprised by the arrival of the explorers Vilhjalmur Stefansson, Rudolph Martin Anderson, and "Billy" Natkusiak, an energetic and highly competent Eskimo from the Seward Peninsula of Alaska. The three were on an expedition sponsored by New York's American Museum of Natural History. They had been living at the bottom of Franklin Bay and had learned from the Inuit that a ship was wintering to the east of them.

Stefansson was anxious to meet the supposedly isolated Inuinnait whom he had heard about from Charlie Klengenberg and Billy Mogg, and no doubt he was dismayed that another foreigner had reached them first. Stefansson asked Bernard to accompany him on a trip to other untouched Inuinnait groups, pro-posing that Rudolph Anderson could take care of the *Teddy Bear* in his absence. Bernard wrote that Stefansson tried to persuade him by saying "it would be a big feather in my cap! I declined. A big feather in his hat but not in mine!"

Stefansson, who was known to take credit for the efforts of others, conde-scendingly wrote in his diary, "It was a disappointment to me to find a ship in Coronation Gulf." No doubt Stefansson felt that the presence of a trader would spoil the Inuinnait's isolation, but he ignored the fact that the Inuinnait eagerly sought out Bernard for his trade goods — manufactured items that made their lives easier and for which, to them, he received insignificant payment.[39]

As spring 1911 wore on, more Inuinnait visited Bernard, trading fox, wolver-ine, wolf, polar bear, and caribou skins in return for his goods. The visitors were astonished when Bernard played his gramophone for them. At the beginning of May Tulugak and Bernard took in their traps. On June 12 the schooner was afloat. A week later the *Teddy Bear* was underway, heading west for Baillie Is-land. Bernard arrived there on August 15, 1911, one day after the last ship had headed outside for the winter. To his dismay he discovered that Ira Rank's ship-ment of trade goods had not reached the island as he had expected.[40]

Charlie Klengenberg was also at Baillie. After the loss of the *Ivy* in the winter of 1909–1910 he had sailed a whaleboat to the Mackenzie delta and there had repaired a run-down riverboat, the scow-schooner *Laura Waugh*. He then sailed

Joe Bernard's schooner *Teddy Bear* in winter quarters in Coronation
Gulf, 1911. White fox pelts are bleaching in the rigging.
American Museum of Natural History Library, No. 15229.

Joe Bernard in Coronation Gulf entertaining Inuinnait with his
gramophone, which is on the sled. Joseph Bernard Collection,
Archives, University of Alaska–Fairbanks, box 4, folder 14, book 24.

the scow east and wintered in Liverpool Bay, near Baillie Island. Bernard was
dumbfounded to learn that Klengenberg had the idea of sailing "this tub" to
Banks Island with his family. "He is insanely proposing to continue on to Banks
Island in it," Bernard wrote. "He does not have a crew to help him, either, only
his family. The oldest member is a girl of 17 years. We are trying to persuade
him not to dare such a voyage [at] this time of year in an old scow." Klengenberg must have heeded their advice because he probably wintered again in
Liverpool Bay.[41]

At Baillie Island Tulugak and his family left the *Teddy Bear,* having decided
to stay in the settlement there. Joe had planned to spend the winter of 1911–1912
on Banks Island, but with the Tulugak family's departure Joe was left without
a crew, so he made up his mind to winter the *Teddy Bear* there, inside the protection of the Baillie Island sandspit in company with Fritz Wolki's *Rosie H.*
He was joined at Baillie in September by a group of Nunatamiut who had

arrived in a whaleboat from west of the Mackenzie River. They announced
that four or five families would also follow them to Baillie. These former Alaskans were presumably drawn there by the opportunity for trapping in an under-
exploited area, but it turned out that the winter of 1911–1912 coincided with a
low point in the population cycle of the arctic foxes in the region, and in any
case, the immediate Baillie area did not usually yield many furs. This caused
Bernard considerable concern for the welfare of these Inuit who, he felt, were
neglecting their basic subsistence hunting and were concentrating too intently
on trapping, expecting that they would be able to trade their furs for "white
man's food."[42]

At Baillie, Bernard was fortunate to meet a friend of Wolki's, "Old John
Cole" (Johan Kuhl), a German sailmaker and a veteran arctic whaleman. Old
John had been aboard the *Rosie H.* but signed on with Joe to try his luck in
trapping. They built a house and storage shed on shore. Joe and Old John then
began their winter routine, running a trapline and trading with the Inuit, one
party of which informed him that Martin ("Matt") Andreasen was wintering
with his small schooner *North Star* near the eastern entrance to the Mackenzie delta and that he had built a camp ninety miles west of Baillie, at Warren
Point. Furthermore, Matt's brother Ole was camped on the northern tip of the
Tuktoyaktuk Peninsula, and their partner Fred Jacobsen was about halfway between them. Joe knew them well: they had all been based in Nome when they
were involved in the coastal trade on the Chukchi Peninsula. Clearly the frontier of the trapper-traders was quickly expanding eastward in Canada's Western
Arctic.[43]

On August 7, 1912, the whaler-trader Captain C. T. Pedersen brought the
Elvira into Baillie Island, and Joe received his first mail in two years, a letter
from Ira Rank in Nome. He began packing his furs to send them out to Rank,
and when Captain Steven Cottle, commanding the *Belvedere*, touched at the
island, Joe sent a shipment of 400 white fox pelts to Rank.[44]

Joe and Old John set off from Baillie Island aboard the *Teddy Bear* on August
22, 1912. They paused at Horton River to land Fred Jacobsen and his wife and
their winter outfit, then headed east to the Parry Peninsula to salvage more gear
from the wreck of the *Alexander* and continued on along the mainland shore,
"searching and worrying about where we were going to find quarters," Joe wrote.
On September 22, 300 miles east of Baillie Island, amid gales in Dolphin and
Union Strait, they came upon an uncharted harbor, the entrance of which was
concealed behind several outlying islands. It offered good protection, "a perfect
shelter from all winds," and there were a number of Inuit camped nearby.[45]

Joe and Old John immediately began hunting and fishing and moving their gear ashore. In November they started setting out their traps. During a sled trip in mid-November Joe met a group of Inuinnait from the Coppermine River. Unlike his friends from the Asiak River, these Inuinnait were arrogant and overbearing. "These Coppermine Eskimos are a very quarrelsome lot but my good friend of last year, Okomea, and his family were here. It was good to see them. And especially so because I had some trouble."

> While trading with one of them a woman insisted on taking a cup. It was the only one I had with me. When I refused to let her have it she decided to have it anyway. I had to take it from her[,] then the men closed in around me as if making ready to fight, muttering. I flashed my revolver and they stood back. Okomea, at this point, told them I was alright and they stopped.
>
>   I noticed that some of these Eskimos were wearing some white men's clothing and Priest's vestments. I tried to get information about where they got these things but I could not get a word out of them and those persons who were wearing the vestments disappeared into their houses. Okomea advised me not to camp with these Eskimos so I took my sled about 5 miles away. Okomea came along to stay with me as he did not trust them either.[46]

Joe became suspicious about the Inuinnait with the ecclesiastical vestments. Although he did not know it at the time, it turned out that he had stumbled onto the first evidence that two of this group had murdered the Roman Catholic priests, fathers Jean-Baptiste Rouvière and Guillaume Le Roux, who in 1912 had traveled overland from Great Bear Lake to proselytize among the Inuinnait. In 1914, when Bernard returned to Herschel Island, he mentioned these priests' vestments to the police. Then in spring 1915 the trader D'Arcy Arden sent word from Great Bear Lake that Inuit had been seen on the coast with vestments and a breviary. A police patrol was dispatched, and in 1916 the murderers were in police custody. They were eventually tried in Edmonton (with Patsy Klengenberg serving as the interpreter) and sentenced to life imprisonment. They served two years in loose captivity before they were returned to their homelands.[47]

   That winter, 1912–1913, Joe and Old John put out long traplines and both enjoyed good success, sometimes comically: "John . . . does not take a gun with him on his daily rounds of the trap line but carries a game bag full of bait. Well, he saw a fox in one of his traps so he dropped his bag and started out for the fox. Then another fox ran off with his bag. John did not miss his bait sack until he was ready to bait the trap which had the fox. He then looked around, saw the other fox dragging his sack but could not shoot of course, so he had to run after the thief. But the fox kept to a 50-yard lead ahead of John and even took time out once in awhile to rest. John said the fox gave him a good run before it

Joe Bernard and the crew of the *Teddy Bear* at
Nome, undated. Glenbow Museum, NC-1-762.

dropped the bag and made for the hills." At the end of the season Joe had taken
517 fox skins by trade and trapping.[48]

The *Teddy Bear* was underway again on July 22, 1913. They had hoped to go
outside to Nome, but the summer of 1913 was very icy in the Western Arctic.
They found the ice to be so heavy and closely packed that they were unable to
make significant progress in Dolphin and Union Strait and were forced to winter in Lady Richardson Bay on southwest Victoria Island. They were only about
seventy miles from their last wintering site.

By the beginning of October 1913 the *Teddy Bear* was in winter quarters in
Lady Richardson Bay and her cargo was cached ashore, ready for Joe's fifth winter on this voyage. At the beginning of November the men began again setting
out their traplines. They trapped and traded throughout the winter; however,
in April 1914 they discovered that the schooner was leaking badly. They were
forced to bail it out regularly, up to 100 buckets per day, for the rest of the winter. At the beginning of June they moved ashore to a tent and allowed the water
to rise in the schooner. "It is just too much for us to keep the water out," Bernard
wrote. "I cut a hole through the ice and found that it is 7 feet, 4 inches thick. I
decided to let the schooner fill up because with the ice this thick it will hold her

up; she will be lifted with it [as it melts in spring] and she will not sink." They resumed bailing in July and, with block and tackle, hauled the schooner to the beach, careened it to caulk the hull, and then refloated it. On August 6, 1914, they started again for Nome.

Nine days later, at the entrance to Darnley Bay, Joe was surprised to see Charlie Klengenberg coming out to the *Teddy Bear* in a whaleboat. It turned out that Klengenberg had wintered near there, probably in Pearce Point Harbour. Bernard sold him all of his remaining trade goods and told him about the trapping and trading opportunities in Coronation Gulf. In 1916 Klengenberg would relocate there.

On the nineteenth they were at Baillie Island, where Joe had planned to leave Old John to rejoin Fritz Wolki, but they learned that Wolki had left the day before for the outside, so Old John decided to stay aboard to help Joe work the schooner to Nome. At Baillie they met Joe's friend Dr. Rudolph Martin Anderson, in command of the Southern Party of the Canadian Arctic Expedition. Anderson's fleet now included the schooners *North Star* and *Alaska*, and he was searching for a place to overwinter to carry out his explorations. Bernard advised using his harbor of 1912–1913, which they did, from 1914 to 1916. Anderson wrote that the expedition named it Bernard Harbour "partly in honor of Captain Bernard's pioneer energy in discovering its suitability and using it as a ship station and in recognition of his unusual kindness and rectitude as a pioneer of trade."

Joe and Old John reached Charlie Brower's trading station at Barrow on September 10. They then sailed along the coast to Point Hope, where Joe picked up Arthur Rank—Ira Rank's brother—at Rank's U.S. Mercantile Company outpost. Three days later they were at Nome, and Joe stored his goods in Rank's warehouse before taking the *Teddy Bear* to Safety Sound, twenty miles east of Nome, to lay it up for the winter.

In addition to his furs, Joe had collected "over two tons of Eskimo artifacts, ornithological and natural history specimens," some of which he sold to the University of Pennsylvania's Museum of Archaeology and Anthropology and many others he donated to a number of museums.[49]

When the *Teddy Bear* departed Victoria Island in 1914 it is unlikely that Bernard understood the changes that he and Klengenberg and Mogg had initiated through their presence among the Inuinnait, nor that their success would encourage other traders to enter the region. But Diamond Jenness, the anthropologist who was based at Bernard Harbour from 1914 to 1916 as a member of the Canadian Arctic Expedition, saw the situation very clearly. In the epilogue to his narrative of those years, *The People of the Twilight*, he warned that the fur trade had transformed Inuinnait society from collectivist to individualist: "Even as we sailed away traders entered their country seeking fox-furs; and for those pelts[,] so useless for real clothing[,] they offered rifles, shot-guns, steel tools, and other goods that promised to make life easier. So the Eskimos abandoned their communal seal hunts and scattered in isolated families along the coasts in order to trap white foxes during the winter when the fur of that animal reaches its prime. Their dispersal loosened the old communal ties that held the families together. The men no longer labored for the entire group, but hunted and trapped each one for his family alone. . . . The commercial world of the white man had caught the Eskimos in its mesh, destroying their self-sufficiency and independence, and made them economically its slaves. Only in one respect did it benefit them: it lessened the danger of those unpredictable famines which had overtaken them every ten or fifteen years."[50] Jenness's clear-eyed statement was an accurate evaluation of the changes in Inuinnait lifeways that had resulted from their participation in the fur trade.

Part 3

———————◆•◆———————

Heyday of the Western Arctic Fur Trade, 1914 to 1929

Although the arctic fur trade would soon enter a fifteen-year period of expansion, the news was otherwise in autumn 1914 when the trading vessels reached Nome, Seattle, and San Francisco, and their crews learned of the outbreak of war in Europe. Previously the price of white fox pelts had been on a rise, driven in part by their increased use by fur dyers who had converted the furs into a dozen exotic shades of "champagne, canary, orange, porpoise blue and pink, solferino, emeraldo, and poignant purple."[1]

But the result of the commencement of hostilities was immediate for trappers and traders: the demand for fur garments evaporated and the fur market collapsed. The British Board of Trade suspended the fur auctions in London; later, Russia did the same. "Nearly all foreign markets were closed to American shippers . . . and the almost instant loss of so large a percentage of the trade paralyzed the fur business in the United States," wrote A. L. Belden. "Prices of skins declined sharply; merchants . . . augmented the depression by limiting their purchases to comparatively small lots at low figures." And in the winter of 1914–1915 the Hudson's Bay Company ordered its posts to halt buying furs. This action caused hardship and resentment among its Native customers, who suddenly had no market for their pelts—although some HBC traders quietly advanced supplies to the Natives and kept a separate set of books to tide them over until the company resumed purchasing skins.[2]

In 1913 white fox pelts had sold at between $20 and $50 in auctions in Great Britain and the United States, and at Barrow they had ranged from $12 to $15; nevertheless, in 1914, when the trader Charlie Madsen returned to Nome from the Chukchi Peninsula aboard the schooner *Challenge* carrying 1,700 white fox skins, three tons of walrus ivory, sable skins, 20,000 seal skins, and other furs, he arrived about three weeks after news of the war. "The fox skins . . . were now worth only $5.00," he remembered. Other Northerners who reached Seattle discovered that their furs were worth 75 percent less than they had been in 1913.

"The American fur market was completely disorganized; prices offered by different buyers varied widely, and all were low." Charlie's ivory, worth fifty cents per pound when he left for the Chukchi Peninsula, was now only half that, and the value of his sable, seal, polar bear, and walrus skins had done a nosedive as well. "The bottom dropped out of the fur market," Olaf Swenson declared. "There is no use in trying to hide the fact that the European war has struck a hard blow to the fur trade of the world," reported the journal *Hunter-Trapper-Trader.* The only possible response was to hold onto the skins until fur prices might rise again, as Louis Lane tried to do when he reached Seattle with a cargo of 700 white foxes aboard his motor schooner *Polar Bear.*[3]

In the Arctic the news was devastating for the trappers and their families. "The war in Europe has ruined the Arctic fur market," declared the *Seattle Post-Intelligencer.* "The Eskimos are asking the same prices as in the past years and consequently there are no buyers. They wanted from $10 to $15 per skin and believed that the traders were trying to swindle them when they explained that the war had destroyed the market for furs in Europe." The trader William D. Clark reported from Fort Yukon in 1915: "War has hit the Alaskan trapper nearly as hard as it did the Belgians."

Many trappers in the North, both Native and non-Native, abandoned trapping during the winter of 1914–1915 to focus primarily on subsistence hunting and fishing. According to a report in *Fur News Magazine,* very few Natives in northern Alaska "will do any trapping as long as the present low prices of fur prevail. Under the present conditions it is easier and pays as well for the natives to shoot seals as to trap foxes."

And trappers in Western Arctic Canada made similar choices. Inspector J. W. Phillips of the Mounted Police reported, "Owing to the extremely low prices being paid for pelts none of the natives are making any attempt to secure any quantity of furs. Their attention is being given to hunting moose and caribou, and in this they show good sense." Nevertheless some trappers must have stayed the course, because despite the low prices that traders were forced to offer, at H. Liebes and Company's Barrow station Charlie Brower bought more than 2,000 fox skins.[4]

Oddly enough, in the midst of the carnage of war in 1915 the price of furs began to edge up again, and Northerners began to return to intensive trapping. It was the American market that helped them, through, in part, a curious fad for wearing fur in summer, while at the same time floor-length full-fur evening wraps came into vogue. "As the year 1915 advanced . . . a sudden and quite general demand sprang up in America for furs, chiefly neckpieces composed of single skins, to be worn during the 'good old summer-time,'" noted A. L. Belden. "This unexpected outlet resulted in the consumption of a large number of fine, medium and common peltries at better prices than had prevailed in the immediately preceding winter. Values continued to increase as the months passed, and the raw fur collection season of 1915–16 opened with a strong competitive demand for skins of all kinds. . . . The American export trade in furs, which was nearly destroyed by the European war, recovered somewhat in 1916, reaching a total valuation of approximately eight million dollars during the fiscal year ending June 30, 1916."[5]

The American craze for summer furs began in New York and moved outward from there. By mid-1916 it had spread across the country, and by 1919 it had reached "startling proportions." Simultaneously the United States became the world's largest fur market, and fur auction exchanges were founded in New York and St. Louis. In fact, while the Hudson's Bay Company was focused on wartime supply contracts and was slow to respond to competitors, many Canadian furs were sold in American markets. And likewise, without the dyed furs from Leipzig, American fur dyers took up the challenge themselves and soon were producing first-class dyed furs of all kinds.[6]

Despite the ongoing war, the price of furs continued to rise, to the benefit of trappers throughout North America. Referring to the turmoil in Russia and its subsequent revolutions, the fur trade economist and historian Harold Innis wrote, "the decline in export of furs from Russia caused a further pronounced rise in prices, especially from 1916–1919." By 1916 the best large white foxes had advanced to an average of about $25.00, a fact which was reflected on the arctic coast the following year when H. Liebes and Company's ship *Herman* was paying, depending on the quality of the pelt, from $10.00 to $15.00 in trade goods, and in 1918 at Liebes's Barrow station Charlie Brower paid $20.00 to $25.00 in trade. By 1919, large number-ones were fetching $50.00 at city auctions. In 1920, during a short-lived price spike, white fox prices at the Hudson's Bay Company's spring sales in London averaged $62.25, and in Montreal they were selling for $60.00 to $70.00. It is little wonder that Northerners were again drawn to the substantial profits that trapping, temporarily at least, offered them.[7]

Referring to the years 1918 to 1920, Agnes Laut stated: "Summer furs have been in fashion in every part of America, not only neck pieces but hat trimmings and edges for elaborate gowns; the fashion shows not a sign of abating. Those who cannot afford real silver fox, or sable at $1000 per, buy white fox dyed in imitation of silver fox, or Chinese goat dyed in imitation of no fox that ever was on land or sea—and are happy; and swell the swelling chorus for furs, more furs, and yet more furs." By the year 1920 total purchases of furs in the United States rose to $100 million, up from $40 million before the outbreak of the war, and auction houses were proving so successful at selling consignment furs that the Hudson's Bay Company was forced to abandon its practice of selling only its own pelts.[8]

The Hudson's Bay Company's J. W. Anderson described the fur bubble. "During the final years of World War I raw fur prices on the world market reached astronomical heights, with the result that every Tom, Dick, and Harry rushed into the fur trade. And it was easy to make money too! If you operated from a railroad point, all you required was a toboggan, a few dogs, camp equipment and a roll of dollar bills. You would visit some nearby Indian camps and by the time you returned to the railroad a week or so later, fur values had again advanced. It was as easy as that!"[9]

And then the bubble burst. The fur market had been showing signs of the jitters as early as March 1919, as speculators drove it higher, but with the onset of a severe postwar economic recession (which lasted from January 1920 to July 1921) the fur market slumped badly from the effects of extreme deflation, unemployment, a drop in business activity, and a decline in the stock market. By October 1920 fur prices had dropped 60 percent below the prices that had been paid in 1919. From *Fur Trade Review:* "The wave of speculation which swept over the entire fur trade in 1919 and 1920 was caused principally by outsiders who 'got in' on what most of them thought was a 'good thing.'" There was so much unsold inventory on the market in New York and London that the autumn fur sales of 1920 were postponed until January 1921.[10]

By 1922, however, the recession was over. There was a rapid return to prosperity, and with the onset of the Roaring Twenties the market stabilized and white fox prices at the Hudson's Bay Company's sales in London averaged more than $40. *Fur Trade Review* reported, "When the popular . . . fashion turned to fox scarfs [sic] in 1922 the blue fox came into its own. The demand was so great and the supply so small that the fur men were forced to turn to imitation blue fox and so the white fox was dyed to resemble the genuine Alaska blue fox with fairly satisfactory results." And fur prices began a mostly steady rise, which reached its peak in 1929.[11]

This rise, in turn, stimulated small entrepreneurs to invest their capital in fur farms. Many began ranch-raising silver foxes or blue foxes, the pelts of which sold at the highest prices, but a few, including some Eskimos in Alaska, specialized in raising white foxes. Consequently the fur farming industry in Alaska

expanded rapidly: by 1922 fur farmers had leased over 150 islands for propagation, and by 1925 there were 391 fox farms, mostly on islands, and 33 permits
were issued for capturing and propagating white foxes. Presumably many of the
latter were granted for small one-family operations. Tony Polet's grandson, Bill
Boucher, told me that one of the largest farms was owned by George Goshaw
at Shishmaref on the Seward Peninsula, where he experimented with mutation
breeding, and that many people in Nome had small fox farms at their outlying
camps.

The global supply of farmed white fox pelts developed swiftly, and in 1925
it was estimated that the annual farmed production was 30,000 from North
America, 25,000 from Asia, and 10,000 from Europe. By 1926 the United States
had approximately 2,500 fur farms raising a variety of species, and Canada had
nearly as many. According to *Fur Trade Review*, in 1929, 11,000 fur farms world-
wide were breeding silver foxes. But as Sarah Isto, a historian of Alaskan fur
farming, has noted, the supply from the farms themselves led to a decline in
prices. "There is little evidence that demand had fallen. Instead, supply had
risen. . . . The rising volume from Alaska and elsewhere contributed to dropping prices." Despite the general rise in white fox prices from 1922 to 1929, the
rate of gain was uneven and the prices that "wild fur" — in distinction to "farmed
fur" — received suffered from this new competition, in part because the quality
of the farmed pelts was more consistent.[12]

By 1929 white fox prices at the Hudson's Bay Company's sales in London
averaged $58.32, and northern trappers were receiving $35.00 to $50.00 in trade
goods for prime large number-one pelts. In northern Alaska in the late 1920s the
market became so hot that fur buyers began using aircraft to scour the region,
and in 1929 Edward Darlington Jones wrote to his wife from Nome, "There is
no chance to get [a] good fox skin at Nome as they have all been bought up by
fur buyers and most sent out by air mail."[13]

Easy credit was one of the factors driving prices upward, allowing many fur
dealers and manufacturers to overextend themselves, despite the prophetic
warning in 1928 by Melvin A. Traylor, president of the First National Bank
of Chicago, who stated flatly: "The nation has been mistaking the richness of
credit for the richness of capital. . . . This credit must be paid. A day of reckoning must come."[14]

Fur Trade Review echoed the dizzy days of the fur trade in the 1920s:

July 1922: "The long neglected black fox and the scarce white fox have again
come into their own." "Long haired pelts again in demand."[15]

Actress Lantelme Durrer in a coat trimmed in
white fox fur, ca. 1925. Getty Images 3374886.

July 1926: "General advance in prices." "London auction results" (white fox
up 22.5 percent over April).[16]

September 1927: "Heavy import of furs. Gain of 25 per cent in value for first
half of 1927."[17]

March 1928: "Alaska fur catch 1927" (2,819 white fox average $44.25). "Raw fur
prices in this season of 1927–28 at higher levels than were even experienced
in the mad year of 1920."

April 1928: "Dyed white foxes are finding favor this season."[18]

June 1928: "Bright outlook for next season."[19]

January 1929: "Fur auctions expanding." "Numerous failures in the New York
market have not depressed 1928–29 pelt values—world demand has absorbed
last winter's catch."[20]

March 1929: "Strong market in London." (The top price for white fox is
$71.00, for blues $215.00.)[21]

May 1929: (In Seattle) "White fox—sold well" (The best lot sold for $75.00, with the sale averaging $47.50). (In New York, white fox) "poor condition, sold exceedingly well" (Top price $69.00.) (Blue fox) "excellent condition, sold exceedingly well." (Top price $175.00.)[22]

Six months before the Great Crash a typically giddy assessment of the super-heated state of the market appeared April 5, 1929, in the *Seattle Post-Intelligencer*:

FINE PELTS HIGH IN LOCAL FUR MARKET
Prices Reach Record Mark On Exchange;
1928 Volume May Be Exceeded At Auctions

The makings of fur coats are sky-high!

Fine pelts handled by the Seattle Fur Exchange are bringing the highest price in the history of the Northwest, according to J. E. Agnew, treasurer and general manager of the Fur Exchange. That applies to fox, mink, lynx, and all fine furs, Agnew continued.

Sales made at the twelve monthly auctions conducted by the Seattle Fur Exchange totaled $5,000,000 in 1928. . . .

Business in the first quarter of 1929 is running 25 per cent ahead of the corresponding period of 1928, Agnew reports.

As we shall see, the rise in fox prices allowed many northern trappers and traders more than a decade of prosperity, and in return for their efforts, they received material goods—boats, outboard motors, camping equipment, firearms, manufactured foodstuffs, tents, phonographs, sewing machines, and many other things—in amounts that they had not previously enjoyed. Their prosperity was short-lived.

5

REVOLUTION AND CIVIL WAR ON THE CHUKCHI PENINSULA

For the peoples of Chukotka—the Chukchi, the Yupik, and other societies—the first three decades of the twentieth century were chaotic, destabilizing, and disruptive. They endured, first, weak tsarist government control and free-booting American trade from Nome, then, after the Treaty of Portsmouth in 1905, an aggressive Japanese penetration of their territories, followed by an inchoate series of governmental edicts that took place between the outbreak of the Russian Revolutions in 1917 and the final Soviet seizure of the peninsula in 1923, followed again by ever-changing decrees, regulations, and increasingly coercive state management and controls.

THE TSARIST REGIME, REVOLUTION, CIVIL WAR, AND SOVIET CONTROL

By the mid-nineteenth century the peoples of Chukotka had become integrated within global markets for whalebone, furs, and walrus ivory (chapter 3). But after the founding of Nome, Alaska, in 1899 their association with foreign trade increased yet again as Americans, Europeans, and Russians established trading posts at more than a dozen coastal sites on the Chukchi Peninsula. Nevertheless, with the collapse of the market for whalebone in the first decade of the twentieth century and the nearly simultaneous rise in the prices of furs, new challenges and opportunities suddenly faced the Chukotkans.

In the first decades of the twentieth century one manifestation of the rising price of fox pelts was that a number of Yupik from the southeastern Chukchi Peninsula began to expand into new locations. Some moved to St. Lawrence Island, Alaska, which is a highly productive area for white fox trapping. Others moved to Emma Harbor in Provideniya Bay, where there was a government storehouse and Julius Tomsen ("Billy Thompson") had a trading post. A larger number of Yupik from Cape Chaplin recolonized nearby islands. Still others moved more than 200 miles westward to establish new settlements on the mostly uninhabited shores of Kresta Bay and the Gulf of Anadyr. White foxes had not previously been trapped there, and the immigrants could sell their goods at the summer trade fair in the town of Novo-Mariinsk (today, Anadyr), which they had been visiting since the 1880s on long and difficult trading expeditions in groups of ten to fifteen large skin boats.

An outcome of this dispersal to Kresta Bay was that the Yupik established trading relationships with the interior-dwelling Chukchi by exchanging coastal products and manufactured goods for reindeer skins and meat, some of which the Yupik traded onward at Anadyr. For about twenty years, 1915–1935, at least 250 to 300 people were "on the move," stated the ethnohistorians Igor Krupnik and Michael Chlenov, "and scores of new villages and camps were quickly established" in Kresta Bay and on the shore of the Gulf of Anadyr.

Because trapping was now the focus of their efforts, life in these new settlements was different than it had been at Cape Chaplin. Similar to the experience of the Eskimos in northern Alaska, it required that the trappers had to spread out in small numbers to maximize their fur catch. According to Krupnik and Chlenov, "winter fox trapping took much more of the [Yupik] settlers' time than it had in their native land [near Cape Chaplin]. It also compelled the trappers to disperse to personal trapping lines and grounds. The migrants had to reorient their former way of residence by breaking into small camps or one or two houses or winter tents." "For the Asiatic Yupik, their 'New Land' around Kresta Bay became a lasting monument to the era of commercial trapping."[1]

In the early decades of the twentieth century several foreign entrepreneurs also expanded their operations to the Chukchi Peninsula. Among the smaller operators was the Abraham Wittenberg family of Nome, merchants who had arrived from Seattle in 1904 and, like Tony Polet and Ira Rank, had established a general merchandise business there. Wittenberg and his son Leo chartered and owned schooners, such as the *Sea Wolf* and *Challenge,* for the coastal trade in Chukotka, Alaska, and Western Arctic Canada, and in 1917 they began trading as far as Kamchatka. In 1919 they joined with Leo Seidenverg, forming the Seidenverg-Wittenberg Trading Company, chartering the freighting-and-trading schooner *Bender Brothers,* and setting up a store in Petropavlovsk, Kamchatka.[2]

Similarly, in 1921 the newly formed Phoenix Northern Trading Company of Seattle and Tacoma, Washington, acquired the assets of the one-year-old Siberian Commercial Company of Seattle, assets that included a trading post on Senyavin Strait, near Cape Chaplin, and the gasoline auxiliary schooner *Iskum*. The principals sought to raise $85,000 via a prospectus that cheerfully declared, "The people that get in business early and stay with the country cannot make a mistake . . . fortunes can be made . . . in trading and transportation." This, of course, ignored the fact that there were already more than a dozen posts on the peninsula, in addition to the visits of the Nome fleet and other maritime traders. With upbeat hyperbole the prospectus outlined the coastal trade procedure: "The trader drops anchor in front of the village, and the whole population pile their furs, etc., in their boats and come aboard, where they barter their stuff for all kinds of merchandize. They get necessities . . . first, then if they have anything left to trade, their fancy runs to candy[,] chewing gum, clothes, notions, alarm clocks, lamps, coal oil, beads, gaudy handkerchiefs and even phonographs. As soon as the trader can get their stuff he heads for the next village, where the same thing is repeated." The prospectus added, "The farther north he goes[,] the better prices he gets—anywhere from 300 per cent to 1,000 per cent. One thousand per cent is not uncommon from North Cape [Cape Schmidt] to the Kolyma River."

On the *Iskum*'s voyage of 1922 James M. Ashton listed the merchandise the schooner carried for trade. "Axes, saws, knives and various line of hardware; guns, ammunition, tools and cooking utensils; lanterns and lamps; animal traps, sleeping bags, tents, matches, candles, condensed milk, flour, sugar, tea, chocolate, molasses, tobacco and pipes; heavy shirts and sweaters; thread and needles, thimbles, pins etc.; soap, combs, phonographs, mouth organs and other minor musical instruments; goggles and eye-glasses of different types; pants and overalls, and highly colored calicos as well as other dry goods; necklaces, beads and many other notions."

In return the *Iskum* received "fox skins of all kinds; polar, brown and grizzly bear skins; Arctic wolf, wolverine, reindeer and fawn skins; hair seal and ugruk [bearded seal] skins; whalebone, walrus skins, and all grades of walrus ivory, both raw and decorative; the feathers and down of Arctic birds; the teeth of extinct mammoths; native slippers, moccasins, gloves, belts, pouches; also many very beautiful ivory curios."[3]

Other traders also joined the rush. For example, the entrepreneurial Karaev family expanded their operations throughout the region (chapter 3), with bases at Petropavlovsk in Kamchatka and on the Kolyma River, added posts on the peninsula to a total of four, and bought the auxiliary power schooners *Avacha*, *Flyer*, and *Alaska* to supply their stations via Seattle and Nome. Their presence on the peninsula was immediately felt by Nome's traders: in 1917 the schooner *Ram* returned to Nome from "Siberia" with the report that trade had fallen off because "the Russian traders have established stations at numerous points and are picking up the cream of the furs caught by the natives."[4]

And for a time the Japanese had an effect equal to the other foreign traders. As a result of the Treaty of Portsmouth of 1905, the Japanese had received fishing rights to the Russian Far East, and a fisheries convention that was concluded two years later resulted in a consortium of Japanese companies sending 20,000 workers to the coasts annually. In turn the Japanese ignored Russian authorities and participated in an illicit trade in alcohol at many coastal points, activities that the tsarist government was unable to control, nor were the Red or White guards while they were fighting with each other during the civil war after the tsar's abdication.

At first, the events of the two Russian Revolutions of 1917 and subsequent civil war had little effect in Chukotka and Kamchatka. "When 'mainland' authorities got around to checking out the Northeast," wrote the historian John J. Stephan, "the locals showed they could accommodate to every shift in the political winds. . . . On Chukotka officials appointed by the Provisional Government in 1917 stayed in office until the end of 1919, adding or dropping the word 'soviet' from their nomenclature as circumstances required."[5]

While the Reds and the White Guards were engaged in their internecine slaughter, the Soviets briefly established nominal jurisdiction in Kamchatka in 1917 but were ousted in 1918, when a Japanese-sponsored group took control, only to be ousted themselves in 1922. In 1918 the Soviets, who were in tenuous control of the region at that time, issued an order that all trading vessels must clear customs at Petropavlovsk, Kamchatka, a requirement that "practically prohibits small vessels from attempting to trade," as one Hudson's Bay Company man put it. The following year the Soviet government nationalized the fur trade and commenced buying furs at set prices. And in 1920 the Soviets issued regulations for the Chukchi Peninsula that required all traders to comply with three stipulations: they must obtain a trading license at Anadyr; they must have a Russian speaker aboard the ship; and they must trade only at Soviet establishments, not with the Natives. That year Abraham Wittenberg arrived at Petropavlovsk in the *Bender Brothers* to find the Reds in control. In "payment" for his trade goods he was forced to accept 10 million rubles of worthless White Guard currency.[6]

These regulations caused the Nome Chamber of Commerce to complain that the merchants from Seattle would get the best of the trade because there were very few Russian speakers in Nome. Nevertheless, for a few more years trading vessels from both ports were able to operate as usual, without observing any state controls. In the winter of 1920–1921, for example, Gus Masik and a partner from Nome secretly overwintered a schooner on Karaginsky Island off the coast of Kamchatka, and the following winter Masik trapped in the Kolyma River delta with Arnout Castel. But things would soon change.[7]

Describing the chaos in Chukotka, Igor Krupnik and Michael Chlenov wrote, "The preceding years of civil war between the Bolsheviks and various White Guard regimes saw incessant changes in administrations. Various 'governors' and 'representatives' of the Soviet and White Guard arrived in the summer by a trade steamer coming from Petropavlovsk or Anadyr. The activity of such short-term administrators was mostly restricted to the district center in Uelen and to a few nearby Chukchi villages, as well as to Provideniya Bay, and their power did not expand beyond levying taxes on American and Russian traders."[8]

In the muddled years prior to the complete Soviet takeover in 1923 seizures and corruption were common. Although "the country [had been] open and free to trade, most traders met with a different local order of government at every port," *Fur Trade Review* reported, "often they were taxed, their merchandise was requisitioned and never paid for, or, in some cases, confiscated and there was no appeal." In 1920 the *Seattle Post-Intelligencer* stated that the captain of the Hibbard-Swenson trader *Chukotsk* reported that "no trading vessels have approached these ports because of the depredations of roving bands of marauders, which bands operate under the guise of agents of the Moscow government."[9]

But the Soviet government at the outset was so weak and disorganized that in 1920, out of necessity, it created a puppet state, the "Far Eastern Republic," to rule the territories east of Lake Baikal as a buffer to the Japanese. This "republic" was nominally independent but in fact was controlled by Moscow, and it was absorbed into the Russian Soviet Federated Socialist Republic in 1922. For their part, the Japanese sponsored the White Guard's "Amur Government" in 1921 but were forced to withdraw from the region the following year.

In Chukotka nominal Soviet control had been established in 1919, when a Revolutionary Committee was formed by two Bolsheviks at Novo-Mariinsk (Anadyr). The "committee" declared the nationalization of fisheries, cancelled the Natives' debts to the merchants, and confiscated the property of foreign entrepreneurs. Five weeks later, in January 1920, local traders shot the two communists, but the Bolsheviks regained control of the town in August, when a force arrived from Petropavlovsk. After sporadic fighting throughout the region they were able to establish complete control only in 1923, and in several towns and settlements they installed "plenipotentiaries" who were invested with full power and the authority to govern. It appears that these officials had only sketchy directives from their superiors and, lacking a legal code, issued orders—

often arbitrary and vague—that they made up on the spot and later frequently contradicted, a fact that caused confusion and resistance among the residents and traders alike.

Amidst this turmoil the Soviet administration slowly extended its rule over the peninsula. "A few handpicked local Russian executives," wrote Igor Krupnik and Michael Chlenov, "made all key policy decisions, usually under general orders from their high offices in the provincial city of Petropavlovsk or in the new administrative hub in Anadyr." In 1922, for example, the trader Fedor Karaev was appointed as the "plenipotentiary" of the "Chukchi and Anadyr Districts" by the Soviets. This seems surprising in that a capitalist trader had been given control over eastern Chukotka by a communist regime, but it is likely that the Soviets had no one else to turn to. "An industrious businessman well familiar with the area he was appointed to govern, Karaev tried to incorporate the existing network of trading agents, the majority of his trade partners or representatives, into the nascent soviet system." Karaev, a capable administrator, established seven agencies throughout the region, appointing among them "Terugyi, Chukchi trader; Iosif Pavlov, creole guard at the Provideniya storehouse, Magometh Dobriev, trader . . . ; Nechipurenko, Karaev's deputy, Russian communist; Rawtergin, Chukchi hunter; Vaal [Bengt Vold], Norwegian trader; and Olaf Swenson" as his agents. Karaev's authority did not last long; he was replaced in quick succession by two communist officials and his appointees were removed.[10]

OLAF SWENSON, THE INDEPENDENT TRADERS,
AND THE SOVIETS

Olaf Swenson was one of the better-financed entrants to the Chukotka trade. Swenson had been active on the peninsula since the early days of the Northeastern Siberian Company's operations (chapter 3). In 1912 he secured funding from the Hibbard-Stewart Company of Seattle, a company that specialized in dealing in fur, hide, and wool. Swenson's language skills, in both Russian and Chukchi, and his good relations with the Natives proved to be very useful. His voyages usually started on the Kamchatka coast and worked north in late June to Anadyr, where he would attend the annual fur fair, then sail to Nome to send his fur cargo to Seattle before loading with more supplies. He would spend July and August trading for furs at various coastal settlements throughout the Chukchi and Beaufort seas.

The following year, 1913, the newly formed subsidiary, the Hibbard-Swenson Company, bought the former whaleship *Belvedere* and chartered other smaller vessels as the trade required, establishing posts at a number of places, with warehouses at Anadyr. "It had been our custom," Swenson wrote, "to pick out a local spot, put a good man in charge there, and finance him against the business he would do for us, letting him operate in his own name and extend credit according to his own judgment." At the height of his operations Swenson may have had more than thirty agents and independent traders in his organization, which spanned the coasts of the Sea of Okhotsk, Kamchatka, and in Chukotka as far west as the Kolyma River, resulting in a reported turnover of approximately $1 million per year.

Swenson was, however, very unlucky with his ships. The *Belvedere* was crushed by pack ice on the north coast of the Chukchi Peninsula in 1919, and in 1920 his *Kolyma* was wrecked in a storm on Sledge Island, near Nome. To replace the *Belvedere* Swenson bought another old whaler and renamed it *Kamchatka*. It caught fire and burned up south of the Aleutians in 1922, forcing Swenson and his crew to spend four days in their boats before reaching land. And, as we shall see, he was to lose another vessel as well.

In 1922 Hibbard-Stewart, with fortunate timing, decided to withdraw from the Siberian trade, and Swenson used the opportunity to create a larger trading organization. He secured partnerships with several trading houses, including Bryner and Company of Vladivostok, Denbigh Brothers of Vladivostok and Hakodate, and two other Russian trading firms that had interests in various endeavors throughout the Far East and northeastern Asia. Hibbard-Stewart then transferred its Siberian assets to Swenson's new company, and with these partners he established Olaf Swenson and Company, of which he was president and treasurer. "It is said that the . . . firms constitute the most powerful trading factors ever brought together in the history of the Siberian fur trade," declared *Fur Trade Review*. "This new organization will not, however, confine its activities solely to furs but will engage in general trading, shipping, financing, mining and development work of every kind and carry on the big fur and trading business of the old Hibbard Swenson Company but on a far greater scale than heretofore and . . . plans eventually to operate its own line of ships between Seattle and Vladivostok."[11]

In the meantime the Soviets, who had seized Olaf Swenson's warehouse in Anadyr in 1920, had by 1923 confiscated all his trading posts and inventory, filing suit against him for unpaid taxes on a claim of 600,000 gold rubles. Swenson had to travel to Moscow to protest the seizure of his property.

At the same time—and in the same confiscatory atmosphere—Sigurdur K. ("Chris") Gudmanson, an Icelander, sailed the motor schooner *Polar Bear* to the Kolyma River, reaching the town of Nizhne Kolymsk, 1,000 miles by water from Nome. There he was warmly received, to say the least, because his was the first trading vessel to visit in two or three years. The Soviets likewise seized his cargo and vessel. Gudmanson was forced to go overland to Yakutsk to seek redress, which he obtained, but on his return to Nizhne Kolymsk he found that high water in the spring flood had stranded the schooner, rendering it impossible to refloat. Gudmanson had to travel back to Nome aboard Arnout Castel's small schooner *Belinda*, which had wintered in the Kolyma delta with Gus Masik aboard.[12]

There was a strong economic imperative for the Soviet seizures: the government was insolvent. The trading vessels had been exporting substantial numbers of Chukotkan furs, and fur exports were one of the few sources of hard currency available to the Soviet Union. In 1921 the *Seattle Post-Intelligencer* reported that $300,000 worth of furs were exported from "Siberia" through Nome, and in fact, from 1924 to 1929 fur exports amounted to 10 to 15.3 percent of all Soviet exports.

"In the meantime," Mary-Kay Wilmers stated, "desperate American dealers begged their government to put pressure on the soviet bureaucracy. ('I can't make out how it is that a rotten government, in my estimation, like the Soviet crowd can dictate to us and close our Americans out of Siberia because of some whim while we allow their subjects to do business in competition with American firms right in our own home,' a New York furrier wrote to the US Secretary of Commerce in 1924.)" As D. A. Holmes put it about the Soviets, "The present government has not yet had time to work out just what to do with its great empire. It is now experimenting with a system of government monopoly in trade; and who can say how this, as well as the experiment in Sovietism itself, will work out?"[13]

Nevertheless, during the navigation season of 1923 the situation was so confused and fluid in Chukotka that Olaf Swenson's schooner *Chukotsk* prudently returned to Nome in June, having done no trading because of the "unsettled political situation," and H. Liebes and Company's schooner *Arctic* did the same "for fear of seizure." Those decisions turned out to have been wise because at the same time the Soviets seized the schooner *Belinda*, Tony Polet's and Sam Malsago's chartered *White Mountain*, Olaf Swenson's *Silver Wave* and *Blue Sea*, and the Phoenix Northern Trading Company's *Iskum* on charges of "ignoring the license and tax laws as laid down by the Soviet" on the grounds that they had not paid for trading licenses from the new authorities in Petropavlosk, Kamchatka. The Soviets also "arrested" any trade goods and furs ashore. They claimed a tax on fur exports of two-and-one-half gold rubles per white fox skin, twenty rubles on polar bear skins, and the confiscation of all blue and silver fox skins, which were the most valuable and which were declared to be state property.

The Soviets compelled the owners of the *White Mountain* to "sell" the schooner to the government (which did not pay for it). The *Blue Sea*, before it was released, was taken to Anadyr and used to transport a detachment of soldiers to the Kolyma River to fight the Whites. But by one means or another, the two other schooners were able to make their escape. The *Iskum*'s crew managed to overpower the two guards that had been stationed aboard, placed them in irons, and headed for Nome. Captain Jack Hammer and the *Silver Wave* were seized because the Reds had found a check from Olaf Swenson in the pocket of a White Guard officer whom they had executed. That Swenson had presumably traded with the enemy was deemed to be sufficient grounds for the Reds' seizure of all of Swenson's properties. According to the *Seattle Post-Intelligencer*, "It was only because Captain Hammer was clever enough to persuade the soviet authorities that Swenson had nothing to do with the vessel that he was released."

At Anadyr the Soviets also fleeced Max Gottschalk of $1,000. Gottschalk had had many brushes with Russian authorities since the beginning of the century—including a charge of murder—and on leaving Anadyr, he headed to Provideniya Bay, where he knew there was a government coal depot. His crew loaded eighty tons of the Russian coal aboard his schooner, which, on reaching Nome, he sold at $35 per ton, thus, he claimed, recouping his stolen money. Actually he "recouped" it more than twofold.

The Soviets likewise took Billy Thompson's schooner *Trader* at his post in Emma Harbor and ordered Thompson to sail it to Anadyr. Thompson, no fool, duly left Emma Harbor, but once he had cleared the headlands of Provideniya Bay, he steered not west toward Anadyr but east to Nome to make his escape. On his arrival in Nome he reported in the *Nome Nugget* that traders were required to obtain a license from the Soviet government in Petropavlovsk, Kamchatka (about 1,500 miles from Nome), and that fox skins were now prohibited from export "until the government has first adjusted the laws" to allow it. He added that "the present government officials at Anadyr are an illiterate lot of men who pass a law and never stop to consider the results of having a bad law passed."

Famine was often the result of these confiscatory tactics, and the confusing, contradictory, and occasionally corrupt actions by the Soviets had the effect, the *Seattle Post-Intelligencer* stated on July 3, 1923, that "isolated villages in Far Northern and Northeastern Siberia are faced by an ammunition and food shortage as a result of the detention at [Cape Dezhnev] of American trading vessels and the policy of the soviet government in discouraging trade by foreigners. . . . The posts depend largely upon the American traders for ammunition used in hunting and for many important items of food. . . . The policy of the soviet government with regard to trading licenses has been such however, that traders have been discouraged from any attempts to reach the villages this year, and consequently a shortage of food is imminent."

The following summer, 1924, C. T. Pedersen's *Nanuk* "only narrowly escaped seizure by the Russians," although he was forced to forfeit $2,000 to secure his release. Pedersen felt fortunate that his ship and cargo had not been confiscated. In 1925 the Soviets commandeered the cargo of the Nome schooner *Ram*, which, under charter to Sam Malsago, had been wrecked on the coast of the Chukchi Peninsula. The *Ram*'s captain, Victor Jacobsen, who enjoyed a reputation for free-bootery similar to Max Gottschalk's, made his way back to Nome aboard the *Blue Sea*. According to the *Seattle Post-Intelligencer*, Jacobsen reported the "arrest of Sam Malsagow, well-known Russian trader, and two members of the crew[,] . . . charged with taking furs out of Siberia illegally. They are to be transported to Petropavlovsk on a Soviet freighter for trial. The only reason he could assign for his release by the Russians was that he talked longer and louder than his captors."[14]

THE HUDSON'S BAY COMPANY, SOVIET DISORGANIZATION, AND OLAF SWENSON

During this chaotic period the best financed of all the entrants into the northeast Asia trade was the Hudson's Bay Company. In 1919 it joined with two other firms to begin their "Siberian Venture," an initiative to explore trading into the Sea of Okhotsk, Kamchatka, and Chukotka. Believing that the situation in northeasternmost Asia presented opportunities for entering the fur trade there, the company took a majority position in a consortium with the Sale and Frazar Company of Japan and Count Berg, a Russian. The rationale for the Siberian Venture was the optimistic (and naïve) belief that "although the Communists had acquired supreme power in Moscow in 1917, the operation of their economic policy for the abolition of capital and private ownership had not penetrated to North-east Siberia, nor was there any indication that such a policy would be extended to such remote regions, and therefore the Company were justified in developing their trade on private lines." The company's leadership would regret this decision.

In 1920 the HBC began freighting supplies to the coastal posts that the Karaev brothers operated, with the contractual understanding that, in return for supplying the Karaevs with supplies and merchandise for operating their posts, the HBC would receive the furs they collected. The following year, 1921, Sale and Frazar and Count Berg withdrew from the initiative, but the HBC's directors decided to continue alone and entered into agreements with local trading companies to supply posts on the Sea of Okhotsk, on the Kamchatka Peninsula, and on the Chukchi Peninsula in return for the fur catch.

Things went badly from the start. Partially because of its own planning the HBC encountered logistical difficulties in shipping the trade goods to the various ports, and it appears that the Karaev Brothers may have been playing on both sides by trading on their own account with their Kamchatka and Chukotsky Peninsula Company. By summer 1922, the HBC's leadership had planned to sever its ties with the Karaevs but found that the political conditions at Anadyr by then had become so confused that no action was taken.

To make matters worse, that summer proved to be very icy on the Asian coast. The HBC's steam-powered icebreaker *Baychimo*, which had already been damaged by grounding on the Kamchatka coast, ran into heavy fields of ice at Cape Dezhnev. It was forced to turn back before reaching Cape Schmidt on the north coast of the Chukchi Peninsula, and it had to abandon plans to supply posts on the west coast of Kamchatka.[15]

According to a Hudson's Bay Company report, in March 1923, the Soviet government in Vladivostok had "claimed a monopoly of the fur wealth of the districts in which the Hudson's Bay Company had already established its extensive trading organization, and the Company was faced with the alternative of negotiating with the Provisional Government for a continuance of trade, or complete withdrawal and liquidation."

Had they been omniscient, the HBC's leadership would surely have chosen liquidation at that point, because in 1923, to avoid a large loss, the company entered into a one-year agreement with the Soviet government to supply its existing posts, with the option of renewal for another year, "the net profits from which were to be equally divided" between the HBC and the government "in the expectation that the Government would cooperate and render every possible assistance." The HBC was, however, sadly disappointed in this arrangement because of the changeable and often contradictory ad hoc regulations that the Soviets imposed at various locations, which included "restrictions and the submission of exorbitant demands for taxes by local governing authorities" and the seizure of HBC property.

In early 1924 the company attempted to achieve an understanding with the government in Moscow to reach "more reasonable terms and conditions," but it was unsuccessful because the Soviets "were of the opinion that the monopoly operations in the prescribed districts could be made productive of considerable profit."

Faced with an impossible situation, and without any Soviet cooperation in an endeavor in which the communists were manifestly unprepared, the HBC decided to cut its losses, but even then they found that "various oppressive conditions were imposed . . . to which the Company were compelled to agree." In essence the Soviets unilaterally seized all of the HBC's property and goods and allowed only a fraction of the HBC's fur to be exported.

The *Seattle Post-Intelligencer* reported on the state of affairs: "An agreement made with the Soviet several years ago has expired. Hundreds of thousands of dollars were spent in establishing posts and experienced Russian and Siberian traders were engaged. Great stores of trade goods have been sent in to the country and high-powered launches were included in the special equipment sent to Kamchatka. Diplomacy failed, however, and the venture has been dropped." The Hudson's Bay Company had very deep pockets at that time, but in withdrawing from the Siberian Venture it was forced to write off a loss of approximately $1 million.[16]

The withdrawal of the HBC and the seizure of the American trading vessels put the Soviets in an extremely difficult position, as they came to realize that because of their actions they now had no sources for supplying northeasternmost Asia. But despite the confiscations, the Soviet-controlled peninsula still presented a lure to a few maritime traders. In 1926, Tony Polet and Leo Seidenverg outfitted the motor vessel *Nome* for a trading trip to Anadyr, speculating that the Soviets would welcome a supply of goods.

> However upon arrival at Anadyr they found it was impossible to do any trading, although the people wanted and needed the stock of goods very badly. Do [sic] to the restrictions placed against foreign vessels trading, the people of Anadyr realizing that they needed the stock of goods on this vessel, they voluntarily raised nearly $10,000 and asked the Soviet officials to take this money and purchase the cargo and place it in the government store so that they might be able to repurchase it. But this arrangement was tabooed by the government official in charge of the store[,] refusing to have anything to do with it.
>
> It was learned that the soviet government supply vessel had recently arrived there with supplies . . . but the class of goods were [sic] much inferior to what the vessel from Nome carried. In fact they stated that that the potatoes brought to Anadyr by the soviet vessel were dumped overboard because they were in a rotted condition and that the other goods were of a cheap variety

which the people did not care to buy. After waiting a considerable length of time for the Nome vessel to be released by the Soviet officials they sailed back to Nome without having accomplished any business.

The *Nome Nugget* reported in 1926 that Charlie Carpendale, who had been a trader near Cape Dezhnev for two decades, "was fined recently $2000 which is 50% of the money earned by him while working for the Hudson [*sic*] Bay Company." And "Mr. Wall [Bengt Vold], another trader at [Cape Serdtze Kamen], was fined $2000 for some minor offense and later assessed another $2000." In 1927, when the schooner yacht *Northern Light* touched there briefly on a sport hunting expedition, the owner, John Borden, described meeting Bengt Vold: "A Mr. Wall (Norwegian trader) . . . said he had been living here for 17 years and wanted to get out as Bolsheviks had confiscated his schooner and taken everything he had for taxes. . . . These Chukchees hate the Russians who treat them very badly. They keep them as poor as possible so as to get their furs cheaply. . . . The Russian steamer that we saw last week at [Cape Dezhnev] stopped here three days ago but left no food or ammunition for the natives." He noted that "The Chukchees wanted flour, tea, 30–30 cart[ridge]s, plug tobacco (pipe), lump sugar, knives, pipes, needles and calico."

A month later the *Nugget* added:

> The old traders are permitted to trade by the Soviet government. The license costs about $100.00, but the taxes kill them when the year is ended. Books must be kept. A certain amount of expense is allowed and trade is but [permitted to] make 10%: anything over that goes to the government stores and all goods [must be] bought from them and there is only one price to all traders and natives.
>
> Before this new law went into operation in 1925 it cost one old trader 3,000 roubles[,] about $1,700 for two years 1923–24[,] and he never had over $6,000 in trade goods at any time. For those who work for wages[,] no matter how small[,] the government takes 14% of those wages: and this in a land where there is not a hospital or mail service. Everything goes through the government and they will tell you that the land was in darkness during the independent traders [time] but the native knows different and prefer darkness to the so-called light under government trading.

Within a few years many of the resident traders, including Charlie Carpendale, had fled the region, and the majority of the trading vessels had ceased visiting the Chukchi Peninsula, although a few played a cat-and-mouse game with the Soviet authorities for a while.[17]

Olaf Swenson, however, was one trader who did eventually obtain a trading license, and his vessels were able to trade legally, often reaching as far west as the Kolyma River. It is highly ironic that the Soviets were forced to turn to Swenson, an honest businessman and trader, who was roundly vilified in print as a scoundrel and pirate by Soviet-era historians. In 1925, after tedious negotiations with the Soviet trading organization Dalgostorg, during which he may have retrieved some of his seized property, Swenson entered into a contract to provide the government with trade goods in Kamchatka and Chukotka on a "cost plus a fixed percentage" (the amount of which Swenson did not specify) in return for furs at set prices which he would then sell in the United States.

The following year, 1926, he signed a five-year contract with the Soviets to supply them with 600 tons of supplies annually. The agreement was expanded in 1928, with Swenson gaining the financial backing of New York fur dealers, among them Albert Herskovits and Sons. This arrangement appears to have been the expedient—and the only—avenue available for the Soviets, who lacked any other means of providing essential supplies to the inhabitants of the region.

"The Swenson outfit has some agreement with the Russians," wrote Captain Edward Darlington Jones of the U.S. Coast Guard cutter *Northland*, "so that they could not dispose of a skin before they reach Seattle—they are more like freighters than traders and are not permitted to do any trading at all in Siberia. They are told what supplies to bring in and deliver them at their destination— they are there given the furs to bring out and must take what is handed to them."

Although Swenson had to overcome a number of difficult logistical problems to fulfill his part of the agreement for delivering cargo as far west as the Kolyma River, one of his greatest challenges was in coping with the sea ice itself. In 1926 he bought the three-masted schooner *Nanuk* from C. T. Pedersen, and in 1928, because he had been awarded a second contract by the Soviets, he purchased the Norwegian schooner *Elisif*.

"The ice conditions north of Bering Strait in the Chukchi Sea in 1928 were very bad," wrote Robert Gleason, the *Nanuk*'s radio operator. "After several weeks trying to work her way through the ice, *Nanuk*'s propeller was severely damaged and she returned to Seattle under sail. Enroute home, much of her cargo was unloaded at Teller, Alaska, to be stored until the next summer." Worse, the *Elisif* was unable to reach the Kolyma River and was frozen in for the winter near Cape Schmidt, three miles off the north coast of the Chukchi Peninsula. By spring 1929, Swenson's backers were anxious to retrieve the 6,400 white fox pelts (worth $600,000) aboard the *Elisif*. They arranged for the pioneering bush pilot Noel Wien to fly to the ship, 600 miles northwest of Nome.

The *Nanuk*, frozen in at Cape Schmidt, Chukotka, 1930. A biplane is
next to the ship, ready to fly furs out to Nome. George Lounsbury
Collection, Archives, University of Alaska–Fairbanks, UAF 2006-0102-00033.

The furs weighed about 4,400 pounds, and Wien calculated that he would require four flights to bring them all out. The Soviets granted permission for the
flights.

The temperature stood at 40 degrees below zero in early March when Wien
touched down on a rough handmade ice strip near the ship. "I learned that
this was fairly warm compared to what it had been," wrote Wien. The Soviet
"governor," who was on the spot, then asked Wien to fly to a newly established
colony on Wrangel Island, about 100 miles north of there, to take out its furs.
The colony, as we shall see, had not been supplied since its founding in 1926.
Wien offered to do it for $500. The "governor" declined. "It's a good thing he
didn't take me up on it. . . . I found out the 'aviation' gas they said they had
ashore at [Cape Schmidt] was about ten years old. . . . It was very poor grade gas
and very old. . . . That Russian gas couldn't have got us back to Alaska."

Wien departed the next day with 1,725 fox skins worth $150,000. Shortly after
reaching Nome he received word that the Soviet authorities had cancelled his
permission for more flights, apparently because of his unwillingness to fly to

Olaf Swenson and his daughter Marion at Cape
Schmidt, Chukotka, 1930. They are standing under
the wing of the biplane that will carry them to Nome.
George Lounsbury Collection, Archives, University
of Alaska–Fairbanks, UAF-2006-0102-00035.

Wrangel Island. The *Elisif* broke out in summer but was soon severely holed
by the ice and had to be run ashore near Cape Billings. The crew of twenty was
then forced to sail more than 400 in their launches, as far as Little Diomede
Island, where they were rescued by the U.S. Coast Guard cutter *Northland*.

Things went no better for Swenson when the *Nanuk*, on a resupply voyage
to the *Elisif* and to the Kolyma River, was frozen in for the winter of 1929–1930
at roughly the same spot. Swenson had obtained insurance on only half of his
cargo, and his seventeen-year-old daughter Marion was aboard the ship. He
chartered the equally famous pioneering polar pilot Carl Ben Eielson to fly
them and his furs out. The first trip, without Swenson or Marion as passengers, went successfully, but on the second trip Eielson flew into a blizzard and

crashed on a sandspit east of the ship, killing both himself and his mechanic Earl Borland. Search parties by aircraft and dog teams immediately started out, but the wreck was not located until January 1930. Swenson and Marion finally flew out in February. In April and May most of the furs were flown out by Joe Crosson and others. In August 1930 the *Nanuk* reached Seattle. "From almost every standpoint, the voyage had been a disaster," stated Robert Gleason. "Less than half the fur had been taken out; two lives had been lost; one airplane had been destroyed and three other airplanes damaged." In Captain Edward Darlington Jones's estimation, Swenson took "desperate chances" with his ships to secure his profits. Certainly Swenson's record of losing ships would support Jones's assessment.

Swenson had purchased the Danish motor vessel *Karise* to replace the *Elisif* and to rendezvous with the *Nanuk*. The ship succeeded in reaching the Kolyma River in September 1930, but on the return voyage it, too, was frozen in and was forced to spend the winter of 1930–1931 west of Cape Serdtse Kamen. In 1931 the Soviets sent the schooner *Chukotka* to resupply the settlements, but it also was caught by the ice and was crushed, sinking off the north coast of the Chukchi Peninsula with the loss of lives.

Unfortunately for Swenson, however, the Soviets did not renew his five-year contract, and by 1931 one of Swenson's backers, Albert Herskovits and Sons, was faced with a fur market in steep decline and was unsure about continuing the Siberian operations. Consequently 1931 became Swenson's last year in active trading there. From 1931 until 1933 he traveled to Russia to conclude his business. Under the headline "Olaf Swenson Leaves Seattle," the December 1932 issue of *Fur Trade Review* declared, "Swenson . . . will be missed from the lanes of the trading fleet next spring. Mr. Swenson has liquidated the Swenson Fur Trading Company and may invest in a Moscow business. He is now on his way to Russia. He spent much of his time there last summer."

Swenson chartered the *Karise* to the Hudson's Bay Company for its Western Arctic resupply in 1932 and in 1933 sold it to Amtorg, a Soviet trading company. In 1932 he chartered the *Nanuk* to MGM motion pictures. In 1932–1933 the *Nanuk* wintered on the Seward Peninsula at Teller, Alaska—because ice had blocked it from reaching Barrow—for the filming of *Eskimo: Mala the Magnificent*. In 1933 MGM bought the ship. It appeared as the *Hispaniola* in *Treasure Island* and as HMS *Pandora* in *Mutiny on the Bounty*. Swenson died in Seattle in 1938, apparently a suicide.

Soviet historians of the Cold War era branded Swenson as the foulest sort of capitalist exploiter, but it is an inescapable fact that the Soviets desperately needed his services, and without Swenson's supplies, the Chukchi and Yupik of the region, who were hard-pressed by the meager stocks that the Soviets offered, would have been in even worse straits.[18]

THE SITUATION FOR THE YUPIK AND THE CHUKCHI

The communist takeover was disastrous for the Natives. A ponderous bureaucracy was imposed on them, and a Soviet administration was set up in the village of Uelen, near Cape Dezhnev. "The new Communist officials immediately pressed for tighter control over commercial and native communication across Bering Strait," wrote Igor Krupnik. "Border posts were established, and foreign traders and visitors were banned from entry without special papers and visas." In 1924 "a Soviet district officer from Uelen visited Big Diomede Island and prohibited any unregistered trade between the islanders and passing American schooners. He promised instead to send a Soviet trade vessel with better Russian supplies. This ship, however, never arrived. The next Soviet official, in 1925, recorded strong pro-American sympathies and the islanders' deep suspicion of the Soviet Regime."

In spite of the Soviets' regulations on Native trade, a few Yupik from Cape Dezhnev still risked the trip to Nome, and Diamond Jenness, who was carrying out archaeological excavations at Cape Prince of Wales, Alaska, may have witnessed the final voyage: "In the summer of 1926, while I was excavating some ruins at Wales, on the American side of the strait, an umiak manned by Siberian Eskimos called here on its way to Nome to purchase supplies, and called again on the return trip. One of its crew then told me in a queer Eskimo-English jargon, that fighting had broken out near his home between what I assumed to be Soviet Russians and White Russians. Although it was impossible to confirm his report, some disturbance probably did occur about that time, because since 1926 not a single boatload of Siberian natives has made its way over to the Alaskan side, nor have any Alaskan natives crossed over to Siberia."

Those few traders that still chanced a visit to the Chukchi Peninsula often preferred to stop at the Yupik village of Nuvuqaq on the steep escarpment of Cape Dezhnev, rather than at the Chukchi settlement at Uelen, a few miles to the northwest, where the authorities were stationed. Nuvuqaq is a poor trapping area, but located as it is at the narrows of Bering Strait it had unique access to Little Diomede Island in American waters and to Nome, to the profit of the Nuvuqaqmiit. Thus, once again, the local Yupik served briefly as middlemen in the trade, as they had for centuries, across Bering Strait.

While the Soviets were consolidating their control, the American side of the

strait held a greater lure for the Natives. A number of Iñupiat from Little Diomede Island, Alaska, were drawn to the Seward Peninsula and Nome; they were
replaced by Iñupiat from Big Diomede, who were attracted to Little Diomede
for its Lutheran mission school; and some Yupik from Cape Dezhnev moved to
Big Diomede and, later, to Little Diomede.[19]

Despite the prohibition of trade with foreigners, some Yupik from Cape
Chaplin also occasionally managed to cross into United States waters to the
village of Gambell on St. Lawrence Island. In 1929 Captain Edward Darlington
Jones wrote to his wife: "A number of Siberian Eskimos who are at Gambell . . .
said they were out hunting and got blown away from their own coast. I think
they really came over for a visit and to trade[,] which the Soviet Government
prohibits."[20]

"When the Reds took over the country and declared a monopoly," Olaf Swenson stated, "the government confiscated all business and fixed prices. Fur prices
dropped from an average of between seventy-five and ninety per cent of retail
market value to about fifty per cent. The natives couldn't get a decent price for
their year's labor and they couldn't obtain the merchandise they wanted and
needed. . . . Now, with the Soviet monopoly in force, they got only such things
as the Soviets saw fit to send them." He added, "Luxuries were completely taboo
and the natives had to content themselves with a pretty grim, dull selection of
absolute necessities, and not too many of these. There is no question that the
standard of living in Siberia dropped sharply and promptly as soon as the Soviets came into power there."[21]

In Nome in 1924 the Danish explorer Knud Rasmussen had just completed
an epic journey from Hudson Bay to Bering Strait. There he chartered Joe
Bernard's schooner *Teddy Bear.* Hoping to complete his ethnographic investigations by studying the Yupik on the Chukchi Peninsula, Rasmussen and Bernard
arrived at "Emmatown" southwest of Cape Dezhnev. In his book *Across Arctic
America* Rasmussen described his visit in a chapter entitled "The Bolshevik
Contrast." Offering a glimpse of what life was like for the Natives and for the
traders under the new regime, he wrote:

> There is a small township there consisting of a few Tchukchi families, some
> traders, and the Soviet representative. We are not particularly anxious to run
> right into the arms of the frontier police, but we shall have to meet them
> sooner or later. Captain Bernard and I were both pretty certain that we were
> in for a trying day, . . . we were met by a well known trader Charley Carpen-
> dale, who has lived here for a generation. He at once introduced us to . . . the
> frontier guard Allayeff. . . .

We had hardly got our boat hauled up on shore before Allayeff requested us to accompany him to the police station. Here, with the energetic assistance of Bernard, I endeavored to explain my errand, and the reason for my having no passport, at the same time requesting permission to stay for a month among the Eskimos of [Cape Dezhnev]. I promised, of course, that no trading should take place with the natives.

Allayeff declared that he had no authority to give me any such permission, and that if we did not put to sea again at once he would be obliged to send me under escort to the Governor at [Uelen]. . . . I was then led over to the Tchukchi village, where a team of twelve dogs was in readiness. . . . It was at once evident that these people were of a different type from the cheery, noisy Eskimos. The men looked serious, and from their expression, appeared to regard me as some dangerous criminal. Curious types there were among them, but all looked poor and ill cared for. Women came out from the big dome-shaped walrus hide tents; they were not unaccustomed to seeing people carried off never to return. A few dirty children clustered round the sledge.

All my papers had been taken from me and handed to the Tchukchi who is to take me to the Governor. . . . Some distance out we encountered another sledge coming from the opposite direction; it proved to be a Tchukchi, who spoke a few words of English, and we halted for a few minutes' talk. . . . He was very interested in my doings. Was I a trader? Had we any sort of goods on board our ship, and would we trade with him, somewhere out of sight along the shore?

I explained that I wished to conform to the law of the land, at which he protested, urging that the shops were all empty, and one could not even purchase ammunition. To make my own position clearer, I told him a little story I had heard myself regarding one of the American traders a few weeks before our arrival at [Cape Dezhnev]. He had been informed, through one of the Eskimos on Diomede Island, that the Russian authorities had no objection to his landing at [Cape Dezhnev] and trading with the natives there. Trusting to his safe conduct, he went across, and started bartering, only to find himself immediately seized and accused of illicit trading. All the ready cash on board his vessel, some $2000, was confiscated; the trader himself got away, thankful that they had not taken his ship as well. But when the Eskimo intermediary on Diomede Island heard what had happened to his friend, he crossed to the mainland himself to complain of having been made the instrument of a plot in defiance of good faith. All he got for his pains was a fine of $25 for insulting the authorities, and the fine being doubled each time he renewed his protest, he was at last obliged to give in. My Tchukchi friend nodded sadly, as one who understood all too well.

When Rasmussen reached Uelen he encountered the same confusion and contradictory rules that the American traders had endured. He was allowed to stay only twenty-four hours, but he was able to speak with several of the Russian traders at the settlement and gained a brief view of what life for them was like under the Soviet government.

> I began by calling on the traders, who were assembled in a small house, and discussed with them the situation generally. They were all Russians, but in spite of this, their position was worse than my own. The Soviet monopoly forbade them to trade on their own account, while at the same time, the government offered them no other means of making a living, and no opportunity of getting out of the country. One of these unfortunates, whose name I will not mention, fumbled in an old chest full of oddments, and pulled out a huge bundle of notes—paper roubles from the time of the Czars. These were his savings; rouble on rouble hoarded up by years of economy; and now, he declared, worth less than so much cigarette paper. I asked how many there were.
>
> "What does it matter?" he answered. "I used to know the whole sum to a kopek, but now, I cannot say. Thirty thousand, a hundred thousand roubles, it makes no difference either way."
>
> One old trader named Gobrinoff, who had suffered the same fate, burst out suddenly into a foolish mirthless laugh, and the rest of us fell silent.
>
> These bankrupt traders speak no ill of the Soviet, in spite of the fact that they, like everyone else in the district, have to look forward to a winter without tea or coffee, perhaps without tobacco, though, as they explain almost apologetically, there will be plenty of walrus meat and blubber. It is something of a degradation in their old age; they were wealthy merchants once, men of distinction in the place, and are now reduced to eating the blubber of charity and seeking the warmth of the native yarrangs as soon as the winter drives them from their own wooden huts, which they have no fuel to make them habitable.[22]

Six years later, in 1930, Captain Edward Darlington Jones visited Little Diomede Island aboard the U.S. Coast Guard cutter *Northland*. He wrote to his wife on June 23: "There are several Siberian natives here—they have to tell me at great length, through an interpreter, how badly the Russians treat them. Take their property away. Live in their houses and pay nothing for it, threaten them with rifles, will not let them go hunting etc. etc. I can only tell them that I am very sorry and warn them not to go to the mainland of Alaska. If they do, some U.S. Marshall will get hold of them, lock them up, get us to deport them. My idea is that these people have been going back and forth for centuries—long before whites came here—and I have no intention of stopping them."[23]

WRANGEL ISLAND

In the midst of the chaos of the Soviet takeover came the attempt by the explorer Vilhjalmur Stefansson to claim Wrangel Island for Britain.

Wrangel Island lies mostly above the seventy-first parallel of latitude at the boundary of the Chukchi and East Siberian seas, approximately ninety miles from the closest point on the Chukchi Peninsula. Speculation among Europeans about the existence of the island had been posited since 1824, when F. P. Vrangel, a Russian explorer, recorded Native reports suggesting that new land lay north of the Chukchi Peninsula, but the island was first seen by foreigners only in 1849, during the British search for the missing Franklin expedition. In the 1860s a handful of whaleships occasionally cruised near there for a few days, and Eduard Dallman, a German whaler and trader from Hawaii, had set foot there, but the first widely recognized landing did not take place until 1881, when parties from the U.S. revenue cutter *Corwin* and USS *Rodgers* landed briefly. The first Russians to visit the island were a group of hydrographers from the icebreakers *Taymyr* and *Vaygach* on an oceanographic exploration of the region in 1911. In 1916 the tsarist government claimed the island, and others nearby, for Russia.[24]

In 1914, a group of survivors from the wreck of Vilhjalmur Stefansson's Canadian Arctic Expedition ship *Karluk*, which had been crushed by ice in the Chukchi Sea, struggled ashore after a two-month trip over the floes and lived there for six months before they were rescued in September by Olaf Swenson's schooner *King and Winge*. On July 1, 1914—Canada's Dominion Day—the survivors had raised the flag of Great Britain. Because these men were thought to have been the first human beings to live on the island, based on their occupation Stefansson believed that Britain, via Canada, had a claim to its sovereignty.

With fox prices rising, a few adventurous trappers had planned expeditions to the island, assuming that virgin trapping territory awaited them there. Arnout Castel, with Gus Masik, had intended to take the schooner *Belinda* to the island for two winters. Heavy ice, however, prevented them from getting that far, and they wintered instead in the Kolyma River delta.

But in 1921 Stefansson cobbled together a hastily planned expedition and sent four relatively inexperienced university students, accompanied by a young Eskimo woman, Ada Blackjack—who would serve as the expedition's seamstress—to live on the island for two years. They were to trap foxes and to establish British sovereignty. Then in 1922, in a summer of exceptionally heavy ice, at Stefansson's request, Carl Lomen in Nome hired Joe Bernard and his *Teddy Bear* to resupply the party, but the ice defeated Bernard, and he was unable to reach the island. Speculation then went out widely in the press that the party must be in danger of starvation from a lack of supplies.

In 1923, during the preparations for another relief expedition (this time via the motor vessel *Donaldson*), the Soviet government sent word to Nome that the *Donaldson* must stop at Anadyr to receive permission to visit the island and that it must take aboard a detachment of Red Guards who would collect taxes from the party. This demand was ignored, and the *Donaldson* sailed for Wrangel in August. When the *Donaldson* reached the island only Ada Blackjack and her cat remained alive.

Stefansson, continuing his quixotic quest, had also sent another party aboard the *Donaldson*. The group comprised twelve Point Hope Eskimos—men, women, and children, including Peter Kunaŋnauraq (chapter 7)—and Charles Wells, an experienced trapper. But Stefansson soon realized that neither Canada nor the United States was likely to back his claim to Wrangel, and in May 1924 he sold his "rights" to the island to Carl Lomen, whose family were owners of large reindeer herds on the Seward Peninsula.

That same year the Soviets dispatched an icebreaker, the *Krasny Oktiabr* (*Red October*), carrying a detachment of infantry, to arrest the party and to assert Russian sovereignty. Word of this expedition spread quickly, and the U.S. revenue cutter *Bear*, the *Herman*, and the schooner *Silver Wave* all unsuccessfully attempted to evacuate the party. On August 26, 1924, the Soviets arrived, arrested the trappers, confiscated their catch (157 fox pelts, 40 polar bear skins, 2 polar bear cubs, and 4 gunny sacks of walrus ivory), and sent the party south to Vladivostok on the icebreaker. Charles Wells and two of the children died during their captivity. The Eskimos were eventually deported to China, where the American Red Cross arranged for their transportation. In January 1925 they sailed from Harbin to Kobe, Japan, then to Seattle, and eventually back to Point Hope.

"Thus ended Stefansson's bold, injudicious Wrangel Island 'adventure,'" stated the diplomatic historian Gordon W. Smith. "In retrospect, it is difficult to comprehend how he or anyone else could ever have believed that it would end otherwise. Apart from all other considerations, Soviet Russia—given the climate of the times and her attitude toward the rest of the world—would not remain passive indefinitely in the face of a Canadian, British, American, or any other 'capitalistic' attempt to appropriate island territory so close to its Arctic coast."[25]

During his brief visit to Cape Dezhnev in 1924 Knud Rasmussen wrote, "Scientists do not appear to be popular after Vilhjalmur Stefansson's exploit in planting the British flag on Wrangel Island, which the Russians regard as Russian territory. . . . All unsuspecting, I had tumbled into a political wasps' nest. . . . I was shown out; requested to leave."

In response to Stefansson's adventure the Soviets decided that they must confirm clear sovereignty to the island by establishing a settlement there. In 1926 they sent the ice-strengthened ship *Stavropol* with equipment and supplies for the new colony. On the first of August it reached Emma Harbor in Provideniya Bay to recruit Native hunters with their families by emphasizing the opportunities for trapping on the island. After a stop at Cape Chaplin the ship moved on north with a complement of fifty-five Yupik and a few other locals. On August 11 they began unloading supplies at Rodgers Harbor on Wrangel Island.

The colony got off to a shaky start, enduring several crises, including an outbreak of scurvy and the death of one of the leaders. Moreover, in 1927 heavy ice prevented the *Stavropol* from breaking through to resupply the colony. The summer of 1928 was the same, similar to the difficulties that the Hudson's Bay Company would experience at the Fort Ross post at Bellot Strait (chapter 1). Only in late August 1929 was the icebreaker *Fedor Litke* able to reach the island, carrying a large cargo of supplies, new buildings, 100 tons of coal, and a radio station. But during those three winters the Yupik, who had been dispersed into trapping camps around the island and whose trapping skills were clearly superior to those of Stefansson's party, had traded 500 fox skins, 300 polar bear skins, and two and a half tons of walrus ivory at the local Soviet store.

In 1931 the relief vessel *Chukotka* tried to reach the island but was sunk by ice. The following summer was the same: ice stopped the resupply vessel, but two float planes did land and returned with 1,000 fox pelts. The next year, 1933, the freighter *Chelyuskin* was also trapped by the ice, and, heavily damaged, it drifted in the southern Chukchi Sea for a number of months. The crew was evacuated by aircraft before it sank, forcing the population on the island to go on very short rations.

Finally, in 1934 the icebreaker *Krassin* managed to reach Wrangel with building materials and staff for a meteorological station, as well as two new Yupik families. But the autumn walrus hunt failed because Konstantin Semenchuk, the autocratic station leader, forced the Yupik to haul supplies rather than pursue game for their winter stores. Scurvy again broke out in winter. The lack of walrus meat also meant that there was no bait for the traps. The trappers asked Semenchuk to advance supplies to them on credit. He refused their request, thus placing the Natives in a life-threatening situation, wherein they were eventually forced to eat their dogs and their skin boat covers, which made it impossible for them to run traplines or to hunt for walrus in autumn. As many as seventeen (one-third of the Yupik population) starved to death there in the winter of 1934–1935. Semenchuk was later removed and all of the debts that the Natives had incurred were cancelled. Semenchuk and his assistant were tried in Moscow by state prosecutor Andrey Vishinsky, "the main theoretician of Stalin's jurisprudence and the future star of the Moscow show trials," wrote Yuri Slezkine. The men were executed.[26]

GROWTH OF THE TRADE IN
NORTHERN ALASKA

POPULATION DISPERSAL

Although only a few Native families had previously wintered on the north coast of Alaska between Barrow and the Canadian border, by 1914 more families had begun moving there for fox trapping (chapter 4). Although some ceased trapping in the winter of 1914–1915 because of low fur prices, a gradual dispersal of the population had commenced. Groups of one or two families set up camps fifteen to thirty miles apart in two regions, one on the coast east of Barrow and the other west of the Canadian border. Within a few years the early immigrants were joined by interior-dwelling Eskimo families, many of whom moved north to the coast. A few camps were also located on the inland rivers, and a dozen families had taken up residence below the treeline on the south slope of the Brooks Range. In summer some of these interior-dwellers traveled to the coast for seasonal hunting, fishing, and trading.

By 1916 the American fur market had begun to rise again, and Charlie Brower was quick to catch the trend. "When whaling went by the board there was nothing for the Eskimo to do around here," Brower wrote. "For several years I tried to get them to spread out to where there was some chance of them catching fur. . . . I got some of the best to go. Then I had to put a station where they could get supplies when they needed them. There was a lot of competition with all the small traders coming in every summer. If there was no place [the Natives] could go with their skins, many just held onto them until the schooners arrived and sold to them. I, who fitted them out, was the loser."[1]

But Brower did have some success in encouraging the Barrow Natives to disperse, although the missionaries wanted them to remain in the settlement. He also faced stiff resistance from the government schoolteacher, who wished to keep them concentrated in the village. Archdeacon Hudson Stuck visited Barrow in 1918 on a circuit of northern Alaska and described the situation:

> Mr. Brower had a controversy with the Bureau of Education over the policy of Eskimo concentration to which it seems committed perhaps somewhat bureaucratically at this place, holding that there were too many people gathered at Point Barrow for the prosperity of the community; and he had "outfitted" a number of men with grub that they might take their families and go far off where there was better prospect of white foxes than in the overtrapped neighbourhood of Point Barrow. Of course he was the agent of a furrier's house and it was his business to secure furs, but there is little now besides furs that an Eskimo who uses "white man's grub" can procure to trade for the same. Even for the sealing, the daily bread-winning of the Eskimos, the gathering of many people at one place is not favourable for a plentiful provision of food, and the problem of fuel, always a serious one in an Eskimo community, was rendered more pressing by a large population, and was indeed more pressing at Point Barrow than at any other place we visited.[2]

"I had to almost force many to even leave the village during the trapping season," Brower recalled. "The missionaries wanted them to stay around so they could attend church three times every week. I thought that they could be religious out in the country as well as here and still make a living. We finally got them to trap[,] as they found there was no credit [at the store] for those who did not try to do something for themselves." For those who did move away to concentrate on trapping, the reward was considerable. At that time, "an industrious trapper," wrote the geologist Ernest de Koven Leffingwell, "could catch fifty to one hundred skins each season in northern Alaska, which would yield about $2,000."[3]

Brower swiftly established a number of small posts on the coast. First, in 1916 he bought Hansen's Store in Barrow and its outpost at Wainwright. Hansen's had been set up by Captain John Backland Sr. in 1913 to sell his cargo after his trading schooner *Transit* had been stove by ice and run ashore near the village. In the same year Brower offered his former partner, Tom Gordon, the opportunity to set up a post at Demarcation Point (which the company named "Icy Reef Station"), only a few miles from the Canadian border. Gordon had the post up and running in 1917.

In 1917 Brower also persuaded his friend Arthur James ("Jim") Allen to move from Point Hope to manage both the Wainwright station and its outpost fifty miles southwest of there at Icy Cape. (The names "Icy Cape Post" on the Chukchi Sea and "Icy Reef Station" on the Beaufort Sea, which are located 400

Fred Hopson and Charlie Brower at Barrow,
1917. Charlie wears sealskin trousers. Arnold
Liebes Collection, N4323. © Arnold Liebes,
California Academy of Sciences.

miles apart, have occasionally caused much confusion.) By 1925 Brower had set
up another post at Barter Island, west of Demarcation Point, where Tom Gordon had by then moved, leaving his son Mickey in charge of the Demarcation
Point post.

A number of visitors to Brower's main station at Barrow remarked about its
neatness and the variety of the goods he stocked. Clarence L. Andrews, who
stopped there in the summer of 1924, wrote: "The front of the building was the
storeroom. The shelves were piled with prints, factory cloth, and calicoes in
bolts, blankets in bales, cartridges in stacks on the shelves, steel traps hanging
by their chains along the wall in heavy bunches, the cases of well-oiled rifles

Landing Tom Gordon's stores from the *Herman* to establish the H. Liebes post at Demarcation Point, 1917. Two whaleboats have been rafted together to carry freight. Arnold Liebes Collection, P711. © Arnold Liebes, California Academy of Sciences.

and shotguns, in the corner shoulder guns and darting guns for the whale hunt, flenzing [*sic*] knives, all the paraphernalia of the world in which they lived. Primus oil lamps, dog harness, and thermos bottles for the trails, fur [parkas], bales of sox, Eskimo *mukluks.*"[4]

For a number of years Brower had been sending boats to the traditional Iñupiaq trading rendezvous at Niġliq in the Colville River delta, but in 1918 he expanded his operations in the area. To get the furs in the Colville River area before the arrival of the Nome trading schooners Brower built a post at Beechey Point, twenty-five miles east of the Colville delta, and convinced a few Native families to move there as well. His agent at Beechey was Antone ("Tony") Edwardsen, who formerly had been with Backland's Hansen's Store. Each summer Edwardsen took his launch from Beechey Point to Barrow, collecting furs at coastal camps along the way, while the Gordons did the same from Demarcation Point and Barter Island.

A few Native trappers also sailed to Barrow in their own boats to await the arrival of the "outside" ships. A handful of independent traders likewise set up posts on the coast, and they, too, usually headed to Barrow for supplies in summer or waited for the outside ships to reach their camps. Thus, by the early 1920s, the trapping families on the coast were benefiting from reasonably reliable access to supplies year-round, and consequently Charlie Brower ceased sending the annual boat to the Niġliq rendezvous in the Colville delta.[5]

Brower's efforts to encourage trappers to disperse from Barrow did meet with success: According to the United States Censuses, from 1910 to 1920 the population of Barrow declined by more than a quarter. Soon there were winter trapping camps spaced about one day's dog team travel apart at all points along the north coast. Because of this dispersal, the larger villages of northwest Alaska—such as Barrow, Wainwright, and Point Hope—gradually evolved into a demographic condition that included a core element of permanently resident Native inhabitants that were surrounded at some distance by a satellite population that lived "on the land" during winter to engage in trapping or reindeer herding. Many of these "satellite" families left their children with grandparents or relatives in the villages to allow them to attend school. They visited their children when they returned to the villages for trade and for Thanksgiving, Christmas, and Easter holidays. "The grandparents were very valuable to the children," Brower's daughter Sadie Neakok remembered. "They were the ones who raised the kids." Many of these families would be reunited after the close of the trapping season, when the trapping families returned home and reunited for spring and summer hunting and fishing.[6]

H. LIEBES AND COMPANY AND C. T. PEDERSEN

By the second decade of the twentieth century the maritime fur trade in northern Alaska had consolidated: two large firms and a few smaller ones carried trade goods to posts throughout the region. Although Nome merchants— including Ira Rank, Tony Polet, and the Seidenverg and Wittenberg families— outfitted a few coastal trading schooners to supply independent trappers and traders, the two largest and best-financed operators were H. Liebes and Company and Captain John Backland Sr.'s Midnight Sun Trading Company. John Backland had a salmon cannery, the Midnight Sun Packing Company, in the town of Kotzebue and had posts at a few coastal settlements, such as Shishmaref and Point Hope. He also carried freight and government supplies as far as Barrow.

Though H. Liebes and Company had been in partnership with Charlie Brower's Cape Smythe Whaling and Trading Company since 1893, until 1914 it had concentrated its northern voyages on a mixture of whaling and fur trading. By then, however, faced with diminishing returns from whaling and rising profits from trading, the company signed on Captain C. T. Pedersen to be the

H. Liebes and Company's trading ship *Herman* ca. 1922.
Courtesy of Richard S. Finnie, author's collection.

master of their ship the *Herman*, succeeding Captain Hartson Bodfish, who had retired.

Pedersen had been a whaler and trader in the Western Arctic since 1894 and had acquired a well-deserved, Arctic-wide reputation for honesty, integrity, masterful marine skills, and supreme proficiency in ice navigation. He served as captain of the *Herman* until 1922, trading, taking a few whales, and bringing out thousands of furs annually. In 1923, because the *Herman* had become too small for the volume of H. Liebes and Company's trade, Pedersen was instructed to find a larger vessel. He bought a 669-ton, four-masted schooner and installed a 350-horsepower engine. The company renamed it the *Arctic*.

In May 1923, however, Leon Liebes, the hot-tempered president of the company, fired Pedersen in a bitter dispute over his salary. Pedersen quickly wired Albert Herskovits and Sons in New York. They were also backing Olaf Swenson and had been interested in hiring Pedersen. Such was his reputation that they immediately agreed to send $96,000 for the purchase of a ship and supplies. Together they founded the Northern Whaling and Trading Company, in which Pedersen held a 20 percent interest.

Captain C. T. Pedersen aboard the *Herman*,
ca. 1916. Courtesy of the New Bedford Whaling
Museum, Ted Pedersen Collection.

Not wanting to lose the 1923 season—but by then far behind the usual date
of departure for the arctic trading vessels—Pedersen quickly bought a three-
masted lumber schooner (which he later renamed *Nanuk*) and frantically set
about preparing it for arctic work by installing an engine and sheathing the hull
with ironbark for protection from the ice. He left San Francisco six weeks after
the *Arctic* had departed for the North, but by driving his ship relentlessly he
caught up with the *Arctic* at Icy Cape and worked through the floes ahead of it,
dodging ice all the way.

Southwest of Barrow, Pedersen's skill as an ice pilot immediately paid off.
Ever alert to changes in wind, current, and ice, he noticed that the pack ice
was closing up, and turning his ship, he immediately headed south to safer
water. But the *Arctic*'s captain, John Bertonccini, was not as nimble, and when
the floes closed around the ship, they bent the propeller so badly that it was
jammed against the *Arctic*'s stern post, rendering the engine inoperable. The

C. T. Pedersen's ship *Nanuk* in the ice, ca. 1925. A crow's nest is mounted at the top of the mainmast, giving Captain Pedersen better visibility for directing the ship through leads amid the floes. Courtesy of the New Bedford Whaling Museum, Ted Pedersen Collection.

Arctic did not carry a coffer dam to cover the stern, thus to allow the crew to change the propeller blades, and the captain apparently did not think to build one. The crew spent three days cutting off the bent blade, and thus impaired they were able to proceed only slowly, with the ship vibrating violently from the unbalanced propeller.

That year H. Liebes and Company had contracted with the Royal Canadian Mounted Police for $37,000 to deliver materials for a new detachment post at Cambridge Bay on Victoria Island, but the crippled *Arctic*, well behind Pedersen, only managed to get as far as Baillie Island in Canada. There it offloaded the cargo and headed for home at once—despite the fact that there was very little ice that summer in Amundsen Gulf.

Pedersen estimated that he "cleaned up at least 90% of the furs" on the north coast of Alaska and the Western Arctic that year. Southbound at the end of the season, when he passed Barrow he had more than 5,000 white fox pelts aboard his ship.

The following summer, 1924, was very different and turned out to be one of the iciest in memory. Even in the Bering Sea Pedersen had to use black powder to blast the floes to keep his ship moving through the pack ice. The *Arctic* and the Hudson's Bay Company's 635-ton schooner *Lady Kindersley* were not as fortunate. When the *Arctic* reached Barrow laden with a cargo valued at $150,000, Bertonccini found heavy ice that prevented the ship from moving to the relatively safe water east of the point. Brower saw that the ice conditions there were very dangerous and urged Bertonccini to move the ship inside the protection of the barrier of ground ice—a pressure ridge that piles up about a quarter of a mile off shore on the shallows that parallel the coast in sixty feet of water. Despite the fact that Bertonccini had had decades of experience aboard ships in the Western Arctic, he did not heed Brower's advice, and he secured the ship to an ice floe about a mile and a half offshore and sixteen miles south of Barrow.

There he waited for five days for the floes to open. But then the pack ice came grinding in and shoved a piece though the bottom of the *Arctic*. The crew scrambled to salvage as much cargo as possible, rushing to offload it onto the shore-fast ice, but twelve hours later, when the pressure of the floes eased up, the ship settled to the bottom. Brower managed to salvage some of its supplies.

Joe Bernard and his *Teddy Bear* had also been trapped near Barrow, but he had managed to keep his schooner safe, and when the ice eased off, John Bertonccini made his way south aboard the *Teddy Bear*. When Bertonccini reached San Francisco, H. Liebes fired him. H. Liebes and Company found itself now

Unloading Charlie Brower's supplies from H. Liebes and Company's ship *Arctic*, 1923.
Natives serve as longshoremen, carrying the goods up the beach to the warehouse.
Arnold Liebes Collection, P1002. © Arnold Liebes, California Academy of Sciences.

without an arctic ship or a captain, and, forced to eat crow, the company offered
to rehire Pedersen at a salary of $10,000. Pedersen refused.

Aboard the Hudson's Bay Company's ship *Lady Kindersley* Captain Gus
Foellmer made the same mistake that Bertonccini had made. The ship was
hauling supplies for the HBC's Western Arctic posts as well as radio transmitting
equipment for a government station that was to be built at Herschel Island.
The *Lady Kindersley* left Vancouver in late June and reached Barrow on August
2. Like Bertonccini, Foellmer secured his ship outside the grounded pressure
ridge rather than moving it between the ridge and the shore, where the pressure
ridge would have protected his ship from the moving pack ice. But Foellmer
was waiting for a quantity of reindeer meat to be delivered to the ship and in
that exposed position had allowed the *Kindersley*'s semi-diesel engine to cool.
When the pack ice came shoving back in, the crew did not have time to heat
up the cylinder heads to get the engine started.

Hurriedly salvaging cargo from the *Arctic*, 1924. The pack ice closed in on the
ship and crushed its hull but held it afloat for a few hours. When the pressure
of the ice eased, the ship sank. Rauner Special Collections Library, Dartmouth
College, Stef MSS-4, C. L. Andrews Papers, box 1, folder 3.
Courtesy of Dartmouth College Library.

On August 4 the ice surrounded the ship and hauled it off, damaging the
rudder so badly that the *Lady Kindersley* could turn only to port. The crew
jury-rigged a rudder, but the *Lady Kindersley* carried no dynamite or blasting
powder to break up the floes, so it drifted helplessly for twenty-eight days, first
drifting more than 60 miles east of Barrow. The *Kindersley*'s supercargo Percival
("Percy") Patmore had been stranded ashore on August 4. He chartered Joe
Bernard and the *Teddy Bear* to stand by near the ship at the ice edge, but when
the crew tried to abandon the ship and walk to the schooner the jumbled and
milling floes were so dangerous that they were forced to return to the doomed
vessel. Driven by the wind, the ice then carried the *Lady Kindersley* 200 miles
back westward, to a position approximately 120 miles northwest of Point Barrow.

Now in great danger for their lives if the ship were to be crushed so far from
shore, on August 31 the crew abandoned it again and scrambled south over jumbled floating pressure ridges toward the U.S. Bureau of Education's ship *Boxer*,
which was standing by seven miles away. The *Boxer* had been asked to assist by
Percy Patmore. Using a wireless set that Bertonccini had salvaged from the *Arctic*, he coordinated the rescue effort. The crew found milling ice a mile south of
the *Kindersley*, but Patmore had hired several Eskimos with their umiaqs to go

Wreck of the *Arctic*, 1924. Courtesy of Richard S. Finnie, author's collection.

out aboard the *Boxer*. They reached the stranded men and ferried them back to the rescue ship. The HBC's icebreaker *Baychimo* arrived the next day, having been hurriedly ordered from duties in the HBC's Siberian Venture (chapter 5). The *Baychimo*'s crew collected the men but could not find the wreck. They searched fruitlessly for two weeks before heading south.

But the hulk of the abandoned *Lady Kindersley* did not sink immediately. In fact, the pack ice carried it for two years. In 1925 the wreck was spotted in the ice near Kolyuchin Bay on the north coast of the Chukchi Peninsula, 500 miles southwest of Point Barrow, where Natives boarded the ship and salvaged some supplies, and the following year it turned up nearby again. Driven by wind and current, it had presumably been carried in a great gyre around the Chukchi Sea. Then it vanished.[7]

To replace the *Arctic*, in 1925 H. Liebes and Company renamed a whaling schooner the *Charles Brower*. In 1927 the ship ran aground on a reef near St. Lawrence Island, badly damaging the hull. After some tense days the crew managed jury repairs, and the ship hobbled to Nome, where valuable time was wasted in further repairs. It ended up costing H. Liebes and Company $16,000 to fix the damage.[8]

The Hudson's Bay Company's ships at Tree River, ca, 1923. *Left to right: Lady Kindersley, Fort MacPherson* [sic], *and El Sueno*. RCMP fonds, e010836867. © Government of Canada. Reproduced with the permission of Library and Archives Canada.

In any case, prior to the *Brower's* stranding, under Leon Liebes's erratic leadership H. Liebes and Company had decided to withdraw from the arctic fur trade. This came about for several reasons but probably because the competition from C. T. Pedersen and small independent traders had cut into the company's profits. In fact, in late 1925 H. Liebes and Company offered to sell the *Brower* and its northern Alaska stations to Herskovits. Herskovits made an offer for the Liebes properties, which was accepted, but at the last minute Leon Liebes demanded that the Northern Whaling and Trading Company must assume all of its outstanding liabilities. Pedersen knew that Charlie Klengenberg was suing H. Liebes and Company for $75,000 for breach of contract in not delivering his supplies in 1922 and 1923, and Pedersen assumed that Klengenberg would win the court judgment, which he did (chapter 7); consequently Pedersen and Herskovits withdrew from the negotiations. Then, in 1926, H. Liebes and Company sent word to Charlie Brower at Barrow, requesting him to return to San Francisco for discussions about the future of their partnership. On September 14, 1926, Brower remembered that he "called at the Cos office, everything was upset. H. Liebes and Co were tired of the Alaska business." Although Brower tried to find an investor in New York to buy out H. Liebes and Company, in 1927 the company reluctantly sent him back north aboard the *Brower* with a small outfit and with orders to sell the outposts. Henceforth supplies for the Barrow station would be shipped aboard John Backland's four-masted schooner the *C. S. Holmes*. In 1928 the company sold the *Charles Brower* to the Soviet trading company Amtorg, and Charlie Brower sold the Icy Cape and Wain-

The *Patterson*'s deck cargo, 1935. Starting from aft: three basket sleds, boats, fuel drums, sacks of coal, and fuel drums. On the left, meat hangs on a line strung between a boat's davits. Courtesy of the New Bedford Whaling Museum, Keith Smith Collection.

wright stations to Jim Allen, the Beechey Point station to Tony Edwardsen, and the Demarcation Point and Barter Island stations to Tom Gordon and his son Mickey. H. Liebes and Company's timing of the sale could hardly have been better, as we shall see.[9]

Like Brower and Liebes, Pedersen and Herskovits worked quickly to take advantage of the rise in white fox prices. In 1924 Pedersen hired Jack Smith to set up a post at Collinson Point in Camden Bay and two years later established John Hegness at Cape Halkett to open a post and a white fox farm. By 1925 Pedersen's trade had grown to such an extent that the 261-ton *Nanuk* was too small for the growing volume of his northbound freight. In the winter of 1925–1926 he sold the ship to Olaf Swenson. Pedersen then bought the 580-ton *Patterson*, which he strengthened for arctic work, and continued his annual voyages, hauling freight and supplies each year until his final voyage in 1936.

Philip Masqin Campbell, a Yupik of St. Lawrence Island, served as a deck hand (and later as crew chief) for Pedersen aboard the *Herman*, the *Nanuk*,

Visitors aboard the *Patterson* at
Wainwright, 1936. In the foreground are slices of bowhead
whale skin and blubber, a delicacy
called *maktak*. Courtesy of the
New Bedford Whaling Museum,
Keith Smith Collection.

and the *Patterson*. He told me that Pedersen followed a routine in his trading
practice. On his northern voyage he would stop at several camps and towns on
St. Lawrence Island, trading for furs and taking aboard five Native men for
crew. In the years before the Soviet takeover on the Chukchi Peninsula he also
would stop at Cape Chaplin and several other Native settlements, including
Uelen, then head across Bering Strait to the Diomede Islands, and King Island,
buying, among many other things, ivory carvings, before going to Nome to pick
up extra supplies and fresh produce that had been shipped north for him.

Pedersen then continued onward, stopping at villages before reaching Point
Hope, where he usually signed on an additional eight men for the crew at a
salary of $50 to $110 per month. There he also bought quantities of bowhead
whale skin and blubber (*maktak*), which had been taken by the Natives during
the spring whaling season. He would sell the maktak, which was a delicacy to
the Northerners, at Herschel for $50 to $150 per sealskin "poke."

Then Pedersen visited all the coastal villages and camps north of Point Hope.
Pedersen, who was usually the first seaborne trader to arrive each year, would

stop briefly at Native camps if he spotted a flag flying from a pole on shore, even for just one tent. Hubert Koonuk, describing how the Native store in Point Hope was often out of supplies by spring, recalled: "We didn't have money but we had the furs, the foxes, polar bears, sealskins, that we could trade with. . . . Captain Pedersen was the one who would buy anything, like skins, maktak, oil. . . . There was another ship that always came after Pedersen but we didn't have too much left because Captain Pedersen always came early, even while there is still ice, and got all of the things we had to sell."[10]

Warren Neakok remembered Pedersen's visits: "While we were there on the spit . . . , as soon as the ice breaks up the ocean breaks up. Pretty icy but Captain Pedersen would come up. He used to be the first boat to come up. And every time he came up he used to stop there. Anchored in front of us and my grandfather would do some shopping. Sometimes he had more than two big sacks of white foxes or red foxes and would take them out. My grandfather had a wooden whale boat. That whale boat was a pretty big size, about 30 feet. Fill it up. . . . Supplies for all winter. . . . They stored that stuff . . . that they got from Pedersen, groceries, crackers, coffee, sugar, whatever he had. . . . Pedersen learned Eskimo too."[11]

"He thus was able to get first choice of all the skins and furs from the natives along the coast waiting to do trade with the pelts they had saved from the previous trapping season," David Greist stated. The trapper would quickly launch his boat and come out to the *Patterson* with his furs. "I would stand by in the captain's cabin where Captain Pedersen was receiving furs from the natives. He would hold up a white fox, blow on the fur, shake it out and then say, 'Sixty dollars.' This was, of course, in trade; no cash was exchanged. Then the Eskimo could say, 'I want 30-30 rifle and plenty ammunition.' [Pedersen's] son or I would run to the hold, get a rifle and several boxes of ammunition to make up the sixty dollars. It went on like that all day. Some of the natives would have twenty-five or thirty foxes to trade. They would end up with a lot of merchandise. Then they would load everything into their umiaks, go ashore and we would sail on to the next village." Philip Masqin Campbell recalled that in 1928 the highest price Pedersen paid (in trade goods) was $65 for a prime large white fox and $200 for a blue fox.[12]

The Natives were the beneficiaries of this steady supply of goods, goods that were now available from the posts year-round and in summer from the ships, but the rising price of fox pelts also had an ancillary effect in distracting the Eskimo reindeer herders from carefully tending to their herds; instead they increased their focus on fox trapping as a sideline. "The high price of white fox tempts the natives to neglect their reindeer," reported the botanist A. E. Porsild.

"Several herds [I] visited had shown a steady decrease in the last few years because the owners devoted most of their time to trapping, and depended on the
reindeer all winter for dog feed."[13]

The exception to this state of material abundance came in the very icy summer of 1924, when the *Arctic* and the *Lady Kindersley* were lost near Barrow.
"We ate only ptarmigan, that was all we had to eat," stated Roxy Ekowana,
remembering the winter of 1924–1925. "Because the supply boat had been
wrecked that year we did not have any white man's food. . . . The people had a
lot of fox skins but no place to trade them in, so everyone was short of supplies
that year." Levi Kagona Greist and Elizabeth Qalliñiq Greist recalled, "That
time Liebes' boat, the *Arctic*, is wrecked. Nobody can get any flour. . . . People
had a hard time, but nobody was dying, because there were a lot of young people, a lot of hunters—mountain sheep, caribou, seal and everything."[14]

In the summer of 1929 confidence in the fur market remained equally high
for northern trappers and traders. Captain Edward Darlington Jones of the U.S.
Coast Guard wrote to his wife from Nome at the end of June: "The coast natives
have had a very profitable year—big catch of foxes and very high prices—They
are not at all interested in small sales of ivory and have done very little carv-
ing. They want suits of clothes, outboard motors, phonographs, radio sets, good
binoculars etc." Aboard the *C. S. Holmes* the following summer Captain John
Backland Jr. carried seven prepaid boats to St. Lawrence Island, the result of
1929's prices in the overheated fur market.[15]

Because of the rise in fox prices the years from 1914 to 1929 in northern Alaska
were characterized by a general dispersal of the Eskimo population to trapping
camps throughout the region and an increasing availability of manufactured
goods and other supplies, items which they could no longer do without and
which made their lives easier, an abundance that the Eskimos embraced—but
an abundance that would soon wane (chapter 9).

7

COMPETITION AMONG TRADERS IN WESTERN ARCTIC CANADA

ALASKAN IMMIGRANTS AND THEIR SCHOONERS

From roughly 1915 to 1923 a second wave of Alaskan Nunatamiut immigrants entered Western Arctic Canada to trap white foxes throughout the region and muskrats and mink in the fur-rich Mackenzie delta. The delta muskrats have a heavy, dense underfur; fur manufacturers found that their pelts could be sheared and dyed to become imitation fur seal garments, selling in the middle price range of the retail fur market as "Hudson seal." In 1923 a headline in *Fur Trade Review* announced, "Hudson Seal the Backbone of the Trade." By the mid-1920s Hudson seal jackets were widely in vogue, as were skirts and evening wraps trimmed with white fox.

By this time the interior of Alaska's North Slope was largely deserted, and those Alaskan immigrants, who became known as *Uummarmiut* ("people of the ever-greens and willows") within the Inuvialuit population, quickly gained a reputation for energetic enterprise (chapter 4). By 1924 the Alaskan Eskimo immigrants were estimated to have become 75 percent of the local Inuit population. But their presence in the delta was resented by the Indigenous Siglit, who, in condominium with the Gwich'in, had always used the delta as a hunting reserve, a region that had never before supported a year-round population. The Siglit, who had become clustered in the northeast part of the delta near Kittigazuit, felt that the Alaskan immigrants overharvested the area. Referring to the original Inuit inhabitants of the region, the Siglit trapper Nuligak stated: "Long ago the Kitigariuit Inuit [Siglit], the real inhabitants of this land, avoided building their homes in the Delta. The Indians [Gwich'in] did the same. For them the Delta was the hunting-land, the trapping ground. When the hunting season was past, they would return home, keeping the mouth of the Mackenzie as a park where no

Western Arctic Canada.

one had the right to build or spend a whole year there. Game was abundant. The Nunatarmeut [*sic*], coming in from Alaska, began to build houses and live there the whole year round. They hunted mink everywhere, even during the summer by canoe, so much so that they laid bare the whole country. Now there is no more game in the Delta and the trapping is very poor." Nuligak added, "In those days, many Nunatarmeut were full of vanity because, once they had left Alaska to live in the Delta of the Mackenzie, they had left a miserable life for a plentiful one."[1]

The Nunatamiut immigrants were quickly joined by foreign trappers and traders who descended the Mackenzie and invaded the delta. In the period from 1920 to 1929 there were twenty-seven posts at thirteen locations in the delta and the competition among them kept fur prices high. The Alaskan immigrants' response to the foreigners' arrival was to move farther north in the delta and then to expand east onto the coast, to Baillie Island, to the coasts of Franklin and Darnley bays, and to the mainland shore of Amundsen Gulf.

The human geographer Peter Usher summarized the distinction between the two Inuit groups. "Many whites had commented on the differences between the Mackenzie [Siglit] and Alaskan [Nunatamiut] Eskimos, from the earliest days, and in general favoured the latter on the grounds of their greater familiarity with white culture and language, and their greater 'ambition' and sophistication in trapping and hunting. The Mackenzie Eskimos from the start considered the Alaskans as interlopers, and blamed them for despoiling the country . . . and in later years they were blamed for the destruction of fur and game in the delta. The Alaskan Eskimos were interested in producing a cash crop in order to amass wealth beyond the daily needs of shelter and food, and were willing and able to employ superior technology, greater commercial sophistication and increased geographical mobility to do so."[2]

Many of the Alaskan immigrants in Western Arctic Canada did become wealthy through hard work and shrewd trading. Some, in fact, enjoyed annual incomes far higher than those of average Canadians in the South, and this wealth allowed them to purchase wooden watercraft: whaleboats and "schooners," as well as other expensive equipment. "The high prices between 1920 and 1930 meant that if a trapper took 300 foxes (easily possible during the peak year of the fox cycle)," Keith Crowe observed, "he could earn from $9,000 to $18,000. This was at a time when most Canadians earned only $1,000 a year or less." At Aklavik, for example, an Alaskan immigrant, the entrepreneurial Pokiak, "purchased a complete electric lighting system from the Anglican mission at Shingle Point, and installed it in his own house. He was probably the first Eskimo to have an electrically lighted house," according to Superintendent James Ritchie of the Royal Canadian Mounted Police.[3]

From the beginning of the whaling fleet's arrival at Herschel Island in the 1890s a whaleboat (*umiuraq*) was a very saleable item and proved to be superior to the traditional skin boat (umiaq) in some respects. By the winter of 1906–1907 the explorer Alfred Harrison noted, "Nowadays nearly every Nūnātāmā owns an ōmeūrak, or whale-boat, which has latterly nearly ousted the ōmiak . . . amongst them." He added that the Indigenous Siglit owned only "one or two" whaleboats. In the 1920s the whaleboat, whether with sail power alone, or in rare cases fitted with an inboard engine, was highly desired. Some whale-boats were built in New Bedford, Massachusetts, and shipped by rail to San Francisco, where others were also built. Captain C. T. Pedersen, for example, carried them aboard his ships and continued to sell them to Natives long after he himself had ceased whale hunting. Sail-powered whaleboats often sold for $1,000 in the 1920s. Some Native hunters fitted them with brackets to mount outboard motors.[4]

In Canada's Western Arctic, however, the preferred (and more expensive) vessel for both the foreign trappers and the Inuit was the "schooner." "Schoon-ers" were usually about thirty to forty-five feet in length, fitted with a variety of rigs (not necessarily classic schooner rigs), many of which had inboard gasoline engines and were called "gas boats." Some of these schooners were carried from Vancouver and San Francisco as deck cargo aboard ships, but a larger number were built in Edmonton. The Hudson's Bay Company and the Northern Trad-ing Company sold these on credit, and the debt was usually paid off in furs in two or three years because, as the *Edmonton Journal* reported, "the Eskimos are found to be dependable people to deal with."[5]

The Edmonton boats were built by the Alberta Motor Boat Company and the Northern Boat Building Company, which alternated summer work of building sleighs with winter work of building boats. The schooners were loaded aboard rail cars and carried north to the Mackenzie watershed, then towed downstream to Fort Fitzgerald (formerly called Smith Landing), where they were loaded onto carts and hauled sixteen miles overland around the Slave River rapids, then launched again at Fort Smith for the passage across Great Slave Lake and down the Mackenzie River, a total of 1,900 miles from Edmonton to Aklavik, where their new owners usually took possession of them. By 1922 the Hudson's Bay Company had begun building the schooners at Fort McMurray, thereby simplifying the transportation of the hulls.

These boats were given memorable names by the builders: *Bluenose, Henry Ford,* and *Mayflower,* after the famous Grand Banks fishing schooners that raced off Nova Scotia. Among others were *White Fox, Blue Fox, Golden Hind, Arctic Blue Nose,* and *Saucy Jane.* By 1924 the *Edmonton Bulletin* reported that "Innotuk" had bought five schooners, four of which he sold to others, and that the Northern Boat Building Company had built a total of thirty-six schooners for the Western Arctic Inuit. "Georgia pine and sturdy oak are used in building these northern boats; ribs, keel, stem, all are of solid oak to stand the squeeze of the ice floes," the *Edmonton Journal* stated. "The schooners are the last word in finish, even to the Blue Peter to fly at the masthead when the trip starts, and a weather glass to tap every morning. Innotuk will have everything of the best, and so stipulates; therefore he gets it."[6]

On a research trip down the Mackenzie River the economist and fur trade historian Harold Innis described the prosperity that the Inuvialuit enjoyed because of the boom in the fur trade. He noted that at Aklavik "competition [against the Hudson's Bay Company] has become more serious in the Western Arctic with the sale of small schooners to the Eskimo. The schooners are . . . valued at about $3,000 or $3,500 to $4,500 with gasoline power attached. In 1924 the Eskimo fleet at Aklavik totaled thirty-nine schooners, of which nineteen had auxiliary power, and twenty-eight whale and other boats, of which two had power. These were valued at a total of $128,000 and had been bought within five years. The Eskimo are able to visit various points to secure highest prices for furs and lowest prices for goods."

The Danish explorer Knud Rasmussen was astonished at the difference between the Inuvialuit in Western Arctic Canada, who were deeply involved in the fur trade, and the Inuit who lived farther to the east and who had not yet embraced it. In 1924 Rasmussen was traveling westward "across Arctic America" from Hudson Bay by dog team. He had moved through regions where Inuit had experienced only peripheral contact with the fur trade. In March, however, Rasmussen came upon Inuvialuit trappers, probably at Pearce Point Harbour.

At Cape Lyon we encountered the first Eskimo immigrants from Alaska, who, like white trappers, were now seeking their fortune in the country of their "wild" tribal kinsmen. They were extremely hospitable, spoke fluent English, and soon proved to be thoroughly businesslike. We did not take long to discover that we were in the land of the Almighty Dollar. A joint of caribou meat such as would have been given us freely as a token of welcome among tribes farther east, here cost $8, and when we wanted a man and a sledge to help us one day's journey on ahead, . . . the price asked for was $25. We thought perhaps, for a moment, with regret of the kindly folk we had left, who would have helped us on our way for a week and been only too pleased, without any question of payment. But the principle here was unquestionably right; the

Eskimos had now to compete with the white men, and if they were to make ends meet, it was necessary to ask a fair payment for services rendered.

He added, "The Eskimo hunters were no poor savages in kayaks; they owned schooners and called one another 'Captain.'"

The following summer, 1925, the explorer L. T. Burwash visited Baillie Island at the beginning of a trip toward Hudson Bay and formed a similar impression of these entrepreneurial Inuvialuit. "The modern influence of the west is strongly marked, the people being much more advanced in business ideas than those to the eastward," he wrote. "They are awaking to a very clear idea of modern values in practically all lines, and now follow the world post war system of combining to use the power of the producer periodically to advance prices."[7]

The Siglit trapper Nuligak may have been one of the first of the Indigenous Mackenzie Inuit to purchase a schooner. "I went to Aklavik to sell my foxes. Then I sent for a schooner through the Northern Traders Company. . . . That summer of 1926 I owned a schooner at last! It was a brand-new one, built that year, and called the *Bonnie Belle*. It was forty feet long, with a Frisco Standard heavy duty ten horsepower machine. . . . It worked beautifully." As the decade of the 1920s wore on, however, and as the price of white fox pelts rose, the schooners became larger and the price for them increased. For example, in 1928 Patsy Klengenberg and his brother-in-law Ikey Bolt bought the schooner *Nauya* from the Hudson's Bay Company for $8,500.[8]

INDEPENDENT TRAPPER-TRADERS

The surge in white fox prices in the second decade of the twentieth century also led to a second wave of small boats and trappers entering the remote parts of the Western Arctic. Like Wrangel Island in the Chukchi Sea, Banks Island in the Beaufort Sea seemed to have the potential for rich trapping grounds, and the island had been a traditional hunting area for the Kangiryuarmiut, a group of the Northern Inuinnait (formerly called the Copper Inuit). In fact, in the winter of 1914–1915 a few members of the Canadian Arctic Expedition, including its Inuit employees, experimented with trapping and caught a large number of white foxes in the vicinity of their camp at Cape Kellett at the southwest corner of the island.

Joe Bernard had planned to spend the winter of 1911–1912 on Banks Island but was unable to do so because of a lack of a crew (chapter 4). Although several other persons had also intended to trap on Banks Island before 1916, C. T. Pedersen was among the first to sponsor commercial trapping there when he landed a group of Point Hope Iñupiat—Peter Kunaŋnauraq and his family and Ataŋana and his family—at Masik River, but despite Pedersen's best efforts, two very icy summers prevented him from resupplying them. Pedersen wrote, "I tried to get over to Banks Land in 1917 and 1918, but found too much ice, but got over there in 1919 and picked up the trappers." Roy Vincent, Ataŋana's adopted son, told me that by 1919 the party had run so low on ammunition that they would only shoot caribou when two were in line and overlapping, so that they could retrieve the bullet from the carcass of the second one. Roy added that Billy Natkusiak, who had earlier been with Joe Bernard, was also on the island then, and to get supplies, he and Peter Kunaŋnauraq were forced to undertake the extremely dangerous seventy-mile crossing of Amundsen Gulf, traveling across moving ice floes, to reach a trading post on the mainland.

Natkusiak (chapter 4), also known as "Billy Banksland," had immigrated to Western Arctic Canada from the Seward Peninsula of Alaska. He remained on the island from 1917 to 1921 with his small schooner *North Star* (which Martin Andreasen had sold to the Canadian Arctic Expedition and which Billy had received in lieu of wages for his service). In 1921 Pedersen, suspecting that Natkusiak might need help, went to Banks Island looking for him. His "engine was out of commission and he had failed to get out. . . . We steamed along through slack ice to Masik River, and two or three miles offshore, watching for a tent on the beach, but no luck, so I headed for Baillie Island. We had proceeded only a mile or so, when I gave a last look through my glasses towards Masik River, and saw a dark square against the hills. I saw that it was a flag, so headed back and found the 'North Star' some distance in from the mouth of the river, but could see only her mast and flag. I sent our launch in and towed the 'North Star' out to us. Poor Billy Natkusiak was so excited that he could hardly speak, as he had not seen anyone for several years. Most of his white foxes had been thrown away, as they had rotted while hanging up in the damp hold of his vessel during the summer months. We took him in tow, and landed him at [Baillie Island] the following morning." Pedersen had planned to put another ten or twelve Iñupiat trapping families on the island, outfitted with three years' supplies, but in March 1920 the island was declared to be a game preserve for Canadian Inuit. Banks Island would not be colonized again until 1928 (chapter 10).[9]

JIM CRAWFORD, LEO WITTENBERG, GUS MASIK, OTTO BINDER, AND HAROLD NOICE ENTER THE REGION

James R. Crawford had been the first officer of the schooner *Mary Sachs* when the Canadian Arctic Expedition bought it at Nome in 1913, and Crawford continued working for the expedition at a salary of $125 per month for six months of the year, with the understanding that he would be allowed to trap foxes during the winter months. In 1914 he helped to set up the expedition's base camp on Banks Island at Cape Kellett, and in spring 1915, with Billy Natkusiak and George H. Wilkins, he had encountered a group of Inuinnait near Minto Inlet on Victoria Island. Wilkins described their meeting: "Crawford emptied a half-pound tobacco can just as we were about to start . . . when the woman asked for it. He asked her what she would give for it, but she had no idea what to offer, so he pointed to a fox skin. She seemed delighted to think that a fox skin was worth so much and was willing to trade any amount more at the same price. She produced a bundle of about forty. They had heard, they said, that white men wanted these skins but did not think that it was true, for nobody ever came and asked them for skins before. They had caught these with deadfalls during the last three years. I told them that other white men would very likely come next year who would give them good trade for the skins, but that we had far too heavy a load to think of taking any more with us."

Crawford, however, had a fondness for alcohol and consequently was fired from the expedition at Herschel Island in summer 1915. But that autumn, at Unalaska in the Aleutians, he had managed to buy the schooner *Challenge*, and the following year he obtained a trading outfit from Abraham Wittenberg in Nome. Wittenberg's son Leo would act as supercargo for the voyage. The *Challenge* was a relatively weak craft, but its small size and comparatively shallow draft made it suitable for coastal work.

In 1916 the *Challenge* was among the first vessels to enter Western Arctic Canada with the specific plan to trap and to trade for white fox pelts. In addition to Crawford and Wittenberg, the *Challenge* carried Gus Masik and Otto Binder, who would trap on their own from a camp at DeSalis Bay on southeastern Banks Island. After Crawford had deposited Masik and Binder he headed east about eighty miles to Victoria Island, where he planned to overwinter. The following summer Crawford sold the schooner at a good profit to Vilhjalmur Stefansson's Canadian Arctic Expedition, which was badly in need of another vessel. But Crawford and some of the crew, including "Nick Chucaluk and his wife Susie," chose to remain on Banks Island to continue trapping for another two years. Wittenberg, however, was arrested at Baillie Island for falsification of customs papers—or as one person put it, for "smuggling"—and spent six months in police custody at Herschel.

When Stefansson reached Baillie Island in 1917 he immediately sold the *Challenge* to Otto Binder, Harold Noice, and A. A. Carroll, a representative of the Northern Trading Company who was scouting for trade opportunities east of Baillie. With several others, including "the Eskimo Kimona and his family," they planned to take the vessel into Coronation Gulf for trapping and trade with the Inuinnait. According to Stefansson, "Binder and Carroll had their eyes on fur and a fortune," but he added that during the winter of 1917–1918 the schooner "was wrecked in winter quarters on the mainland coast of Amundsen Gulf." Noice remained in the region for a few years, trading in winter and carrying out archaeological excavations in summer. In 1918 Binder joined the Hudson's Bay Company's post at Tree River.[10]

CHARLIE KLENGENBERG

At the same time Charlie Klengenberg (chapter 4) was probing new areas for trapping and trading opportunities. Acting both on Joe Bernard's advice of 1914 and on the advice of his son Patsy, who had been an interpreter for the Canadian Arctic Expedition at Bernard Harbour from 1914 to 1916, he took his family in the scow-schooner *Laura Waugh* to the Coppermine River area in Coronation Gulf. There he found unexploited trapping territory and acquired large collections of white foxes, both on his own and in trade with the Inuinnait. His presence in the area from 1916 to 1923 allowed him to intercept furs that Inuinnait were carrying westward to the newly established Hudson's Bay Company post at Bernard Harbour, giving him the first pick of the pelts.

Klengenberg expanded his operations in 1919. He set up his daughter Etna Klengenberg and her husband Ikey Bolt, a native of Point Hope, Alaska, on southwestern Victoria Island at Rymer Point, near the entrance to Dolphin and Union Strait. In 1920 he and Patsy scouted Bathurst Inlet, and in 1925 Patsy opened a post on Wilmot Island at its northeastern entrance. The following year, 1926, Charlie's daughter Lena built a post at Cape Krusenstern on the mainland, near Dolphin and Union Strait, thus giving the Klengenberg family trading control of a large area of Coronation Gulf.[11]

Klengenberg knew, however, that he needed to have a more serviceable boat than his river scow. In February 1921 he packed a large load of his best furs onto three sleds, and, with Patsy and an Inuk named Kohar, set off for Herschel Island, 700 miles to the west, where he waited for break up. He then hired a whaleboat to cover the 175 miles to Aklavik. There he sold his furs and bought a forty-foot double-ended power boat, loaded it with supplies, and headed east for Rymer Point.

In late August, on his way back to the point, he encountered C. T. Pedersen in command of H. Liebes and Company's *Herman*. Pedersen bought 506 fox skins from Klengenberg for $11,000. Klengenberg then placed an order with

Diamond Jenness's photograph of the Klengenberg family with
their scow-schooner at Baillie Island, July 26, 1916. *Left to right:*
Etna, Jorgen, Qimniq holding Bob, Patsy, Andrew, Charlie, and
Lena. e0022801198. © Government of Canada. Reproduced
with the permission of Library and Archives Canada.

H. Liebes and Company to send him a large cargo of lumber and supplies, paying a $6,000 cash advance for the outfit, to be delivered to Rymer Point the next
summer, or the following one if the ship were to be unable to reach him in 1922.

But 1922 proved to be a very difficult ice year—the Hudson's Bay Company's
Lady Kindersley, bound for Coronation Gulf, was able to reach only Herschel
Island, and Pedersen was unable to advance east of Baillie Island. Fearful of
being frozen in for the winter, he returned to San Francisco with Klengenberg's
goods. Klengenberg was forced to travel to the Hudson's Bay Company's post
at Tree River to get supplies to last him the winter. The HBC's trader at Tree
River would sell Klengenberg only a minimal amount of supplies at high prices
because he did not want Klengenberg to have surplus goods to trade against the
company.

In 1923 Pedersen was fired by Leon Liebes (chapter 6), and H. Liebes and
Company's ship *Arctic* was damaged by ice before it passed Point Barrow. The

Charlie Klengenberg's house near the Coppermine River, 1916–1917.
The house is banked with blocks of snow for insulation. Joseph Bernard
Collection, Archives, University of Alaska–Fairbanks, UAF-0764-00139.

Arctic could only reach Baillie Island and it turned back, again without delivering Klengenberg's supplies. At Rymer Point, because no ship had arrived with
his outfit, Klengenberg, now very short of provisions, realized that he was in a
tight spot and had to act quickly. Leaving 850 skins behind on Victoria Island,
he loaded more than 2,000 aboard his boat—as well as several sleds and dog
teams—and with his sons Andrew and Jorgen he departed for Herschel, reaching the island just before freeze up. He stored half of his furs with the Royal
Canadian Mounted Police (RCMP) at Herschel and set off with his sleds to
Aklavik. At Aklavik Klengenberg found that his load was too heavy for further
transport, so he sold 416 skins to the Northern Trading Company and transferred the rest of his load to toboggans. With the help of Gwich'in guides he
crossed the mountains to Rampart House in the Yukon Territory and headed
onward, to the port of Seward on the Pacific Coast, where he and his sons took
a passenger ship to Seattle. It was his first visit "outside" since 1907.

    In Seattle Klengenberg sold his skins at the Seattle Fur Exchange and was
lucky in catching a rising fur market. "For the first time in my life I had plenty
of money, and could pay cash for whatever took my eye," he remembered.
Klengenberg then engaged a San Francisco law firm and brought suit against
H. Liebes and Company, claiming damages of $75,000 for breach of contract
in not delivering his supplies. Klengenberg won, but H. Liebes and Company

appealed the verdict, and several years later the case finally reached the U.S. Supreme Court, which declined to hear it.[12]

That winter, 1923–1924, Klengenberg sold to C. T. Pedersen, sight unseen, the cache of more than 1,000 furs that he had left at Herschel Island. Klengenberg, as we know, was energetic, resilient, and entrepreneurial — with a capacity for truth that was both fungible and elastic. He claimed that it was an "average" batch of skins: ones and twos with a few "blue backs" and culls. Pedersen, like many in the North, was suspicious of Klengenberg's honesty, but the fur market was rising then, so he paid Klengenberg $35,500 for the collection. But when he retrieved the skins at Herschel, he found that the collection was "of very poor grade," containing only "256 medium and small #1, 412 twos, 114 twos low, 318 threes, 82 fours, 3 fours damaged worthless," and demanded that he be repaid $8,060. Klengenberg wrote to the RCMP at Herschel, instructing them to turn over an additional 381 skins to Pedersen.

Nevertheless, Klengenberg, in Seattle that winter, needed to return to his family on Victoria Island. In February 1924 he bought the three-masted schooner *Maid of Orleans*, and fitted it for arctic work with ironbark sheathing and a 150-horsepower engine. When he departed Seattle, in addition to his supplies Klengenberg carried materials for a schoolhouse as well as Miss Alice Supplee, who would be the tutor for his children, and Oliver Morris, his engineer. Oliver and Alice would marry and remain in the North for many years.[13]

But Klengenberg was in for a bad surprise at Herschel Island. When the *Maid of Orleans* arrived there he learned that foreign vessels would henceforth not be allowed to proceed past Herschel Island for coastwise trade. On January 5, 1924, the commissioner of customs and excise had written to the Royal Canadian Mounted Police:

> It appears from information recently conveyed to this Department that Captain C. T. Pedersen of the trading Schooner "Herman" and other United States whalers have for some years past been in the habit of trading with the natives located in Canada along the shores of the Beaufort Sea. It further appears . . . that the Officer of the Royal Canadian Mounted Police, who is acting as Customs Officer at Herschel Island, has permitted United States vessels to report at Herschel Island and then land their goods at various places in Canadian territory and pay duty to the Police Officer on board the vessel as such supplies are landed at the various places referred to.
>
> You are instructed to notify the Royal Canadian Mounted Police Officer, acting as Customs Officer at Herschel Island that this practice cannot be continued, as it is contrary to the provisions of the law. He is to be instructed that foreign vessels reporting at Herschel Island are required to make Inward re-

port of all goods carried by them, and be also required to pay duty and excise taxes lawfully payable on all such goods, with the exception of such ships' stores as are necessary for the return voyage of the vessel from Herschel island to the foreign port of first call. You are also directed to instruct the Officer at Herschel Island that he is to refuse coastwise clearance to foreign vessels who wish to do coasting trade business with Canadian citizens along the coast of the Beaufort Sea.[14]

Klengenberg was stunned:

I dropped anchor at Herschel Island. The Acting Customs Officer of the Mounted Police came on board. He told me that since I had left Seattle there had been a new Canadian regulation made . . . by which no ship of American register would be allowed to trade coastwise in Canadian waters. My ship and cargo was held by the police. They would not allow me to trade there, or to go on to Victoria Island.

I protested. I sent despatches through to Ottawa, explaining my situation, and how I had sailed in ignorance of any such new law to be made. It got me nothing. Ottawa was obdurate as usual. . . . Finally some word came through to the police. I was told that I would be permitted to go on to Victoria Island, but with only enough supplies to be landed to serve for the immediate use of my own family. I was not to put a single pound ashore for trading purposes, nor could I even land the building material which I had for the proposed new trading posts and the school-house. . . .

They put Constable Macdonald [*sic*] aboard the *Maid of Orleans* when she sailed, to see that their orders were obeyed to the last ounce. . . . He certainly did watch everything. . . . He allowed only the barest necessities for my family to be landed. . . . Then I was ordered to take my schooner and all her cargo . . . back to Herschel Island, there to be held pending further instructions from Ottawa.

On the return trip Constable Macdonald disappeared. He must have fallen overboard, but none of the crew saw the accident happen. . . . After a vain search of about thirty hours I turned and proceeded to Herschel Island. I reported the loss of Constable Macdonald, and an inquiry was held, and all members of my crew as well as myself were closely questioned. No more could be done at the time and the inquiry was adjourned.[15]

A number of people suspected Klengenberg of having committed another murder, but nothing could be proved, and, luckily for Klengenberg, Constable McDonald's notebook, which was found aboard, showed that Klengenberg had obeyed his orders. Henry Larsen, navigator on the *Maid of Orleans* (and a future RCMP superintendent), wrote: "Inspector Caulkin was not a man to take anything at face value. He ordered everything on board taken ashore to be checked in the police storehouse. Every single item was checked off on the list the captain had for customs purposes, and luckily for him, every item missing was found recorded in MacDonald's notebook."

"On Herschel Island we had some more bad news," Larsen continued. "The Hudson's Bay Company ship *Lady Kindersley* had been crushed by the ice near Point Barrow. . . . *Lady Kindersley* had seven hundred tons of supplies destined for the island, and this was a hard blow to the traders there. Klengenberg could have sold his cargo twice over if he had only paid the duty as required, but that he refused to do. Yet he gave the Mounted Police and the locals what they needed and left one man behind to look after the rest of his supplies when we sailed again on September 10. . . . We headed westward and quickly ran into heavy ice. About two hundred miles from Point Barrow we came to a complete stop. . . . We soon became stuck and barely managed to get free again just in time before we would have been frozen in for good. . . . Reluctantly Klengenberg decided to return to Herschel Island, where we knew we would at least find a good harbor. There was no doubt that the pack ice had arrived for the winter."[16]

In 1925 Klengenberg was again allowed to supply his family before heading west and going outside. In 1926, however, to comply with the new customs regulations, he became a citizen of Canada and put the *Maid of Orleans* under Canadian registry. He changed its name to *Old Maid No. 2* because the ship registry would not allow duplicate names, and two other vessels were at that time named *Maid of Orleans* and *Old Maid*. He loaded $60,000 worth of supplies aboard the schooner and headed north to visit his posts at Rymer Point, Cape Krusenstern, and Wilmot Island. On his return in September he was reported to be carrying $100,000 worth of furs, which he again sold at the Seattle Fur Exchange.

In 1927, though, Charlie learned by letter that there had been a poor fur catch in the Western Arctic and made up his mind not to sail north that year. Klengenberg's sons Andrew and Jorgen were with him in the South, and they "were furious," according to Henry Larsen. "They wanted him to turn the ship over to them and asked me to come with them, but this was not to be, and they had to wait another year before they could return to their home."

In 1928 the U.S. Court of Appeals ruled in favor of Klengenberg in his suit against H. Liebes and Company, and he was awarded the $75,000. Klengenberg sold the *Old Maid No. 2* to the Hudson's Bay Company and retired from the Arctic. Henceforth his children would trade with the HBC. Thus the HBC had eliminated one of its competitors. The company sent the *Old Maid No. 2*

The *Maid of Orleans* housed over in preparation for winter at Herschel Island, October 4, 1924. A change in the Canadian trading laws prevented Klengenberg from trading east of the island, although he was allowed to supply his family on Victoria Island with provisions for the winter. Klengenberg Collection, Archives, University of Alaska–Fairbanks, UAF-1975-0085-00007.

north again in 1929 and 1930 but then laid the schooner up and sold it in 1934. Klengenberg died in Vancouver on May 4, 1931. In June of that year Patsy Klengenberg returned to Victoria Island aboard one of the first aircraft to visit the region. He scattered his father's ashes at Rymer Point.[17]

Richard S. Finnie summarized Klengenberg's career: "Klengenberg's death was symbolic of the passing of an era in the Arctic in which radio and airplanes played no part, when adventurers trod new land and met new people in the course of seeking the elusive white fox."[18]

JOE BERNARD

In 1916 Joe Bernard returned to the Western Arctic with his schooner *Teddy Bear*. He had spent the years 1909 to 1914 pushing his explorations eastward into Coronation Gulf (chapter 4). But although in 1914 he had professed to have become tired of the Arctic, he later wrote of his change of heart, "After I made my rounds of family, friends, museums, universities and exhibiting my Eskimo collection, I became restless. I . . . decided that arctic life was better than this.

So I returned to Seattle in May, 1916, to purchase supplies for another voyage into the mid-arctic."[19]

He left Nome August 21 with a crew that included two trappers, and after a stormy passage he arrived at Barrow. There he collected the supplies that John Backland Sr. had carried north for him from Seattle aboard the *C. S. Holmes*, departing Barrow on August 31 so heavily laden with forty-five tons of supplies that the *Teddy Bear* had only four inches of freeboard. At Herschel Island on September 10, 1916, Bernard learned that two days previously the *Challenge*, with Jim Crawford, Leo Wittenberg, Gus Masik, and Otto Binder aboard, had departed for Banks and Victoria islands.

Arriving at Baillie Island on September 15, Joe was surprised at the transformation that had taken place in only two years: the Hudson's Bay Company now had a post there and the Church of England had established a mission. After giving his friend Fritz Wolki a lift to his camp at Horton River, Joe headed on east and passed his wintering site of 1912–1913 at Bernard Harbour, where the Hudson's Bay Company was establishing a post. On September 26 he was near the mouth of the Coppermine River. There he found Charlie Klengenberg and his family in their house, with his scow-schooner hauled out on shore. Two days later Joe was in his old anchorage in the mouth of the Asiak River, beginning to prepare for winter. By mid-November Inuinnait had begun arriving to trade with him, and among them were his old friend Okomea and his family.

Charlie and Patsy Klengenberg also paid him a visit. A few days later he traveled west with Charlie's son-in-law Ikey Bolt and came upon a village of Inuinnait near the mouth of the Coppermine River. "There were about 150 men, women and children and twice as many dogs surrounding our sled. Everybody yelling 'Yo! He come back!' . . . Everyone was grabbing at my hands to welcome me. . . . I could understand some of their remarks to one another: 'He has not changed much.' 'He has more gray hair.' 'He is not afraid of the crowd.' 'He seems glad to be back.'"

On returning to the Asiak River, Joe was reminded how fast things were changing there too.

Many Eskimos were wanting to trade. I obtained a lot of fine summer caribou skins, some caribou skin clothing and bows and arrows. The natives all wanted in turn, snow knives, powder, primers and dishes. When I was here in 1910 these people were primitive, hunting deer with bows and arrows. Now, already all [sic] most all of them are using rifles, only a few using the old method in necessity.

Two sleds of Eskimos came in from Tree River with some caribou to trade. I obtained meat of 13 caribou and a brown bear skin and other small items. I got all of this for very little trade: powder, primers[,] a dishpan and a few snow knives. One of them left all he had traded on deck, saying he would get them in a couple of days after he came back from hunting in the east.

"I found conditions much changed from 1911," Joe told Diamond Jenness in 1920. "In the migration of caribou there were not half the number as in 1910–1911, and none stayed in the vicinity during the winter as they did then. I also find a great change with the natives, for the best in a few cases but for the worse for others."[20]

Like his friends Fritz Wolki and "Old John" Kuhl, Joe had found life outside far less pleasant than life in the Arctic. Remembering Christmas Day 1916 he wrote: "As I sat in my little cabin recalling the difference between this Christmas day and the one of a year ago when I was down in the sunny south, I was struck with the contrast. There, we had everything and fine warm weather; here, a land of ice and snow with the same things happening from day to day; one day simply following another: cold and stormy. Yet it is here that I feel the most peace."[21]

During the winter of 1916–1917 Bernard ran a trapline and traded with the In- uinnait. Most productive for them, however, was Joe's introduction of gill nets —which had not previously been part of their tool kit—for fishing in summer and autumn. Formerly they had speared fish in summer at stone weirs built in rivers and fished through the ice with hook and line. In spring 1917, when the northward caribou migration was underway, a large group of Inuinnait from Ba- thurst Inlet visited his camp. They were followed later by the prospector-trader D'Arcy Arden and the Roman Catholic priest Father Frapsance, who had trav- eled north from Great Bear Lake together. Arden was an energetic young Ca- nadian who from 1914 to 1916 lived at the northeast corner of Great Bear Lake. Arden would soon establish a trading post and fur farm at Fort Norman (today, Tulita, NWT), where the Great Bear River joins the Mackenzie. In 1919 he was instrumental in convincing a group of Inuinnait from the Coppermine River area to trade at the fort by guaranteeing their safety from the Indigenous Athapaskan group, the Sahtú Dené. Thus Arden, too, became a factor in the expansion of the Western Arctic fur trade.[22]

Charlie Klengenberg's son Patsy—who was bilingual and who moved easily among the foreign trapper-traders and the Indigenous Inuit—also visited Joe, but his mission was not trade, but courtship. "Patsy is on his way to Bernard Harbor to get his sweetheart," Joe wrote. "He is all dressed up in his best clothes and loaded with presents for his girl's family. Her father is Kepokea, a very well- respected Eskimo who had worked with the Canadian Arctic Expedition in 1914–15 when they were at Bernard Harbor. Diamon [sic] Jenness, the expedition's ethnologist, had given Kepokea many things which he saved for the time when his girl would be of age. These will now be Patsy's. I knew Kepokea in 1910 and also when I was at Lady Richardson Bay in 1913–14. I have a very fine opinion of the family. So, Patsy now has permission from Charlie to bring the girl home."[23]

At the beginning of June 1917, Bernard was surprised at the arrival of Inspector Francis H. French of the Mounted Police. French had traveled overland from Chesterfield Inlet on Hudson Bay to investigate the murders of the prospector George Street and sport hunter Harry Radford, who had vanished in 1912, as well as to probe the murders of Fathers Rouvière and Le Roux (chapter 4). French's "Bathurst Inlet Patrol" would traverse more than 5,000 miles before its return.

The *Teddy Bear* was underway again in early August 1917. But first, Joe had collected as much driftwood as he could, because he knew it would be scarce where he was headed. With two Inuit added to the crew, and with dogs and sleds aboard, he followed the southern shore of Victoria Island, passed through Dease Strait, and entered Queen Maud Gulf. But then, instead of keeping on eastward and crossing the gulf, he turned northeast and entered Victoria Strait, searching for a group of Inuit that he had heard about from Stefansson. There, on August 16, advancing drift ice trapped him amid the reefs behind Taylor Island at the southeastern corner of Victoria Island. To his annoyance the ice surrounded the schooner and prevented him from proceeding farther east. It would keep him captive there for two winters: "As soon as we were in this bay the ice closed in on the entry and never left or opened until the first of September, 1919. For two years it held us prisoner in this deserted land, deserted indeed, for no native abides nearer than Cambridge bay except for an accidental bear hunt in the latter part of March some years; but they never stop long, as the game is scarce and they fear starvation."[24]

The *Teddy Bear* was only the fourth foreign vessel to enter Queen Maud Gulf. The first two were Sir John Franklin's ships *Erebus* and *Terror*, which sank there. They were followed by Roald Amundsen's sloop *Gjøa*. From 1903 to 1905 it wintered in a small harbor on southeastern King William Island while on its way to completing the first ship transit of the Northwest Passage.

The winter of 1917–1918 at Taylor Island was relatively uneventful. The trapping and hunting were only adequate, and the first Inuit to visit their camp did not arrive until March. One of the visitors carried a German-made rifle that Joe had traded to someone the previous winter, but no cartridges were available for its exotic caliber, so the man had returned to using his bow and arrows. Most interesting, however, was that the group also had a collection of foreign items.

Kongonlikak brought down a little box of tools, bits of iron, brass and copper. Among them was a brass label, 2 inches in diameter, which had stamped on it the Coat of Arms of England! On close examination I find that it was a label from a tin of potatoes and the stamp clearly read: "Edwards Preserved Potatoes." Below the coat-of-arms were the words: "By Royal Letters Patent." It looked to be very old. I asked where it came from and the little girl said she had picked it up on the land of *Elikhook*. The man pointed south saying it was a small island. (I later learned that this was a small island just south of the Admiralty Islands). He said that the label came from some white men who had come in a ship a long time ago. The ship was crushed by the ice near this land and all the men had died. He knew of this from his father. He told me that there were 2 ships, one had been crushed on a large island he called *Pohonhean*, near King William Land. This must be Sir John Franklin's ships.

A few days later the Inuit produced more material from Sir John Franklin's ships. "I asked them where they found it. They picked it up on a small island which they call *Okotulik*. They had sawed it up to make various implements."

On August 19, 1918, the schooner was afloat, but it soon became clear to Joe that he was going nowhere that summer. "It looks as though we will have to stay here for another year as the young ice is making today."[25]

Resigned to spending another winter at Taylor Island, Joe began preparations by cutting sod for a house on shore, caching provisions, hunting for caribou and seals, and unrigging the *Teddy Bear*. Later he set out his traps and built a set gun for bears and a seal gun loaded with a spear, positioned over a breathing hole. "The second winter was a tough one," he later stated to Diamond Jenness.

> Most of our provisions were gone and we had no fuel left, nor was there any chance of getting any seal.
>
> In December, I, with a young native whom I had engaged in the summer, went over to the westward looking for game or the natives . . . and as we hadn't seen anything of game I desired to go to the natives. The weather was extremely cold and stormy. After nine days we found the natives in Wellington bay. They were very friendly. They had but little meat or fish and no oil. Most of the houses were in darkness and they could not, it seems, get any seal, and they were fearing starvation and were moving west to the natives of Bathurst inlet, so we had to turn back without obtaining but little help, a little dried fish and a few frozen fish. After nine days of the worst kind of weather and travelling I have seen[,] we got home, having left two dogs on the trail and the rest of them so fagged out they couldn't stand up.[26]

Back at his camp, on Christmas Day he celebrated by cooking some evaporated potatoes and roasting two owls. He wrote, "I thank God for his many blessings." "So we had to put through the winter as best we could, using naphtha (distillate) mixed with moss and ashes for fuel in February."

In early February 1919, he and local Inuinnait, Payula and Anoyou and his family, set off to cross Victoria Strait toward the mainland in search of other Inuit. By the beginning of March they were very low on food, forcing them to eat one of the sled dogs and to return to their camp at Taylor Island. "We made three unsuccessful attempts to cross Victoria Strait, finally in April I succeeded in getting across and found the natives near the mouth of Sherman Inlet. They too had not fared too good during the dark days. Two families were reported to have starved to death in Simpson strait."[27]

In early April they came upon a small village of Inuit families hunting at seals' breathing holes. This group, the Ililirmiut, possessed pieces of glass and more iron than the people farther to the west. Bernard assumed that these things had also come from Franklin's ships. No doubt he was correct because the remains of HMS *Erebus* were discovered nearby in 2014 and the hulk of HMS *Terror* was located on southwestern King William Island in 2016.

Bernard then traveled into Sherman Inlet, and on Easter Sunday, April 15, 1919, he wrote, "It does not look like I will be celebrating like I would like to but I fed myself the very best we had in camp: boiled caribou tongue and some hard bread."

Joe found that these Inuit had also obtained a quantity of firearms and ammunition via intra-Inuit trade. The manufactured goods probably originated from Hudson's Bay Company posts that had been established on tributary waters of Hudson Bay at Chesterfield Inlet in 1911 and at Baker Lake in 1914. The goods had gained value at every exchange between middlemen and by the time they reached the Ililirmiut they were very expensive. Joe recorded the prices that the Ililirmiut paid to their neighbors to the east: "one pound of powder for 3 fox skins; a piece of lead 4 inches square by ¼ inch thick for 2 fox skins; 100 shotgun primers for 1 fox skin; a 1-quart granite pot for 2 fox skins." He added, "This is a pitiful return."

Joe and his companions returned to Taylor Island on May 16, and soon a group of Inuit turned up from Cambridge Bay. "One of them grabbed both of my hands, saying 'You come back next year to the Kehelarmiut. Come, come, we want you back.' I certainly would like to go back, they are the finest Eskimos I have ever met in the Arctic."[28]

"It was the first of September, 1919, before we could get out of this bay; even then it was only after a hard bucking with ice." The schooner was underway again, headed west, but the season was already well advanced. In mid-September, the *Teddy Bear* was in Coronation Gulf, where Joe was surprised to see Otto Binder coming out to the schooner in a dory. After the wreck of the *Challenge*, Otto had remained at Tree River. Until 1918 he had worked for the Northern Trading Company, but they closed the post and the Hudson's Bay Company had relocated there, so Otto had joined the HBC. Joe was glad to be able to buy supplies from Binder because, with his late start from his winter quarters at Taylor Island, it was clear that he would have to spend yet another winter in the Arctic (see endnote).[29]

The Mounted Police were also setting up a post at Tree River in 1919, and Joe learned that, thanks to Charlie Klengenberg, he had become the object of a police investigation:

> What a thing friendship is! Charlie Klengenberg had been up to tricks again. At first I did not know he was the one who started the police investigating me! After I introduced myself I learned that the police have been looking for me all over the Arctic and even on the Atlantic coast.
>
> It seems that when the police were investigating the Street and Radford murders they had gone to the Coppermine River where they found out that an Eskimo woman had also been murdered. The natives had laid out the body but when the police went to examine it, they could not find it. Then they interviewed Charlie Klengenberg. "Oh, hell!" he told them, "Bernard took the body and pickled it! Why he'd collect any kind of specimens!"
>
> So the inspector asked me today, "Is there anything to this?" I replied, "I think it would be pretty strange for me to kidnap a dead woman." (And when I returned to Nome I learned that the police had even contacted some people there about this collection I had supposedly made. They were ready to believe it knowing of my readiness to collect anything. Since I had several barrels of salted seal skins in storage in Nome the stories went around town that in one of them was the dead woman's body!)

On September 25 Bernard reached his old anchorage at the mouth of the Asiak River and the next day began gathering driftwood and preparing for winter. "We trapped all winter, getting wolves, wolverines and fox. The fox were not very plentiful but we had plenty of meat all winter and enough wood."

The next year, at the beginning of August 1920, the *Teddy Bear* was off again. On September 5, at Herschel Island, Joe cleared with the Mounted Police and pressed ahead. "God alone knows how we managed to dodge all of the ice-bergs but we got by them somehow. We rounded Point Barrow while it was blowing half a gale. There was a vessel laying there and we were completely out of food. The wind was too heavy for us to get aboard the ship so I told Anderson we might just as well tighten our belts and take advantage of the favorable wind.

He was quite willing, saying, 'We have lived on dried salmon for quite some time so I guess we can stand it for a couple of days more.'"

Exhausted, they reached Nome on September 13. "We had sailed over 1200 miles in 13 days!" Joe then laid up the *Teddy Bear* and headed south with his collection of furs and artifacts, some of which he sold to museums, some to collectors, and others to Ye Olde Curiosity Shop in Seattle.

Despite his genuine concern for the welfare of northern Natives, Joe had become an agent of their change. The annual report of the Mounted Police for the year 1917 had stated, "The most striking feature in the Arctic is the extension of the trade eastward as far as the mouth of the Coppermine River. . . . The lure of new trading fields has attracted traders and trappers with the hopes of profitable [trade] among the Eskimo, hitherto untouched." And in fact, by the winter of 1922–1923 — and perhaps the previous winter as well — Martin Andreasen and Peter Brandt were wintering on the schooner *Anna Olga* at Tree River. Oliver D. Morris also entered the region, trapping in Coronation Gulf and setting up camps at several locations, including one at Joe Bernard's old site on the Asiak River from 1926 to 1928. All were decent men, but they became vectors of transformation by their presence in the region.

Joe Bernard reached Ottawa on December 22, 1920. There he met the anthropologist Diamond Jenness, who had been with the Canadian Arctic Expedition at Bernard Harbour from 1914 to 1916. On the basis of Joe's report Jenness wrote:

> [Bernard] stated that the Copper Eskimo country had undergone a profound change during the last few years. Four Hudson's Bay Company trading posts had been established, one at Bernard harbour, one at the mouth of the Coppermine river, a third at the mouth of Tree river and a fourth at Kent peninsula. The Eskimos were leaving their winter sealing grounds about two months earlier than usual, and devoting their attention to the trapping of foxes. In the winter of 1919 all the inhabitants of southeast Victoria island migrated to Kent peninsula, where a large supply of blubber fuel had been accumulated by the trader in order that the natives might be able to give all their time to trapping. Hardly a bow remained in the country, nearly every man possessing a rifle. Caribou meat [rather than fish or seals] had therefore become the predominant article of food, and the destruction of the caribou was proceeding so rapidly that within ten years, he believed, hardly one would be left in the vicinity of Coronation gulf. The old copper culture had given place to one of iron — even the copper ice-pick had disappeared. . . . Clearly, for better or for worse, the new era has dawned.[30]

Joe Bernard returned to Nome the following spring, 1921, and he and the *Teddy Bear* were immediately chartered by a party from the Standard Oil Company to deliver it to Alaska's North Slope to prospect for petroleum. In Nome later that summer, Olaf Swenson chartered him to take ten tons of trade goods to Swenson's station at Anadyr, but, as Joe wrote with his characteristic understatement, "in the fall of 1921 I had the misfortune to be shipwrecked on the coast of Siberia" at Puoten lagoon, southwest of Cape Dezhnev. He and his crew cobbled together a shelter on shore out of the cargo, and "after we were established in winter quarters, I spent as much time as possible in the villages, gathering folk lore and other information about the lives of the natives." They managed to get the schooner afloat the following summer and returned to Nome, where he was immediately chartered to attempt to resupply Stefansson's colonists on Wrangel Island, but heavy ice on the north coast of the Chukchi Peninsula prevented the *Teddy Bear* from approaching the island. In 1924, after a trip to Barrow and during which he had assisted in the rescue of the crew of the *Lady Kindersley* (chapter 6), Knud Rasmussen chartered him to sail to Cape Dezhnev, but the Soviets denied him permission to stay (chapter 5). Joe did not return to the Arctic. He sailed to Cordova, on the Pacific coast of Alaska, in 1925 and remained there, serving as harbormaster for many years. He died at the Pioneer Home in Sitka in 1972 at the age of ninety-three.

THE HUDSON'S BAY COMPANY
AND H. LIEBES AND COMPANY

During the years 1912 to 1929, the Hudson's Bay Company steadily expanded its operations into the Western Arctic. But in reality the company had been advancing toward the region since 1876, when it completed the ninety-mile trail from Edmonton to the Athabasca River at Athabasca Landing (today, Athabasca, Alberta) in the Mackenzie watershed. This initiative immediately rendered obsolete the former trade route from tidewater on Hudson Bay, via Methye Portage, to the Clearwater River in the Mackenzie drainage. Supplies now could be hauled northward from Edmonton by carts and then carried down the Athabasca, Slave, and Mackenzie rivers by scows, with a portage around the Slave River rapids.

The completion of the Canadian Pacific Railroad in 1885 gave independent traders access to the southern regions of Western Canada and, as an unintended consequence of building the Athabasca Landing Trail, allowed them to enter the Mackenzie watershed as well, thereby challenging the Hudson's Bay Company's monopoly. By 1883, however, the company further improved its transportation system by launching the steamer *Grahame* to operate on the Athabasca and Slave rivers, and three years later it launched the propeller steamer *Wrig-*

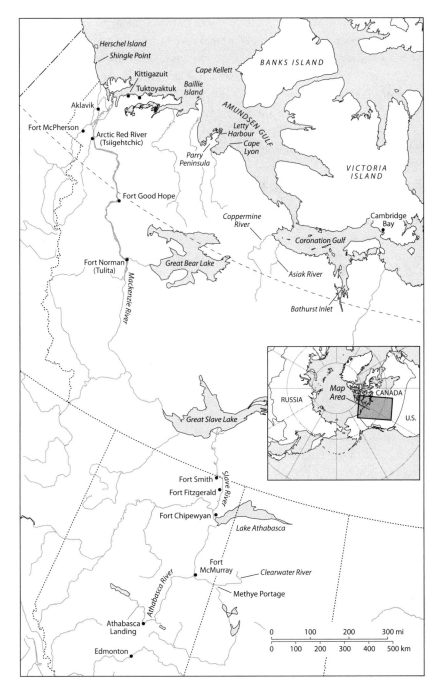

Western Arctic Canada and the Mackenzie River drainage.

ley to service its posts on Great Slave Lake and the Mackenzie River. Then, in 1888 the sternwheeler *Athabasca* was put in operation for service between Fort McMurray, Alberta, and Athabasca Landing. Three years later the railroad reached Edmonton, thus eliminating the need for steamboat transportation via the North Saskatchewan River. At the same time the Athabasca Landing Trail was being upgraded into a wagon road with regular stagecoach service.

In 1897 the news of the discovery of gold in the Yukon resulted in a massive influx of fortune-seekers descending the Mackenzie to Fort McPherson on the Peel River. They then headed up the Rat River and over McDougal Pass to the Yukon, a movement that also increased the number of white trappers in the Northwest Territories. More competition for the Hudson's Bay Company arrived when John A. McDougall and Richard Secord founded McDougall and Secord in Edmonton: "general merchants, wholesale and retail; buyers and exporters of raw furs; dealers in land scrip and north west lands; outfitters for survey parties, traders, trappers, miners and others for the north, and suppliers for country stores." Another rival entered the trade in 1899, when the Parisian furriers Revillon Frères opened an establishment in Edmonton.[31]

Then the Hislop and Nagle Trading Company presented another challenge to the HBC by setting up eight posts in the lower Mackenzie region. By 1910 its fur returns had grown to such an extent that it no longer sold its furs in Edmonton; instead, it sold them at C. M. Lampson and Company's fur auctions in London. In 1911 Hislop and Nagle was acquired by the Northern Trading Company (later named Northern Traders) of Edmonton, which began to send large outfits to its Mackenzie posts via the Northern Transportation Company. As one HBC man summarized it, the "growth of Edmonton as a mercantile centre has led to the invasion of the entire North by traders equipped there."[32]

By that date the Hudson's Bay Company was also facing opposition in its southern operations because of the expanding transportation networks and the new availability of information about current fur prices, keeping the HBC's profit margins there relatively modest. But in response to the continuing rise in white fox prices, the leadership of the HBC perceived the opportunity to engage in the barter trade in the Western Arctic, where it was assumed that the company would enjoy greater profit margins and less competition. Consequently in 1912 the decision was made to advance onto the coast and to purchase a schooner "as a means of consolidating and retaining the trade in the Western Arctic and Mackenzie River District."[33]

That year the company "hurriedly" sent supplies down river and established a post at Aklavik in the Mackenzie delta with an outpost at Kittigazuit, close to the shore of the Beaufort Sea. Apart from a short-lived post that it had operated at Anderson River in the mid-nineteenth century, it was the first downstream advance by the company since the founding of the Peel's River Post (later named Fort McPherson) in 1840.

With that initiative, the company entered an area where the Natives had been the beneficiaries of competition among multiple vendors since the arrival of the whaling fleet two decades before. As a result, the Inuvialuit, who for centuries had been skillful in trading with other Inuit and Athapaskan societies, were canny traders who were fully capable of playing one dealer against another. "Unlike other parts of the Canadian Arctic," Peter Usher observed, "the new Western Arctic fur trade was characterized by individual enterprise, competitive trade, and an abundance of material goods, an economic milieu already familiar to the Eskimos of the region from the whaling days." Heather Robertson, the editor of Richard Bonnycastle's diary of his years with the Hudson's Bay Company in the Western Arctic, put it more strongly: "The Hudson's Bay Company was smug, slow-moving, top-heavy Johnny-come-lately to one of the most sophisticated and viciously competitive commercial frontiers in the world. [It was] accustomed to a 200-year tradition of monopoly, the deference of politicians, and a free hand with the natives."

In fact, on its arrival in the delta the HBC quickly discovered that the Inuvialuit were holding onto their furs to buy boats and schooners from the ships at Herschel Island, and the company immediately encountered competition from Christian Sten at Shingle Point and a few other independent traders, such as Martin Andreasen. Andreasen made annual 2,500-mile round-trip voyages aboard his small schooner *North Star* from the delta to Nome, where Ira Rank outfitted him.

Although one of the original reasons for the HBC's expansion was "with a view to combating the growing opposition in the lower Mackenzie River," an equally compelling argument for this initiative was that it might allow the company to supply its posts on the lower Mackenzie by sea and thus to force its rival, Hislop and Nagle, "to abandon their opposition" at Arctic Red River (today, Tsiigehtchic) and Fort Good Hope. The HBC was aware that while it could land 100-pound sacks of flour at Fort McPherson at a cost of $16.50 and sell them for $30, the San Francisco whalers at Herschel Island bought sacks of "an inferior grade" of flour at a cost of $1.80 in San Francisco and sold them at the island for $10. Even though the ocean route via Bering Strait might involve risks, the company estimated that it cost $160 to $300 per ton of freight (see glossary) to haul their supplies via the Mackenzie drainage, but that it would cost only $25 to $35 per ton if the supplies were carried by ship from West Coast ports to Herschel Island. The company's estimate of the cost per ton of shipping supplies via Bering Strait would prove to be exceedingly optimistic: by 1915 it would be paying $85 per ton for a cargo of approximately 300 tons.[34]

Accordingly, the company's leadership made the decision to set up a post at Herschel Island to serve as a transshipment base for the lower Mackenzie and for future posts in the Western Arctic. The plan was to establish the post in 1913, and the company received an offer from Ira Rank, who was managing the schooner *Bender Brothers*, to carry freight from Seattle to the island at $35 per ton, but when the company finally got around to offering a contract for the schooner's service, it learned that the ship had already sailed with another cargo. Because of this and because the company found it difficult to send a sufficient number of men to the island to build the post that year, the plan was deferred.[35]

In 1914 the company chartered the 345-ton *Ruby*, a shallow-draft schooner used for freighting cargo to the Kuskokwim River in southwest Alaska. It would carry supplies from Vancouver to Herschel at a rate of $40 per ton. The company's new sixty-five-foot gasoline-powered schooner *Fort MacPherson* [*sic*] would accompany it to the island, but the *Ruby*'s captain, Louis Knaflich, lacked experience in ice piloting in the Chukchi and Beaufort seas, and the schooner, though sturdy, was not ice-strengthened. As if to foretell future problems with the ocean route, when the *Ruby* reached Point Barrow on August 20, "the sight here was appalling," recalled Christian ("Christy") Harding, who was to be the HBC's post manager at Herschel. "The ice was jammed on the beach mountains high; ice everywhere. This was all on the move with tide and current, crashing and breaking up as it moved along . . . when a heavy fog came on. We hit a large cake of ice and could see the ship buckle and the decks heave up. A large hole was punched in the ship above the water mark, through which a man could crawl. . . . The captain informed me that no ship could live in such heavy ice, and decided to abandon the venture." Captain Knaflich managed to work out of the milling pack and sensibly turned back. They stowed the cargo and the *Fort MacPherson* at Teller, Alaska, near Nome, leaving Christy Harding and his wife to watch over them.

The following year the cost of the freight had risen to $85 per ton, and on August 14, 1915, the *Ruby*, now under the command of Captain Steven Cottle, a veteran whaleman who had previously been the captain of the *Belvedere*—and who was well versed in ice work from his long career in the Western Arctic—finally reached Herschel. The HBC men quickly put up a store, a dwelling house, and outbuildings. Later they added a forty-foot by eighty-foot warehouse.

In 1916 the Hudson's Bay Company shipped no supplies to the island from the West Coast. But more opposition had already arrived in the form of two in-

The Hudson's Bay Company's schooner *Fort MacPherson* at Herschel
Island, winter 1915–1916. To prevent damage from the ice, the boat was
hauled ashore by winching it alternately from the bow and stern and
skidding it on planks. RCMP fonds, e10836733. © Government of Canada.
Reproduced with the permission of Library and Archives Canada.

dependent trading schooners. Alexander Allen's *El Sueno* overwintered at Warren Point, east of the Mackenzie delta, and Martin Andreasen's newly acquired
Anna Olga was not far away at Atkinson Point. Christy Harding, awakening to
the competitive climate of trade in the Western Arctic, wrote: "These schooners
keep the natives in a state of dissatisfaction." In his post journal on December
1, 1915, he grumbled, "I am obliged to pay $5.00 each for the Best Foxes, or
otherwise they will be held for the first trading schooner that calls here." By
March 1916 he had increased the price he would pay for a good white fox pelt
to $7.00. Recognizing the global integration of the fur trade, he stated, "It seems
remarkable that the markets of the world controls [*sic*] the prices of furs even in
this land."[36]

Yet another adversary for the HBC arrived in 1917 when H. Liebes and Company began to expand its trade into Western Arctic Canada. And H. Liebes had
outfitted their ship *Herman* with a wireless radio set to keep it ahead of its competitors by knowing up-to-date fur prices. After delivering 321 tons of the Hudson's Bay Company's own freight to Herschel, the *Herman*'s crew dismantled a

The Hudson's Bay Company buildings at Herschel Island, 1930. The large building
on the left is the warehouse. The store is to the right. In the foreground a barge and
a schooner are on shore. Courtesy of Richard S. Finnie, author's collection.

whaleship's storehouse, the "Karluk House," which the company had bought
for $100 from its owner in San Francisco, and loaded it aboard the ship. Then it
proceeded farther along the coast, to Shingle Point, near the outer perimeter of
the Mackenzie delta, where the crew reassembled the house, and Ole Andreasen,
Martin Andreasen's brother, was installed as the trader. That year H. Liebes had
also planned to establish posts at Baillie Island and Kittigazuit, but heavy ice
prevented the *Herman* from reaching Baillie Island and low water in the Mackenzie delta made it impossible to get to Kittigazuit. The Kittigazuit materials
were left at Shingle Point to be installed later in the year. In 1918 H. Liebes also
built a post at Aklavik.[37]

But that wasn't the Hudson's Bay Company's only problem at Herschel Island. It was now bracketed by H. Liebes and Company's posts at Shingle Point,
about sixty miles southeast of Herschel, and about the same distance to the west
of the island was the Liebes station at Demarcation Point, a few miles beyond
the Alaska border, which sold goods cheaper than the HBC and hence paid
higher prices for the pelts.

The HBC was also hampered by its own procedures and by its high-handed
treatment of its customers. In 1918 the Episcopal priest Archdeacon Hudson
Stuck visited the post at Herschel Island on his way to Fort Yukon. Arriving from

Barrow, where competition among traders was more vigorous, he was appalled when he observed the Hudson's Bay Company's manner of dealing with its customers. "The Hudson's Bay method of business," he wrote,

> is primitive beyond what would be tolerated anywhere in Alaska. The shop or store is wholly unwarmed—for fear of fire; such canned goods as would spoil by freezing are kept in the dwelling and there is no stove or any means of heating the store. This, I was informed, is the custom at every Hudson's Bay post. No trader who had a competitor could afford to treat his customers in such a way. It was not particularly cold weather while we were at Herschel Island; indeed, the first touch of spring was in the air; but the inside of the store was like a frozen vault. Yet whatever the temperature, he who would trade at the store must stand and make his purchases unwarmed. . . .
>
> The prices were as high in proportion as the Alaskan prices—in either case "all that the trade will stand." . . . The last reports from the fur market received at Point Barrow quoted white foxes at thirty dollars. . . . Mr. Brower was paying twenty for foxes; at Demarcation Point Mr. Gordon was paying fifteen, and here at Herschel Island the Hudson's Bay agent was paying twelve. . . . all of these prices "in trade" of course, so that there was the large profit on goods sold as well as the profit on the furs.

Stuck recognized that competitors were making life difficult for the HBC at the island: "When it is remembered that the Hudson's Bay post at Herschel Island is flanked on the west at Demarcation Point and again on the east by a station of a San Francisco fur house, and that independent fur buyers from the interior make visits every winter to the coast, it will be seen that the Great Company's monopoly is altogether of the past, and it may be expected that it will be compelled to meet competition in prices, and perhaps adopt a more accommodating attitude towards its customers; the 'take it or leave it' days are done."[38]

In 1925 Charlie Brower formed a similar opinion of the company's brusque trading behavior when he visited the island aboard the H. Liebes schooner *Charles Brower*. "The Hudson [*sic*] Bay Co. are not well liked by any of the trappers or traders I saw here and certainly while I was there they did no business. Pedersen [aboard the *Nanuk*] getting everything that came in, several thousand fox skins besides other furs. . . . I wanted to buy some heavy flannel and a heavy blanket, such as the Hudson Bay Co. carry. Going ashore I went to the store here. Their clerk would not sell them to me, saying he did no business with an opposition company. Leaving the store Mr. West their head agent met me and I asked him the reason why. I got no satisfactory answer, but West did let me buy what I wanted, charging me more than they usually do to others. This habit of not selling to their customers what they want or only part of it and then

The Hudson's Bay Company's buildings on the sandspit
at Baillie Island, 1925. Burwash [1927]: opposite p. 13.

changing their prices at every sale makes them many enemies, especially they
are disliked by the Mounted Police."[39]

In response to its growing competition at Herschel and in the Mackenzie
delta, in 1916 the company had returned to its strategy of expansion eastward
by setting up posts at Baillie Island and at Bernard Harbour in Dolphin and
Union Strait. In 1917 the company bought the *El Sueno* from Alexander Allen
for $2,400. It would serve as a supply boat. The company moved farther in
1918—into Coronation Gulf at Tree River—and in 1920 it established an outpost of Aklavik at Shingle Point on the Yukon coast, and another post on the
Kent Peninsula, east of Tree River.

The following year, 1921, it launched the ill-fated, 187-foot auxiliary schooner
Lady Kindersley to supply the Western Arctic posts via Bering Strait (chapter
6). The company also bought H. Liebes and Company's three Canadian posts
(Shingle Point, Aklavik, and Kittigazuit), thereby removing some of the competition, and it built a post at Clarence Lagoon a few miles east of the international boundary in Canadian territory—an attempt to keep furs from going to
H. Liebes and Company's post at Demarcation Point, Alaska. In 1925, however,
the HBC admitted defeat and closed that post because, according to Hugh Conn,
the Western Arctic district inspector, "there would never be enough business to
warrant our continuing to operate the Post, as the American trader has his post

located on American territory six miles from us. He has no customs duty to pay on numerous trade articles, and can undersell us in almost everything."

In 1923 the HBC continued its expansion by adding posts on Victoria Island in Prince Albert Sound and Cambridge Bay and at Simpson Strait on King William Island. On September 21 the explorer Knud Rasmussen was camped with Inuit at Simpson Strait and, somewhat stunned, witnessed the eastward growth of the fur trade as the HBC's pioneering party arrived there. "An hour later the vessel was at anchor close inshore, and a motor boat came sputtering up to the beach with two white men on board, who introduced themselves as Peter Norberg of Hernoesand, Sweden, and Henry Bjoern of Prestoe, Denmark. . . . They had come up to establish a station for the Hudson's Bay Company on King William's Land. The vessel was called *El Sueno* and had originally been a private yacht stationed at San Francisco. To our unaccustomed eyes, she seemed a very frigate; though she was but twenty tons. And in this cockle-shell of a craft, without engines even, and with a heavy boat in tow, Peter Norberg had forced a way through the most difficult part of the North-west Passage, namely Queen Maud Gulf, a piece of seamanship the extent of which he himself was far from realizing. They had no charts and no technical aids to navigation whatever."

In 1924 the company purchased the assets of the overextended Lamson and Hubbard Canadian Company, thereby eliminating some of its competition in the Mackenzie drainage, and in the deal it simultaneously acquired Lamson and Hubbard's subsidiary, the Alberta and Arctic Transportation Company, which allowed the HBC to move freight more efficiently in the entire Mackenzie watershed. In 1926 it also bought 54 percent of the shares of Revillon Frères and gained complete control ten years later, thus removing another opponent. By 1929 the Northern Traders Company was under severe financial pressure, and the HBC secretly loaned it $200,000 in return for 51 percent of its shares as collateral. The HBC also received an option to buy the company outright if the loan was not repaid. The HBC eventually bought the company.

Although the loss of the *Lady Kindersley* in 1924 temporarily forced the closure of the Cambridge Bay post for lack of supplies, in 1925 the company sent the *Baychimo* to supply the Western Arctic and bought Roald Amundsen's 120-foot exploration ship *Maud*, which had been seized by creditors in Seattle. It was renamed *Baymaud*, and it was acquired as much to keep this ice-strengthened vessel out of the hands of competitors as to help shuttle supplies to posts in the Western Arctic. "The *Baymaud* had not been a practical type of ship for the company to have," Dudley Copland, an HBC man wrote, "but then it was the policy to acquire any vessel offered for sale that was suitable for working ice. This discouraged any opposition in the Arctic."

The company sent the *Baymaud* north to overwinter at Cambridge Bay in 1926. The HBC also set up posts at Inman River on the mainland of Amundsen Gulf, at Perry River on the mainland shore of Queen Maud Gulf, and at Rymer Point and Cape Krusenstern—these two posts to compete with the Klengenbergs. In 1927 it built posts at Letty Harbour on the Parry Peninsula, at Pearce Point Harbour near Cape Lyon, as well as one in Bathurst Inlet, and two in Coronation Gulf, while also moving the post at Simpson Strait to a better site at Gjoa Haven on King William Island. In 1928 it built a post at Coppermine (today, Kugluktuk, Nunavut) and moved the post in Prince Albert Sound farther north to Walker Bay on the government's directive.

In 1927 the company sent its schooner *Fort James* from Newfoundland, via the Eastern Arctic, to overwinter in Oscar Bay on the west coast of the Boothia Peninsula and experimented with supplying it—as well as the King William Island and Queen Maud Gulf posts—overland via a tractor trailer "cat train" from tidewater at Hudson Bay. But in 1929 heavy ice forced the *Fort James* to winter at Gjoa Haven and prevented it from reaching Cambridge Bay. In 1930 the sea ice conditions in that area were better, allowing the schooner to return to the Atlantic, and the experiment was abandoned. In 1934 the *Fort James* was assigned to the company's Western Arctic fleet and sailed there via the Panama Canal. It was crushed in the ice and sank in Dolphin and Union Strait in 1937. The company's next experiment with supplying its Western Arctic posts from the east would be Fort Ross (chapter 1).

Major L. T. Burwash, conducting a government survey of the lands from the Mackenzie delta to Hudson Bay, described the eastward growth of the fur trade: "During the past 15 years civilization has steadily extended its outposts until in 1925 not more than five hundred miles of our Arctic coast line . . . remained unaffected by the trader and the white trapper." Thus from 1915, when the company built its Herschel Island post, to 1928, it had placed more than two dozen posts in the Western Arctic. It had expanded eastward about 600 miles into the Western Arctic Waterway, and it had bought out some of its rivals—but it was not alone in this rush for white fox pelts, and it would use every means possible to throttle its competition, as we shall see.[40]

C. T. PEDERSEN AND THE CANALASKA COMPANY

In 1924 Captain C. T. Pedersen barely escaped having the *Nanuk* seized by the Soviets (chapter 5), but more bad news awaited him in Canada. When he reached Herschel, like Klengenberg he was astonished at the new customs regulations of which he had been given no prior knowledge. As Peter Usher put it, "The Dominion Government . . . was under considerable pressure from the Hudson's Bay Company and other Canadian trading interests to enact measures which would offset the advantages the Americans enjoyed." Consequently the Northwest Game Act of 1917 had been amended. "In 1924, a longstanding regulation prohibiting coastal trade by foreign ships was invoked by the Customs and Excise Branch with regard to the Western Arctic. . . . This was partly in response to lobbying by the Hudson's Bay Company and others, but it also reflected fears of increasing U.S. interest in the Canadian trade (which did not in fact materialize) following the Soviet exclusion of American traders from the Kamchatka-Anadyr coast in 1923."[41]

Nor did the police allow Pedersen to proceed east of Herschel to collect debts that he had accumulated before 1924. It was claimed that the government had sent notice of the change in the regulations to the usual foreign traders (H. Liebes and Company, Pedersen, Klengenberg, and others), but Pedersen did not receive it, and, of course, neither did Klengenberg. RCMP Inspector Caulkin required Pedersen to unload his entire trade cargo on shore and to pay a duty of approximately 35 percent on it. The commissioner of taxation also attempted to levy income tax on Pedersen for the years 1917 to 1924.

In October of that year Pedersen wrote to O. S. Finnie, the director of the Canadian government's Northwest Territories and Yukon Branch, "Had I received your notice prohibiting American vessels doing such trading as we have been accustomed to do on the Arctic coast of Canada . . . I could have saved my partners thousands of dollars which are now tied up in such trade goods as we used to dispose of in the Northwest Territory. I am leaving for our home office in New York on or about October 20th and will proceed to Ottawa as soon as possible. I will esteem it a great privilege if you will grant me an interview."[42]

Not surprisingly, the Hudson's Bay Company had been instrumental in effecting this change because Pedersen, especially, had cut into its profits. The company's report on the Western Arctic District for 1923–1924 to Fur Trade Commissioner Angus Brabant gloated: "The new trapping and trading regulations and the enforcement of the laws regarding foreign vessels and coastwise trade, will . . . be detrimental to the American competition which in the past has been very aggressive. Trapping licenses for 'foreigners' are now $150.00, trading licenses $300.00 and foreign vessels are [not] allowed to enter into coastwise traffic, which means that while they may bring cargoes to Herschel, they cannot go East from Post to Post."

In 1925 Pedersen arrived prepared and, according to regulations, offloaded his cargo onto shore, where he set up five tents, one of them twenty feet by forty feet, to conduct his trade. That summer, at Shingle Point, the explorer

C. T. Pedersen's *Nanuk*, trading at Herschel Island, 1924. A gangplank has been rigged to move the cargo ashore. A schooner is on the right. Klengenberg Collection, Archives, University of Alaska–Fairbanks, UAF-1975-0085-00091.

L. T. Burwash witnessed the trappers heading to Herschel to trade with Pedersen, some of them from 300 miles away at Baillie Island. "During the day numerous Eskimo schooners passed sailing westward to Herschel. Many of these had come from points as far east as Baillie Island, and all were intent on reaching Herschel in time to trade with Capt. Pedersen, whose ship was anchored at that point. Capt. Pedersen is a most popular trader, not only with the natives, but also with free traders and unattached white trappers along the coast. The majority of the free traders operating in the western Arctic look to him to replenish their outfits."[43]

Despite the new regulations, the fact is Pedersen was beating the Hudson's Bay Company hands down, and by then most of the trappers had acquired schooners and could sail to Herschel to meet Pedersen. The inspection report for the company's Western Arctic District for 1925, sent by General Inspector Hugh Conn to Fur Trade Commissioner Angus Brabant, evaluated the competition. "Our chief competitors are the American traders who visit [Herschel Island] every summer. Captain Peterson [*sic*] is the strongest of these. He is probably the best navigator in the Western Arctic. . . . His boat is run at very low cost: He told me that his fuel never cost more than $10.00 per day. His other operating expenses are correspondingly low. As a result, his costlanded [*sic*] on sugar, flour, gasoline, coal oil, and all other heavy articles is lower than ours, and he is satisfied with a comparatively small profit, this Post [Herschel Island] has great difficulty in holding the trade. Captain Peterson is one of the best known and the most popular man in the Arctic. He has a good reputation for fair dealing, and commands the respect of the Missionaries, Police and other Government officials. We cannot wonder that the feeling amongst the white trappers and the delta natives is so strong in his favour."[44]

Angus Brabant confirmed and elaborated this assessment in his report to the HBC's governor and committee: "Competition in the Western Section of the District, and as far east as Baillie Island, is most severe, and our Company is hard put at times to maintain their trade. Of the American traders Captain Peterson [*sic*] is the most aggressive and the most successful. This trader visits Herschel Island with a large and well assorted stock of goods each season, and as he sells his merchandise at about our cost-landed, and in many cases lower, especially flour, ammunition and groceries, the natives naturally are anxious to encourage his visits. . . . Besides the native trade, which this year was fairly extensive, Peterson has numerous customers of the trapper-trader type who deal with him exclusively. The people operate in the Delta and as far east as Baillie Island, and when White Foxes are numerous, as was the case this year, their trade collectively amounts to a considerable sum."[45]

Pedersen expressed some of his concerns about the Canadian regulations in a letter to O. S. Finnie on March 17, 1926:

I am wondering if something can be done about modifying the customs regulations at Herschel Island. At present we are required to land the entire cargo of trade goods and pay duty thereon, regardless of the amount we may sell. This arrangement is not so bad in a good fur year, but it would be a great hardship on us in a poor year. At present we have two small stations on the Alaska coast between Barrow and Herschel Island; and because of the shortness of the Arctic summer, we can not afford to lay around waiting for favorable ice and weather conditions on this open coast on our way in, therefor [*sic*] we would have to carry these goods as far as Herschel and land them on our way out. . . . This year I am taking up a much larger outfit[,] as I intend to draw from this stock to establish one or two more posts on the North Coast of Alaska. You can readily understand that if I stop to put up buildings and land supplies for these posts, the trappers and traders, who have made the hazardous trip in small boats from Baillie Island in order to obtain their supplies from us at Herschel Island, will have to wait so long at Herschel that it will be almost impossible for them to return to their homes before freezeup. Even when we arrive early at the Island they are in a hurry to get back home in order to put up the necessary fish for the winter.[46]

The Canalaska Company's buildings at Herschel Island, ca. 1935. The
second building on the left is the bonded warehouse. The store is to its right.
A schooner and two whaleboats are on shore to the right of the store. Courtesy
of the New Bedford Whaling Museum, Keith Smith Collection.

By 1925 Pedersen's business had grown to such a size that the *Nanuk* was too
small to carry his cargo (chapter 6). During the winter he traveled to New York
to consult with Albert Herskovits to devise new methods about how to approach
the problems of cargo and of complying with the Canadian customs regulations.
Their solution was to purchase a much larger ship, the 580-ton *Patterson*, and to
form a Canadian corporation, the Canalaska Trading Company, Ltd., with headquarters at Vancouver, B.C., which in turn would own a Canadian-registered
supply vessel. That same winter Canalaska built a motor vessel, the *Nigalik*, in
Vancouver at a cost of $38,000. It was a sturdy, seaworthy vessel, seventy-two feet
long, with a cruising range of up to 4,000 miles and a cargo capacity of eighty
tons. It would be used to supply the posts that the company planned to establish
in Western Arctic Canada and it would meet the *Patterson* at Herschel, swap-
ping the posts' furs for trade goods.

Writing to Herskovits in New York, Hugh Clarke, who would manage Canalaska's field operations, outlined the initial strategy: Canalaska's plan was to be
nimble and go wherever the furs were located, to "settle down on the most stra-
tegic places" between the Kent Peninsula and the Boothia Peninsula to cut off

Captain and Mrs. C. T. Pedersen, ca. 1930.
Courtesy of Richard S. Finnie,
author's collection.

the furs going to Klengenberg's and the Hudson's Bay Company's posts. "They will be entirely temporary posts, capable of being moved from year to year, as circumstances dictate, depending on the movement of the natives. Permanent posts have proved expensive to the Hudson's Bay Co. . . . We are sure we will not be able to carry lumber enough from Herschel for small shacks as intended, so as a consequence, we have had two tents made 12 x 14. These we will stretch over a wooden frame and cover with a snow house, and which will be just as warm as a lumber house and are more mobile."

Clarke continued, summing up his opinion of the strengths and weaknesses of Canalaska's competitors:

Our competition will be the Klingenberg [*sic*] and the Hudson's Bay Co. The former in my estimation will be the harder nut to crack, as he is a rustler. The Hudson's Bay Co. have men not acquainted with the country, cannot speak the language, and are more or less generally disinterested and dissatisfied, and

The Canalaska Company's *Nigalik* delivering supplies at Baillie Island, ca. 1935.
Courtesy of the New Bedford Whaling Museum, Keith Smith Collection.

as long as they are drawing their salary do not worry very much about their
trade. They are hampered by poor transportation, deep draft vessels. They
have the money and resources, but we do not look upon them half as seriously
as we do Klingenberg. . . .

Our policy will be never to boost prices but we will employ native traders
(the smartest and most influential men among the natives)[,] outfit these men
with goods and place them amongst the trappers, and if they get the foxes for
us, we will make it a point to see that they are always the best provisioned,
dressed, and equipped natives amongst their own people. . . . And they without doubt are the foxgetters.

The Hudson's Bay Co. have sometimes had men of this nature. He has
traded all winter for them, and turned them in hundreds of foxes whose total
cost would be about $4.00. They [the HBC] have stuck to facts and figures,
contended the Foxes should have cost but $3.00, and turned him out for the
summer with nothing to keep him. Our policy will be as long as the cost of
foxes he trades are not out of reason, to always see that he is well equipped.[47]

Canalaska, in fact, did employ two highly competent Inuit traders: George
Porter Sr. (the son of whaling captain George W. Porter) and Angulalik, whom
it outfitted to run his own post at Perry River on Queen Maud Gulf. George

Porter Sr. told me that Inuit from as far away as Somerset Island visited his post for trade.

"One of the major differences Inuit found between working with Pedersen and working for the Bay," Robin McGrath wrote, "was that while a Bay employee could be reasonably sure of security with modest pay . . . no Bay employee (and certainly no Native Bay employee) was likely to get rich. The salaries, even for non-Natives, were not high, and limits were put on how much independent trapping employees were allowed to do. Canalaska, as a supplier rather than an employer, allowed post workers to trap as much as they cared to, and once the trade goods were paid for, the workers could make and keep as much profit as the market would support."

But this rapid expansion of the trading posts put strains on the trading families; for example, to educate his children it was necessary for George Porter Sr. to send them to an Anglican residential school in Aklavik, a thousand miles to the west of Gjoa Haven. His son George Porter Jr. described being sent away to Aklavik the age of six and not seeing his parents for six years. At age fifteen, when he finished school, he had to find his own way back to Gjoa Haven with no money and in charge of his ten-year-old sister Mary. It took them months, hitching rides on several boats, to reach home.[48]

To keep up with current fox prices and to prevent the competition from knowing Canalaska's price structure, Hugh Clarke advised Herskovits, "We have opportunity on our trip from the East [toward Herschel Island] next year to purchase Foxes at Baillie Island, from white trappers, but not having had any communication with the outside world for a year or more, the prices of Foxes may have changed considerably in the meantime. I would suggest . . . that you send a message by wireless to Aklavik, in the Spring, addressed to us at Baillie Island, it would be advisable to have it reach Aklavik not later than March 1st. . . . I would suggest you state in the wire the maximum price we can pay for good White Foxes, and as other eyes will see it besides ours, that the amount be made in the wire just two thirds of the true amount, to wit, if you wish to notify us we are to pay not over thirty dollars, the wire should read twenty dollars."[49]

The Hudson's Bay Company may have learned of Pedersen's and Herskovits's plans from the December 1925 issue of *Fur Trade Review*. Worried about the competition and hoping to stifle all opposition in the Western Arctic, Angus Brabant, the HBC's fur trade commissioner, wrote to O. S. Finnie, warning: "If these plans materialize and with Klinkenberg doing his share, your Department will have more than its hands full to protect the interests of the natives and the conservation of the game and other resources of that territory."

Finnie, an honest and dedicated civil servant who worked to maintain market

The independent trader Angulalik and family at his Perry
River post (Kuugjuaq), Nunavut, 1950. Library and Archives
Canada/Department of Indian Affairs and Northern Development
fonds, a211288. © Government of Canada. Reproduced with
the permission of Library and Archives Canada.

competition in the Western Arctic and to prevent monopoly control of the fur trade, politely acknowledged the receipt of Brabant's letter, replying, "With the establishment of wireless stations at Aklavik and Herschel and possibly other stations this year, the Department will be able to secure first-hand information concerning conditions in the North and be in a position to take immediate steps for further protection of the natives if necessary."[50]

In fact, steps had already been taken to protect the Natives: in 1918 Victoria Island had been designated as a game preserve for the Inuit; two years later Banks Island was added. And within a few years all of the Arctic Islands and the mainland north and east of Bathurst Inlet were set aside as well. "No whites were allowed to trap or hunt in the preserve, and very strict limits were put on the establishment of new trading posts on the Arctic Islands," wrote Peter Usher.

Angulalik in his storehouse, undated. Fox pelts hang from
the rafters. e010674364. © Government of Canada. Reproduced
with the permission of Library and Archives Canada.

"These regulations by implication ensured that any subsequent opening of new
trapping grounds would have to be effected by the Eskimos themselves." The
regulations were strengthened in 1926, requiring traders "to obtain a license for
each post operated, specifying the location."

Furthermore, "an amendment in 1929 stipulated that all trade be conducted
in permanent buildings, open for business at least eight months of the year.
This regulation, enacted under pressure from trading concerns with a large
fixed investment in posts and outfits, was designed to eliminate the schooner
trade and the practice known as 'tripping.' In the latter, itinerant traders sledged
out to the trapping camps and traded with the Eskimos in mid-season, obtaining furs for lower prices, and as a result increasing the defaults on debts to the
established posts. The Canalaska Company and the smaller free traders along
the coast were required to establish permanent posts in order to continue their
activities."[51]

Pedersen's letter to O. S. Finnie of March 17, 1926, must have been effective
because in April 1926 Herschel Island was designated as a port of entry and a
warehousing port by the Department of Customs and Excise. Pedersen received

permission from the department to build a bonded warehouse at Herschel in the name of the Northern Whaling and Trading Company, Inc., of New York. He purchased a half acre of land near the RCMP's quarters on the sandspit at Pauline Cove, where the water was deepest, thus allowing the *Patterson* to lie alongside within a few yards of the shore.

The *Patterson* and the *Nigalik* reached Herschel in summer 1926. Immediately the crews began building the bonded warehouse and a store. From then on goods could be landed in bond at the warehouse without paying customs duty. The warehouse had two locks; the RCMP held the key to one of them, and the other was Pedersen's. When goods were removed from the bonded warehouse and transferred to the store, the police made note of them in an inventory.

The police acted as customs officers at Herschel. One customs official described the RCMP's assignment and the ponderous procedure by which the taxes were collected:

> checking off the cargoes landed from foreign vessels, and comparing them with the ship's manifest, so as to assess the Customs and Excise taxes payable. . . . Payment of duty was by blank draft, which was sent to the Collector of Customs at Edmonton, with the necessary Customs forms, on the winter mail. . . . No money was collected from Peterson [*sic*] for duty and taxes when the entries were made and the goods released to him at Herschel Island in the summer. When the entries were received at Edmonton the following February or March, no money was received, only blank drafts, and when the entries had been checked at Edmonton, I used to have to fill in the drafts for the proper amounts and to advise Peterson in California of the amounts. These drafts were drawn on a firm in New York by the name of Herskovitz [*sic*] & Company, and I used to fill them in and hand them to the Imperial Bank at Edmonton for collection . . . the duty used to amount to between thirty and forty thousand dollars, and of course, the goods had been imported and released the preceding summer.[52]

In 1926 Canalaska expanded the Natives' access to trade goods by establishing posts in Bathurst Inlet and at White Bear Point on the south shore of Queen Maud Gulf, and the next year, three more, including Cambridge Bay and Gjoa Haven. Canalaska would establish three more posts in the early 1930s, at Read Island, Walker Bay, and briefly at Cape Krusenstern. The *Nigalik* would winter in the Arctic, usually at Cambridge Bay, and in summer collect the posts' furs and carry them to Herschel, where it met the *Patterson*. In 1929 Canalaska added the auxiliary schooner *Emma* to help supply the posts.[53]

Many Natives and independent traders and trappers made the annual voyage in their schooners to Herschel to trade with Pedersen. His sons Charlie and Teddy described to me the trade procedure at the island. The trapper would board the ship with his skins, Pedersen would grade them quickly, giving each one a shake and then stating the price to a clerk who was standing by, keeping the record. When the trade was complete the trapper would receive his credit and proceed to the store on shore to select his merchandise and supplies. The store was illuminated by electric light from power run off the *Patterson's* generator.

Pedersen, who was known for his honesty and willingness to help anyone, also served as a sort of banker for a number of trappers, Native and non-Native, by advancing supplies to them on credit and by paying their income taxes and trappers' licenses. Pedersen's integrity and accommodating friendliness secured the loyalty of most of the independent trapper-traders.[54]

An HBC report noted that the company's trade at Baillie Island had fallen off because of Pedersen's competition at Herschel Island:

> All this type of business was lost to Baillie Island when, following those years when extremely high prices were paid for fur, these same natives were able to purchase large schooners (many bought from Captain Pedersen) and consequently were able to take the longer and more hazardous trip to Herschel Island. Once arrived there, they found wider, cheaper and more varied assortments of goods than they previously had been in the habit of being able to buy and received higher prices for their fur.
>
> In addition, Pedersen overlooked no opportunity to firmly cement this connection through the provision of such essential facilities as would ordinarily be found in a small shipyard. Pedersen's boat "The Patterson," was in many respects a travelling shipyard, carrying a varied supply of Ship's Chandlery, spare engine parts and the necessary supplies for making repairs to hulls, etc. Arrangements were also made whereby boats could be hauled out and repairs effectively undertaken by competent workmen. Taking the long term view, such services were obviously essential if the natives were to continue to make these trips to Herschel Island without serious impediment, and undoubtedly Pedersen's efforts in this regard were adequately repaid.[55]

Each summer a fleet of schooners owned by Natives and independent trapper-traders congregated at Herschel Island to await Pedersen's arrival. For the month of August Herschel had all the raucous activity and noisy ambience of any fur trade rendezvous, with the trappers and their families arriving with high expectations for the price of their winter's catch. The harbor there was cluttered

with dozens of schooners and many whaleboats awaiting Pedersen's arrival.
O. S. Finnie's son, the journalist Richard S. Finnie, described the assembly at
Herschel in 1930:

> Each day come several Eskimo-owned schooners, fur-laden from Banks Island
> and far-flung points along the mainland. They line up in festive array, paral-
> leling one another against the gravelly beach. . . . From a half-dozen phono-
> graphs blares incongruous jazz while the Eskimos hold reunion tea-parties.
> Old friends and relatives, separated for a year or longer, have adventures to
> recount and inexhaustible stores of gossip. . . . And thus they chatter and
> laugh, the phonographs and dogs furnishing an obligato. Each boat has its
> quota of sled dogs, and these are tethered on shore—howling, snarling and
> fighting over big salmon trout just taken from the nets.
>
> Foxes were plentiful during the past winter, and nearly everyone is prosper-
> ous. One native family has brought in more than a thousand pelts, and the
> current price averages around thirty dollars apiece. What will these Macken-
> zie Delta Eskimos do with so much credit? Why, they will buy new schoon-
> ers, all manner of household goods, fancy civilized clothing, rifles and ammu-
> nition galore, groceries, sewing machines, outboard motors for their canoes
> and whaleboats, and phonographs and radios. One or two of them may even
> bank their surplus capital. . . .
>
> More interesting than the freight brought by the trading ships are the half-
> dozen passengers, most of them homeward bound Northerners. Arctic trap-
> pers will live ascetically and labor arduously for years to acquire small for-
> tunes. Then, with few exceptions, they will hurry to the bright lights, travel
> luxuriously and spend money like drunken sailors. They usually go broke
> inside of a year or two, but by that time they are thoroughly disgusted with
> civilization anyway. Most of them, having had the foresight to invest in return
> fare and a fresh outfit while their capital was still intact, land back in the
> Arctic with happy recollections and big headaches, quite content and ready
> to renew their hand-to-hand struggle with Nature.[56]

Because of Pedersen's presence in Canada's Western Arctic the Northerners
were the beneficiaries of his opposition to the Hudson's Bay Company and
its attempts to gain control of the trade. Pedersen's goods were of higher quality, his prices were lower, his deliveries were more reliable, and Captain and
Mrs. Pedersen's accommodating personalities were far more attractive to customers than the HBC's detachment and disinterest. Pedersen's annual visits to
the island were anticipated by Natives and non-Natives alike. It was a happy
time for all, and the Natives were treated fairly because of Pedersen's presence.

Part 4

Decline of the Western Arctic
Fur Trade, 1929 to ca. 1950

The boom of the 1920s continued until 1929 and then came the crash. In September the London stock exchange imploded after a fraudulent scheme was exposed, a month later in New York the Dow Jones Industrial Average lost a quarter of its value, and in November it was down 45 percent. The Great Depression had begun, and its effects would essentially persist until the later 1930s. By 1933 close to 11,000 of 25,000 banks in the United States had failed and a quarter of the workforce was unemployed.[1]

The collapse immediately affected the fur market. From *Fur Trade Review*, January 1930, a report headlined "Trade at a low ebb" read: "The New York skin market reached a low ebb during December. The large number of failures throughout the fur trade of the country, totaling for the year over 350 cases with liabilities of over fourteen million dollars, depleted the fur trade of the little purchasing strength left to it following the declining business of the last quarter of the year. Sales dropped week after week until there was practically no demand save the spasmodic purchase of small quantities of skins by individuals."

Albert Herskovits, C. T. Pedersen's partner in the Northern Whaling and Trading Company and the Canalaska Trading Company, summarized the boom and bust in the same issue of *Fur Trade Review*: "Warning after warning was issued by those who know and study the economics of business and apply it to the fur industry, yet to no avail. Prices in all markets advanced to record heights in 1928, and the few who tried to stem the reckless bidding up of skin values were powerless, and had no choice but to follow the crowd. Our fur industry was swept along with the business of the entire country."

Fur merchants worldwide immediately felt the effects, and by late 1931, for example, the Leipzig Fair's business had fallen off to such an extent that it offered to underwrite fur buyers' travel expenses if they would purchase furs valued at 100 times the cost of their travel. By 1934 the retail fur market had shrunk to 30 percent of its 1929 annual turnover. At first the trappers, traders, merchants, and trade periodicals confidently maintained that things would soon return to "normal." But as Sarah Isto noted about Alaskan fur farms, many of which had been established in the heady years before the 1930s: "As the Great Depression settled over the United States, smothering the vibrant fur markets of the 1920s, Alaska fur farmers watched their income tumble. Blue fox pelts that had sold for $101 in 1929 fell to $21 by 1932. Mink slid from $21 to $6, and Silver fox toppled from $125 to $41. At first, many fur farmers, their associations and their journals clung to the optimism of the boom years. Markets had fluctuated in the past."[2]

"The wealthier classes and the urban white-collar workers formed the heart of the demand for fur garments," the economist Victor Fuchs stated. But the fact was that disposable funds in the upper-income groups had shrunk dramatically. Women's fashions changed and many designers abandoned the fur market. In London in 1931 white fox prices, which had occasionally stood above $60 for large prime pelts a few years earlier, fell to an average of $23.10. In 1934 the global demand for furs was feeble, and white fox was particularly weak. In the 1930s, depending on the quality of the fur collection, white fox prices usually spanned $12 to $24 in Seattle auctions. The fur market revived somewhat at the end of the 1930s, but the war brought on the beginning of the development of synthetic cold-weather clothing for the military, and "by the end of World War II, the army and air force were using fur only for ruffs." By the 1950s the use of synthetic materials for lightweight, durable warm clothing became widespread.[3]

Postwar demographics and changes in style and fashion also affected the fur market. "The profound changes in place and manner of living which have taken place during the last decade have also contributed to the relative depression of the fur industry," Victor Fuchs wrote in 1956. "The interregional movement of population is one such change. It has resulted in large increases in population for areas where furs are relatively unimportant, and very small increases for the major fur consuming states." Fuchs had outlined the death knell of the once-robust arctic fox trade.[4]

8

STATE OWNERSHIP OF THE TRADE ON THE CHUKCHI PENINSULA

In the 1930s the central focus of the Soviet government's policies toward the Native peoples of the North was collectivization. "Whatever economic arguments were adduced in the Communist Party's assertions of the need to collectivise the hunting, fishing and herding activities of the Siberian peoples, the real aim was to proletarianise them by binding them in collectives subordinated to the superstructure of the Soviet state," stated the historian James Forsyth. "The Siberian native peoples . . . had to be disciplined, deprived of their leadership, and reduced to the level of serfs handing over their produce (especially furs) to the Soviet Russian state."[1]

In contrast, Soviet writers declared boldly and without embarrassment "that the occupation of Siberia was on the whole a peaceful process, that incorporation into Russia was of more benefit than harm to the native peoples because it brought them into contact with a 'higher culture,' and that there was no resemblance between Russian rule and other colonial régimes under which native peoples were cruelly exploited. Distortion and the hushing-up of facts reached a preposterous level in Soviet writings about the post-revolutionary period: while on the one hand it is asserted that 'Leninist nationalities policy' led the world in humanity and justice in dealing with minority peoples, including those of Siberia, the facts of the actual suffering they underwent during enforced acculturation to Soviet Russian social and political institutions—in particular collectivization, denomadisation and the destruction of traditional cultures and occupations—have been almost totally suppressed."[2]

In 1924 the Soviet government established the Committee for Assisting Peoples of the Far North. It was divided between conservatives, including three eminent ethnographers (Waldemar Bogoras, Waldemar Jochelson, and Lev Sternberg), who wished to maintain Native land reserves, and radicals, who wanted speedy industrial development. Bogoras, for example, advocated allowing the Chukchi to continue their traditional lifeways with as little intervention as possible. According to James Forsyth, "This view received little consideration from the Bolsheviks, who had as little doubt as any tsarist empire builders of Russia's right to possess the whole of northern Asia." By the end of the decade the radicals had gained control of the committee.[3]

Although "the first measures of the Soviet government were aimed at protecting the population against exploitation by the traders and the liquidation of cultural backwardness," wrote the Soviet linguist Georgii A. Menovshchikov, in 1928 the Soviet government embarked on its first Five-Year Plan, a "great leap forward" for industrial development. This coincided with the beginning of the Soviet Union's policy of collectivization, shifting away from giving economic assistance—such as it was—to the Indigenous peoples and toward developing political structure.

One manifestation of this was the hunt for "kulaks," wealthy Natives who in the doctrine of Marxism-Leninism were exploiters of the poorer Natives. For the Chukchi reindeer herders, writes Bathsheba Demuth, "this meant the creation of state farms (*sovkozy*) and collective farms (*kolhozy*). In both cases small-scale herders were to pool their deer, and the rich 'exploiting' class, or kulaks, would relinquish their stock for the common good. . . . In response, wealthier Chukchi chose to burn the tundra and slaughtered their reindeer herds en masse rather than hand their animals over to the state."

But the authorities' attempts to reeducate the Natives about the glories of sovietization faced serious obstacles. "It is, after all," wrote Alan Wood, "a bit tricky to translate such things as 'labour theory of surplus value,' 'dialectical materialism,' 'the bourgeois-democratic revolution' and the 'dictatorship of the proletariat' into a language whose native speakers have no understanding of, or vocabulary for, such economic and ideological constructs." As Yuri Slezkine has noted, one Koryak, when pressed to denounce Koryak kulaks, "expressed a popular view when he declared: 'We don't have people who don't help the poor; if they see that you are hungry, they feed you.'" Nevertheless, "This primitive communism . . . was not seen as a virtue by the communists," stated James Forsyth, "but on the contrary was considered to be a disguised form of exploitation and social parasitism."[4]

To spread Soviet influence the authorities established cultural bases (*kultbazy*) in Chukotka. These bases included a boarding school (which thus separated children from their families), a nursing station, a store, and a radio station, among other things. One was built for Chukchi near Chaun Bay, and another amalgamated both Yupik and Chukchi in Lavrentiya Bay. The anthropologist Debra L. Schindler has noted that the purpose of the kultbazy was twofold: "to oversee the economic education of the indigenous population and to supervise the modernization of indigenous lifestyles," resulting in reeducation of the Natives.[5]

"In reality the new communist state was no less inclined than the old tsarist one to make the colonial natives pay for the privilege of being ruled by the Russians," James Forsyth observed. Beginning in 1926 the government consequently enforced a trading system in which the Natives traded their furs in return for credits at cooperative stores that were stocked by state purchasing agencies. In distinction to the old barter system, which had comprised several buyers competing for the Natives' furs, in the state-controlled monopsony there was only one buyer, therefore demand from only one source, and the state was free to fix the prices it paid for the furs. In turn the state gave credits to the cooperatives for firearms, ammunition, and trapping materials to increase the fur harvest.[6]

In the coastal settlements of the Chukchi Peninsula the cooperatives evolved into collective units that were organized into brigades (*artels*), such as for seasonal marine mammal hunting, winter fox trapping, and women's sewing collectives. According to the anthropologist Victor Shnirelman, these small cooperatives "were efficient enough in terms of subsistence economy, but not enough to supply the State with the expected surplus." Consequently the cooperatives were enlarged and consolidated, allowing greater governmental control, and burdened with even greater bureaucracy by merging small groups of people, including Yupik and Chukchi, an arrangement that Soviet ethnographers proudly proclaimed as a "progressive process" which "liquidates the fragmentation of small ethnic groups . . . and presents them with a possibility for rapid and limitless cultural development." According to one report, by 1938, 95 percent of the Yupik economy had been collectivized.[7]

Worse, the Russian agents who staffed the cooperatives were often assigned from far away. They usually found their new postings depressing and isolated, and they felt little motivation to engage in mutually beneficial relationships with the trappers, which had been the traders' custom prior to the Soviet takeover. "Part of the problem," wrote Yuri Slezkine, "was the unwillingness of the imported agents to play by the local rules: they avoided traditional 'friendship' arrangements, broke the laws of hospitality, and refused to provide their clients with long-term loans. . . . Before long the agent's employers would give up on the tundra as a serious source of income. As a result, the north was increasingly becoming a dumping ground for shoddy goods that could not be sold elsewhere. Trading posts were filled with scissors that did not cut, wicks that did not fit lamps, and binoculars through which nothing could be seen, as well as goods of less than vital importance in the tundra such as high-heeled shoes or mirrors decorated with pictures of naked women."[8]

The government secured further centralization of control in 1932 when it established the Chukchi National Area for the entire peninsula, lumping together Chukchi and Yupik in one administrative unit with its capital at Anadyr. As Terence Armstrong has noted: "The constitutional arrangements, which gave the impression, as intended, that the minority peoples had full control of their own affairs, were entirely misleading. . . . The 'National Districts,' such as the Chukchi and six others in the north, had less autonomy than an English county."

"From this time on," Igor Krupnik and Michael Chlenov stated, "various federal and local agencies controlled by the Communist Party made and introduced all of the decisions regarding the Chukchi Peninsula and its residents." At the same time the government established the General Directorate of the Northern Sea Route (*Glavsevmorput*), which was in charge of shipping in the Northeast Passage and the adjacent arctic regions that lay between Bering Strait and Murmansk on the Barents Sea. Glavsevmorput controlled all of Chukotka east of Kresta Bay, and an ancillary result of this was the rise of the town of Provideniya at Emma Harbor in Provideniya Bay as a port city and regional center.

But throughout the 1930s the Soviets continually had severe difficulties in supplying the settlements that were located between Bering Strait and the Kolyma River: three ships were lost, many were damaged by the ice, and others were frozen in at sea and drifted throughout the winter. To the west, the Union Gold Trust, which in 1938 became the Far East Construction Trust (*Dalstroy*), controlled the lands, within which the secret police, the NKVD, operated its infamous and brutal Gulag of forced-labor camps.

"Yet for the Yupik and for all of the residents of the country a new era had begun. Changes, both sweeping and staggering, were not long in coming." By 1938 most Yupik men were forced to work in "collectives" for the purpose of "centralized production and distribution" of hunting and fishing, while others were assigned to winter trapping, dog team postal service, or summer cargo transportation.[9]

In 1930 the Soviet government centralized its fur exports by establishing *Soyuzpushnina*, a marketing syndicate that paid for furs and set prices. "While the export market is handled in an efficient, flexible manner," observed Victor Fuchs, "the internal market is run in a stiff and mechanical fashion. The failure to adjust internal prices to changing supply and demand conditions is a characteristic weakness of Soviet planning." "The state fur-trading agency," Yuri Slezkine noted, "found that it was sometimes easier and cheaper to bypass the natives and get the furs through its own means. One such means was to open game reserves, forbid the local hunters from entering and hunt relentlessly throughout the year. When all the animals had been exterminated, the 'reserve' would be closed."

Although the United States recognized the Soviet Union in 1933 and exchanged embassies in 1934, allowing for increased trade between the two nations, and although the Soviet Union became the world's largest fur exporter in the 1930s, the state-controlled fur industry in Chukotka never became significantly profitable. In the 1950s—long after the world market for farmed furs had become sophisticated and saturated—the government experimented with fur farming at various places throughout the Arctic, raising silver fox, blue fox, and mink in Chukotka. By 1962 the government had established nineteen fur farms there.

But according to Victor Shnirelman: "The results were very disappointing more frequently than not. Feeding conditions were inappropriate for this kind of industry in most of the northern regions, equipment was almost non-existent and the workers lacked training. Fur animals were fed valuable reindeer meat and other farm flesh as well as fish and sea-mammal meat, whereas people themselves had to eat canned meat and fish of worse quality." By this time in Chukotka the expenses for fur farming were twice the amount of its returns. "Nevertheless, despite its obvious lack of economic sense fur-farming was emphatically supported by the State bureaucracy: its only advantage was to provide inhabitants with jobs."[10]

Thus the Yupik, the Chukchi, and other Native groups of northeasternmost Asia had lost the freedom of their pre-Soviet days. They had been concentrated in settlements that often comprised more than one ethnic group, their lifeways had been forcibly changed and collectivized by the Soviet state, and their participation in the fur trade had been degraded to the status of laborers.

9

CONTRACTION OF TRADE IN
NORTHERN ALASKA

For the inhabitants of northern Alaska and Western Arctic Canada the decade of the 1930s was almost the inverse of the prosperity they had enjoyed in the 1920s. Not only was the price of white fox pelts less than half of what it had been, but the decade was marked by several summers with very difficult ice conditions and several winters with very poor fur harvests.

Charlie Brower thought the 1929–1930 trapping season was the worst he had ever experienced, and in January 1930 C. T. Pedersen wrote, "There must be nearly 200 trappers in the two villages at Barrow and they had caught less than 50 foxes by Xmas time." To make matters worse, in 1930–1931 diphtheria was epidemic among the Eskimos along the northwest coast, and influenza broke out in the town of Kotzebue, curtailing trapping, which in any case yielded another poor fur harvest. Fur harvests were again low in 1932–1933, 1935–1936, and 1936–1937.[1]

In 1930–1931 there was also a poor fur catch on St. Lawrence Island, and when R. M. Gilmore, a wildlife biologist, visited the village of Gambell in June he immediately noticed the effect the slump in fur prices had wrought on the Natives' lives. "Prosperity was once theirs and consequently they bought $1000 whale boats and erected houses of lumber. They can't understand the depression of 1929–30 but they have been brought into full realization of it. In addition the last two years have been very lean as far as hunting went and so many of them are living entirely on Eskimo food again." In 1931 Alaska Governor George A. Parks reported to the secretary of the Interior that "low prices on furs have reduced the incomes of the [Native] people almost to the vanishing point."[2]

Despite this bleak outlook, and despite the fact that trapping had become far less remunerative, some Natives continued to leave the Barrow area for coastal

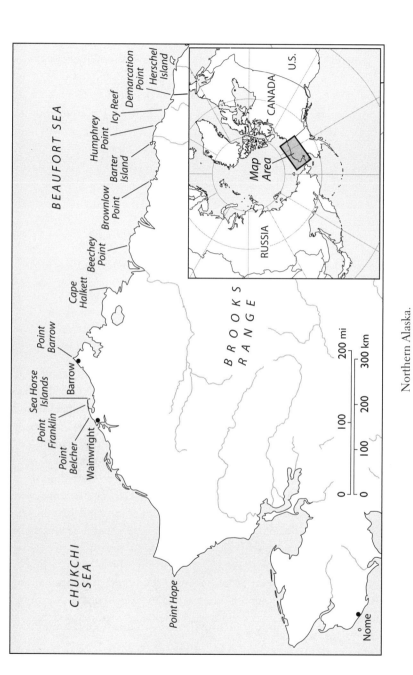

Northern Alaska.

points, where they could combine trapping with subsistence hunting and fishing. Fortunately for them, however, the walrus, whale, and caribou populations had substantially recovered from the low levels where they had stood at the turn of the century. "Eskimos of northwest Alaska are going back to nature for livelihood and prosperity," *Fur Trade Review* declared in November 1932. "The decline in raw furs has resulted in a sort of depression reaching far-flung villages of the Arctic coast. The natives, unable to afford more of white man's chow and the modern store clothes, have decided to take to the trail followed by their forefathers and trap, hunt and live as in days of old. . . . All this activity has been caused by the white man's business decline, which has extended to . . . the Arctic rim of northern Alaska and Canada. There is no market for their furs as in former years."[3]

THE *PATTERSON* AND THE *BAYCHIMO*

In addition to the decline in fur harvests, the summers of 1930, 1931, 1932, 1933, 1935, and 1936 were noted for very difficult ice conditions. David Greist, a young college student, was working his passage back to his parents' home at Barrow aboard C. T. Pedersen's *Patterson*. He remembered the summer of 1931:

> The arctic ice pack broke up very late, much more so than usual, and then, because of erratic currents and contrary winds, its vast field menaced all shipping for long weeks. . . . We dodged ice, fought ice, blasted ourselves free repeatedly with dynamite and gunpowder and, for many days slowly and painfully worked our passage through menacing ice fields toward the North.
>
> One of the methods of cracking the ice field was by using black gunpowder that came in 5-pound cans. I would knock a hole into the can's top with a screw driver; insert a 2-foot fuse into the can and seal it with Fels Naptha yellow soap. The gun powder was then lashed to a long 2 x 4. One of us would light the fuse and two other fellows would thrust the can as far under the ice as they could and then would run away a short distance and wait for the explosion.
>
> If we cracked the ice, we retrieved what was left of the two by four, climbed aboard the ship and Captain Pedersen would then order full speed ahead. The ship's bow would run up onto the ice and the weight of the ship would widen the crack. On several occasions we did this . . . all day long and the ship moved perhaps the distance of one mile.[4]

That year, 1931, the *Patterson* reached Herschel Island only on August 26, its latest arrival there—thirty-six days after having reached Barrow, which is only 400 miles to the west, a distance which normally would have been covered in

The crew of the *Patterson* using gunpowder charges to blast a path through the ice. The charge is fixed to the end of the pole. The man at the right is lighting the fuse, and the others will shove the pole under the ice, where the charge will explode. Courtesy of Richard S. Finnie, author's collection.

less than two days' steady travel. Because of the heavy ice he had encountered, Pedersen knew that his ship was in danger of being frozen in for the winter—and possibly crushed by the floes—unless he could get out quickly. He and the crew worked frantically to offload the cargo, to swap the trade goods with the supply boats that had arrived from his eastern posts, and to buy furs from the visiting trappers. Exhausted, they hurriedly departed Herschel Island for the west ten days later, but that was only the beginning of their trials.

They fought the encroaching pack ice for most of the 400 miles to Point Barrow, where it seemed that they would be frozen in for the winter. They narrowly made it past the point, but when they rounded the shoals off Icy Cape, 150 miles to the southwest, the pack immediately closed in behind them, driving hard on shore, where it remained for the rest of the winter.

The Hudson's Bay Company's *Baychimo*, like the *Patterson*, had arrived at Herschel Island only on August 26, and because of the heavy ice conditions Captain Sydney Cornwell wanted to offload the cargo for the Western Arctic

The Hudson's Bay Company's *Baychimo* at Shingle Point, 1925. A barge, used for towing supplies ashore, is secured alongside. Burwash [1927]: opposite p. 13.

posts there, at the island, and to ship it onward via schooners, but he was over-ruled by HBC Commissioner Ralph Parsons and by Western Arctic District Manager Richard Bonnycastle, whose orders were to visit the company's posts to compile their annual reports on the status of the company's Western Arctic operations. At the end of its supply mission the *Baychimo* left Herschel, west-bound, eight days after the *Patterson* had departed, but Captain Cornwell—a short, pudgy martinet with an explosive temper—was not as skilled as Captain Pedersen, nor as steady, as we shall see.

In fact, six years earlier, in 1925, when Cornwell had been on his first voyage to the Western Arctic aboard the *Baychimo*, his assigned task had been to supply the Hudson's Bay Company's posts as far east as Cambridge Bay. On that return voyage, when the outbound *Baychimo* reached Herschel Island on August 31, 1925, Cornwell, with ice pilot Gus Foellmer (the former master of the *Lady Kindersley*), found thick floes barring the way. Despite repeated attempts to head west, they spent four weeks without being able to leave the island. Finally, on September 28, 1925, the floes eased up somewhat and allowed them to pro-ceed. Fighting ice all the way, they reached Barrow on October 2, one of the latest dates that a ship had passed the point.

At Barrow Charlie Brower remembered the autumn of 1925:

[Charlie Klengenberg's] Maid of Orleans when here reported the Bay Chimo still east of Herschel Island and that the ice was heavy from there in, she having a hard time getting out. As the Bay Chimo did not show up on October 1st, we all gave her up for the year, expecting that as she was leaking badly she would be abandoned and the crew go up the river. . . . I heard someone thumping on my door, . . . there was the captain and several men from the Bay Chimo, wanting me to get up and tell them any news there was to tell. . . .

Six boys from here [that] they had taken as crew were glad enough to get home. Mr. Patmore [formerly the purser of the *Lady Kindersley*] was still the supercargo for the Hudson Bay Co. He left me with $60.00 each for the men that had helped rescue the crew of the Lady Kindersley the year before, he also had a medal for each of them. . . . After breakfast they all went aboard and were soon out of sight, going south as fast as they could. Her bow was badly bashed in, they were leaking badly[,] still they were homeward bound.

Captain Cornwell reported to the company at the end of the 1925 voyage: "After being held up so long at Herschel Island no one expected us to get out this season—or, if we did clear Herschel Island—to get round Point Barrow at this late date. I am told this is the first time—or at least for forty years—that a ship has left Herschel Island and gained the outside so late as this in the season."

Although everyone understood that they had been lucky to get out in 1925, for Cornwell and for the *Baychimo* the next five summers (1926 to 1930) presented manageable ice and weather conditions, and despite receiving damage almost every year from multiple groundings in the barely charted waters, the 230-foot steamer had carried out its assignments, a fact which perhaps lulled everyone into thinking that the annual voyage from Vancouver to the Western Arctic posts was practicable for such a sturdy and powerful ship.[5]

And probably because of this string of successful voyages, in 1930 the company had ordered the *Baychimo* to attempt an eastbound traverse of the Northwest Passage. But, as if a portent of things to come, west of Herschel Island the ice had twisted its rudder and broken two and a half of its propeller blades, so the plan was abandoned.

The following summer, in the icy year of 1931, the *Baychimo* delivered supplies and collected furs at the company's posts in the Western Arctic as usual, steaming as far east as Coppermine before departing from Herschel Island on September 13, 1931. But the ship left the island four days after the *Patterson* had barely squeaked past Icy Cape, just ahead of the encroaching pack ice. On that date the *Baychimo* was still more than 500 miles to the east. At once the ship met heavy pack ice, and it took five days to work through 400 miles of floes to Point Barrow, resulting in the loss of a blade from the propeller.

When it reached Barrow the *Baychimo* was already far behind schedule for the usual date of getting out of the Arctic. Charlie Brower recalled: "The Bay

Chimo returned on the 18th but the ice was all in along the coast[.] [It] had great difficulty in making the point[.] From there down to the station there was a lead of water inside the ground ice so she came along as far as here[.] Below the station the pack ice was in on the beach. So here she anchored half a mile from the house unable to proceed." "On the night of the 22nd the wind hauled to the east and the ice moved off outside the ridge, but still there was no chance for the Bay Chimo to get out and go south."

On September 22 they tried to buck through the grounded pressure ridge without success, so Brower sent his son David with a crew and a supply of dynamite to blast a hole through it. "Then began one of the darndest performances I've ever seen," Richard Bonnycastle recorded in his diary. "Trying to break through the narrow barrier of loose ice pans cemented together with new slush ice & jammed fairly tight. . . . In this little predicament which required patience & common sense the Captain lost his head completely, swore at his officers & men in most unjust fashion, became panicky and pessimistic & altogether most objectionable & impossible."

By backing and filling and bucking again the ship began to make a little headway, but it was brought to a halt off Point Belcher, where it was without shelter and nakedly exposed to the pack ice, and it was forced to return fifteen miles to a somewhat safer position off Point Franklin. On October 8, now low on coal—and with the temperature below zero—it appeared that the *Baychimo* was stuck for the winter, so the crew began building a fifteen-by-forty-five-foot house on shore, using tarpaulins, lumber, the ship's hatch covers, and driftwood logs for uprights. They then hauled the ship's supplies and coal to the camp. Captain Cornwell also wanted to take his cargo of twenty bales of fur to store it in Jim Allen's warehouse at Wainwright, but Bonnycastle refused to allow this on the grounds that the costs of transportation and warehousing would be too expensive. It was a poor decision, and consequently $30,000 worth of furs, ivory, and other cargo (by the company's estimate) was left onboard the ship.

Accepting that the ship was now frozen in for the winter, on October 9 the company authorized Bonnycastle to charter planes from Northern Air Transport in Nome to fly out the passengers and nonessential personnel. Three days later the crew began staking out a landing strip on the ice. The planes arrived on the fifteenth and Bonnycastle, Scotty Gall, and Percy Patmore flew out to complete arrangements for housing, onward transportation, and resupplying the crew that remained behind. In all, nineteen men were evacuated. Oliver Morris, with his wife Alice and their children, were passengers aboard the *Baychimo*, returning from several years' trapping and trading in Canada's Coronation Gulf. They sensibly decided to spend the winter at Wainwright. Cornwell

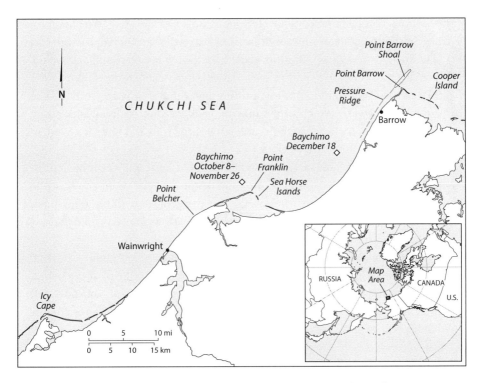

The *Baychimo*'s drift in 1931 after being carried away by the pack ice.

and seventeen men would stay onshore at the camp with the ship's wireless radio set, keeping watch over the *Baychimo*.

At Wainwright Jim Allen wrote, "Just before Thanksgiving we had one of the lowest barometers I'd ever seen in the Arctic. The day before Thanksgiving the wind blew up and at night it was a gale. The rise and fall of the tide in the Arctic Ocean is normally about three feet but that night it went up about six, an event that never had been known before. Captain Cornwall [*sic*] had come to visit Ellnou [Allen's wife] and me for the holiday. He worried all Thanksgiving Day about his ship but it was impossible for him to return to where she was. Two days after Thanksgiving he started back with one of the natives and my dog team. He had just gone a little way when he met two of his men. They reported that the ship had drifted away." The three-day gale had kept them inside their cabin, and when it was over, the ship was nowhere to be seen, replaced by pressure ridges estimated to be forty feet or higher.

It was assumed that the ship had gone down, but, like the *Lady Kindersley*, it inexplicably stayed afloat amid the floes. A few weeks later, Oliver Morris and two Iñupiat companions were traveling along the coast and spotted it about five miles offshore, eighteen miles southwest of Barrow. Even though the price of white fox pelts was down, the furs aboard the *Baychimo* were still very valuable. With great difficulty, and in great danger, they reached the ship over the jumbled floes and found that it was sitting upright atop a large ice floe. The incalculably powerful force of the moving pack ice during the Thanksgiving storm must have shoved a pan right under the ship's hull and lifted it up, out of the water, and onto its own drydock.

Morris and his friends salvaged fourteen bales of fur, each weighing approximately 130 pounds. But this load proved to be too heavy for their dog teams to pull, so Morris cached four bales on the ice and kept on with the remainder, storing them in Charlie Brower's warehouse at Barrow. He requested $15,000 from the Hudson's Bay Company for the salvage.

Morris then returned to the *Baychimo*'s camp and told Captain Cornwell that he had boarded the ship more than thirty miles northeast of their hut. Cornwell started out at once and found the ship, now fifteen miles offshore, but the ice was so confused and broken that he could not reach it, and it is unclear what his visit might have achieved.[6]

On December 18 Leslie Melvin, an energetic novice trapper, was on his way to Nome from Barter Island via dog team, having resigned from a poorly planned venture with Gus Masik. Melvin was then in company with Dr. James A. Ford, a young archaeologist from the Smithsonian Institution who was wintering at Barrow. They followed Morris's tracks out to the ship. "Suddenly we looked up and found the stern of the great ship towering over us," Les Melvin recalled. "Her rudder and propeller were high above the ice. The immense pressure of the converging ice fields had slipped along her rounded bilges and lifted her above the ice instead of crushing her like an eggshell. We found a ladder lashed to the rail and signs of Morris having boarded the vessel. Jim Ford set about searching for some food while I made up a pack of the furs scattered about where Morris had left them. I also took two flags from the ship, and the captain's hat. We hurried away from the vessel, for a wind was beginning to blow. It was very dark. The traveling was terrible." When they reached shore, Melvin and Ford went to Morris's camp. "He bawled us out for taking such a chance. Said furs were no good for a dead man."

Melvin and Ford returned to the ship on December 20 to try to salvage some of Morris's discarded furs. They left shore two hours before the arrival of the brief, faint, twilight of the solstice. "When light enough we got on a hummock and looked around," Jim Ford wrote. "There she was, close at hand and dead ahead. We went aboard but didn't have enough information—couldn't find the fur locker and nearly everything that we wanted was there . . . everything and we couldn't find it! . . . After two hours we left and made a quick trip to our camp. The next day we came to Barrow. We found out where everything was—got drawings, etc. and were planning to each take a team and a native and return with Morris but next morning there was a slight wind out of the east and a decided barometer drop. Morris and I decided to wait but Melvin went down. He arrived in time to see the [ship] moving offshore."

News about the *Baychimo* had gone out over the radio and at once adventurers began planning to use aircraft to search for the ship, but they were unable to find it. In mid-February 1932, assuming that the vessel was lost, the HBC arranged for the remaining crew to be flown out and ordered them to abandon the camp.

But the pack ice, winds, and currents of the Chukchi Sea proved otherwise. In fact the ship reappeared at Barrow in mid-March 1932, and it was next seen seven miles off Wainwright in August, where Jim Allen, with a crew of about twenty, went out to it to try to salvage the launch. They took some small items, but fog closed in and they were forced to leave. The U.S. Coast Guard cutter *Northland* was nearby and also searched, but fog set in once again, and the *Baychimo* vanished into arctic mists. The ship then reappeared, and a party of twenty-eight set out from Wainwright, crossed seven miles of ice, and salvaged some firearms and clothing.[7]

Once again the ship was assumed to have been lost, but in 1933, to the amazement of all, the *Baychimo* was spotted again, now twelve miles off Wainwright. C. T. Pedersen saw it from the *Patterson*, and Captain John Backland Jr. caught sight of the *Baychimo* four miles away from his schooner *C. S. Holmes*, when both ships were locked in the ice about seventy miles southwest of Barrow. "One of the oddest sights of the voyage," Backland reported, "was an Eskimo who came aboard our ship after visiting the Baychimo. He had found the captain's uniform left on the other ship and proudly wore his four stripes." And at the same time Isobel Wylie Hutchison, an intrepid Scottish botanist who was traveling north as a passenger with Ira Rank and the crew of the schooner *Trader*, fought through the floes and on August 11 caught up with the ship, still aboard its ice raft, "her giant hull, rust-stained and battered . . . looming tower-like above the little *Trader*," she wrote. "A strange spectacle the decks presented. . . . The hold was open to the winds, but its half-rifled depths still contained sacks of mineral ore, caribou skins, and cargo of various descriptions. . . . On a sack of sinew thread stood a rusted but unused typewriter. Parkas from the eastern Arctic were here. . . . Writing-paper, photograph films, ledgers of the Hudson's Bay Company, typewriter ribbons. . . . Charts of all seas of the world

Ira Rank (right) with the crew of the *Trader*, 1933.
Isobel Wylie Hutchison Collection. Reproduced by
permission of the National Library of Scotland.

lay scattered upon the decks of the pilot-house. In the dining room the natives
were already busy wrenching the wire mattresses from the sofas and unfixing
the pivot-chairs from the floor. A breakfast menu tossed in the doorway indi-
cated that the crew of the unlucky ship were at least in no danger of starvation,
for there was a choice of some six courses."

To everyone's surprise in September 1934 the *Baychimo* reappeared yet again.
It was drifting north near Barrow, and C. T. Pedersen went searching for it
with the *Patterson*. "It was snowing so hard that we could not see ½ a mile," he
remembered. "I steamed north the 12 miles to the point, hoping that the snow
would let up, but it got thicker and thicker on the surface and began to freeze
up, so I turned south for home. The trader [Charlie Brower] at Barrow told
me that her stern was only about 14 feet from the water, so I had blasts ready to
drop her down. With good weather, we could have towed her down to Teller
(Port Clarence), and sent for a tug to tow her down to Vancouver. She was seen

The *Trader* in the ice, heading toward the *Baychimo*, 1933. Isobel Wylie Hutchison Collection. Reproduced by permission of the National Library of Scotland.

The *Trader* reaches the *Baychimo*, 1933. The schooner is visible on the left. Isobel Wylie Hutchison Collection. Reproduced by permission of the National Library of Scotland.

again in 1935, and later again, according to reports, so they called her the 'Ghost Ship.'" Natives at Barrow spotted the *Baychimo* far out in the pack ice in February 1936 but did not attempt to board it. There were a few other reports of the ship afterward, but nothing verifiable.[8]

END OF THE DECADE

As the decade of the 1930s wore on, more misfortune appeared for the inhabitants of northern Alaska. The summer of 1933 was so cold and icy in the Bering, Chukchi, and Beaufort seas that it was very difficult for John Backland Jr. with the *C. S. Holmes*—which lacked auxiliary power—to reach Barrow with badly needed supplies. And in 1934 a citywide fire destroyed much of Nome, including the warehouses of several merchants, among them Ira Rank's U.S. Mercantile Company. Furthermore, in 1934 and 1936 violent maritime labor strikes erupted in the West Coast ports of the United States and Canada, causing many to worry that, without shipping, all of Alaska would be on very short rations for the winter. These, among other factors, forced C. T. Pedersen to cease sailing the *Patterson* north after the 1936 season (chapter 10), and John Backland Jr. did not operate the *C. S. Holmes* after the 1937 season because of labor troubles and the loss of a government freighting contract.[9]

Reindeer herding, too, which had steadily increased in northern and western Alaska since the beginning of the century—and which the government considered to be an important source of food and income for the Natives—also suffered a steep downturn. The number of reindeer in Alaska fell from about 360,000 at the beginning of the 1930s, to 250,000 in 1940, to 25,000 in 1950, and the herds near Barrow suffered a proportionate decline, the result of overgrazed ranges, the herders' lack of attention to their herds, wolf and bear predation, losses by reindeer joining migrating caribou herds, and government mismanagement.[10]

Worse, the trapping seasons spanning 1933–1934 to 1937–1938 turned out to be so poor in northern Alaska that Charlie Brower exported an average of only 327 white fox skins each season. In 1933 Arnold Liebes decided to leave H. Liebes and Company to set up a retail fur business on his own in San Francisco. He continued his association with Brower until 1938, when Brower recorded the last fur shipments in his ledger.

By spring 1937 the *Seattle Post-Intelligencer* reported that the "Eskimos of Northern Alaska are migrating toward the Canadian border." This became the third wave of Alaskan Iñupiat immigrants into Western Arctic Canada. At the same time some "inland" families that had migrated to the Alaskan coast twenty or thirty years earlier had begun to return to their homelands in the Brooks

The C. S. *Holmes* at Barrow, ca. 1935. San Francisco
Maritime National Historical Park, G6.9241n.

Range, where the caribou herds had recovered to near their former numbers.
"The year 1934 marked the beginning of a journey back into the mountains for
at least four Iñupiat families," stated Edwin Hall and his coauthors. "The first
steps were tentative, as they kept within relatively easy reach of the sea and its
resources. . . . The settlement pattern [that] developed . . . involved spending
summers in the general Colville River delta region as they had done previously,
but travelling to the foothills, and later the mountains, for the winter months. . . .
Trapping of fur bearers increased, because furs were one of the few sources of
income available to the inland Iñupiat at the time. Wolves, in particular, were
sought because the Territory [of Alaska] paid a bounty on this species. . . . The
primary trade goods desired by the inland Iñupiat at this time were salt, tea,
coffee, flour, and other groceries. Having a sufficient supply of ammunition was
considered critical, and scarcity often was the impetus for a trip to the nearest
trading post; usually a trip made each spring and fall." For example, on one
trip to the Beechey Point post the inlanders were recorded as having bought a
modest supply of seventeen boxes of rifle and shotgun cartridges, tobacco and
chewing tobacco, one pair of snow glasses, two knives, two packs of matches,
cigarette papers, two spools of thread, a pencil, eight yards of cloth, two pounds
of coffee, two pounds of tea, three pounds of salt, twenty-five pounds of flour,
and ten pounds of sugar.[11]

Captain John Backland Jr. aboard the *C. S. Holmes* in Seattle before
heading north, ca. 1935. Courtesy of Elsie Backland, author's collection.

In 1937 the Reverend Fred Klerekoper, traveling by dog team, recorded
only seven small trading posts on the coast between Barrow and the Canadian
border: Oliver Morris at Cape Halkett, Jack Smith at Beechey Point, Henry
Chamberlain at Brownlow Point, Tom Gordon at Barter Island, Gus Masik east
of Barter Island, John Olson at Icy Reef, and Mickey Gordon at Demarcation
Point. But their days were numbered, and by then only a few ships carried supplies as far north as Barrow. In 1938 Oliver Morris tore down his house at Cape
Halkett and moved it to Barrow, where he would trade for a few years, and Ira
Rank, carrying small stores in the *Trader*, was alone in visiting the north Alaska
coast between Barrow and the Canadian border. He found the coast east of
Barrow almost deserted. Where once there had been camps of one or two families every twenty or thirty miles on the coast, except for a few persons at Cape
Halkett, Beechey Point, and Brownlow Point, there were only five families between Humphrey Point and the Canadian border. All of the trading posts located east of Barrow were small operations. Describing the trading posts on the
Kuskokwim River, the Smithsonian Institution's Aleš Hrdlička could have been
speaking about those on the north coast of Alaska as well: "These storekeepers
. . . sell mostly on credit and get in return such furs as the natives secure. A few

in the best places and with management may get fairly well-off in years, but most just about exist, though they sell at 100 or more percent profit."[12]

In February 1939 Charlie Brower wrote to John Backland Jr.: "It has been a rotten season with hardly any fur. To date I have collected two hundred and two foxes of all kinds. . . . Furs are getting scarcer every season. . . . One does not dare to extend much credit for it never comes back. Not that some of the Eskimo are not honest but they have no resource."

The trade was so poor in 1939 and 1940 that Ira Rank had been unsure whether he would go north the following summer. He died in 1940, by which time there were only three traders remaining on the north coast: Jack Smith, Henry Chamberlain, and John Olson.

Because Pedersen and Backland no longer came north, according to the Eskimo trapper Isaac Akootchook, the Gordons could no longer get supplies and closed their stores, and John Olson and Henry Chamberlain had to take their boats to Barrow for their outfits. With the posts closing in the late 1930s and early 1940s some families moved to Barrow, while others relocated to Canada. Tom Gordon died in 1938, and no one took over his post at Barter Island (today, Kaktovik). Alex Gordon, for example, moved from Alaska to the Yukon coast in 1944 and, two years later, to Aklavik. Jack Smith and John Olson died in 1942, and Henry Chamberlain closed his post in 1943. In 1945 Oliver Morris sold his post at Barrow to Tom and David Brower, and that year Jim Allen died at Wainwright.[13]

The low fur prices and poor fur harvests depressed the Eskimo trapping activity in northern and northwestern Alaska. In 1940 Charlie Brower declared, "This has been the worst year I have ever put in at Barrow. No furs and what we have there is no sale for at prices that does not pay to collect them. Then all the village has been sick with measles and are just beginning to get around again. Everyone has been hungry and I am broke trying to keep things going."

Charlie Brower died in 1945, a time when the militarization of Alaska was beginning to provide some wage labor jobs to the Natives, and by then, as Ernest S. Burch Jr. wrote, "virtually all of the native population of Northwest Alaska was concentrated permanently in school-mission-store communities," which were located at productive places for subsistence hunting and fishing. Burch could well have been referring to all of northwestern Alaska and Western Arctic Canada. The majority of the population of northern Alaska was by then centered in villages of about 100 to 350 persons at Point Hope, Point Lay, Wainwright, and Barrow.[14]

10

Toward Monopoly Control
in Western Arctic Canada

THE BANKSLANDERS

During the optimism of the 1920s, no attempt was made to recolonize Banks Island until 1928, despite the fact that its productivity for trapping had been proven by Billy Natkusiak and others. By then, however, the Mackenzie delta and surrounding regions had become saturated with trappers, resulting in declining catches. The mink harvest in the delta, for example, fell from 21,205 in 1923–1924 to 3,630 in 1927–1928. The overall fur catch in the region was low in the winter of 1923–1924, and although the catch rebounded the following winter, it declined again in 1925–1926, when catches at Aklavik and in the Mackenzie delta were reported by the RCMP as "very poor, and had it not been for the muskrat season, some trappers would have fended poorly." The fur harvest in 1926–1927 was the same, and white foxes were scarce. The problem was made worse in the winter of 1927–1928, when an influx of red foxes, preying on the arctic foxes on the North Slope of Alaska and the Yukon, resulted in a comparatively meager harvest.[1]

Having been encouraged by C. T. Pedersen and others, three enterprising trappers—Lenny Inglangasak, David Pirktuqana, and "Old Adam" Onoalayak, all from Baillie Island—in autumn 1928 crossed from Cape Parry to Banks Island with their schooners, families, dogs, and equipment to overwinter on the southwest coast. "In what was a poor winter on the mainland," Peter Usher wrote, "they did moderately well, with over 100 foxes each. The next year, the same men returned to trap again. Inoalayak brought his son-in-law, Jim Wolki; Inglanasak [sic] brought Alex Stefansson and Pannigabluk (Stefansson's mother), while Pektukana [sic] brought a Copper Eskimo by the name of Nakitok, who had been his trapping partner for some years at Pearce Point. In addition, Allen Okpik, from the Delta, had purchased a schooner and outfit from Ole Andreason at Atkinson Point, and he brought his family, including three grown sons . . . to Banks Island. The Baillie Islanders got 200 to 500 foxes each, and the Okpik family got over 1,100 between them . . . they had gained a fortune. The reputation of the Island was established. The news prompted the equivalent of a gold rush amongst the elite, schooner-owning trappers who could obtain the necessary outfits."[2]

Before long the families had dispersed and established more than a dozen camps at most of the river mouths and harbors on the west, southwest, and southeast coasts of the island, sites that were chosen for good hunting and trapping, fresh water, and protected harbors, among other benefits. The families often changed locations after a winter or two at a particular site. Thus began a routine for the "Bankslanders," all of whom were Inuit. At Herschel Island or Aklavik (and later at Tuktoyaktuk) they traded for their winter outfits. "The Bankslanders always prepared their furs with considerable care," Usher noted, "and accordingly tended to receive prices well above the average tariff."

"Their yearly outfits were also more costly than the average, amounting to a minimum of $3,000 to $5,000 per family. Coal and gasoline were a major expense, as were capital goods such as rifles, traps, canvas, ammunition and dog feed. The annual purchase of groceries included not only such staples as flour, lard, sugar and tea, but tinned fruits and vegetables as well." The winter supplies also often included 100 pounds of cornmeal per dog because the trappers found that their teams performed better when they were fed a cooked mixture of seal meat and cornmeal. Usher continued, "Moreover, the Bankslanders in most years could afford additional durable goods such as washing machines, sewing machines, phonographs, radios, watches, binoculars and cameras. A few of the best trappers were also able to afford new schooners, costing $10,000 to $15,000. Usually the trappers required credit for part of their outfits, but in good years they could purchase their entire outfit on the basis of the previous year's catch and still have money left over. Some trappers kept such surplus monies in bank accounts in Edmonton or Vancouver through 'The Bay' or Captain Pedersen."

The schooners, laden with a year's supplies—and often with an extra family or two aboard as paying passengers—would usually gather in the harbor at Baillie Island or the Booth Islands to await favorable conditions for crossing to Banks. Depending on their point of departure, the distance to be covered was 70 to 120 miles. In autumn, when fog and gales were always a worry, the crossing was made by dead reckoning, heading directly for Sachs Harbour or for Nelson Head at the southern tip of the island, which, at 2,450 feet, is visible from Cape

Parry in very clear weather. When they reached the island they steered for their winter sites.

On arriving at the wintering place, the Bankslanders unloaded the schooner and then pulled it out of the water, skidding it sideways, on planks. First they buried a beam or a log (a "deadman") in the beach and used it as an anchor for a triple-purchase block and tackle to winch the bow and stern alternately a few feet at a time, as they "walked" the schooner up the beach. The family also built a frame from the lumber they had brought with them and covered it with a canvas wall tent, ten by twelve feet or twelve by fourteen. It was heated by a small coal stove.

There is little driftwood on the island, and because the coal cost as much as $200 per ton, this fuel was often augmented by seal blubber. These dwellings could require as much as three to five tons of coal for the winter. The traps, harnesses, and sleds then had to be overhauled for the season to come, and as soon as the rivers froze, ice blocks had to be cut and hauled to the camp. "They would saw good size ice blocks and put ice around the tent with enough space for a person to go through," Agnes White remembered. "For the top of the tent, they put moss, and a window on the roof. It was warm! It never frosted. . . . On cracks they would *quunataq* it ('slush it')."[3]

Before the autumn fox molt was complete and the pelts had become prime, the hunters focused on taking seals and caribou, while the children hunted for hares and ptarmigan. Each man tried to have twenty or thirty seals in stock before the start of the trapping season. When the trapping season opened, the men, usually working in groups of two or three, set out their traps on lines along the coast or in the river valleys, over distances that took a week or two to cover. On the trail they lived in snow houses or double-walled tents and cooked over Primus stoves fueled by kerosene, which was much lighter to carry than coal. Occasionally a man would reset his trapline at mid-season, but when the season closed at the end of March, all traps were pulled and put aboard the schooner—because the trappers often spent the following winter elsewhere, and in years with heavy summer ice, they might not be able to return to the island at all.

At the end of the trapping season the men returned to seal and caribou hunting, and the women helped with preparing the pelts. This was followed by goose hunting and fishing in the month or so before it was time to ready the schooners for the summer's voyage. They painted the boat and put the engine into working order before launching. The physiologist E. O. Hohn, who was on a visit to the island, outlined the procedure: "The boats were resting with the keel supported by a few beams laid crosswise. These were greased with seal blubber and thus became skids. Using a jack against the keel and with every man in the place pushing with his back against the boat alternately at the stern and the bow, the boats were shifted a foot or so at a time and finally broadside into the water. However, their launching didn't mean we were free to go. There was open water for about a mile offshore, but beyond that the ice was still unbroken. Every day we'd climb the nearest of the coast hills behind the settlement and examine the lay of the open water."

"Everything was put on board," wrote Peter Usher, "dogs, travelling and camping equipment, traps, meat, the winter's fox catch, even the canvas and lumber from the tents, because there was no guarantee that the party would return to the same spot next year." For ballast on the southbound voyage Fred Carpenter loaded gunny sacks full of gravel aboard his schooner. In Aklavik the gravel would find eager buyers, who would use it for covering footpaths amid the town's delta mud.

The families then waited for the ice and weather to allow them to cross Amundsen Gulf. The fleet would often rendezvous at Sachs Harbour before crossing to the mainland in convoy. E. O. Hohn described one voyage with Fred Carpenter and his family aboard the schooner *North Star*.

> On top of 18 people we had 50 sled dogs chained on deck and a captive wolf, kept for breeding with the dogs. The Bankslanders have to travel with all their essential equipment. As ice conditions sometime prevent their return to the island, they must be prepared to put in a winter's trapping wherever they may happen to get stuck. That's why we had the dogs as well as two sleds tied to the railing, and sacks full of fox traps.
>
> The loading of the dogs was quite a game—hardly any of them would walk the gang plank, so we simply hauled them up by the chains fixed to their tight collars. I feared this would break their necks but it seems they can take it. The wolf was a more awkward proposition. First a long chain was manipulated around his neck and this was held tight by a man on each side, then he was knocked on the head with a piece of two-by-four till he was pretty groggy and a muzzle slipped on. After that he was no more of a problem than the dogs.

The precaution of taking everything with them was well founded. Heavy ice thwarted the Bankslanders from returning to the island in 1936 and in 1941, forcing them to spend the winter of 1936–1937 on the mainland, southwest of Baillie Island in North Star Harbour, where the trapping was poor; an early freeze up caught them at Aklavik for the winter of 1941–1942. In the very icy summer of 1933 the floes were so thick that they could not even leave Banks to get supplies at Herschel Island, and only with great difficulty were a few able to reach the HBC post at Walker Bay. "The ice never went all summer and it froze over again," Jim Wolki remembered. "We already had ran out of pretty well everything when we wintered. There was lots of owl and we were trapping them. So we were quite healthy. Then in the fall, after freeze up, we got a few seals. We had few shells [ammunition] and there was hardly any caribou at Banks Island. After freeze up, we didn't drink tea anymore, we ran out, no more flour too, no more coffee. Whatever food we had, we all ran out but we still had a little bit of gas since we had some left for the schooner. We used gas for travelling, that's the only thing we had left, saving it for the Primus stove." That winter Jim Wolki and two others crossed more than seventy miles of Amundsen Gulf over moving sea ice to get supplies at Letty Harbour on the Parry Peninsula—a very dangerous crossing. It was three months before they were able to return to their families on Banks Island.[4]

The sandy soils of Banks Island nevertheless proved to be prime trapping grounds, and for the Banksland trappers the first seven winters there included two peak years in the white fox population cycle, yielding a total of $300,000 worth of furs. The Bankslanders quickly gained a reputation throughout Western Arctic Canada for their hard work and resilience—and for their trapping skills. Their fur harvests were such, for example, that in 1935 at Herschel Island Jim Wolki and Fred Carpenter ordered a fifty-seven-foot schooner from C. T. Pedersen. The George Kneass shipyard in San Francisco built the *North Star*, and in 1936 Pedersen carried it to Herschel Island as deck cargo aboard the *Patterson*. He sold it to them for $23,000. At the same time another Bankslander had sufficient funds to be able to spend the winter of 1935–1936 with his family in San Francisco and Vancouver and returned to the island with money to spare.[5]

After the poor winter of 1936–1937 on the mainland in North Star Harbour, the Bankslanders went again to the island to enjoy another peak in the white fox cycle, catching a total of 6,500 foxes, with one family taking a record of 1,300. According to Peter Usher, "This bumper harvest, however, coincided with a nadir in the market price. . . . The 1,300 foxes, which brought about $15,000 . . . would have fetched $100,000 ten years previously. Still, earnings were sufficient for most families to clear long-standing debts and even have some credit left. The Bankslanders enjoyed a second peak harvest of almost 5,500 foxes in 1940–41, and furthermore enjoyed the advantages of a rising market."[6]

During the war years and after, the Bankslanders' fortunes suffered from the early freeze up of 1944, resulting in a winter in the fox-poor Booth Islands at Cape Parry, and in 1946 heavy ice prevented three of the schooners from getting to the mainland. The fox harvest of 1946–1947 was plentiful, but the prices were low, and an early freeze up in 1947 held the fleet at Sachs Harbour, thereby saturating the area with twenty-five trappers. The result of these misfortunes

The *Patterson* carrying the *North Star* as deck cargo toward Herschel
Island, 1936. Courtesy of Teddy Pedersen, author's collection.

forced most of the Banks Island trappers deeply into debt, with some owing
$6,000 to $8,000. "Commodity prices, and particularly food prices, were soar-
ing, and the traders were not prepared to advance new outfits of the size required for a Banksland winter." This, plus an epidemic of influenza in the Mackenzie delta that sickened many of the islanders in 1948 and an early freeze up,
simultaneously kept them in the delta for the winter, where their presence and
competition was resented by the local Inuvialuit.

But things began to change for the better when the government decided that
a Native presence on Banks Island would help to confirm Canada's sovereignty
over its Arctic Islands, and at the same time the fur market began to rise a
bit. "Laco" Hunt was a government administrator at Aklavik. He wrote, "Fred
Carpenter was a skilled seaman. . . . As it turned out, he wanted desperately to
return to Banks Island. I told him that the government would guarantee his
group's debts with various traders, and promised to fly to the island the following spring with the medical officer. I wanted him to know that the government
was indeed concerned about the Bankslanders' welfare. Fred agreed to do all
he could to persuade a selected number of Inuit to travel with him and Wolkie
[*sic*] back to the island."

Nine trappers received an outfit and a small government stipend, and in September 1951, aboard two schooners, they set off for the island from Tuktoyaktuk.
Their arrival coincided with another peak in the fox cycle, although an invasion

The *North Star,* loaded and preparing to depart from Aklavik for Banks
Island, 1950s. Courtesy of Sven Johansson, author's collection.

of wolves resulted in the loss of a quarter of their catches for several years. The
government then created the "Eskimo Loan Fund," providing assistance to the
trappers. Consequently more families returned to the island in the following
years. In 1953 the RCMP stationed an officer at Sachs Harbour, and two years
later a meteorological station was established. At the same time the North
American air defense system, the Distant Early Warning Line ("DEW Line"),
began construction, providing the opportunity for wage labor in the Canadian
Arctic until 1957. Regular air service soon came to Sachs Harbour as well.

With growing assistance now available to the settlers, Banks Island families
began leaving their outlying camps and moving to Sachs Harbour, creating a
permanent settlement. The concentration of population there was complete by
1961, which also marked the last voyage to Banks Island of the iconic schooner
North Star.[7]

THE HUDSON'S BAY COMPANY AND C. T. PEDERSEN

The 1930s were not kind to the Hudson's Bay Company. In 1931 the company
posted a trading loss of $3,731,670 and a net deficit of $2,224,325. Faced with
these heavy shortfalls, the company reduced its employees' salaries by 10 percent and omitted its dividend to its shareholders, which it did not resume until
1938. But in fact the company's entire Western Arctic District was a mess.

Loading the sled dogs aboard the *North Star* at Aklavik, 1950s. Courtesy of Sven Johansson, author's collection.

During the boom years of the 1920s the HBC's traders had liberally advanced debt throughout the district. "With the increase in the price of fur and the competition among the traders to secure that fur the natives were given anything they asked for," wrote RCMP Corporal G. M. Wall. He stated that in one year alone "twenty-six power schooners were brought into the country and in many instances very little paid on them in advance. Large outfits were given on credit." Describing the 1926 season, he added, "I . . . was informed that $3,000 in credit was nothing, some of the best hunters getting up to $5,000." In 1928 the district posted a loss of $183,000, largely due to lax administrative oversight of its traders and inconsistent directives from its leadership. Richard Bonnycastle described the chaos after an inspection tour of the posts in 1928, "There is nothing stable, no continuity of policy, tremendous overhead, everything done on the spur of the moment without any thought to the future or consideration of the past." He continued, "Scarcely any progress is being made in the Western Arctic at all. Commissioner [Angus] Brabant sets up Fort Harman, Fort Hearne, Ellice River, Perry River, and practically closes Cambridge Bay; [Inspector Hugh]

Sled dogs tethered on the bow of the *North Star* prior to departure for
Banks Island, 1950s. Courtesy of Sven Johansson, author's collection.

Conn comes along determined to close Harman, Hearne, Ellice and Perry River,
opens Pearce Point, Coppermine, and Kugaryuk, moves Bathurst, King William Land and Fort Brabant. . . . Next year someone else will come along and
decide on new locations and abandon old ones." Despite this, by 1931 Bonnycastle, who faced strong resistance from many of the company's field men, had
made some progress by closing posts, getting rid of unsalable goods, winning
over some of C. T. Pedersen's non-Inuit customers, and persuading the Klengenberg family to trade with the HBC.[8]

Then in 1932, to replace the *Baychimo* (chapter 9), the company chartered
Olaf Swenson's motor vessel *Karise* to carry supplies to Herschel Island, but as a
precaution it also chartered an aircraft to meet the outbound ship at Barrow to
fly a load of furs south. The ship returned without incident, but it proved to be
small for the job, and the following year Swenson sold it to the Soviets.

In any case, in 1933 the company chartered the steamer *Anyox* for the voyage
to the Western Arctic and to carry supplies for the RCMP as well. North of
Icy Cape in the Chukchi Sea pack ice closed in on the ship, surrounded it,
and swept it northward. Near Point Barrow on July 27 it was crushed by the
floes. "Water deluged the hold. A call for help was sent out and the pumps
were started, but the vessel listed, water extinguished the fires of one boiler and
flowed to within an inch of the other's bed plates. The engine room crew . . .
sloshed grimly about in the black water, pouring coal into the single boiler to

keep the pumps going. Their shovels . . . kept her afloat until the United States coast guard cutter Northland steamed to the rescue."

The *Northland* then sent a collision mat to the *Anyox*. "The canvas was made fast by manila lines to the steamer's side above the hole, other lines being made fast to the lower edge and drawn under the keel and taut on the other side by the vessel's winches." With the *Northland* standing by, the patch slowed the leak enough for the pumps to cope. The voyage was abandoned, and the *Anyox* headed south. It was beached at Teller, Alaska, for additional temporary repairs. The ship hobbled into Vancouver on August 24, 1933, and the company sold whatever cargo that had not been spoiled.[9]

The loss of the Western Arctic supplies put the company in a tight spot. Unless it acted quickly all of its Western Arctic posts would be on very short rations and its Inuit customers would surely suffer. Scrambling, it sent its sternwheeler *Distributor* back down the Mackenzie with a second outfit. The *Distributor* reached Aklavik on August 30, where a fleet of nineteen schooners—fourteen of them owned and operated by Inuit—had been hastily assembled to carry the supplies onward. "On September 1 ten vessels left for Herschel Island with freight for that point and cargo for the [RCMP's patrol vessel] *St. Roch*, which was all ready for a rush trip through to Cambridge Bay before freeze-up. . . . On September 2 the *Rob Roy*, *Sea Wolf*, *Sea Otter*, *Anna Olga*, and *Bonnie Belle* pulled out for posts as far distant as [Walker Bay], Coppermine, and Bathurst Inlet." The trapper Nuligak remembered the event: "I was paid $40 a ton to go to Baillie Island, and made $450." The *Sea Otter*, however, carrying supplies for the company's post at Walker Bay on western Victoria Island, ran into heavy ice on the way and was forced to winter more than eighty miles west of there, in DeSalis Bay on Banks Island.[10]

With its seaborne transportation system now in disarray, in 1933 the company's senior planners were forced to reexamine their strategy for delivering supplies to the Western Arctic and to acknowledge the litany of problems with their route via Bering Strait: the failure of the *Ruby* to reach Herschel Island in 1914; the inability of the *Lady Kindersley* to proceed past Herschel in 1922 and its loss in 1924; the *Baychimo*'s hairbreadth escape in 1925, its almost yearly damage since then, and its abandonment in 1931; the unsuitability of the *Karise* in 1932; and the near loss of the *Anyox* in 1933.

The only practicable alternative to the ocean supply route was to ship outfits down the Mackenzie system. Although the cost of delivering the supplies by river had been much greater than delivery by sea, this system became much more efficient in 1925 when the Alberta and Great Waterways Railroad's "end of steel" reached Fort McMurray, Alberta, on the Clearwater River, thus bypassing all the rapids in the Mackenzie drainage except the Slave River rapids. These four sets of very dangerous rapids, where the river drops 240 feet over a distance of sixteen miles, required that northbound freight had to be unloaded at Fort Fitzgerald, Alberta, and hauled over a sixteen-mile portage road to Fort Smith, Northwest Territories. The road had been steadily improved by the Ryan brothers' transportation company, and instead of the former method of employing oxen and carts to move the freight over a swampy corduroy road, Mickey and Pat Ryan used tractors and large wagons for the haulage over their sand and clay road. In 1931 the government contracted with Ryan Brothers Transport to maintain the road and gave them exclusive rights to haul freight over it.

Nevertheless, as early as 1928 the HBC's leadership had foreseen that a change in its Western Arctic supply system might be necessary and had sent Captain Thomas Smellie to scout the mouth of the Mackenzie for a suitable port on the Beaufort Sea, while simultaneously the government surveyor and explorer L. T. Burwash used the schooner *Ptarmigan* for a similar mission. "Considerable time was spent in exploring the delta of the Mackenzie," he wrote, "to find a water route by which river steamers might reach a point where direct connection could be made with ocean-going craft."

In 1934, as a result of the undeniably greater reliability of the river route, the company established a transshipment port at Tuktoyaktuk, a shallow harbor twenty miles beyond its post in the delta at Kittigazuit (which it closed that year). Supplies would now be barged downriver to Aklavik by the *Distributor* and hauled onward by a tug to Tuktoyaktuk. There the cargo would be transferred to schooners for distribution to the company's Western Arctic posts. To help the *Aklavik* and *Fort MacPherson* with the cargo distribution the company sent its schooner *Fort James* from Newfoundland to the Western Arctic via the Panama Canal and brought the motor vessel *Margaret A.* down the Mackenzie from Fort Smith.

But the company had an equally compelling reason for setting up a post at Tuktoyaktuk: it lies about 180 miles east of Herschel Island by water, and, because foreign vessels were prohibited from sailing east of Herschel (chapter 7), the assumption was that the HBC would be able to capture the trade of the schooners that were heading past "Tuk" to the island to trade with C. T. Pedersen. "The Canalaska Trading Company was the Hudson's Bay Company's principal competition on the arctic coast," wrote Dudley Copland, a loyal company man. "It came under the direction of an old whaling master, Captain C. T. Pedersen, a shrewd and experienced trader, and a highly qualified shipmaster and ice-master. . . . Since Canalaska was American-owned, their supply ship the M.V. *Patterson* was not permitted to enter Canadian waters beyond the port of entry at Herschel Island. So their subsidiary vessels which wintered in the Arctic, had to travel to Herschel Island to get their trade supplies. The establishment of a freight trans-shipment centre by the Hudson's Bay Company at Tuktoyaktuk was a serious threat to the business which Captain Pedersen had carried on with the Banks Island Inuit; now they could be intercepted at Tuktoyaktuk on their way to Herschel Island."[11]

This assumption ignored the profound loyalty that many trappers held for Pedersen. Unlike the Hudson's Bay Company's inventory, Pedersen carried a wide variety of high-quality trade goods that were perfectly suited to the requirements of northern life. His prices, too, were lower than the HBC's, and he kept them low by rigorously controlling his labor costs. For example, by staffing the *Patterson* with a skeleton crew on leaving San Francisco, he would then take on a dozen Yupik and Iñupiat to work as deckhands and longshoremen for the arctic cruise.[12]

In 1933, the year when the *Anyox* was damaged and forced to turn back, Pedersen's was the only ship from outside to reach Herschel, and the supplies he carried saved many of the Inuit, the trapper-traders, the police, and the missionaries from a winter of privation. In fact, when the *Anyox* failed to reach Herschel, the Anglican mission at Shingle Point found itself very low on supplies. The Reverend Harold Webster wrote: "The Inspector of the RCM Police suggested that I send a radiogram to Captain Pedersen asking if I could obtain supplies from his warehouse. He replied immediately that I was to get the keys from the RCM Police at Herschel Island, and take whatever supplies I needed. It took several dog teams to move the supplies of staple foods, canned meats, dehydrated vegetables and clothing from Herschel Island to Shingle Point but our emergency was over, thanks to the Captain's generous response."[13]

The Hudson's Bay Company had been wary of Pedersen since 1914, when he was on his first voyage in command of H. Liebes and Company's *Herman*, and as the years passed, Pedersen's share of the Western Arctic trade grew. Most important—and to the benefit of all residents in the Western Arctic—Pedersen's presence forced the HBC to compete with his prices and prevented it from establishing a trading monopoly.

The mid-1930s were, however, a time of low fox prices and poor fur harvests, and Pedersen's trade produced only modest profits, despite his Olympian efforts to serve his customers. The Canalaska post at Gjoa Haven was forced to close temporarily in 1932 because his supply schooner *Emma* was unable to reach King William Island; it was wrecked in Queen Maud Gulf in 1932, leaving the Gjoa Haven post without fresh supplies. In 1934, Johnny Togluk's schooner *Hazel*, en route to Walker Bay from Herschel Island with Canalaska supplies, was wrecked in Prince Albert Sound, with very little freight saved. And in 1935 the autumn set in so swiftly that to avoid being trapped for the winter Pedersen was forced to leave the island hurriedly on August 27, with the land already covered in snow. He only barely made it out past Point Barrow. Violent labor strikes in the West Coast ports of Canada and the United States compounded his problems.[14]

After the shipping season of 1936, the government—no doubt with the encouragement of the HBC—closed Herschel Island's customs facilities and designated Tuktoyaktuk as a port of entry. Its harbor was too shallow for the *Patterson*'s deep draft. The change in location was the final blow for Pedersen; the *Patterson*'s 1936 voyage was its last to Herschel Island. Because the profits from the Northern Whaling and Trading Company (the U.S. company) and Canalaska Trading Company (the Canadian company) had been declining during the 1930s, he and Albert Herskovits and Sons made the decision to sell their assets.

When faced with rivals, the Hudson's Bay Company's modus operandi was, as we have seen, to buy out the opposition. In January 1937 Pedersen and Herskovits met with the HBC's fur trade commissioner Ralph Parsons in Montreal to propose selling Canalaska to the HBC. Their opening offer for Canalaska's buildings and equipment (including all watercraft, with the exception of the *Patterson*), inventories, and accounts receivable was $280,000.

"Pedersen's offer to sell out is just exactly what we have been expecting," crowed Richard Bonnycastle.

> He is in a very weak position. He has had a very tough row to hoe the past few years. We are closing in on him. Our Tuktoyaktuk operations have hit his Herschel Island trade very hard. We have taken all his outside transport business away from him and most of the independent traders who dealt with him have quit the country or switched to us. We have stepped up our trade at Cambridge Bay which was his stronghold and are opening two new posts at Perry River and Boothia Peninsula [Fort Ross] which will hurt him badly. On top of this has come this difficult ice year. His best trappers have not reached their trapping ground, three of his posts received no fresh supplies, his King William Land manager is frozen in 800 miles away, one of his supply boats is a wreck while his main boat the "Nigalik" requires repairs which means replacing it temporarily at least, and therefore more capital . . . and we feel he will sell out at almost any price. . . . We should recommend very favourable consideration of this opportunity to close out a most difficult competitor in the Western Arctic where there is only room for one large trading concern.[15]

The negotiations proceeded in secrecy in 1937, and in June an understanding was reached: the agreement gave the HBC the option to purchase, on or before

August 5, 1938, the *Nigalik*, Canalaska's buildings and equipment, and any supplies left on hand.[16]

Pedersen then began to wind down his business. In 1937 the Northern Whaling and Trading Company sold the *Patterson* to Charles Gilkey and associates of Seattle, who planned to carry only heavy freight as far as Barrow. The HBC agreed to allow Pedersen, at his expense, to ship his supplies down the Mackenzie on the company's equipment and to carry him and his employees to Tuktoyaktuk. At Tuktoyaktuk in 1937 Pedersen hauled the *Nigalik* out for inspection. He then went to Herschel Island by boat with his supplies and quietly tried to collect some of his outstanding debts, while at the same time the HBC's trader closed the buildings there. In 1938 the HBC bought all assets of the Canalaska Trading Company for $26,000. In 1938 and 1939 Pedersen returned to Tuktoyaktuk to conclude his business. A line in the December 1939 issue of the HBC's magazine *The Beaver* stated, "This will be the captain's last business trip to the Arctic."

Describing the end of an era in the Western Arctic, Peter Usher wrote, "In 1938, Captain Pedersen sold his interests to the Hudson's Bay Company. Although he had maintained a good share of the trade to the end, it no longer yielded much profit. . . . The Hudson's Bay Company's profits on the fur trade were no doubt falling off as well. . . . However, Pedersen could not balance his losses against the profits of a large chain of department stores in Western Canada." Pedersen told his son Charlie that he had been forced to sell Canalaska for "ten cents on the dollar" of its actual value.[17]

"The decline in trading activity along the Arctic coast after 1930 was sharp and uninterrupted," Peter Usher stated. "The creation of the Arctic Islands Game Preserve, which by 1926 included all of the Arctic Islands as well as the mainland east of Bathurst Inlet, had a profound effect on post locations. Because whites could not trap in the Preserve, all but a few independents were effectively prevented from trading there as well. . . . The Canalaska Company withdrew in 1938, and many independents left the country around that time. . . . Although [the Hudson's Bay Company] had opened 35 posts in the region prior to 1940, by the end of that year only 9 were still in operation. [L. F. "Slim"] Semmler, an independent who had operated several posts, mainly in Coronation Gulf, withdrew to the Mackenzie Delta in 1948. During the severe decline in fox prices around 1950, little or no profit could be obtained from the fur trade, and at several traditional locations the only trading outlets were operated by the Roman Catholic Mission."[18]

In the late 1930s the trapping was for the most part poor in the Western Arctic Waterway. At the end of February 1937 Ole Andreasen, at Richardson Island, on the coast of Victoria Island, wrote to Patsy Klengenberg at his post on Wilmot Island, at the entrance to Bathurst Inlet, "To bad fox trapping is very poor here. Hope some fox comes around soon." Patsy Klengenberg, who had helped to establish the Fort Ross post in summer 1937 (chapter 1), had returned west from there aboard the *Aklavik*, and, searching for new trapping and hunting grounds, had set up camp in Terror Bay on southwest King William Island. Lamenting the lack of game he found in that area, he wrote in his diary on January 31, 1938, "I sure pick the rotten place thes fall, but we down know these New Lands." A day later he added, "Thes is sure getting my goad we would have done bittir if I star at Wilonot Island. The foxes are not here."[19]

In 1938 the government restricted trapping licenses in the Northwest Territories to Natives and the few non-Natives who already possessed them. According to Peter Usher, "This brought a gradual but inevitable end to the era of the white trapper in the north, and to a lesser extent to the independent trader as well. . . . The outbreak of war hastened the decline of the white trapping and trading community, as many left to enlist in the armed forces. By the early 1950s there were only half as many posts [in the Northwest Territories] as fifteen years before; the decline being largely due to the folding of the larger companies and the departure of the independents." Elsewhere he stated, "By 1950 'The Bay' had triumphed completely, primarily because of its greater size and ability to withstand the losses incurred by such disasters as bad fox years, bad ice years when supply vessels could not get in, or even the loss of a supply vessel."[20]

With the exception of Slim Semmler and a few others, the Hudson's Bay Company had effectively achieved monopoly control in Western Arctic Canada.

CONCLUSION

In some ways the Hudson's Bay Company's experiment at Fort Ross mirrored the entire quest for arctic furs in that era, embracing as it did at first a confident response to the market for fox pelts, a response that had created not only Native population movements but also temporary wealth and benefits for the northern trappers and traders. But the market for northern furs was based not only on distant fur markets but, at its essence, on popular tastes and economic confidence among the retail customers for those furs. Most important, the market was dictated by the fashion industry, and "fashion" is, of course, notoriously fickle. And just as fashion had called for white fox in the early twentieth century, by midcentury it had developed other tastes.

With the end of the Second World War the fur markets saw the rise of demand for durable, short-haired furs, such as mink, which by then was produced in a variety of mutation colors by fur farms. Although in the 1920s mink had sold poorly because of inferior color, by the 1940s mink ranchers had overcome this problem. Because of the consistency of quality of the farmed mink, by 1945 mink amounted to almost 80 percent of the Seattle Fur Auction's sales and fox sales had fallen proportionally.

"The period just after World War Two was a prestigious one for furs in fashion, when elegance came back and was enjoyed by more women than ever before," stated the historian of fashion Elizabeth Ewing. "This elegance was ushered in by Christian Dior's New Look of February 1947. . . . It was to be the great age of the mink coat, which was to dominate the fashion world and become the most sought-after of furs by fashionable women all over the world."[21]

In 1956 a director of the Hudson's Bay Company, the furrier J. G. Links, summarized the change in the market's taste in furs and the lack of interest in fox furs in particular: "This must not be allowed to become a funeral oration. Besides, there is plenty of blue fox still sold and worn, and white fox can never be supplanted entirely. What a fall is this, though, from the days when a hundred thousand silver foxes . . . would be offered for sale, and eagerly competed for in one London auction alone. And what has become of all the other foxes, . . . all of which could be seen across some proud shoulders in the days when to be bereft of a fox was almost to be naked? If it is not to be a funeral oration I must certainly avoid mention of red fox and most other kinds, for it is impossible to speak of them except in the past tense. . . . Whether they have a future I do not know . . . but revulsions of taste have brought about other tumbles. Sometimes the victim has recovered, sometimes not. . . . Let us draw a veil over the story of fox and proceed to something more cheerful."[22]

"Although the war years brought higher prices and breathed new life into the [arctic] trapping economy," Peter Usher wrote, "its days were numbered. White fox prices in the [Northwest Territories] fell from a high of $36.00 in 1945 to $6.50 in 1950." Elsewhere Usher declared, "The end of the decade [of the 1940s] saw an economic depression worse in its effects than that of the 1930s. Another severe drop in fur prices, coupled with the steep post-war increase in the cost of living, caused great hardships throughout the North."[23]

"The end of the traditional fur trade era," he added, "came with the declining fox prices and the resulting Arctic-wide depression of the late 1940's." In the Northwest Territories "between 1945 and 1950," the Cree trapper Maxwell Paupanekis remembered, "the long-haired fur went right down in price, especially the fox, lynx, and fisher and this was the time that trapping almost collapsed. This was very hard for the trapper who had made his living on the trapline for a long time." All Northerners echoed his feelings.[24]

The activities of the trappers in the Arctic and the rewards they received for their hard work were ultimately governed by the tastes of couturiers and furriers thousands of miles away in the great urban centers of Europe and North America. And the market for white fox pelts never fully recovered from the pain of the Great Depression. Then the market for long-haired furs shrank dramatically. As the Hudson's Bay Company noted, "by the late 1930s the demand for long haired furs had fallen sharply and prices dipped below an economic level." That market was replaced by the desire for short-haired, more durable furs, such as mink, a market in which fur farming, mutation breeding, and advanced fur dyeing techniques were producing a wide variety of pelt colors.

By the end of the 1930s monopolies had been established in Chukotka and Western Arctic Canada, and in Alaska competition among buyers of furs and sellers of trade goods had decreased dramatically. Apart from some cooperative stores, the few Roman Catholic missions in Canada that bought furs, and a small number of independent traders and buyers, by the 1940s in northern Alaska and Western Arctic Canada the only other significant avenues for marketing furs were via fur auction houses in the South, while at the same time mail order catalogues provided some sources of goods. In evaluating monopolies in general, the venture capitalist Ted Forstmann stated: "Monopolies invariably produce bad products at high prices."[25]

A market for white fox pelts exists to this day, but the price — and the reward for the trapper and for the trapper's family — has never returned to the glory days of the 1920s.

CHRONOLOGY

1848	The Bering Strait whaling grounds are discovered. During the second half of the nineteenth century whaling vessels trade with Natives for baleen, walrus ivory, and furs throughout the Bering, Chukchi, and Beaufort seas.
Mid-nineteenth century	Fur is used as an ornamental article of fashion. The mass production of metal traps begins, allowing trappers to increase their catches many-fold beyond the use of deadfall traps. Metal traps reach northwestern Alaska in the 1870s.
1870–1900	Swift growth in the North American domestic fur market. A severe decrease in the caribou herds of northern Alaska occurs because of a cyclical decline in the population and possibly because of overharvest by the Natives through the use of repeating firearms. In the late 1880s this decline causes many interior-dwelling Alaskan Eskimos to begin to migrate northward and eastward toward Canada's Western Arctic.
1876	The Hudson's Bay Company completes the construction of a trail from Edmonton to Athabasca Landing, bypassing the cumbersome 200-year-old supply route from Hudson Bay via Methye Portage.
1883	To increase the efficiency of its northern supply route the Hudson's Bay Company launches the steamer *Grahame* to operate on the Athabasca and Slave rivers in the Mackenzie drainage.
1885	The completion of the Canadian Pacific Railroad allows competitors to challenge the Hudson's Bay Company's monopoly in western Canada.
1886	The Hudson's Bay Company launches the propeller steamer *Wrigley* for service to its posts on Great Slave Lake and the Mackenzie River.
1888	The Hudson's Bay Company launches the sternwheeler *Athabasca* for service between Fort McMurray and Athabasca Landing.

| 1890–1891 | Whaleships begin wintering at Herschel Island. For the next twenty years Inuit and Gwich'in sell large amounts of caribou meat to the fleet. The whalers also purchase furs, providing the Natives with access to sources of supplies other than the Hudson's Bay Company. |

1891 Dyed white fox begins to come into vogue.

The railroad reaches Edmonton, avoiding the need for steamboat transportation on the North Saskatchewan River, again simplifying the supply route to the North.

1893 Charles D. Brower and his partners in the Cape Smythe Whaling and Trading Company at Barrow, Alaska, become agents for the furriers H. Liebes and Company of San Francisco.

1894 In response to the beginning of a trend for dyed furs, most of the white foxes from Alaska and Siberia that are sold in London go to fur dyers in Leipzig.

1895–1914 The demand for furs of all types is strong and prices rise.

1896 Gold is discovered in the Klondike on the Yukon River.

1897–1899 The trail to Athabasca Landing from Edmonton is improved into a wagon road with regular stagecoach service.

1897–1908 McDougall and Secord, wholesale merchants of Edmonton, outfit fur traders and buyers in competition with the Hudson's Bay Company.

1898 The Yukon gold rush brings a massive influx of foreigners to the region. They arrive by descending the Mackenzie River and crossing the mountains to the Yukon River, by hiking over Chilkoot Pass to the upper Yukon River, and by ascending the Yukon from St. Michael, Alaska.

Gold is discovered near Cape Nome.

Seattle becomes a major supply point for the Yukon and northern and western Alaska.

1898–1899 An unfounded rumor of gold on the Kobuk River of Alaska induces many miners to overwinter there.

1899 The Nome gold rush begins. As many as 20,000 persons arrive there during the summer. A resident fleet of small schooners soon begins to trade throughout the region.

1900 A measles epidemic strikes the inhabitants of northern Alaska and the Mackenzie region, reducing the Native population.

Siberian Yupik begin to visit Nome for trade.

Ca. 1900– early 1930s Because of a lack of caribou in northeastern Alaska the Brooks Range is largely deserted by Eskimos, who are now located at coastal sites in northern Alaska and Western Arctic Canada. A few families move south over the Brooks Range to trap for furs in Koyukuk River watershed.

1902 By this date 30,000 white fox skins are being tanned and dyed in Leipzig each year.

Another epidemic of measles rages throughout northern Alaska and the Mackenzie region. At Barrow 120 persons die, and among the Indigenous Mackenzie Inuit perhaps 400 remain alive, 20 percent of the size of the population that existed a century earlier.

The Hislop and Nagle Trading Company expands its operations to the lower Mackenzie River to compete with the Hudson's Bay Company.

John Rosene's Northeastern Siberian Company gains a concession from the tsarist government of Russia to conduct mining exploration and to operate trading posts on the Chukchi Peninsula.

Ca. 1902   Ira Rank and his brother acquire the U.S. Mercantile Company in Nome and begin outfitting schooners for coastal trade throughout the region.

1903   A Mounted Police detachment is established at Fort McPherson, with patrols to Herschel Island. A permanent post is established at Herschel Island the following year.

1904–1905   The Russo-Japanese War leaves the coast of the Chukchi Peninsula unpatrolled. In 1905 the Treaty of Portsmouth concludes the Russo-Japanese War. As a result Japan receives, among other concessions, the right to operate coastal fisheries in Kamchatka and Chukotka.

1905–1906   Charlie Klengenberg overwinters the schooner *Olga* on southwest Victoria Island and trades with the Inuinnait, who had previously had no contact with the fur trade.

Ca. 1907   The Parisian couturier Paul Poiret introduces the natural uncorseted look in women's fashion, killing the market for whalebone corset stays and contributing to the increasing popularity of fur garments. In 1908 the price of whalebone collapses, shifting the focus of the Western Arctic industry from whaling to fur trapping and trading.

1909   With the decline in mining activity on the Seward Peninsula more Nome merchants seek opportunities in the coastal fur trade, outfitting small trading vessels to overwinter on the coasts of the Bering, Chukchi, and Beaufort seas.

A few Iñupiat (Eskimo) families in northern Alaska start to concentrate on fox trapping, beginning a trend that leads to the dispersal of the population along the north coast.

Elaborate fur stoles and muffs are in vogue, increasing the demand for northern furs.

Ca. 1910   A dispersal of the Yupik population on the Chukchi Peninsula commences when a group from Cape Chaplin moves west to largely unpopulated areas in the vicinity of Kresta Bay for trapping opportunities.

1911   Hislop and Nagle sells its assets to the Northern Trading Company, which, in competition with the Hudson's Bay Company, sends large outfits to its Mackenzie posts via the Northern Transportation Company.

1912	The Hudson's Bay Company initiates its expansion to the Western Arctic coast by building posts at Aklavik and Kittigazuit.
Ca. 1913	A second wave of Alaskan Iñupiat emigrants begins entering Western Arctic Canada for fur trapping opportunities.
1914	The Cape Smythe Whaling and Trading Company ceases commercial shore whaling at Barrow. Charlie Brower encourages his employees to concentrate on fox trapping, increasing the dispersal of the population on the north coast of Alaska.
	The First World War begins. Fox prices collapse because of a lack of demand for fashionable furs.
1914–1915	The British Board of Trade suspends London fur auctions. The Hudson's Bay Company halts buying furs, causing hardship and resentment among its Native customers in northern Canada. Many Northerners temporarily cease trapping and return to subsistence hunting and fishing because of low fur prices.
1914–1918	The disruption of the First World War gives North American fur merchants the opportunity to challenge European dominance. Many Canadian furs go to U.S. markets. Fur dealers invest in auction companies.
1915	The Hudson's Bay Company establishes its post at Herschel Island.
	The Alberta and Great Waterways Railroad reaches the Athabasca River, thereby bypassing the Athabasca Landing Trail, further simplifying freight transport from Edmonton.
1916	Because of a fad for fur trimming, American demand causes white fox prices at auction to rise from $6.50 per pelt in late 1914 to $23.00 in 1916.
	With the supply of German fur dyes cut off, U.S. chemists begin to develop their own.
1917	Responding to the rise in white fox prices, H. Liebes and Company sets up posts at Demarcation Point, Alaska, and Shingle Point on the Yukon coast. In winter it establishes a post at Kittigazuit in the Mackenzie delta. The following year it sets up a post at Aklavik in the Mackenzie delta.
	Two revolutions take place in St. Petersburg, Russia.
1918	Fur prices continue to rise. White fox prices at the Hudson's Bay Company's sales in London average $30.00 per pelt.
	The Canadian government designates Victoria Island as a game preserve, reserved for Inuit.
	The worldwide influenza pandemic rages throughout the North, resulting in many Native deaths.
1918–1923	Civil war ravages Siberia. Control of Chukotka changes constantly between the Bolsheviks (Reds) and the White Guards.
1919	White fox prices at the Hudson's Bay Company's sales in London reach an average of $48.75.

The Soviet government nationalizes the fur trade, buying furs at set prices.

The number of fur farms expands rapidly in Alaska and Canada. Many European furriers begin to move to New York.

1919–1920   Intense competition among the Hudson's Bay Company, the Northern Trading Company, the Lamson and Hubbard Canadian Company, and independent traders keeps fur prices high in the Mackenzie watershed and the nearby Arctic.

1919–ca. 1928   Responding to the general rise in fur prices, small independent trappers and traders descend the Mackenzie River in numbers.

1920   The Hudson's Bay Company announces plans to build a ship (the *Lady Kindersley*) to supply its Western Arctic posts via Bering Strait.

The Lamson and Hubbard Canadian Company launches the sternwheeler *Distributor* at Fort Smith to serve its posts on Great Slave Lake and the Mackenzie River.

The Canadian government designates Banks Island as a game preserve reserved for Inuit.

1920–1921   A severe but short economic recession takes place in North America and Europe, resulting in extreme deflation, unemployment, a drop in business activity, a decline in the stock market, and a slump in fur prices. Fur auction houses face large losses. In Seattle fur auction prices fall 60 percent from their 1919 level because of lack of demand, excessive speculation, and an oversupply of pelts.

1921   The Alberta and Great Waterways Railroad is extended to Waterways (today, Draper, Alberta) on the Clearwater River, thus further facilitating shipments from Edmonton to the Mackenzie drainage.

1921–1923   Vilhjalmur Stefansson places parties on Wrangel Island to trap for furs and to establish a territorial claim for Great Britain. The Soviets arrest the trapping families in 1923 and confiscate their furs.

1921–1924   The Hudson's Bay Company enters a trading agreement with the Soviets for Kamchatka and Chukotka. The investment is written off in 1924.

1922   In response to the end of the recession of 1920–1921, and with the rapid return to prosperity and rising fur prices, Alaskan Eskimo families continue to move into Canada's Western Arctic to take advantage of trapping opportunities.

An increasing market for white foxes that are dyed to imitate the much more expensive blue foxes results in an average price of $40.05 for white fox pelts in the Hudson's Bay Company's London sales. The market for muskrat skins also accelerates because they are sheared and dyed to become "Hudson seal" garments.

1923   The radio station KDKA in Pittsburgh begins broadcasting coded fur price information to traders in the North, enhancing their ability to respond quickly to the fluctuations in fur prices.

The Seattle Fur Exchange is organized, establishing a large and efficient entity to handle fur sales for trappers and traders.

The Soviets gain control over northeastern Siberia and Chukotka and
seize four American vessels on the grounds of trading without licenses, thus beginning the closure of their coasts to foreign traders.

1924   The Hudson's Bay Company completes the purchase of the Lamson and Hubbard Canadian Company and acquires its transportation subsidiary in the Mackenzie drainage (the Alberta and Arctic
Transportation Company), resulting in further efficiencies for its
northern transportation system.

The Canadian government abruptly prohibits coastal trade east of
Herschel Island by foreign ships, forcing Charlie Klengenberg and
C. T. Pedersen to trade only at the island.

Very heavy ice is encountered in the Bering, Chukchi, and Beaufort
seas, resulting in the loss of H. Liebes and Company's schooner
Arctic and the Hudson's Bay Company's *Lady Kindersley.*

The Edmonton Fur Exchange is established, adding another outlet
for trappers' and traders' furs.

1925   Olaf Swenson secures a permit from the Soviets for exclusive trade in
Chukotka. The arrangement will continue until 1931.

Late 1920s   Hollywood movie stars stimulate the demand for white and silver fox
coats and dresses.

1926   Intra-Native trade across Bering Strait is banned by the Soviets, further isolating the Chukchi and Yupik.

The Soviets establish a colony of Yupik on Wrangel Island, beginning
a permanent Soviet presence there.

1927   Fur prices continue to rise. In the Seattle Fur Exchange's June auction white fox averages $46.75, with the best grades bringing $50.00
to $55.00.

1928   H. Liebes and Company sells its Alaskan trading posts and its supply
ship, the *Charles Brower.*

Three Inuvialuit families colonize Banks Island and enjoy immediate
trapping success, foreshadowing a constant Native presence on the
island.

Influenza is carried down the Mackenzie River, resulting in more
Native deaths.

The Soviet government embarks on the first Five-Year Plan for economic development, establishing a culture base for Chukchi and
Yupik at Lavrentiya.

1929   White fox prices at the Hudson's Bay Company's sales in London
average $58.32. The stock market reaches a ten-year peak on Sep-
tember 3. It crashes on October 29.

With the support of established trading companies, the trade of which
was being undercut by itinerant fur buyers ("trippers") visiting Na-

tive trapping camps, the Canadian government restricts fur buying to existing licensed posts.

Winter air mail flights begin to settlements on the Mackenzie River. Some furs are now carried south by air, simplifying trappers' and traders' access to southern markets.

1930s	Fur prices are generally low. White fox prices drop to about a third of their high.
	The Soviet Union becomes the world's largest fur exporter.
1930	The Soviet government centralizes its fur exports by founding *Soyuzpushnina* to control all fur production and marketing.
1930–1932	As a result of the drop in fur prices the Hudson's Bay Company suffers heavy losses. In 1931 it reduces employees' salaries by 10 percent and omits its dividend to shareholders. The dividend is not resumed until 1938.
1932	Stalin declares all collective farm property in the Soviet Union to be state property.
1934	Worldwide demand for furs is weak. White fox demand is particularly weak.
	The Hudson's Bay Company closes its post at Kittigazuit and transfers it to Tuktoyaktuk to serve as a transportation hub for the Western Arctic and to intercept furs that are being carried to Herschel Island for trade with C. T. Pedersen.
	A citywide fire destroys much of Nome, Alaska, including the warehouses of many merchants and Ira Rank's U.S. Mercantile Company.
	Violent maritime labor strikes in the West Coast ports of the United States and Canada cause difficulties for John Backland Jr.'s and C. T. Pedersen's arctic supply operations.
Mid-1930s and 1940s	Fur prices remain low. Mink becomes a fur of choice, while white fox loses favor, further reducing its price.
	Many Alaskan trading posts close. Some Alaskan Iñupiat emigrate to Western Arctic Canada. Others relocate to coastal school-mission-store towns in Alaska. With fox prices remaining low, some Iñupiat families that had previously lived in the interior of Alaska's North Slope begin to leave coastal settlements and return to their former homelands.
1936	White fox prices at the Hudson's Bay Company's sales in London fall to an average of $14.22.
	Violent maritime labor strikes take place again in the West Coast ports of the United States and Canada, further complicating shipping to the North. The last voyage of C. T. Pedersen's *Patterson* to Herschel Island occurs as a result of labor troubles and declining profits in his arctic trading business.
	Herschel Island is closed as a customs port. Customs services are transferred to Tuktoyaktuk.

1937   Because of labor troubles and the loss of a government contract the last voyage to northern Alaska of John Backland Jr.'s freighting schooner *C. S. Holmes* takes place. Northern Alaskan Natives' access to supplies is reduced further.

In an attempt to simplify shipping supplies to some of its Western Arctic posts, the Hudson's Bay Company establishes its Fort Ross post on Somerset Island. The company's schooner *Aklavik*, arriving at Bellot Strait from the west, meets the ship *Nascopie*, arriving from the Atlantic.

1938   C. T. Pedersen and Albert Herskovits and Sons sell the Canalaska Company to the Hudson's Bay Company; consequently the Hudson's Bay Company establishes effective monopoly control in Western Arctic Canada.

Trapping licenses in the Northwest Territories are restricted to Natives and to those non-Natives who already hold permits.

The last recorded fur shipments take place from Brower's Cape Smythe Whaling and Trading Company to Arnold Liebes in San Francisco.

1940   The last voyage to northern Alaska of Ira Rank's schooner *Trader* occurs because of a lack of customer business.

1948   The Hudson's Bay Company closes its Fort Ross post and relocates to Spence Bay (today, Taloyoak, Nunavut).

1948–1951   Banks Island is temporarily abandoned by the Bankslanders because of low fur prices. They return in 1951 to establish a permanent settlement at Sachs Harbour.

GLOSSARY

Athapaskan	Native American societies that are speakers of Dené languages. A large number of these societies inhabit the subarctic regions of northwestern North America.
Badly sewn	Pelts in which cuts and holes have been poorly repaired.
Bankslanders	Inuit who live on Banks Island.
Baillie Island	The harbor enclosed by Baillie Island and the sandspit at the northern tip of Canada's Bathurst Peninsula. Also the name of the trading post on the sandspit.
Baleen	Also called *whalebone* or *bone*. The keratinous plates that grow from the upper jaw of bowhead whales (*Balaena mysticetus*), with which they filter plankton from the water. Because of its durability and flexibility, in the nineteenth century and the first decade of the twentieth century, baleen was widely employed for corset staying, among many other uses.
Beaming	The process of removing fat and muscle from the skin side of a raw pelt with a scraper by placing it on a beam for support.
Bering Strait	The fifty-mile-wide body of water separating the easternmost point of continental Asia, Cape Dezhnev, from the westernmost point of continental North America, Cape Prince of Wales.
Bering Strait region	For the purposes of this book, the lands and seas surrounding the southern Chukchi Sea and the northern Bering Sea, including the Chukchi Peninsula, St. Lawrence Island, and western and northwestern Alaska.
Bleaching	The application of a bleaching agent to lighten a part, or all of, a pelt, especially to remove the yellow tinge of sea mammal fat from a white fox pelt. Bleaching usually weakens the pelt's *leather*. Preliminary bleaching of arctic fox pelts was carried out by washing and via air drying in the cold and sun of late winter.

Blending	Brushing a dye solution on the tips of the *guard hairs* of a pelt to resemble a more expensive pelt.
Blind set	A trap set out of sight of an animal, such as using a thin wafer of snow to cover a trap.
Blue back	A white fox taken early in winter before the winter molt is complete, not yet fully white, an inferior pelt. See *blue pelt.*
Blue pelt	A bluish color on the skin (*leather*) side of a pelt indicating that the animal was trapped before its pelt had become prime.
Bone	See *baleen.*
Break up	The thaw in spring that fractures sea ice and river ice to allow boat navigation to commence.
Burnt	Pelts that have cracked as the result of fast drying or by grease left on the *leather side* of the pelt.
Cased	A pelt which has been removed intact from an animal, in distinction to an *open pelt*, which has been slit open along the anterior side. A cased skin could be presented *fur out* (the method for foxes) or *fur in* (the method for muskrats).
Catch bone	Baleen that was acquired directly by a trading post's own whaling crews, in distinction to *trade bone.*
Chukchi Peninsula	For the purposes of this book, those lands at the northeasternmost extremity of Asia, lying east of a line between approximately Cape Schmidt on the Chukchi Sea and Kresta Bay in the Gulf of Anadyr on the Bering Sea.
Chukchi people	An Indigenous people of northeasternmost Asia who primarily live in *Chukotka*. A group that is traditionally subdivided into "Reindeer Chukchi" (nomadic reindeer herders living in the interior lands) and "Maritime Chukchi" (sedentary coastal dwellers who concentrate primarily on sea mammal hunting and fishing).
Chukotka	The lands of northeasternmost Asia, east of the Kolyma River.
City collector	A fur buyer who assembles furs into batches large enough to export, or to send to auction, or to sell directly to manufacturing furriers.
Coarse	A pelt hard to the touch, often with stiff, wiry *guard hairs*, often late caught.
Coilspring trap	A trap in which the mechanical energy to close the trap's jaws is stored in coiled springs. This type of trap eventually became cheaper to produce than the *longspring trap.*
Copper Inuit	See *Inuinnait people.*
Corn starch cleaning	Using corn starch powder on a white fox skin to remove oil and yellowing.
Cossack	A military frontiersman in the tsar's service.
Country buyer, country collector	See *tripper.*
Coverage	The quantity of the *guard hairs* on a pelt that cover the *underfur* is described as coverage.

Cross fox	A color phase of the red fox (*Vulpes vulpes*), showing a dark cross on the back and shoulders.
Cubby	In the Arctic a cubby set is often a small housing of snow blocks consisting of three sides and a roof, but open at one end. The bait is placed at the rear of the cubby so that the animal will approach from the open end and step on the trap that is buried in front of it.
Cutter	In fur manufacturing, the cutter is the most highly paid worker because of the person's skill in blending skins together and in conforming them to a pattern.
Deadfall	A trap that captures an animal by releasing a heavy weight and pinning the quarry under it.
Density	The *underfur*'s thickness is described as density.
Dezhnevo	See *Emmatown*.
Dressed	Skins that have been tanned to preserve the pelt and treated to bring out the gloss of the fur.
Dropping	See *letting out*.
Drumming	Furs are cleaned and fluffed by putting them in a revolving drum with hardwood sawdust to absorb excess oils.
Early caught	A pelt taken early in the winter season, often with blue *leather* and less than the usual growth of *guard hair* and *underfur*. See *blue pelt*.
East Cape	Cape Dezhnev. Captain James Cook, RN, charting Bering Strait in 1778, named the easternmost point of land in Asia "East Cape," a name that was in common usage until 1898, when Tsar Nicholas II renamed it in honor of Semyon Dezhnev, who in 1648 became the first foreigner to pass through Bering Strait. The term "East Cape" continued to be used colloquially by mariners and traders well into the twentieth century.
Emma Harbor	An inner bay of Providence Bay on the Chukchi Peninsula, where the modern town of Provideniya is located.
Emmatown	The Chukchi settlement Enmytagyn southwest of Cape Dezhnev, later the site of several trading posts, and the Dezhnevo administrative center.
Eskimo people	In the Bering Strait region *Eskimo* is commonly used as a general reference to include the Iñupiat of northern Alaska, the Inupiat and Yup'ik of western Alaska, and the Yupik who live on St. Lawrence Island and in settlements on the coast of Chukotka and Wrangel Island. In Canada before the 1990s, it was employed to refer to the group now known as the *Inuit*.
Factoring	A process by which a business sells its invoices (accounts receivable) to a third party (a factor) at a discount, providing fast access to capital for the seller.
Farmed fur	Pelts that are ranch-raised; in distinction to *wild fur*.
Finisher	A worker who makes buttonholes and other final details on a fur garment.

Flat	*Guard hairs* lying flat because of a lack of *underfur*, an indication of a weak pelt.
Fleshing	The removal of fat and muscle from the *leather* side of a pelt.
Flouring	Cleaning a *raw pelt* with flour to remove oil from the fur.
Freeze up	The autumn freeze that consolidates sea ice and river ice to end the navigation season for boats.
Full furred	A pelt in prime condition with well-developed *guard hairs* and *underfur*.
Fur in	A *cased* skin with the leather side exposed, in distinction to *fur out*.
Fur out	A *cased* skin with the fur exposed; in distinction to *fur in*.
Fur press	A press used to compress pelts into bales for shipment.
Fur side	The fur side of the pelt, in distinction to the *leather* side.
Glazing	In the late phases of garment manufacture, treating a fur with mild heat to increase luster and prevent matting or curling.
Going outside	Leaving the Western Arctic for the South.
Grade, grading	The classification of furs by quality, size, and color.
Grease burn	A cracked pelt, the result of incomplete removal of fat from the *leather* before it has dried.
Greasy	Pelts on which the fat on the *leather* side has been incompletely removed.
Ground ice	A *pressure ridge* that has grounded in shallow water.
Guard hair	The long glossy hairs that protect the *underfur* of a pelt.
Gwich'in people	An Athapaskan people inhabiting the Porcupine River and adjacent regions of the Yukon and Mackenzie watersheds.
Iceblink	A white glow, the reflection on the underside of low overcast clouds indicating the presence of sea ice; in contrast to *watersky*, which is a dark reflection on the overcast that indicates open water beneath it.
Immature	An *early caught* skin lacking fully developed *guard hair* and *underfur*.
Indian Point	The large Yupik settlement of Ungaziq at Cape Chaplin on the Chukchi Peninsula.
Inuinnait people	Formerly called *Copper Inuit*. A group that traditionally inhabited the lands and waters from southwest Banks Island to near Great Bear Lake and eastward as far as western Queen Maud Gulf, including western and southern Victoria Island and the shores of Coronation Gulf.
Inuit (sing. Inuk)	Ethnonym employed to describe the Natives of Canada's Central and Eastern Arctic (which in this volume include the Inuinnait of Coronation Gulf and Victoria Island). Also broadly applied to those speakers of the Eskimo-Aleut language group.
Inupiat people	The Eskimos of Alaska inhabiting the Seward Peninsula and surrounding areas.
Iñupiat people	The Eskimos inhabiting northern Alaska, a number of whom (the *Nunatamiut*) migrated into Western Arctic Canada from ca. 1890 to ca. 1945.

Inuvialuit people	The Inuit who inhabit westernmost lands and waters of Arctic Canada, descendants of the Indigenous *Siglit* and the *Nunatamiut* immigrants from northern Alaska.
Joiner	A worker who uses a fur sewing machine to join pelt pieces together.
Jump trap	A type of trap on which the spring extends upward from beneath the trap jaws, an *underspring trap*.
Killing the fur	The process by which fur is prepared to accept a dye via the application of chemicals to remove any fatty substance on the hairs.
Kogmolit people (and various spellings)	A loose descriptor employed by *Iñupiat* and *Inuvialuit* to refer to a group of people living "to the east." Thus, to the Alaskan Iñupiat immigrants in Canada, it might refer to the Mackenzie Inuit (*Siglit*). To the Inuvialuit of the Mackenzie delta it might refer to the *Inuinnait*.
Koryak people	A Native group of northeastern Asia. Some Koryak were reindeer herders; others were sedentary coastal dwellers who fished and hunted marine mammals.
Late caught	A pelt that was caught after the fur was *prime*, often with faded color and dry, *rubbed* fur. See *springy*.
Lead	A path of open water amid ice floes.
Leather, leather side	The skin side of a pelt, in distinction to the *fur side*.
Letting out	The process in which pelts are cut into narrow diagonal strips and then sewn together to improve their drape and to allow for more consistent sewing into a larger garment. Also known as *dropping* or *stranding*.
Longspring trap	A type of trap in which the spring (or springs) extends outward beyond the trap jaws.
Loose	A pelt with hairs falling out because of exposed roots in *early caught* skins or from having been scraped too deeply during *fleshing*.
Low	A pelt without fully developed *guard hair* or *underfur*, usually found in *early caught* skins.
Luster	The reflection of light from a pelt's hairs.
Luxury furs	Among northern furs these often include—but are not limited to—white fox, blue fox, red fox, cross fox, silver fox, lynx, ermine, marten, sable, beaver, and mink.
Mackenzie Inuit	The *Siglit*, the easternmost population of the "Western Inuit." In the early nineteenth century various groups of Mackenzie Inuit inhabited the lands and waters from, approximately, Barter Island in Alaska, throughout the North Slope of the Yukon, the coastal zone of the Mackenzie River delta, and eastward as far as Darnley Bay. In the late nineteenth and early twentieth centuries the population was steeply reduced by epidemic diseases.
Mats	Clumps in the *underfur*, the result of poor pelt cleaning.
Mutation	A term applied to controlled breeding of furbearers to produce various shades of color.

Nap	The degree of length of the *guard hairs* extending past the *underfur*.
Nailing	Fastening strips of fur to a board according to the pattern of the garment.
Natsilingmiut (Netsilingmiut) people	The Inuit population that traditionally inhabited the lands and waters from southern Somerset Island to the mainland north of the Back River and nearby drainages.
Northerners	Native and non-Native residents of the Arctic.
North Slope	The lands that border northern Alaska and the Yukon, draining the American Cordillera from the Brooks Range of Alaska and British Mountains of the Yukon.
Northern Alaska	The lands lying north of the Brooks Range, from Cape Lisburne on the Chukchi Sea and eastward to the Canadian border.
Northwestern Alaska	The lands draining into Kotzebue Sound and adjacent regions lying between Bering Strait and Cape Lisburne, including the Noatak, Kobuk, and Selawik watersheds.
Nunatamiut people	*Iñupiat* people who fled famine in the drainages of the Brooks Range, many of whom moved to the North Slope of the Yukon and the Mackenzie River delta. They became known to the Indigenous *Siglit* as *Uummarmiut* ("people of the willows and evergreens").
Open pelt	A pelt which has been removed from the animal by being slit, from nose to tail, down the anterior side of an animal. In distinction to a *cased* pelt which has been removed in one piece.
Overgrown	See *springy*.
Overstretch	A pelt that has been stretched beyond its normal size, resulting in thin *leather* and a *flat*, *weak* appearance.
Outside	To a *Northerner*, going "outside" is traveling out of the Arctic to southern regions.
Outside fleet	Vessels that arrived in the Western Arctic having wintered in the South.
Pelting	The removal of the skin from the animal's body.
Plover Bay	The Yupik settlement of Egheghaq, located on the sandspit at Plover Bay in Providence Bay. It is occasionally used incorrectly to refer to all of Providence Bay.
Plucking	The removal of the *guard hairs* to expose the *underfur*, practiced on muskrat pelts to produce "Hudson seal," in imitation of a fur seal pelt.
Pointing	Gluing badger hair on pelts to imitate a more expensive fur; for example: a red fox pelt can be dyed black and pointed to imitate a *silver fox*.
Pressure ridge	Blocks of sea ice that pile onto others when ice floes are driven together by the forces of wind or current. A grounded pressure ridge, *ground ice*, forms when floes are driven against land-fast ice in shallow water.
Prime	A pelt that was caught at its peak condition, having thick *underfur* and full, glossy *guard hair coverage*, "full of life and flow."
Raw pelt	A fur that has not been tanned and processed.

Resident buyer	A purchaser of manufactured fur garments, acting as an agent for retail furriers.
Rough	Skins which have been heavily *rubbed*, usually late caught.
Rubbed	A pelt that lacks good *guard hair coverage*, caused by an animal rubbing itself against an object, often taken late in the season.
Schooner	In the Western Arctic, a term colloquially used to indicate any small vessel of up to approximately sixty feet in length, often fitted with a small gasoline engine. "Schooners" were used to travel between trapping camps and trading centers in summer and allowed the owners flexibility in choosing the location of the winter camp. In conventional nautical terminology, however, a schooner is a sailing vessel with a fore-and-aft rig, carrying two or more masts.
Set gun	A rifle or shotgun mounted in a fixed position and rigged with a baited line attached to the trigger. When an animal pulled on the bait, the gun discharged. A set gun was often employed for taking polar bears.
Shearing	Shaving a pelt's fur to produce an even texture, often done to muskrat pelts to imitate fur seal and marketed as "Hudson seal."
Shedder	A pelt that shows loss of hair, the result of either being *early caught*, hence not fully developed, or poor pelt handling because of excessive scraping on the *leather* side during *fleshing*.
"Siberia"	In the nineteenth and early twentieth centuries, a colloquial term that was loosely and imprecisely used by foreign traders and whalers in the Western Arctic to refer to Chukotka and nearby lands.
Siberian Eskimo people	*Yupik people* inhabiting St. Lawrence Island, Wrangel Island, and some coastal settlements in eastern Chukotka.
Siglit people	The Indigenous Inuit population of the Yukon's North Slope, lands adjacent to the Mackenzie River delta, and as far east as Darnley Bay. This is in distinction to the *Nunatamiut* immigrants from Alaska, who moved to Western Arctic Canada from about 1890 to 1945. Today the Siglit and Nunatamiut refer to themselves as *Inuvialuit*.
Silver fox	A color phase of a red fox, with dark fur and "silver" *guard hairs*.
Singed	A pelt with curled tips on the *guard hairs*, often the result of rapid drying too close to a source of heat.
Slight	Slight damage to the pelt.
Slip	*Guard hair* and *underfur* that slips off a pelt or pulls out easily, one of the worst types of pelt damage, often the result of rotting before the pelt was dressed. See *tainted*. See *loose*.
Snared	A pelt with fur rubbed off by the snare wire.
Snow set	A trap set in snow.
Springy	A pelt taken late in the season, with its *underfur* beginning to fall out, often lacking *guard hairs*.
Stale	A pelt more than one season old, often with *flat* fur. The *leather* may have become brittle.

Stranding	The process of lengthening and narrowing a skin by cutting and resewing in a series of diagonal strips. Also known as *dropping* or *letting out*.
Summer skin	A pelt taken in the summer, when the fur is *unprime*, often *flat* and lacking *guard hairs*.
Supercargo	The "superintendent of cargo," a member of a trading ship's crew who was in charge of its trading activities, often the person who had chartered the vessel for a trading cruise.
Tainted	One of the worst forms of pelt damage: a pelt that was not quickly removed from the animal, often the result of rotting prior to pelting, creating hairslip and bald patches.
Thin	An *early caught* or *late caught* pelt with patches of hair missing.
Tipping	Coloring the tips of the hairs on a pelt with a brush.
Ton (displacement)	A unit of measurement for the size of a ship, which is determined by the volume of water that the ship displaces, calculated as a unit of approximately 35 cubic feet, equal to the approximate volume of one long ton (2,240 pounds) of seawater.
Ton (mass)	2,000 avoirdupois pounds. A metric ton is 1,000 kilograms.
Ton (measurement)	A unit of volume for cargo freight, usually calculated as approximately 40 cubic feet.
Ton (register)	A unit of measurement for the internal cargo capacity of a ship, usually equal to 100 cubic feet.
Trade bone	*Whalebone* that was purchased in trade, in distinction to *catch bone*, which was acquired by a trading post's own whaling crews.
Trap dog	The small bar that holds the *trap jaws* in ready position and which is released when the trap pan is depressed, allowing the jaws to close.
Trap jaws	The parts of the trap that spring closed when the stored energy of the trap is released, as the result of the quarry stepping on the *trap pan*.
Trapline	The route traveled by a trapper in visiting his traps.
Trap mark	Damage to a pelt from the *trap jaws*.
Trap pan	The plate which the weight of an animal depresses, resulting in the release of the *trap jaws*.
Trap shy	An animal that has narrowly avoided being caught in a trap and has become wary of trap sets.
Tripping, tripper	An itinerant fur buyer who visits trappers in the field.
Uummarmiut people	The term used by the Indigenous *Siglit* to refer to Alaskan immigrants (*Nunatamiut*) in the North Slope of the Yukon and the Mackenzie River delta region: "people of the willows and evergreens."
Underfur	The dense hairs that insulate the animal and support the *guard hairs*. Underfur ideally should be dense and soft.
Underspring trap	See *jump trap*.
Understretch	A pelt that has not been stretched sufficiently, causing wrinkles and a sloppy appearance.
Unprime	A skin taken early in the season before *guard hairs* have developed, often with blue leather. See *blue pelt*.

Utilitarian furs	Less expensive pelts used for day-to-day wear. Among northern furs muskrat was the primary utilitarian fur.
Watersky	A dark reflection on the underside of low overcast clouds indicating open water below; in distinction to *iceblink* on the overcast, which indicates the presence of sea ice beneath.
Weak	A pelt on which the fur is not dense.
Weight	The depth of the *underfur*.
Western Alaska	For the purposes of this book, the lands and waters between Bering Strait and Nunivak Island and adjacent watersheds.
Western Arctic	For the purposes of this book, the lands and seas lying between the Boothia Peninsula of Canada and the greater Bering Strait region, including northern, northwestern, and western Alaska and eastern Chukotka.
Western Arctic Waterway	The transportation route in Canada between the Alaska border and the Boothia Peninsula, including the waters of the eastern Beaufort Sea, Amundsen Gulf, Coronation Gulf, Bathurst Inlet, and Queen Maud Gulf.
Wetted	A skin that was removed from a stretcher before it was fully dry, showing wrinkled leather that has shrunk unevenly.
Whalebone	See *baleen*.
Wild fur	Pelts that are taken in the field, in distinction to *farmed fur*, which is ranch-raised.
Wooly	A pelt missing *guard hairs*, exposing the *underfur*.
Yupik people	A group of Indigenous Eskimoan peoples of St. Lawrence Island and a few settlements in Chukotka and Wrangel Island.
Yup'ik people	A group of Indigenous Eskimoan peoples of western and southwestern Alaska inhabiting the lands and waters between Norton Sound and Bristol Bay.

NOTES

1. FORT ROSS

1. Rowley 2007: 146; Burwash 1931: 64, 104–105; George Burnham 1986: 136–138; Dalton 2006: 161–162, 168.
2. Usher 1971a: 27; Barr 1977: 9; Zaslow 1988: 137; Balikci 1984; J. W. Anderson 1961: 226–230; Copland 1985: 203–204; Finnie 1937: 49; Richard S. Finnie, personal communications to the author; Rowley 2007: 145–149; Graham W. Rowley, personal communications to the author; D. Jenness 1964: 59–61; Captain Thomas Smellie to Fur Trade Commissioner, September 9, 1937, HBCA RG 3/4A/18; log of *Nascopie* 1937, HBCA RG 3/6B/26; Lyall 1979: 108; Ernie Lyall, personal communication to the author; Scotty Gall, personal communication to the author; Dickerson 1988: 156–157.
3. Copland 1985: 214; J. W. Anderson 1961: 230.
4. Heslop 1944: 8–14.
5. J. L. Robinson 1944: 4–7.
6. J. W. Anderson 1944: 45–47.
7. Ibid.: 45–47.
8. J. L. Robinson 1944: 4–7.
9. Ibid.: 4–7; Heslop 1944: 8–14; Dunbar and Greenaway 1956: 159.
10. Murray G. Bowen to James A. Houston, August 20, 1998; James A. Houston to the author, September 25, 1998; J. W. Anderson 1944; Beattie 1991; *Arctic Circular* 1(5): 50–51, May 1948, and 2(1): 11–13, January 1949; C. P. Wilson 1947; Burwash 1931: 104–105.

    In the early twenty-first century, with its far more open ice conditions, the route might have been practicable.

2. WHITE FOX

1. R. M. Anderson 1924: 517; Brower MSc. For a description of other fur bearers that were trapped and traded in the Arctic, see Bockstoce 2009: 41–51.

2. A. R. Harding 1942: 162.
3. Brower MSa: 674–675.
4. John C. George, personal communication to the author.
5. Donald Reid et al. 2012: 120.
6. Brower MSa: 674–675.
7. Scholander et al. 1950; John J. Burns, personal communication to the author; John C. George, personal communication to the author; Hudson's Bay Company 1967: 11; Burt and Grossenheider 1976: 75; Chesemore 1970: 157; Chesemore 1972; Chesemore 1983: 155; Fay and Stephenson 1989; Pamperin et al. 2006; Pielou 1994: 273–274; Austin 1922: 9; Garrott and Eberhardt 1987: 395–406; Donald Reid et al. 2012: 120; Brower MSa: 674–675; Usher 1971b: II, 6–11; Usher 1976b: 207; www.adfg.alaska.gov/index.cfm?adfg=arcticfox.main, accessed April 11, 2015; www.iucnredlist.org/details/899/0, accessed March 23, 2015.
8. A few trappers in the Western Arctic were Polynesians, Cape Verdeans, and Japanese.
9. Hughes 1960: 126–127; Arundale and Schneider 1987: passim; D. Jenness 1957: 28–29.
    In Western Arctic Canada single-family camps were more usual, according to Peter Usher (Peter Usher, personal communication to the author).
10. R. M. Anderson 1924: 518; Usher 1971b: II, 32.
11. Maguire 1988: I, 108; Bockstoce 2009: 51–58, 280; Nelson 1969: 172–174; Murdoch 1885: 92–93; Bernard 1958: I, November 12, 1912; Nuligak 1966: 59–60; *Fur News Magazine* 10(2): 98, August 1909.
12. Gerstell 1985: passim; Roy Vincent Sr., personal communication to the author; John C. George, personal communication to the author; Thomas G. Smith, personal communication to the author; John J. Burns, personal communication to the author; Tom Parr, personal communication to the author; Finnerty 1976: 19; VanStone 1962: 34.
13. Michael Carey, personal communication to the author; Anonymous 1936: 67.
14. Van Valin 1941: 107–108; *Alaska Trappers Manual* 1991: 55.
15. David Greist 2002: 43–44.
16. Waldo Bodfish 1991: 9–10, 85–86; Hall 1997: 71.
17. Swanson 1982: 70.
18. John J. Burns, personal communication to the author; Thomas G. Smith, personal communication to the author; David Greist, personal communication to the author; James A. Houston, personal communication to the author; John C. George, personal communication to author; Brower MSa: 417; Morris 1965; Sonnenfeld 1957: 457–459; Abrahamson 1968: 51; Bailey and Hendee 1926: 15; Washburn 1999: 175; George Burnham 1986: 128; David Greist 2002: 43–44; Haugen 2000: 24; Hall 1997: 71; Poncins 1954: 28–29; Usher 1971b: II, 26–32; Dean Wilson n.d.: 36; Long 1981: 80; Swanson 1982: 70; Nelson 1969: 182; Swenson 1944: 50–51; *Alaska Trappers Manual* 1991: 55; Gilmore MS: June 21–July 12, 1931; *Nome Nugget* December 10, 1931; Van Valin 1941: 107–108; Waldo Bodfish 1991: 9–10, 85–86; Waldo Bodfish, personal communication to the author; R. M. Anderson 1924: 517–518; Hughes 1960: 126; Buckman 2015: 8.
    More recently, innovative trappers have used paper towel sheets, coffee filters, plastic sandwich bags, pieces of white trash bags, synthetic pillow stuffing, fiberglass insu-

lation, and other materials to protect the trap. For attractors some have experimented with surveyor's tape, toothpaste, sardines, red wine, and cheap perfume.

19. David Greist 2002: 54–55; Sonnenfeld 1957: 457; Nagy 1999: 125–126; Thomas G. Smith, personal communication to the author.

20. Stuck MS: March 12, 1918.

21. Thomas G. Smith, personal communication to the author.

22. John J. Burns, personal communication to the author; John C. George, personal communication to the author; Thomas G. Smith, personal communication to the author; David Greist 2002: 54–55; David Greist, personal communication to the author; Okpik 2005: 32; Condon et al. 1996: 71; Usher 1965a: 189; Usher 1965b: 53, 82, 84; Usher 1971b: II, 26; Sonnenfeld 1957: 457; Arundale and Schneider 1987: 63; Chesemore 1972: 265; Brower MSc.

   For trapline locations and distances in Canada's Western Arctic (Northwest Territories and Nunavut), see Freeman 1976, vol. 3.

23. D. Jenness 1957: 18–19.

24. Klerekoper 1977: 2.

25. David Greist 2002: 43; David Greist, personal communication to author; Nelson 1969: 175–177; Peter Usher, personal communication to the author.

26. Usher 1971b: II, 26.

27. Brower MSa: 245, 830; Bernard 1958: I, November 30, December 19, 1910, December 23, 1912, February 8, 1913; Sonnenfeld 1957: 327; Chesemore 1972: 266; Waldo Bodfish 1991: 85–86; Usher 1965b: 54; Ken Deardorf in Zarnke 2013: 174; Collins 2015: 30; L. F. ("Slim") Semmler, personal communication to the author.

28. Thomas G. Smith, personal communication to the author; John C. George, personal communication to the author; John J. Burns, personal communication to the author; Morris 1965; Copland 1985: 157; Swanson 1982: 71; Finnie 1940: 164; Hunter 1983: 18.

29. John J. Burns, personal communication to the author; *Alaska Trappers Manual* 1991: 75.

30. LaDue 1935: 25.

31. Ibid.: 35; Nagy 1999: 131.

32. Bachrach 1930: 82; *Alaska Trappers Manual* 1991: 74–75; North American Fur Auctions 1995: 3; John J. Burns, personal communication to the author; Morris 1965; *Canadian Trapper* November/December 2001: 11–13; *Hunter-Trader-Trapper* 17(1): 23, October 1908; *Fur-Fish-Game* 105(8): 14, August 2008, and 110(8): 50, August 2013; John C. George, personal communication to the author; Thomas G. Smith, personal communication to the author; Usher 1971b: II, 102–108; Hudson's Bay Company n.d.: 8–10; Poncins 1954: 29; French 1977: 94; Pinson 2004: 28; D. Jenness 1957: 38; Paupanekis 1972: 139–140; Bernard 1958: I, May 5, 1913; Nagy 1999: 131; Chesemore 1972: 266; LaDue 1935: 25.

33. George Burnham 1986: 105.

34. Klengenberg v. H. Liebes and Company, Admiralty case no. 18153, testimony of C. T. Pedersen, February 5, 1925, p. 70, and testimony of Christian Klengenberg, folder 2, March 8, 1927, p. 9–10, 16, Northern District of California, San Francisco, NARASB; Mahoney 2013: 155; D. A. Holmes, *Fur Trade Review* September 1925, 52(12): 84–88.

35. Libbey 1983.
36. Carey 2002: 63; Parr 2015b: 55; Zarnke 2013: 153–154.
37. Michael Dederer, personal communication to the author.
38. Gillham 1947: 111–112.
39. Brower MSa: 175, 675; Brown 2007: 103; Pinson 2004: 51; Webster n.d.: 52; George Burnham 1986: 120; Soplu, in North Slope Borough 1980: 81, 191; Bernard 1958: I, 62–63; Usher 1971b: II, 29; Peter Usher, personal communication to the author; Michael Dederer, personal communication to the author; Wendt 1931: 187; Gillham 1947: 111–112; Schroeder 2015: 50; *Alaska Trappers Manual* 1991: 99–100.
40. Seveck 1973: 10.
41. Bailey 1971: 116.
42. Brower MSc: 1916; *Edmonton Journal* October 30, 1909; Stuck MS: January 18, 1918; Mills 1926: 693; Parr 2012: 58–59; Parr 2015a: 54; for example, *Nome Nugget* February 3, 1934, October 23, 1935, November 1, 1935, November 16, 1935.
43. Fuchs 1968: 21.
44. Mills 1926: 693.
45. George Burnham 1986: 131.
46. Washburn 1999: 67; Klengenberg v. H. Liebes and Company, p. 3.
47. Spector 1998: 20.
48. Fuchs 1968: 24; Klengenberg v. H. Liebes and Company, p.23; Sonnenfeld 1957: 290; Michael Dederer, personal communication to the author.
49. Spector 1998: 20–22.
50. Michael Dederer, personal communication to the author.
51. Klengenberg v. H. Liebes and Company, testimony of Joseph E. Agnew, March 6, 1926.
52. Michael Dederer, personal communication to the author; Bachrach 1930: 556; *Seattle Post-Intelligencer* January 10, 1928; Links 1956: 19.
53. Anonymous 1936: 71.
54. Ruttle 1968: 29.
55. Links 1956: 53–54; Ruttle 1968: 9, 15, 26.
56. Bachrach 1930: 69, 87, 286–287; Obard 1987; Petersen 1914: 67; Ruttle 1968; Samet 1950; Saskatchewan 1964; Schroeder 2016b: 48.
57. Links 1956: 24–25.
58. Michael Dederer, personal communication to the author.
59. Links 1956: 20.
60. Bachrach 1930: 556–557; Michael Dederer, personal communication to the author.
61. Links 1956: 27.
62. Manfred Garfunkel, personal communication to the author; Bachrach 1930: 284, 571–580; Taylor 1946: 20–21; Fuchs 1968: 6, 32–34; Mills 1927a; Petersen 1914: 49; Goett 1926: 75–76; Austin 1926.
63. Austin 1926: 55.
64. Poland 1892: 90; *Fur Trade Review* 31(9): 194, May 1904; *Fur Trade Review* 48(9): 102, May 1921.
65. Taylor 1946: 21–22.

66. Austin 1922; Austin 1926: 55; Bachrach 1930: 581–590.
67. *Fur Trade Review* 51(10): 146, July 1924; Austin 1928: 69.
68. Mills 1927a: 14.
69. Bachrach 1930: 284, 571–580.
70. Ewing 1981: 128.
71. Mills 1927b: 137.
72. Anonymous 1936: 66; Taylor 1946: 22–24, 32–33; Mills 1927b; Ben Thylan, personal communication to the author; Irene Spirer, personal communication to the author.
73. Fuchs 1968: passim.

PART 2. DEVELOPMENT OF THE WESTERN
ARCTIC FUR TRADE TO 1914

1. Wilcox 1951: 122, 155.
2. Ewing 1981: 98, 102, 113, 115; Ewing 1978: 60; Callan 1998: 177.
3. Clayton 1966: 71; Fuchs 1968: 4.
4. J. W. Jones 1913: 151–159; Poland 1892: 90; Ray 1990: 52–61, 63–64; Wilcox 1951: 157, 166, 168–170; *Fur Trade Review* 21(8): 115, March 1894, 29(10): 282, June 1902, and 30(3): 529, October 1902.
5. Gernsheim 1963: 92, 94; Ewing 1978: 113; Ewing 1981: 120–121; Wilcox 1951: 156, 158; Links 1956: 57–58; Benioff 1936: 9; J. W. Jones 1913: 153; Bockstoce 1986: 335–338.

3. THE ADVANCE OF THE MARITIME TRADE
IN THE BERING STRAIT REGION

1. Bockstoce 2009: 92–112.
2. Bockstoce 1986: 193–194; Bockstoce and Botkin 1983; Bockstoce and Botkin 1982; Aldrich 1889: 134; Bogoras 1904–1909: 62.
3. Bockstoce 1986: 193; Cook 1926: 147; *Seattle Post-Intelligencer* September 7, 1911, and April 10, 1912; Seveck 1973: 10; Bogoras 1904–1909: 62; whaleship *Frances Palmer* June 17, 1887, KWM 462a, NBWM.
4. Bockstoce 1986: 197–199; Bogoras 1904–1909: 62–63. The *Henrietta* was renamed *Kreiserok* (*Little Cruiser*) and served as a Russian patrol boat until its loss with all hands on October 26, 1889, at Cape Soya on the north coast of Hokkaido.
5. Klingle 2013: 139; Spector 1998: 12–17; Bockstoce 2009: 356.
6. Cole 1984: 38 and passim.
7. Gitlin et al. 2013: 6; Cole 1984: 38.
8. G. B. Gordon 1906: 74–75; *Nome Daily Gold Digger* May 26, 1905.
9. J. W. Anderson 1961: 170; Mahoney 2013: 155.
10. Chapelle n.d.; *Nome Nugget* September 8, 1910.
11. *Nome Nugget* January 19 and May 3, 1912.
12. *Nome Weekly News* October 20, 1906; *Nome Daily Gold Digger* September 7 and 12, 1907; Bogoras 1904–1909: 64, 68.
13. Krupnik and Chlenov 2013: 11.

14. *Nome Daily Gold Digger* September 17, 1909; Owen 2008: 49, 59, 85; Vanderlip and Hulbert 1903; Hanssen 1936: 155–160; Krupnik and Chlenov 2013: 10–15; Igor Krupnik, personal communication to the author, June 30, 2016.

15. Koren 1909: 27; Koren MSc: September 22, 1912, October 7, 1912; *Nome Nugget* March 21, 1913, September 17, 1915, September 25, 1915; *Seattle Post-Intelligencer* March 21, 1913, June 11, 1915; *New York Times* July 23, 1915; Wikan 2000: 109–202; Amory MS 1914–1915; Portenko 1981: 9–11.

16. *Nome Nugget* Mining and Dredging Edition, October 1913; Madsen 1957: 16; *Nome Daily Gold Digger* July 7, 1907, June 22, 1909; Nome Customs Records ledger passim; *Nome Nugget* August 8, 1910, October 3, 1910, August 10, 1911, September 20, 1911, January 19, 1912, August 21, 1916.

17. *Nome Daily Gold Digger* June 24, 1909; *Nome Weekly Nugget* March 14, 1905; Van Valin 1941: 131. Madsen 1957: 16; *Nome Daily Gold Digger* July 7, 1907, June 22, 1909; Nome Customs Records ledger passim; *Nome Nugget* August 8, 1910, October 3, 1910, August 10, 1911, September 20, 1911, August 21, 1916; I am grateful to Igor Krupnik for his observations.

18. *Nome Daily Gold Digger* August 27 and December 31, 1902; Ira Rank to Isobel W. Hutchison, March 10, 1935, Hutchison MSS; Yarzutkina 2014: 372; Bockstoce 1986: 277.

19. Vinkovetsky 2011: 65–66.

20. Krupnik and Chlenov 2013: 11–12.

21. Stephan 1994: 87; Vinkovetsky 2011: 65–66; Krypton 1953: 98; Krupnik and Chlenov 2013: 11–13; Vanderlip and Hulbert 1903: 297.

22. Krypton 1953: 122; Bogoras 1904–1909: 68; Stephan 1994: 86–89; Znamenski 1999a, 1999b; Starokadomskiy 1976: 98.

23. *Nome Daily Gold Digger* September 11, 1906, July 8, August 8 and August 22, September 11 and September 20, 1907, May 30, 1908, July 15, 1909; Gordon 1906: 74–75; Brown 2007: 109–110; W. B. Jones 1927: 58, 157–158.

24. Bogoras 1904–1909: 62.

25. Mackiernan interview passim.

26. Kirillov 1912: 339–340.

27. Bogoras 1904–1909: 68.

4. EXPANSION OF THE TRADE IN NORTHERN ALASKA AND WESTERN ARCTIC CANADA

1. Brower MSa: 443; Brower MSc.

2. Bockstoce 1986: 231–254. Rev. S. R. Spriggs to Sheldon Jackson February 1, 1907, in Jackson 1908: 54.

3. *Seattle Post-Intelligencer* May 11, 1910.

4. Jackson 1908: 53–54; Sonnenfeld 1957: 304.

5. Stefansson 1924: 387.

6. Ibid.: 60–61.

7. Bailey and Hendee 1926: 22; Brower MSb: 21; Driggs to Wood July 3, 1903, St. Thomas Mission papers, ECHS; *Vancouver Province* November 15, 1902.

8. Whittaker 1937: 241–243; Burch 1998: 47, 77, 133, 166, 187, 303, 325, 373; E. S. Burch Jr., personal communication to the author; Hartson Bodfish 1936: 216; Pratt et al.: forthcoming.

9. Simon Paneak in Hall 1997: 39–40 and passim; Brower MSa: 629.

10. Leffingwell 1919: 66–67; Brower MSb: 21, 30; Brower MSa: 629; Stefansson 1909: 606–608; Gubser 1965: 14; S. R. Spriggs to Sheldon Jackson February 1, 1907, Jackson 1908: 46; U.S. Census, 1910; Simon Paneak in Hall 1997: 24–25, 39–40, and passim.

11. *Seattle Post-Intelligencer* November 21, 1909; *Hunter-Trader-Trapper* May 1909, 18(2): 104, 107, August 1913, 26(5): 88–89, November 1913, 27(2): 133; Hartson Bodfish 1936: 78; Brower MSa: 647.

12. Brower MSa: 638, 655; Hartson Bodfish 1936: 280; Bockstoce 1986: 335–337; unidentified newspaper clipping December 18, 1912, Old Dartmouth Historical Society, scrapbook no. 2, NBWM; Swenson 1944: 90–91; *Seattle Post-Intelligencer* February 14, 1913; Kilian 1983; Brower MSc; Brower MSb: 37; Sonnenfeld 1957: 322–323; Tower 1907: 128; *Fur Trade Review* July 1926, 53(10): 52.

13. Brower MSa: 677; Leffingwell 1919: 67; Simon Paneak in Hall 1997: 34; D. Jenness 1918: 94–95, 98; Kakinya and Paneak 1987: 386–391.

14. Burch 2012: passim; Friesen 2013: 63; David Morrison in historymuseum.ca/cmc/exhibitions/archeo/nogap/pinvue/shtml; Crowe 1991: 128; Pálsson 2001: 108; Nuyaviak in Nagy 1994: 55; Whittaker 1937: 225–226; Usher 1971b: 175.

15. Whaleship *Grampus* journal, ODHS 948A, NBWM; Bockstoce 1986: 255–276; Bockstoce and Botkin 1983.

16. Stefansson 1914: 175, 194–195; Bockstoce and Batchelder 1978b; Bockstoce 1986: 255–289; Cook 1926: 74–76; W. S. Mason 1910: 73, 77.

17. Bodfish MS 1897–1899; Hartson Bodfish 1936: 78; Bockstoce 1986: 272–276.

18. Pálsson 2001: 177–178.

19. Stefansson 1922: 127; A. H. Harrison 1908: 97, 251, 259ff. Unfortunately for the new owners, the *Sophia Sutherland* was lost that summer, driven ashore in a gale at Baillie Island. *Seattle Post-Intelligencer* March 13, 1905; Nuligak 1966: 31; Stefansson MS: September 4, 1906, and p. 139; *Edmonton Bulletin* October 6, 1909.

20. Bodfish 1936: 225; whaleship *William Baylies* journal, August 7, 1905, ODHS 955, NBWM; Nuligak 1966: 41; Klengenberg 1932: 128–129; Commissioner, Royal Northwest Mounted Police, to Comptroller, April 13, 1910, RG 18, vol. 487, vol. 391, RNWMP fonds, LAC.

21. Stefansson 1922: 48–56; Stefansson 1921: 306; *San Francisco Chronicle* October 25, 26, and 31, 1907; *Seattle Post-Intelligencer* November 25, 1906, and July 24, 1907; Klengenberg 1932: 61, 195–253; Joseph Bernard 1958: I, 34, 437; A. H. Harrison 1908: 134–135, and MSS: August 1906; Nuligak 1966: 44–45; United States v. Christian J. Klengenberg, Circuit Court of the United States, Ninth District, Northern District of California, Criminal Cases 2182 and 4484, NARASB.

Twenty-five years later Klengenberg dictated his autobiography, *Klengenberg of the Arctic*, to the writer Tom MacInnes (Klengenberg 1932). In regard to his brushes with the law and with other traders, it is a self-serving account, with occasional inaccuracies, distortions, omissions, and factual errors. Moreover, Klengenberg's account was transcribed by a writer who apparently was unfamiliar with the Western Arctic. Mac-Innes also admitted to being hard of hearing and to having difficulty understanding Klengenberg's accent: "Klengenberg's pronunciation was sometimes a bit difficult for my deaf ear, and the way he wrote his scrappy English confused me" (Klengenberg 1932: 352). Klengenberg died in Vancouver, BC, on May 4, 1931, before the manuscript was completed.

"Klinky was one bad bastard, It's a matter of record," said Bill White, a former RCMP constable. But he added, "For such a bad bastard Klinky sure had nice kids" (Patrick White 2004: 80–82).

22. A. H. Harrison 1908: 134–135; Nuligak 1966: 44–45.

23. *San Francisco Chronicle* October 9, 1902; Morrison 1973: 220.

24. Nuligak 1966: 50, 53; *Edmonton Journal* September 21, 1909; Pálsson 2001: 142.

25. Bernard 1958: I, 33; Bodfish's *Herman* journal, September 3, 1909, ODHS 957, NBWM.

26. Brower MSa: 634; U.S. Customs Wreck Report, filed at San Francisco, September 30, 1908, http://alaskashipwreck.com/shipwrecks-by-area/northern-alaska-shipwrecks-2/northern-alaska-shipwrecks/.

27. Bernard 1958: I, 34; Brower MSa: 626–627, 634, 638; Brower MSb: 30–31. *Nome Daily Gold Digger* September 16, 1908.

    Bernard (1958: I, 34) states that he met Klengenberg and the *Olga* near Point Barrow. He confuses the *Olga* with Klengenberg's *Ivy*. By this date the *Olga* was at Nome, having spent the winter of 1908–1909 at Cape Halkett, east of Point Barrow. Mogg was preparing to winter the *Olga* at Nome, but the ship was driven ashore in a strong autumn gale (*Seattle Post-Intelligencer* October 28, 1909).

28. Bernard 1958: I, 40; logbook of *Argo*, September 2, 1909, Leffingwell MS.

29. Report of Sergeant Fitzgerald, *Edmonton Journal* September 3, 1909; Royal Northwest Mounted Police, reports for the years 1908 (p. 143), 1909 (p. 131), and 1910 (pp. 24, 149–151, 181); *Hunter-Trader-Trapper* October 1914, 27(1): 36; Bernard 1958: I, 59.

30. Royal Northwest Mounted Police, report for 1912: 179, 181; Kilian 1983.

31. Bernard 1958: I, 63–64.

32. Ibid.: 72–93, 118–119.

33. Ibid.: 122–130.

34. Ibid.: 141–142.

    Bernard called it the "Kugaryuak River." Later, Hudson's Bay Company men called it the "West Kugaryuak River" or "Little Kugaryuak River" to differentiate it from another Kugaryuak farther east. Others called the Asiak River "Joe's River." To eliminate the confusion, in 1928 the Geographic Board of Canada identified it as the Asiak River (S. Jenness 1995: 15–16, 102–103).

35. Bernard 1958: I, 143.

36. Ibid.: 148–149.

37. Ibid.: 153.

38. Ibid.: 155, 171, 181.

39. Condon 1992; Bernard 1958: I, 189; Pálsson 2001: 259.

40. *Nome Nugget* June 19, 1911.

41. Bernard 1958: I, 249–251, 259; Klengenberg 1932: 263–266.

    Joe also learned from Klengenberg that one of the first entrants into the region for trade, like Joe, had been Samuel ("Scotty") McIntyre, who, in lieu of wages, had acquired the fifty-foot gasoline auxiliary ketch *Argo* from Ernest DeKoven Leffingwell, having assisted him for several years in mapping the Canning River region of northern Alaska. In 1912 McIntyre arrived at Herschel from Flaxman Island with a crew consisting of the whaler-turned-prospector Henry T. ("Ned") Arey, his wife, their son Gallagher, and several other children. The *Argo* was provisioned for a three-year voyage to southeastern Banks Island or western Victoria Island, the area where McIntyre had wintered in 1907–1908 with Billy Mogg, when he was the mate aboard the schooner *Olga*. He had planned to prospect for copper and to trade with the Inuit, but his engine was out of order (and was left behind at Herschel Island), and the ketch was leaking so badly that he was forced into winter quarters for 1912–1913 at Shingle Point on the Yukon coast. The *Argo* spent the winters of 1913–1914 and 1914–1915 in Argo Bay on the east coast of the Parry Peninsula. Until his death in 1927 McIntyre traded primarily on the mainland coast of Western Arctic Canada, ranging as far east as Coronation Gulf, and receiving his supplies from other trading vessels (Bernard 1958, I: 499).

42. Bernard 1958: I, 266 and passim.

43. Ibid.: 280–300. "Old John" Kuhl is often referred as "Old John Cole." *Nome Daily Gold Digger* September 7, 1907.

44. Bernard 1958: I, 349.

45. Ibid.: 362–363.

46. Ibid.: 371–372.

47. Ibid.: 372, 505, and 1958: II, 60; Whalley 1962: 118–119; D. Jenness 1928: 76–80; Richling 2012: 99–100.

48. Bernard 1958: I, 375–376, 411.

49. R. M. Anderson 1943: 766; Bernard 1958: I, 12, 423–494 passim.

    Arthur Rank tried to charter the *Teddy Bear* to return to Point Hope with a winter's stock of goods, but Joe wanted a break from the Arctic. Arthur Rank then chartered the Native-owned schooner *New Jersey*. On the way to Point Hope it was lost with all hands in Kotzebue Sound.

50. D. Jenness 1928: 240.

PART 3. HEYDAY OF THE WESTERN ARCTIC FUR TRADE, 1914 TO 1929

1. Sonnenfeld 1957: 335.

2. Belden 1917: 478–479; Ray 1990: 98, 105.

3. Teien MS: 94, 99, and passim; Arestad 1962; Petersen 1914: 68–69; C. Harding to Fur Trade Commissioner, from Barrow, August 23, 1914, HBCA A.12/FT 295/1(b); Madsen 1957: 253–254; Swenson 1944: 94; *Hunter-Trader-Trapper* November 1914, 29(2): 127, and October 1915, 31(1): 53; *Seattle Post-Intelligencer* October 26, 1914; log of schooner *Ruby*, August 29, 1914, HBCA A.12/FT 295/1(b).

4. *Seattle Post-Intelligencer* October 7, 1914; *Fur News Magazine* 21(4): 10, April 1915; *Nome Nugget* July 6, 1915; Royal Northwest Mounted Police, report for 1915: 189: Brower MSc.

5. Benioff 1936: 9; Belden 1917: 478–480.

6. *Edmonton Bulletin* July 12, 1914; *Fur News Magazine* 24(1): 10 and 30(2): 10; Sonnenfeld 1957: 335–336; Fuchs 1968: 4; A. Ray 1990: 96–97, 170; Laut 1921: 4; *Fur Trade Review* May 1921, 48(9): 102; *Seattle Post-Intelligencer* December 26, 1915, February 18, 1917, December 17, 1918.

7. Innis 1970: 357; *Fur News Magazine* 23(2): 34; *Hunter-Trader-Trapper* January 1916, 31(4): 134, February 1919, 37(5): 86, November 1919, 39(2): 74; Belden 1917: 158; *Seattle Post-Intelligencer* October 22 and November 2, 1915; Liebes 1917, August 4–6, 1917; Norman E. Freakley to James Thomson, October 24, 1918, HBCA A.12/FT 295/1(b).

8. Laut 1921: 6, 25; A. Ray 1990: 102.

9. J. W. Anderson 1961: 138.

10. *Economist* November 8, 2014; *Seattle Post-Intelligencer* October 6, 1920; *Hunter-Trader-Trapper* March 1919, 37(6): 68; *Fur Trade Review* September 1920, 48(1): 138, July 1922, 49(10): 99–100; Sonnenfeld 1957: 336; Isto 2012: passim.

11. *Fur Trade Review* July 1924, 51(10): 146.

12. A. Ray 1990: 128; Wilcox 1951: 159; *Fur Trade Review* March 1921, 48(7): 83, November 1921, 49(3): 180, July 1922, 49(10): 182, and January 1927, 53(4): 138, August 1929, 56(11): 20; *Fur-Fish-Game* February 1929, 49(2), February 1930, 51(2); Sonnenfeld 1957: 336; Ashbrook and Walker 1925: 32–33; Isto 2012: 92–93; Wilcox 1951: 185; William Boucher, personal communication to the author.

13. E. D. Jones MSS: June 9, 1929; *Fur Trade Review* May 1928, 55(8): 52, March 1929, 56(6): 16, and April 1929, 56(7): 48, 55.

14. *Seattle Post-Intelligencer* July 14, 1928.

15. *Fur Trade Review* 49(10): 84.

16. *Fur Trade Review* 53(11): 18–19.

17. *Fur Trade Review* 54(12): 42.

18. *Fur Trade Review* 55(7): 62.

19. *Fur Trade Review* 55(9): 16.

20. *Fur Trade Review* 56(4): 17, 112.

21. *Fur Trade Review* 56(7): 10.

22. *Fur Trade Review* 56(8): 106.

5. REVOLUTION AND CIVIL WAR ON THE CHUKCHI PENINSULA

1. Krupnik and Chlenov 2009; Krupnik and Chlenov 2013: 67–103, 143, 145–146; Krupnik 1994: 57, 63–68; Bockstoce 1986: 136–142.

2. *Nome Nugget* September 25, 1914, and June 22, 1916; *Edmonton Journal* November 6, 1919; *Seattle Post-Intelligencer* August 10, 1913, and June 24, 1922; Masik and Hutchison 1935: 139; Bergman 1927: 34.

3. Phoenix Northern Trading Company [1921?]; Ashton 1928: ix–x, 172–174.

4. S. Jenness 2011: 69–70; Krupnik and Chlenov 2013: 15; *Seattle Post-Intelligencer* De-

cember 10 and 13, 1920; *Nome Nugget* July 2 and August 20, 1917, August 5, September 25, October 2, 1918; J. B. Burnham 1929: 26, 59–60.

5. Stephan 1994: 116–117.

6. HBCA A.12/FT 295/1(b), October 24, 1918; Masik and Hutchison 1935: 139.

7. *Fur Trade Review* May 1927, 54(8): 76–77; Dikov 1989: 146–156; *Nome Nugget* May 29, and June 12, 1920, July 30, 1921; HBCA A.12/FT 295/1(b), October 24, 1918; Masik and Hutchison 1935: 139, 147ff., 160–161.

8. Krupnik and Chlenov 2013: 16.

9. Armstrong 1965: 111, 162–163; Bergman 1927: 28, 60, 86, 148; J. B. Burnham 1929: passim; Forsyth 1992: 243; *Fur Trade Review* July 1925, 52(12): 88; Gapanovich 1933: I, 75–79; Holmes 1925: 88; Krupnik and Chlenov 2013: 15–17; W. B. Lincoln 1994: 316; Mawdsley 2008: 235; Vaté 2005: 86–87; Wood 2011: 187–189; *Seattle Post-Intelligencer* October 6, 1920.

10. Krupnik and Chlenov 2013: 15–16.

11. Forsyth 1992: 237, 243, 263; Swenson 1944: 90–92, 102–109, 118, 127–144, 163, 165; Krupnik and Chlenov 2013: 225; Crow et al. 2010; Brower MSa: 669; Liebes 1917, September 25; *Nome Nugget* July 31, 1920; *Seattle Post-Intelligencer* April 5, 25, 27, May 14, 1921, March 14, 18, 29, 1922, February 7, 1923, November 10, 1925, and August 25, 1938; *Fur Trade Review* May 1922, 49(8): 126–128; Alexander Gumberg to Senator William E. Borah, July 13, 1923, Alexander Gumberg Papers, box 2, WHS.

12. Saul 2006: 105; Krupnik and Chlenov 2013: 16; Dikov 1989: 146–156; *Nome Nugget* June 12 and 19, 1920, June 25 and July 30, 1921; Crow et al. 2010; *Seattle Post-Intelligencer* November 9, 1920.

In 1925 the Soviets managed to refloat and repair the *Polar Bear*, renamed it the *Polyarnaya Zvezda* (*Pole Star*), and used the schooner to transport badly needed supplies to the Kolyma from a cache on the arctic coast. The following year it became the first vessel of modern times used to reach the Lena River delta by sea. It wintered at Yakutsk in 1927–1928. In 1929 it was declared dilapidated and unseaworthy (William Barr, personal communication to the author, September 25 and November 10, 1986; Barr 1988; Ermolaev and Dibner 2009: 64–65, 81).

13. Wilmers 2010: 65; *Seattle Post-Intelligencer* September 12, 1921; Holmes 1925: 88.

14. Forsyth 1992: 247; Willersley 2005: 694; *Nome Nugget* February 25, 1922, June 23, and July 7, 28, and October 6, 1923, and May 5, 16, and August 22, 1925, July 23 and August 27, 1927; *Seattle Post-Intelligencer* June 19, 20, 23, July 3, 27, 29, 30, 31, 1923, and August 21 and September 19, 1925; *Fur Trade Review* September 1923, 50(12): 160–161; Gottschalk MS: 71–75; Hutchison MSS: August 15, 1933; Rasmussen 1927: 364.

15. HBCA H2-222-3-3 and 4; Gapanovich 1933: I, 179; Stefansson 1926: 95; *Nome Nugget* August 19, 1922; Dalton 2006: 48–58.

16. HBCA H2-222-3-3; *Fur Trade Review* October 1923, 51(1): 87–88 and May 1924, 51(8): 85–86; *Seattle Post-Intelligencer* May 7 and July 24, 1924, and August 25, 1938.

17. Forsyth 1992: 247; Wilmers 2010: 65; Willersley 2005: 694; *Nome Nugget* February 25, 1922, June 23, and July 7, 28, and October 6, 1923, and May 5, 16, and August 22, 1925, July 23 and August 27, 1927; *Seattle Post-Intelligencer* September 21, 1921, June 19, 20, 23, July 3, 27, 29, 30, 31, 1923, and August 21 and September 19, 1925; *Fur Trade*

Review September 1923, 50(12) 160–161; Gottschalk MS: 71–75; Willersley 2005: 694; Hutchison MSS: August 15, 1933; Albert Herskovits and Sons to C. T. Pedersen, June 20, 1923, and C. T. Pedersen to Albert Herskovits and Sons, July 5, 1924, Northern Whaling and Trading Company Collection, series 1, nos. 8, 9, 10, UAA; Holmes 1925: 88; Rasmussen 1927: 364.

18. *Nome Nugget* June 27 and August 22, 1925, June 6, July 10, August 21, September 4, 1926, August 27, 1927, October 20, 1928, March 2, 9, August 31, September 14, 21, October 26, November 2, 9, 23, 30, December 7, 1929, January 7, 11, February 1, 22, March 15, April 5, July 12, September 27, 1930, and August 24, 1938; John Borden 1929: July 15 and August 17, 1927; *Seattle Post-Intelligencer* May 7, 1924, September 9, 1925, June 25 and July 1, 1927, June 1, 1928, February 13, March 11, April 1, June 17, July 16, 31, August 12, 13, 31, September 3, November 15, 21, December 29, 31, 1929, January 13, 17, 26, 27, 28, February 9, March 1, 31, July 8, August 4, September 20, 21, 23, 1930, January 9 and August 2, 1931, and August 25, 1938; *Fur Trade Review* August 1927, 54(11): 67, October 1927, 55(1): 42, 44, 46, September 1929, 56(12): 34, March 1930, 57(6): 72, 74, April 1930, 57(7): 67–68, May 1930, 57(8): 30, June 1930, 57(9): 43, July 1930, 57(10): 18–19, 64, September 1930, 57(12): 15–17, December 1932, 60(3): 22; September 1933, 60(12): 37–38; Belov 1959: 217–223; Crow et al. 2010; Courtney Borden 1928: 149; Swenson 1944: passim; Pinson 2004: 135–141; *Seattle Sunday Times* May 8, 1932; Harkey 1974: 234–255; Gleason 1977: 10, 155; E. D. Jones MSS: September 2, 1929, September 27, 1930, and May 11, 1931; Schweitzer and Golovko 1995: 36; Marchenko 2012: 219–220.

19. D. Jenness 1957: 156–157; Jenness and Jenness 2008: 129–130; Krupnik and Chlenov 2013: 113–114; Krupnik and Chlenov 2009; Krupnik 1994.

20. Krupnik 1994: 69; Slezkine 1994: 134, 165, 174, 287–288; Vakhtin 1992: 11; Bobrick 1992: 18–19; Shnirelman 1994: 206; E. D. Jones MSS: June 21, 1929.

21. Swenson 1944: 136–137.

22. Krupnik 1994: 69; Slezkine 1994: 134, 165, 174; Vakhtin 1992: 11; Bobrick 1992: 18–19; Swenson 1944: 136–137; Sablin 2012: 226; Wood 2011: 198; Rasmussen 1927: 361–372.

23. E. D. Jones MSS: June 23, 1930.

24. Bockstoce 1986: 143–146; Bockstoce 2009: 279, 402n33.

25. G. W. Smith 2014: 292.

26. Armstrong 1965: 164–165; *Nome Nugget* September 1, 1919, and August 19, 1922; *Seattle Post-Intelligencer* October 26, 1928, and August 23, 1934; Diubaldo 1967; Hanable 1978; H. G. Jones 1999: 91–102; Seveck 1973: 13; Portenko 1981: 30; Barr 1972; Krupnik and Chlenov 2013: 80–82; Slezkine 1994: 287–288; Stefansson 1926; Rasmussen 1927: 368–369, 378; Hilda Webber, personal communication to the author; Marchenko 2012: 231–237; Igor Krupnik, personal communication to the author, June 30, 2016; Russell Potter, personal communication to the author.

6. GROWTH OF THE TRADE IN NORTHERN ALASKA

1. Brower MSa: 681–682, 694. I have corrected some of Brower's typographical errors.
2. Stuck 1920: 214.
3. Brower MSa: 649, quoted in Blackman 1989: 22; Leffingwell 1919: 66.

4. U.S. Customs Wreck Report, filed September 27, 1913, at Nome, http://alaskaship wreck.com/shipwrecks-by-area/northern-alaska-shipwrecks-2/northern-alaska-ship wrecks; Brower MSa: 668, 670, 694; Andrews 1939: 76.

5. Brower MSa: 694, 737, 776, 780–781; North Slope Borough 1980: 73; Libbey 1983: 16–17; *Fur Farmer Magazine* August 1927, 4(2): 27; Arundale and Schneider 1987: 61.

6. Mikkelsen 1909: passim; Brower MSa: 665; Brower MSb: 37; Leffingwell 1919: 67; D. Jenness 1918: 94; D. Jenness 1957: 12, 136; *Fur News Magazine* 21(4): 10, April 1915; Hall 1997: 72; Chance 1966: 16; Burch 1975: 31–32; Blackman 1989: 22; Koonuk et al. 1987: 46; U.S. Census for Barrow, 1910 and 1920.

7. U.S. Customs Report of Casualty filed at Collection District 31 (Port of Nome); U.S. Customs Report of Casualty filed at Collection District 28 (Port of San Francisco) http://alaskashipwreck.com/shipwrecks-by-area/northern-alaska-shipwrecks-2/north ern-alaska-shipwrecks; Pedersen to Director, February 21, 1924, Northwest Territories and Yukon Branch, Department of the Interior (Northern Administration Branch), RG 85, vol. 747, file 4244, LAC; Brower MSa: 713, 721–726, 787–788; Andrews 1939: 77; G. Newell 1966: 357; Kelly 1951; *Seattle Post-Intelligencer* March 27, 1921, June 18, 1924, and October 26, 1924; Diary of Percy Patmore, 1924, HBCA RG 3/8/3; log of *Lady Kindersley* HBCA C.1/446; interview with Percy Patmore, HBCA E.93/23; Courtney Borden 1928: 265; John Borden 1929: August 20, 1927; *Nome Nugget* July 23, 1927.

8. Brower MSa: 748; Pedersen to O. S. Finnie, April 20, 1925, Records of the Northern Administration Branch (RG 85) vol. 747, file 4244, LAC; Brower MSa: 818–825.

9. Brower MSa: 814, 846, 859–860, 868; Brower MSb: 50, 52; Brower MSc; *Fur Trade Review* June 1933, 60(9): 21 and August 1933, 60(11): 44; Blackman 1989: 22–23; Tom Brower, personal communication to the author.

10. Koonuk et al. 1987: 59–60.

11. Neakok et al. 1985: 17.

12. Philip Masqin Campbell, personal communication to the author; Herbert Kinnee-veauk, personal communication to the author; David Greist 2002: 159–160.

13. Dathan 2012: 64, 70–73.

14. *Seattle Post-Intelligencer* June 18, 1924; North Slope Borough 1980: 115, 142.

15. E. D. Jones MSS: June 29, 1929; *Fur Trade Review* June 1930, 57(9): 25–26.

7. COMPETITION AMONG TRADERS IN WESTERN ARCTIC CANADA

1. *Fur Trade Review* January 1923, 50(4): 124–126; W. C. Black 1961: 70; Wilcox 1951: 182–183; Ewing 1981: 151; Simon Paneak in Hall et al. 1985: 64; Nuligak 1966: 93.

2. Usher 1971b: I, 30; Usher 1975: 318; Robinson and Robinson 1946: 36.

3. Crowe 1991: 113; Royal Canadian Mounted Police, report for the year ended September 30, 1928: 38.

4. Nagy 1994: 1; Murielle Nagy, personal communication to the author, May 16, 2014; Usher 1971b: 25; Coates 1985: 151; W. C. Black 1961: 70; Ferguson 1961: 39; Nuligak 1966: 93, 136–137; *Fur Trade Review* September 1920, 48(1): 154; Gilmore MS: June 20, 1931; Rasmussen 1927: 289, 293–294; Old Dartmouth Historical Society scrapbook T-3, p. 14, NBWM; Harrison 1908: 97.

5. *Edmonton Journal* December 23, 1919.
6. *Edmonton Bulletin* March 24, August 11, and November 17, 1921, March 10, 1923, April 24 and June 21, 1924; *Edmonton Journal* October 30, 1922, May 8, 1928; Okpik 2005: 130.
7. Burwash 1931: 19–20, 104; Usher 1971b: 28; Rasmussen 1927: 294; Innis 1970: 370; Kitto 1930: 56–57, 68; Bonnycastle 1984: 58.
8. Nuligak 1966: 156–157; Bonnycastle 1984: 58.
9. Bernard 1958: I, 251; Condon 1994: 118–119; Usher 1971b: I, 37–38; Manning 1956: 35–36; C. T. Pedersen to Thomas H. Manning, January 31, 1953, Thomas H. Manning Collection, SPRI; Liebes 1917: August 19 and 20, 1917; Rainey 1940 MSS, interview with Peter Kunaŋnauraq, interview with Roy Vincent; author's field notes 1973–1974.
10. S. Jenness 2004: 146, 150, 211, 287; S. Jenness 2011: 265; *Nome Nugget* October 1 and 11, 1915, June 22, September 25, and October 23, 1916, September 22, 1919, June 24 and October 14, 1922; Bernard 1958: II, 5; Masik and Hutchison 1935: 104–107, 120, 122; Stefansson 1943: 598, 668–669; D. Jenness 1921: 545; Noice 1924: 262–263, 268; Stuck 1920: 307; Stuck MS: April 1 and 6, 1918; *Seattle Post-Intelligencer* August 29, 1920, October 5, 1924; *Nome Nugget* June 24 and October 14, 1922; Brower MSa: 706, 707, 709, 767–768; Rasmussen 1927: 290.
    In 1922, however, C. T. Pedersen, acting for H. Liebes and Company, backed Crawford for a trapping and trading voyage in the schooner *Lettie*. Crawford's plan was to land 20 Eskimos from Point Hope, Alaska, on Banks Island. Heavy ice, however, forced him to overwinter at Teller, Alaska, in 1922–1923, but he spent the following winter in Letty [*sic*] Harbour, near Cape Parry, Canada. In 1924 the schooner was wrecked while attempting to enter Wainwright Inlet, Alaska (*Nome Nugget* June 24 and October 14, 1922; Brower MSa: 707, 767–768).
11. Bernard 1958: I, 499; Abrahamson 1964: 41; S. Jenness 1995: 148; S. Jenness 2011: 299–301; Usher 1971a: 111, 167, 175; Klengenberg 1932: 274–277, 332.
12. *Nome Nugget* October 14, 1922; Klengenberg 1932: 330–347 (Klengenberg is in error about his dates); H. Liebes & Co. v. Klengenberg, 23 F.2d 611 (9th Cir. 1928). See my note about the accuracy of Klengenberg's autobiography, chapter 4, note 21.
13. *Edmonton Bulletin* May 16, June 3, September 11, 1924; G. Newell 1966: 353; *Marine Digest* May 31, 1924; Morris 1965; Klengenberg to RCMP, Herschel Island, March 1924, Northern Whaling and Trading Company Collection, series 1, no. 1, UAA.
    When Klengenberg departed Seattle, among his crew was the Norwegian sailor Henry A. Larsen, who would later become captain of the RCMP's ship *St. Roch*, which would achieve the second traverse of the Northwest Passage (Larsen et al. 1967: 11).
14. R. R. Farrow to the Collector of Customs and Excise, Dawson, Yukon Territory, Canada, January 5, 1924, Northern Whaling and Trading Company Collection, series 1, nos. 1–5, UAA; Klengenberg v. H. Liebes and Company, testimony of C. Klengenberg, p. 39, Admiralty case no. 18153, Northern District of California, San Francisco, NARASB.
15. Klengenberg 1932: 346–347; *Edmonton Bulletin* October 15, 1924.
16. Klengenberg 1932: 347; Larsen et al. 1967: 23.
17. Larsen et al. 1967: 23, 33–34, 38; Burwash [1927]: 17; Burwash 1931: 13; Usher 1971a: 175;

Seattle Post-Intelligencer May 9, June 9, and September 12, 1926, June 6, 1930, May 5 and 7, 1931, June 7, 1934; *Edmonton Journal* May 30, 1927, May 10, 1930; *Fur Trade Review* June 1931, 58(9): 24, August 1935, 62(11): 45; G. Newell 1966: 430; Finnie 1940: 185; United States Supreme Court 1927/ 878/ 277 U.S. 596/ 48 S. Ct. 559/ 72 L.Ed. 1006/ 4-4-1928 and 5-4-1928.

The *Old Maid No. 2* soon became a rum runner, sailing under its former name. It was grounded and damaged in British Columbia in 1936 (*Seattle Post-Intelligencer* March 2, 1936) but was refloated, renamed the *Joan G.*, and sailed in the timber trade (Gibson 2000: passim).

18. Finnie 1940: 185.
19. Bernard 1958: I, 516.
20. Bernard 1958: II, 1–29; D. Jenness 1922: 243.
21. Bernard 1958: II, 35.
22. Ibid.: 66; Whalley 1962: 99–100; Cadzow 1920: 7–8; D. Jenness 1922: 152; D. Jenness 1991: 822; Mallory 1989: 145.
23. Bernard 1958: II, 66.
24. D. Jenness 1922: 244.
25. Bernard 1958: II, 135, 139, 159.
26. D. Jenness 1922: 244.
27. Ibid.
28. Bernard 1958: II, 161–292; D. Jenness 1922: 244–248; Balikci 1984: 416; Csonka 1994: 21, 28–29; Usher 1971a: 139–141.
29. In 1922 Binder and RCMP Corporal William A. Doak were murdered at Tree River by Aligoomiak.
30. D. Jenness 1922: 244; Bernard 1958: II, 293–311; Royal Northwest Mounted Police, report for the year ended September 30, 1917: 11; Morris 1965; Usher 1971a: 162–175; D. Jenness 1922: 248–249; Duncan 2000: 110; *Nome Nugget* September 22, 1923.
31. Zinovich 1992: 93, 108; Zaslow 1971: 236, 239–240; Robinson and Robinson 1946: 36; A. Ray 1990: 92.
32. Usher 1971a: 159; Nagle and Zinovich 1989: 19; Zaslow 1971: 240; A. Ray 1990: 104; *Edmonton Journal* September 16, 1910; R. H. Hall to F. C. Ingrams, December 28, 1911, HBCA A.12/FT 295/1(a).
33. F. C. Ingrams to R. H. Hall, February 3, 1912, HBCA A.12/FT 295/1(a).
34. Inspection Report on Fort McPherson post 1910, HBCA A.12/FT 322/2; Usher 1971c: 174–175; Bonnycastle 1984: 97–98; Norman E. Freakley to R. H. Hall, December 11, 1911, HBCA A.12/FT 295/1(a); R. H. Hall to F. C. Ingrams, April 16, 1913, HBCA A.12/FT 295/1(b); W. G. Phillips to A. Brabant, February 19, 1913, HBCA A.12/FT 295/1(b); R. H. Hall to W. Ware, March 31, 1911, HBCA A.12/FT 295/1; F. C. Ingrams to R. H. Hall, December 16, 1911, HBCA A.12/FT 295/1(a); F. C. Ingrams to H. H. Bacon, July 24, 1914, HBCA A.12/FT 295/1(b); report by A. A. Tremayne, HBCA A.12/FT 295/1(a); H. H. Bacon to F. C. Ingrams, November 22 and 26, 1913, HBCA A.12/FT 295/1(b); memorandum from H. H. Bacon, August 14, 1918, HBCA A.12/FT 295/1(b); Usher 1971c: 176–177.
35. R. H. Hall to F. C. Ingrams, April 9, 1913, HBCA A.12/FT 295/1(b); F. C. Ingrams to

R. H. Hall, May 7, 1913, and F. C. Ingrams to N. H. Bacon, May 24, 1913, HBCA A.12/ FT 295/1(b).

36. Log of *Ruby* 1915 and 1916, HBCA 3/27c/1; G. Newell 1966: 241; *The Beaver* December 1925: 22–23; C. Harding 1925; memorandum from H. H. Bacon, August 14, 1918, HBCA A.12/FT 295/1(b); Godsell [ca. 1935]: 260; Brower MSa: 677; Annual Report of the Western Arctic District, 1916–1917, HBCA D.FTR/7, fols. 146–148; Norman E. Freakley to James Thomson, October 24, 1918, HBCA A.12/FT 295/1(b); Liebes 1917; Herschel Island post journal, HBCA 3/27c/1, fol. 65.

37. Liebes 1917; Usher 1971a: 90, 106.

38. HBCA Inspection Reports, Western Arctic District, Season 1925, pp. 3, 4, 53, 55, 60; Royal Canadian Mounted Police, report for the year ending September 30, 1926: 70–71; Stuck 1920: 322–325.

39. Brower MSa: 783–784.

40. *Seattle Post-Intelligencer* March 27, 1921; A. Ray 1990: 154; Crowe 1991: 112; Hunter 1983: 41; Burwash 1931: 64, 104–105; G. Burnham 1986: 136–138; Usher 1971a: 157–158; Usher 1971b: I, 38–39; A. Ray 1990: 162–163; Zaslow 1988: 9; *Fur Trade Review* February 1922, 49(5): 120, February 1926, 53(5): 86; Dalton 2006: 141; Innis 1970: 346–369; A. Ray 1990: 159–161; Rasmussen 1927: 216–217; Burwash [1927]: 7; Copland 1985: 215.

  In 1927 the *Baymaud* carried supplies to the Perry River post in Queen Maud Gulf and returned to Cambridge Bay to serve as a stationary depot ship and radio station. It sank there at anchor in 1930.

41. Usher 1971b: I, 28–29.

42. Pedersen to O. S. Finnie, October 13, 1924, RG 85, vol. 747, file 4244, LAC.

43. Pedersen to O. S. Finnie, November 19, 1925; HBCA General Report, Western Arctic District, Outfit 254, pp. 5–7; Burwash [1927]: 15.

44. HBCA Inspection Reports, Western Arctic District, Season 1925, pp. 3, 4, 53, 55, 60; HBCA Fur Trade Commissioner's Report on Western Arctic District, Season 1925, pp. 1, 3–4.

45. HBCA Fur Trade Commissioner's Report on Western Arctic District, Season 1925, pp. 1, 3–4.

46. C. T. Pedersen to O. S. Finnie, March 17, 1926, RG 85, vol. 747, file 4244, LAC.

47. Usher 1975: 311; C. H. Clarke to Northern Whaling and Trading Company, June 21, 1926, Northern Whaling and Trading Company Collection, series 1, no. 6, UAA.

48. George W. Porter Jr. to Bonnie Hahn, August 17, 1988, author's collection; McGrath MS.

49. C. H. Clarke to Northern Whaling and Trading Company, June 21, 1926.

50. A. Brabant to O. S. Finnie, December 31, 1925, and O. S. Finnie to A. Brabant, January 7, 1926, RG 85, vol. 747, file 4244, LAC.

51. Usher 1971b: I, 29, 37–38.

52. Legg 1962: 125–126.

53. Usher 1971a: 160; *Seattle Post-Intelligencer* July 25, 1929.

54. Charlie Pedersen (March 29, 1988) and Teddy Pedersen (May 5, 1978), personal communication to author; C. T. Pedersen to O. S. Finnie, November 19, 1925, RG 85, vol. 747, file 4244, LAC; *Seattle Post-Intelligencer* July 25, 1929; *Nome Nugget* July 7, 1929.

55. HBCA RG 3/29A/1.
56. Finnie 1940: 17–21.

PART 4. DECLINE OF THE WESTERN ARCTIC
FUR TRADE, 1929 TO CA. 1950

1. *Economist* April 12, 2014: 54 and April 29, 2017: 58.
2. *Fur Trade Review* January 1930, 57(4): 14, 138; *Seattle Post-Intelligencer* November 30, 1931; Isto 2012: 115.
3. Fuchs 1968: 77; *Fur Trade Review* passim 1930–1940, July 1930, 57(10): 90, April 1931, 58(7): 88, 91, October 1931, 59(1): 35, November 1934, 60(2): 34, 54–55; *Seattle Post-Intelligencer* passim 1930–1940; Isto 2012: 148–149, 177; Spector 1998: 38.
4. Fuchs 1968: 77–78.

8. STATE OWNERSHIP OF THE TRADE
ON THE CHUKCHI PENINSULA

1. Forsyth 1992: 291.
2. Ibid.: xvii.
3. Ibid.: 244–246.
4. Demuth 2013: 183–184; Saul 2006: 252–253; Krupnik 1994: 69; Slezkine 1994: 134, 165, 174, 200; Vakhtin 1992: 11; Bobrick 1992: 18–19; Swenson 1944: 136–137; Sablin 2012: 226; Shnirelman 1994: 206; Wood 2011: 198; Menovshchikov 1964: 846.
5. Forsyth 1992: 267, 293; Schindler 1992: 57.
6. Forsyth 1992: 246–248.
7. Shnirelman 1994: 210; Krupnik and Chlenov 2013: 237–238; Hughes 1965: 43–46; Vucinich 1960: 874–875; Igor Krupnik's introduction to Bogoslavskaya et al.: xxvi.
8. Slezkine 1994: 165.
9. Armstrong 1965: 169; Bobrick 1992: 439; Krupnik and Chlenov 2013: 238–248, 268; Antropova and Kuznetsova 1964: 830–831; Marchenko 2012: 219–220, 231–237.
10. www.sojuzpushnina.ru/en/s/50/history.html, accessed August 18, 2016; Saul 2006: 316; Slezkine 1994: 213; Fuchs 1968: 22–23; Wilmers 2010: 216; Ray 1990: 135; Marchenko 2012: 154, 209; Shnirelman 1994: 213–214; Krupnik and Chlenov 2013: 269.

9. CONTRACTION OF TRADE IN NORTHERN ALASKA

1. Spencer 1959: 364–366; Sonnenfeld 1957: 339–340, 344–345; C. T. Pedersen to C. H. Clarke, January 17, 1930, Northern Whaling and Trading Company Collection, series 1, UAA; *Seattle Post-Intelligencer* March 16 and May 10, 1931; *Fur Trade Review* June 1933, 60(9): 38; Brower MSa: 888.
2. E. D. Jones MSS: June 18, 1930; R. M. Gilmore MS: June 20, 1931; *Seattle Post-Intelligencer* November 27, 1931.
3. *Fur Trade Review* May 1931, 58(8): 36, November 1932, 60(2): 15; Chance 1966: 16–17; Andrew Akootchook in North Slope Borough 1980: 3.

4. David Greist 2002: 155.

5. Burn 2012: 185; Dalton 2006: 62, 100–169; Gillingham 1955; Brower MSa: 790–791; Sydney Cornwell to Hudson's Bay Company, 1925, HBCA A.92/22/3.

6. *Seattle Post-Intelligencer* September 30, 1930; Bonnycastle 1936; Bonnycastle MS 1931, HBCA E.154/13; Percival Patmore log, 1931, HBCA RG 3/8/5; *Baychimo* telegrams, 1931, HBCA E.154/21; Brower MSb: 72; *Baychimo* logbook, 1931, HBCA A.92/22/4; *Seattle Post-Intelligencer* December 1 and 4, 1931; A. J. Allen 1978: 206–209; *Fur Trade Review* March 1932, 59(6), April 1932, 59(7): 30; Dalton 2006: 182–221.

7. A. J. Allen 1978: 209; Melvin 1982: 38–39; J. A. Ford MSS, SINAA; *Fur Trade Review* January 1932, 59(4): 17; *Seattle Post-Intelligencer* January 9 and 20, February 5 and 9, March 19, May 11 and 23, August 22, 23, 25, 1932; *Nome Nugget* February 27, March 5 and 19, May 14, August 27, December 3, 1932.

8. *Seattle Post-Intelligencer* October 6, 1933, February 25, March 9, 1936; Hutchison 1934: 109–112; Hutchison MSS; *Nome Nugget* April 21, 1934; Richard S. Finnie, personal communication to the author; Dalton 2006: 234–235.

9. Cole 1984: 157–159; John Backland Jr. to Henry Chamberlain, August 11, 1938, John Backland Jr. Papers, PC.

10. *Fur Trade Review* September 1933, 60(12): 37–38; Dathan 2012: 64; Burch 1975: 31–32; Sonnenfeld 1959; Stern et al. 1980: 56; Olson 1969: 14–15, 54–57.

11. Hall, Gerlach, and Blackman 1985: 65–66, 104n25; Blackman 1989: 22-23.

12. Hrdlička 1943: 285; Klerekoper 1977.

13. *Fur Trade Review* November 1934, 61(2): 34; *Seattle Post-Intelligencer* May to July 1934, passim, April 10, 1937; Brower MSa: 888; Brower MSc; Libbey 1983: 18, 36, 65–66; North Slope Borough 1980: 4, 82, 85, 125, 138, 146; Hutchison MSS, letter from Pete Palsson to Isobel W. Hutchison, January 20, 1939; Gubser 1965: 20, 333; U.S. Census, 1940, Alaska; Nagy 1994: 15; Murielle Nagy, personal communication to the author, April 16, 2014; Morris 1965.

14. Burch 1975: 31–32; Brower to John Backland Jr., February 23, 1939, John Backland Jr. Papers, PC; Brower quoted in Blackman 1989: 23; Alfred M. Bailey MSS; North Slope Borough 1980: 82, 96, 125, 138, 185–186; Libbey 1983: 66; U.S. Census for northern Alaska, 1940.

10. TOWARD MONOPOLY CONTROL IN WESTERN ARCTIC CANADA

1. Usher 1971b: I, 30; Condon 1994: 119; Royal Canadian Mounted Police, report for the year ended September 30, 1924: 41; RCMP, report for the year ended September 30, 1925: 46; RCMP, report for the year ended September 30, 1926: 71; *Fur Trade Review* September 1924, 51(12): 74–75 and February 1928, 55(5): 41; Nuligak 1966: 160–161; C. T. Pedersen to O. S. Finnie, October 25, 1927, RG 85 (Northern Administration Branch), vol. 747, file 4244, LAC; Brower MSa: 277; Sonnenfeld 1957: 339; *Seattle Post-Intelligencer* September 23, 1928.

2. Usher 1971b: I, 39–40; Peter Usher, personal communication to the author, October 15, 2014; Condon et al. 1996: 101–102; Nagy 1999: 47–53.

3. Usher 1971b: I, 45–55; Usher 1976b: II, 210–212; Peter Usher, personal communication

to the author, October 15, 2014; Sven Johansson, personal communication to the author, October 1, 2014, and April 10, 2016; Hohn 1955; Manning 1953; Agnes White in Nagy 1999: 47, 61–62, 75.

4. Persis Gruben n.d.; Charlie and Persis Gruben n.d.; Usher 1971b: I, 45–55; Usher 1976b: II, 210–212; Peter Usher, personal communication to the author, October 15, 2014; Sven Johansson, personal communication to the author, October 1, 2014, and April 10, 2016; Hohn 1955; Manning 1953; *The Beaver* December 1933: 59 and June 1934: 61.

5. Teddy Pedersen, personal communication to the author; Sven Johansson, personal communication to the author; Usher 1971b: I, 52–53. This *North Star* was much larger than Martin Andreasen's and Billy Natkusiak's *North Star.*

6. Usher 1971b: I, 53–54.

7. Ibid.: 55–61; Peter Usher, personal communication to the author, October 15, 2014; Hunt 1983: 108; Gray 2005: 1821.

8. *Fur Trade Review* September 1931, 58(12): 39 and January 1932, 59(4): 83; *Seattle Post-Intelligencer* April 6, 1938; Milne 1975: 188; G. M. Wall quoted in Bonnycastle 1984: 103; Bonnycastle 1984: 39, 97; 143; HBCA A.74/43. Nevertheless in 1935 the Western Arctic District still remained "the number one headache for the Fur Trade Department" (Copland 1985: 184).

9. *Fur Trade Review* August 1933, 60(11): 38 and September 1933, 60(12): 37–38; G. Newell 1966: 425; *Seattle Post-Intelligencer* July 29, 1933; *Nome Nugget* August 15, 1933.

10. *Fur Trade Review* August 1931, 58(11): 63, and January 1932, 59(4): 83; Bonnycastle 1984: 150; *The Beaver* December 1933: 58–59 and March 1934: 58; Nuligak 1966: 172. Nuligak apparently confused the abandonment of the *Anyox* resupply voyage in 1933 with the loss of the *Baychimo* in 1931.

11. Russell 1898: 61; Burwash 1931: 53; Bonnycastle 1984: 21; *The Beaver* March 1934: 57–58 and September 1934: 60; Copland 1985: 191.

12. Philip Masqin Campbell, personal communication to the author, June 11, 1974; Keith Smith, personal communication to the author.

13. Webster 1987: 79.

14. Teddy Pedersen, Charlie Pedersen, and Lincoln Washburn, personal communication to the author; Legg 1962: 125–126; *Fur Trade Review* November 1935, 63(2): 12–13; Usher 1971a: 117; Webster n.d.: 92; George Burnham 1986: 115; *The Beaver* March 1935: 62 and December 1936: 58.

15. R. H. G. Bonnycastle to General Manager, January 19, 1937, HBCA 21 M 161, RG 2/7/211.

16. HBCA A.93/Corr 17/61 Inward, C.C.P. no. 301, December 23, 1937.

17. Post journals 1932–37, HBCA B419/A/1–41; *The Beaver* December 1937: 62, December 1938: 60, and December 1939: 54; Charlie Pedersen, personal communication to the author; Usher 1975; 316, 320. In December 1938 the *Patterson* was "pounded to pieces in the surf," a total loss at Cape Fairweather, Alaska (G. Newell 1966: 466).

18. Usher 1971a: 102.

19. Patrick Klengenberg MS. In 1942 the HBC sold the *Aklavik* to Patsy Klengenberg

for $1.00. It caught fire and sank in Cambridge Bay in 1946. Patsy Klengenberg was drowned while trying to swim to shore.

20. Usher 1971a: 31; Usher 1965a: 51-52.
21. Ewing 1981: 135.
22. Links 1956: 139–140.
23. Hudson's Bay Company 1967: 42; Paupanekis 1972: 140; Usher 1971a: 35; Usher 1975: 317; Schroeder 2016a, 2016b.
24. Usher 1976b: 207; Usher 1975: 317; Spector 1998: 29, 32; Paupanekis 1972: 140.
25. *Wall Street Journal* September 29, 2014.

BIBLIOGRAPHY

ARCHIVAL COLLECTIONS

Alaska State Film Library, Anchorage, AK (ASFL)
   Bowhead Hunting in the Arctic or Cruise of the Whaler "Herman" (video)
Alaska State Library, Juneau, Alaska
   David Brower photographs
   Leslie Melvin Collection
   Various collections
Alaska Trappers Association, Fairbanks, AK (ATA)
   Richard Carroll interview
   Daniel Karmun interview
   Bob Uhl interview
American Museum of Natural History, New York, NY (AMNH)
   Vilhjalmur Stefansson Papers
   Waldemar Bogoras photographs
Anglican Church Archives, Toronto, ON (ACA)
   I. O. Stringer Papers
   St. Matthew Mission journal (Herschel Island)
California Academy of Sciences, San Francisco, CA (CAS)
   Arnold Liebes Collection
   Various collections
California Historical Society, San Francisco, CA (CHS)
   Alaska Commercial Company Collection
   Various collections
Canadian Museum of Nature, Ottawa, ON (CMN)
   Rudolph Martin Anderson Papers
Church Missionary Society, University of Birmingham Library, U.K. (CMS)
   William C. Bompas Collection

Dartmouth College, Rauner Special Collections Library, Hanover, NH (DC)
    Copley Amory Papers
    Charles D. Brower Papers
    Encyclopedia Arctica Collection
    Henry W. Greist Papers
    Ernest de Koven Leffingwell Papers
    C. L. Andrews Papers
    C. T. Pedersen correspondence
    Various collections
Denver Museum of Nature and Science, Denver, CO (DMNS)
    Alfred M. Bailey Papers
Episcopal Church Historical Society, Austin, TX (ECHS)
    John B. Driggs correspondence
    St. Thomas Mission (Point Hope, AK) records
    Hudson Stuck Collection
Explorers Club, New York, NY (EC)
    John B. Burnham Papers
    Various collections
Glenbow Museum, Calgary, AB (GM)
    Lomen Photograph Collection
    Various collections
Harvard University, George A. Baker Business School Library, Allston, MA (HUBBSL)
    Captain George Leavitt Papers
    Various collections
Harvard University, Museum of Comparative Zoology, Cambridge, MA (HUMCZ)
    Johan Koren Papers
    Various collections
Hoover Institution on War, Revolution and Peace, Stanford, CA (HI)
    Frank Golder Collection
Hudson's Bay Company Archives, Archives of Manitoba, Winnipeg, Manitoba (HBCA)
    Biographies
    Post histories
    Ship histories
    Siberian Venture collection
    Various collections
Huntington Library, San Marino, CA (HL)
    Michael A. Healy Collection
    Various collections
Library and Archives Canada, Ottawa, ON (LAC)
    Rudolph Martin Anderson Papers
    Joseph F. Bernard Papers
    C. T. Pedersen Correspondence
    Various collections

Carrie M. McLain Memorial Museum, Nome, AK (CMMM)
    Various collections
National Archives and Records Administration, Washington, DC (NARAW)
    Censuses of the United States, Alaska, 1900–1940
    Revenue Cutter Service Collection
    Various collections
National Archives and Records Administration, San Bruno, CA (NARASB)
    U.S. District Court, Admiralty, Klengenberg v. H. Liebes and Company
National Library of Scotland, Edinburgh, U.K. (NLS)
    Isobel Wylie Hutchison Collection
National Maritime Museum San Francisco, San Francisco, CA (NMMSF)
    John Lyman Papers
    Various collections
New Bedford Whaling Museum, New Bedford, MA (NBWM)
    Hartson Bodfish Collection
    Bernhard Kilian Collection
    Sophie Porter Collection
    Keith Smith Collection
    Various collections
North Slope Borough, Commission on History and Culture, Barrow, AK (NSB)
    Fred Klerekoper diary
Presbyterian Historical Society, Philadelphia, PA (PHS)
    Sheldon Jackson Papers
Prince of Wales Northern Heritage Centre, Yellowknife, NWT (PWNHC)
    Various collections online
Private collections (PC)
    John Backland Jr.
    Bern Will Brown
    John Driggs
    Richard S. Finnie
    Max Gottschalk
    Sven Johansson
    Dunbar Lockwood
    Thomas H. Manning
    E. A. McIlhenny
    Sam Mogg
    Dorothy Cottle Poole
    Froelich G. Rainey
    Keith A. Smith
Provincial Archives of Alberta, Edmonton, AB (PAA)
    Charles Klengenberg album
    Various collections

St. Thomas Mission, Point Hope, AK (STM)
  Diary of Archdeacon Frederick Goodman
  Mission journal
Scott Polar Research Institute, University of Cambridge, Cambridge, U.K. (SPRI)
  Alfred H. Harrison Collection
  Thomas H. Manning Papers
  Charles Swithinbank Papers
  Various collections
Sheldon Jackson College, Sitka, AK (SJC)
  William Healey Dall Papers
  Various collections
Smithsonian Institution Archives, Washington, DC (SIA)
  Frank Ashbrook Papers
  William Healey Dall Papers
  Various collections
Smithsonian Institution, National Anthropological Archives, Suitland, MD (SINAA)
  James A. Ford Papers
United States National Park Service, Cape Krusenstern National Monument (online) (USNPS)
  Bob Uhl journals
University of Alaska, Anchorage, Anchorage, AK (UAA)
  Northern Whaling and Trading Company Collection
  Various collections
University of Alaska–Fairbanks, Rasmuson Library, Fairbanks, AK (UAF)
  Copley Amory journal
  Joseph F. Bernard Papers
  Cape Smythe Whaling and Trading Company shipping ledger
  Charles D. Brower Papers
  Chipp-Ikpikpuk and Meade Rivers Oral History Project, Project Jukebox
    Arnold Brower Sr. interview
    Thomas Brower Sr. interview
    Charlie Edwardson interview
    Adam Leavitt interview
  Don C. Foote Collection
  Charles Klengenberg Collection
  June Metcalfe Collection, Edward S. Curtis typescript
  Oliver Morris interview, Tanana-Yukon Historical Society collection
  Middleton Smith Papers
  Wittenberg Family Collection
  Various collections
University of California, Bancroft Library, Berkeley, CA (BLUC)
  Edward Darlington Jones Papers
  Andrew Jackson Stone diary
  Various collections

University of California, Museum of Vertebrate Zoology, Berkeley, CA (UCMVZ)
    Joseph S. Dixon Papers
    R. M. Gilmore Papers
University of Pennsylvania, Museum of Archaeology and Anthropology (Penn Museum),
    Philadelphia, PA (UP)
    George Byron Gordon Collection
    William Van Valin Collection
    Various collections
University of Toronto Library, Special Collections Archives (UTL)
    Harold A. Innis Papers
University of Washington Libraries, Special Collections Department, Suzallo Library,
    Seattle (UW)
    John Backland Jr. film
    Nome Customs Records, 1909–1924
    John Rosene Collection (Northeastern Siberian Company)
    George C. Teien Collection
    Various collections
Wisconsin Historical Society, Madison (WHS)
    Alexander Gumberg Papers
Yukon Archives, Whitehorse, YT (YA)
    Administration Branch correspondence (Dawson, YT)
    Various collections

PERIODICALS CONSULTED

Arctic Circular 1948–1960
The Beaver 1920–2000
Edmonton Bulletin 1899–1927
Edmonton Journal 1903–1932
Fur News 1907–1920
Fur Trade Review 1887–1936
Hunter-Trader-Trapper 1905–1922
Marine Digest 1923–1940
Nome Daily Gold Digger 1899–1910
Nome Nugget 1901–1939
Nome Weekly News 1900–1906
Seattle Post-Intelligencer 1898–1941

INTERVIEWS AND CORRESPONDENCE

Douglas D. Anderson 1967–present
Lucy Avakana (Barrow, AK) 1974
Elsie Backland (Seattle, WA) 1980–1995
Louvetta Bertonccini (Seattle, WA) 1975

Lincoln Blassi (Gambell, AK) 1969, 1974
Waldo Bodfish (Wainwright, AK) 1970–1972
William Boucher (Fairbanks, AK) 2008–present
Tom Brower (Barrow, AK) 1971–1975
Mary Ferreira Brown (Nome, AK) 1974
Ernest S. ("Tiger") Burch Jr. 1970–2010
John J. Burns (Nome and Fairbanks, AK) 1969–present
Philip Masqin Campbell (Gambell, AK) 1969, 1974
Andy Cockney (Tuktoyaktuk, NWT) 1978, 1990
Paul Fenimore Cooper Jr. 1973–1987
John Cross (Kotzebue, AK) 1970
Michael Dederer (Seattle, WA) 1995
Almond Downey (Kotzebue, AK) 1970
Frank and Ursula Ellanna (Nome, AK) 1970–1976
Richard S. Finnie (San Francisco, CA) 1974–1980
David Frankson (Point Hope, AK) 1970–1978
E. J. ("Scotty") Gall (Victoria, BC) 1983
Manfred ("Freddy") Garfunkel (London, U.K.) 1996
John C. George (Barrow, AK) 1976–present
David Greist (Orlando, FL) 2014–2015
Bonnie Hahn (Nome, AK) 1969–present
Dick and Cynthia Hill (Inuvik, NWT) 1973, 1984–1986
Alfred Hopson (Barrow, AK) 1972, 1973
James A. Houston 1965–2005
Fr. Leonce d'Hurtevent (Paulatuk, NWT) 1978
Samuel Irrigoo (Gambell, AK) 1969, 1974
John Iyapana (Diomede, AK) 1975
Sven Johansson (Victoria, BC) 1973–present
Helen Castel Johnson (Nome, AK) 1972–1977
Eddie Kikoak (Tuktoyaktuk, NWT, and Gjoa Haven, Nunavut) 1980, 1983, 1988
Mary Porter Kikoak (Gjoa Haven, Nunavut) 1988
Bernhard ("Ben") Kilian, (Oakland, CA) 1979–1983
Jimmy Kiligivuk (Point Hope, AK) 1971–1978
Terence Uyuġaluk ("Laurie") Kingik (Point Hope, AK) 1970–1980
Herbert Kinneeveauk (Point Hope, AK) 1970–1978
Angeline Kingik Koonook (Point Hope, AK) 1974–1980
Luke Koonook Sr. (Point Hope, AK) 1974–1980
Chester Lampe (Wales and Barrow, AK) 1973
Fr. Robert LeMeur (Tuktoyaktuk, NWT) 1972–1985
Margaret Andreasen Lennie (Tuktoyaktuk, NWT) 1974
Sam Lennie (Tuktoyaktuk, NWT) 1974
Billy Lyall (Cambridge Bay, Nunavut) 1978–1988
Ernie Lyall (Taloyoak, Nunavut) 1980
Bob and Elizabeth Mackenzie (Herschel Island, YT) 1973–1978

Robert Mayokok (Nome, AK) 1973
Jonas Meeyook (Herschel Island, YT) 1973
Jimmy Memogana (Walker Bay, NWT) 1986
Leslie Melvin (Seattle, WA) 1980
Dwight Milligrock (Nome, AK) 1969–1994
Sam Mogg (Diomede, AK) 1974
Lionel Montpetit (Edmonton, AB) 1977–1990
James Kivetoruk Moses (Nome, AK) 1970–1975
Vincent Nageak (Barrow, AK) 1973
Arthur Nagozruk (Nome, AK) 1970–1974
Bernard Nash Sr. (Point Hope, AK) 1971–1980
Felix Nuvoyaok (Tuktoyaktuk, NWT) 1972–1973
Abe Okpik (Inuvik, NWT) 1968
George Omnik (Point Hope, AK) 1970, 1974
Norman Omnik (Point Hope, AK) 1971–1980
Tom Parr (Columbus, OH) 2014–15
Charlie Pedersen (San Francisco, CA) 1980
Teddy Pedersen (Homer, AK) 1978–1990
Effie Porter (Gjoa Haven, Nunavut) 1980–1994
George Porter Jr. (Gjoa Haven, Nunavut) 1980–1994
George Porter Sr. (Gjoa Haven, Nunavut) 1980
Tommy Porter (Taloyoak, Nunavut) 1980, 1987
Froelich G. Rainey (Philadelphia, PA) 1967–1990
Rosalind Rank 1995
Dorothy Jean Ray (Port Townsend, WA) 1970–2007
Graham Rowley (Ottawa, ON) 1968–2000
L. F. "Slim" Semmler (Inuvik, NWT) 1973, 1990
Peter Semotiuk (Cambridge Bay, Nunavut, and other places) 1972–present
Chester Seveck (Kotzebue and Point Hope, AK) 1974
Leon Shelabarger (Kotzebue, AK) 1970–1975
Charlie ("Grandpa") Slwooko (Gambel and Nome, AK) 1974
Thomas G. Smith (1986, 2015–2016)
Alex Stevenson (Ottawa, ON) 1965
Bob Tuckfield (Point Hope, AK) 1974
Duffy Uglowok (Gambell, AK) 1969
Peter Usher (Ottawa, ON) 1975–present
Roy Vincent (Point Hope, AK) 1971–1978
Glenn and Trish Warner (Bathurst Inlet, NWT) 1987
Lincoln and Tahoe Washburn (New Haven, CT, and Seattle, WA) 1965–1990
Hilda Webber (Point Hope, AK) 1971–1980
Clifford Weyioanna (Shishmaref, AK) 1972
Robin Winks (New Haven, CT) 1999
Jim Wolki (Tuktoyaktuk, NWT) 1972–1974, 1978
Lena Wolki (Sachs Harbour, NWT) 1985

PUBLISHED AND OTHER PRIVATE SOURCES

Abrahamson, G. 1964. *The Copper Eskimos: An Area Economic Survey 1963.* Ottawa: Industrial Division, Northern Administration Branch, Department of Northern Affairs and National Resources.

———. 1968. *Tuktoyaktuk–Cape Parry Area Economic Survey.* Ottawa: Industrial Division, Department of Indian Affairs and Northern Development.

Alaska Trappers Manual. 1991. *Alaska Trappers Manual.* [Fairbanks]: Alaska Department of Fish and Game with the Alaska Trappers Association.

Aldrich, Herbert L. 1889. *Arctic Alaska and Siberia, or Eight Months with the Arctic Whalemen.* Chicago: Rand McNally.

Alexander, W. Louis. 1920a. "Furs from Siberia: Collecting Skins in Northern Regions. . . ." *Fur Trade Review* 48(3): 146–151.

———. 1920b. "The Fur Industry in Siberia before the War." *Fur Trade Review* 48(3): 152–158.

Allen, Arthur James. 1978. *A Whaler and Trader in the Arctic, 1895–1944: My Life with the Bowhead.* Anchorage: Alaska Northwest Publishing.

Alunik, Ishmael. 1998. *Call Me Ishmael: Memories of Ishmael Alunik, Inuvialuk Elder.* Inuvik: Kolausok Ublaaq Enterprises.

Alunik, Ishmael, Eddie D. Kolausok, and David Morrison. 2003. *Across Time and Tundra: The Inuvialuit of the Western Arctic.* Vancouver: Raincoast Books.

Amory, Copley, Jr. MS 1912a. "Description of the Journey from Seattle to Dawson and Down the Yukon . . . 1912. . . ." Rauner Special Collections Library, Dartmouth College, Hanover, NH, MSS-174.

———. MS 1912b. "Journal of a Voyage to Northeastern Alaska: June, July, August and September 1912." Alaska and Polar Regions Department, Rasmuson Library, University of Alaska–Fairbanks.

———. MS 1914–1915. "Journal of a Trip to the Kolyma River Region in Siberia, 1914–1915." Alaska and Polar Regions Department, Rasmuson Library, University of Alaska–Fairbanks.

Amundsen, Roald. 1921. *Nordostpassagen.* . . . Kristiania: Gyldendalske Boghandel.

Anderson, J. W. 1944. "Fort Ross Voyage." *The Beaver* 275(4): 45–47.

———. 1961. *Fur Trader's Story.* Toronto: Ryerson.

Anderson, Rudolf Martin. 1924. "Report on the Natural History Collections of the Expedition." In Vilhjalmur Stefansson, *My Life with the Eskimo.* New York: Macmillan. Pp. 436–527.

———. 1943. "The Work of the Southern Section of the Expedition." In Vilhjalmur Stefansson, *The Friendly Arctic: The Story of Five Years in the Polar Regions.* New York: Macmillan. Pp. 763–783.

———. 1958. "Foreword." In Joseph-Fidèle Bernard, "Arctic Voyages of the Schooner *Teddy Bear.*" Typescript. Alaska and Polar Regions Department, Rasmuson Library, University of Alaska–Fairbanks. Pp. xii–xvii.

———. MSS. Rudolph Martin Andersen Papers, Canadian Museum of Nature, Gatineau, Quebec (CMNAC Anderson 1992 001A and B, 1996 077 Ser. A).

Andrews, Clarence Leroy. 1939. *The Eskimo and His Reindeer in Alaska.* Caldwell, ID: Caxton.

Anonymous. 1936. "Furs." *Fortune* 8(1): 64–74, 120, 123.

——. 1948. "Closing of the Hudson's Bay Company Post at Fort Ross." *Arctic Circular* 1(5): 49–50.

Antropova, V. V., and V. G. Kuznetsova. 1964. "The Chukchi." In M. G. Levin and L. P. Potapov (eds.), *The Peoples of Siberia*. Chicago: University of Chicago Press. Pp. 799–835.

Arestad, Sverre. 1962. "Questing for Gold and Furs in Alaska." *Norwegian-American Studies* 21:54–94. Northfield, MN: Norwegian-American Historical Association.

Armstrong, Terrence. 1965. *Russian Settlement in the North*. Cambridge, U.K.: Cambridge University Press.

Armstrong, Terence, Brian Roberts, and Charles Swithinbank. 1973. *Illustrated Glossary of Snow and Ice*. Cambridge, U.K.: Scott Polar Research Institute.

Arnold, Bridgewater M. 1927. *A Dictionary of Fur Names*. New York: National Association of the Fur Industry.

Arundale, Wendy H., and William S. Schneider. 1987. *Quliaqtuat Iñupiat Nunaŋiññiñ: The Report of the Chipp-Ikpikpuk River and Upper Meade River Oral History Project*. Barrow, AK: North Slope Borough Commission on History, Language, and Culture.

Ashbrook, Frank G., and Ernest P. Walker. 1925. *Blue Fox Farming in Alaska*. U.S. Department of Agriculture Bulletin no. 1350. Washington, DC: Government Printing Office.

Ashton, James M. 1928. *Ice-Bound: A Traveler's Adventures in the Siberian Arctic*. New York: G. P. Putnam's Sons.

Austin, William E. 1922. *Principles and Practice of Fur Dressing and Fur Dyeing*. New York: Van Nostrand.

——. 1926. "The Art of Dressing and Dyeing Furs." *Fur Trade Review* 53(9): 53–56.

——. 1928. "Color Index of Dyed Furs." *Fur Trade Review* 55(4): 66–70.

Bachrach, Max. 1930. *Fur: A Practical Treatise*. New York: Prentice-Hall.

Bailey, Alfred M. 1971. *Field Work of a Museum Naturalist*. Denver: Denver Museum of Natural History.

——. MSS. Alfred M. Bailey Papers, Denver Museum of Nature and Science, Denver, CO.

Bailey, Alfred M., and Russell W. Hendee. 1926. "Notes on the Mammals of Northwestern Alaska." *Journal of Mammalogy* 7(1): 9–28.

Balikci, Asen. 1984. "Netsilik." In David Damas (ed.), *Handbook of North American Indians*, vol. 5: *Arctic*. Washington, DC: Smithsonian Institution. Pp. 415–430.

Barr, William. 1972. "The Voyages of the Taymyr and Vaygach to Ostrov Vrangelya, 1910–1915." *Polar Record* 16(101): 213–234.

——. 1977. "Eskimo Relocation: The Soviet Experience on Ostrov Vrangelya." *Musk-Ox* 20:9–20.

——. 1988. "The Soviet Career of the Schooner *Polar Bear*." *Polar Record* 24(148): 21–29.

Barratt, Glyn. 1977. "Joseph-Fidèle Bernard 'On the Bering Sea Frontier,' 1921–22." *Polar Record* 18(155): 341–349.

Beattie, Judith Hudson. 1991. "Post History: Fort Ross." Hudson's Bay Company Archives, Archives of Manitoba, Winnipeg.

Belden, A. L. 1917. *The Fur Trade of America and Some of the Men Who Made and Maintain It. . . .* New York: Peltries Publishing.

Belov, M. I. 1959. *Sovetskoe Arkticheskoe More Plavanie, 1917–1932. Istoria Otkrytiya i Osvoeniya Severnogo Morskogo Puti,* 3. Leningrad: Izdatel'stvo Morskoy Transport.

Benioff, Fred. 1936. *The Romance of Furs.* San Francisco: Fred Benioff Furs.

Bergman, Sten. 1927. *Through Kamchatka by Dog-Sled and Skis.* London: Seeley, Service.

Bernard, Joseph-Fidèle. 1923. "Local Walrus Protection in Northeast Siberia." *Journal of Mammalogy* 4(4): 224–227.

———. 1958. "Arctic Voyages of the Schooner *Teddy Bear.*" Typescript. Alaska and Polar Regions Department, Rasmuson Library, University of Alaska–Fairbanks.

———. MS. "On the Bering Sea Frontier." Typescript. MG30-B40. Rudolph Martin Anderson and May Bell Allstrand fonds, vol. 11. file 16, Wrangel Island — Bernard, Captain J. Library and Archives Canada, Ottawa.

Bethune, W. C. (comp.). 1937. *Canada's Western Northland: Its History, Resources, Population and Administration.* Ottawa: Department of Mines and Resources, Lands, Parks, and Forests Branch.

Black, J. L. 2013. "Great Expectations: Revisiting Canadian Economic Footprints in Siberia, 1890s–1921." *Sibirica* 12(3): 1–27.

Black, W. C. 1961. "Fur Trapping in the Mackenzie River Delta." *Geographical Bulletin* 16:62–85.

Blackman, Margaret B. 1989. *Sadie Brower Neakok: An Iñupiaq Woman.* Seattle: University of Washington Press.

Bobrick, Benson. 1992. *East of the Sun: The Epic Conquest and Tragic History of Siberia.* New York: Poseidon.

Bockstoce, John R. 1986. *Whales, Ice and Men: The History of Whaling in the Western Arctic.* Seattle: University of Washington Press.

———. 1991. *Arctic Passages: A Unique Small Boat Voyage through the Great Northern Waterway.* New York: Hearst Marine Books.

———. 2006. "Nineteenth-Century Commercial Shipping Losses in the Northern Bering Sea, Chukchi Sea, and Beaufort Sea." *Northern Mariner/Marin du Nord* 16(2): 5–69.

———. 2009. *Furs and Frontiers in the Far North: The Contest among Native and Foreign Nations for the Bering Strait Fur Trade.* New Haven: Yale University Press.

Bockstoce, John R., and Charles F. Batchelder. 1978a. "A Gazetteer of Whalers' Place-Names for the Bering Strait Region and the Western Arctic." *Names: Journal of the American Name Society* 26(3): 258–270.

———. 1978b. "A Chronological List of Commercial Wintering Voyages to the Bering Strait Region and Western Arctic of North America." *American Neptune* 38(2): 81–91.

Bockstoce, John R., and Daniel B. Botkin. 1982. "The Harvest of Pacific Walruses by the Pelagic Whaling Industry, 1848–1914." *Arctic and Alpine Research* 14(3): 183–188.

———. 1983. "The Historical Status and Reduction of the Western Arctic Bowhead Whale Population by the Pelagic Whaling Industry, 1848–1914." In M. F. Tillman and G. P. Donovan (eds.), *Report of the International Whaling Commission.* Special issue no. 5 on Historical Whaling Records [SC/32/PS16]. Pp. 107–141.

Bockstoce, John R., Rob Ingram, and Helene Dobrowolsky. 2012. "Fur Traders." In Christopher R. Burn (ed.), *Herschel Island Qikitaryuk.* Whitehorse: Wildlife Management Advisory Council (North Slope) and University of Calgary Press. Pp. 176–185.

Bodfish, Hartson H. 1936. *Chasing the Bowhead.* Cambridge, MA: Harvard University Press.

——. MS 1897–1899. Trade book. New Bedford Whaling Museum, New Bedford, MA. KWMA58.

——. MS 1909. Trade book. New Bedford Whaling Museum, New Bedford, MA. MSS 17, Series A, S-S1, vol. 1.

Bodfish, Waldo, Sr. (William Schneider, ed.). 1991. *Kusiq: An Eskimo Life History from the Arctic Coast of Alaska.* Fairbanks: University of Alaska Press.

Bogoras, Waldemar. 1904–1909. *The Chukchee.* Memoirs of the American Museum of Natural History, vol. 11. New York: Jessup North Pacific Expedition.

Bogoslavskaya, Lyudmila S., Ivan Slugin, Igor Zagrebin, and Igor Krupnik. 2016. (Marina Bell, tr., Igor Krupnik and Rachel Mason, eds.). *Maritime Hunting Culture of Chukotka: Traditions and Modern Practices.* Anchorage, AK: National Park Service, Shared Beringian Heritage Program.

Bonnycastle, R. H. G. 1931. "S.S. Baychimo Icebound." *The Beaver* 262(3): 364–365.

——. 1936. "Northern Shipwreck." *The Beaver* 266(4): 30–33.

——. 1984. (Heather Robertson, ed.). *Gentleman Adventurer. The Arctic Diaries of R. H. G. Bonnycastle.* Toronto: Lester and Orpen Dennys.

——. MS 1931. Diary. Hudson's Bay Company Archives, Archives of Manitoba, Winnipeg. HBCA 3.154/13.

Borden, John. 1929. *Log of the Auxiliary Schooner Yacht Northern Light.* Chicago: privately printed.

Borden, Mrs. John [Courtney Louise Letts]. 1928. *The Cruise of the Northern Light. Explorations and Hunting in the Alaskan and Siberian Arctic.* New York: Macmillan.

Braund, Stephen R. 1988. *The Skin Boats of Saint Lawrence Island, Alaska.* Seattle: University of Washington Press.

Brice-Bennett, Carol. 1976. "Inuit Land Use in the East-Central Canadian Arctic." In Milton M. R. Freeman (ed.), *Inuit Land Use and Occupancy Project,* vol. 1: *Land Use and Occupancy.* Ottawa: Department of Indian and Northern Affairs. Pp. 63–82.

Brower, Charles. MSa. "The Northernmost American: An Autobiography." Typescript. Rauner Special Collections Library, Dartmouth College, Hanover, NH.

——. MSb. "The Diary of Charles D. Brower, 1886–1945." Typescript. Alaska and Polar Regions Department, Rasmuson Library, University of Alaska–Fairbanks.

——. MSc. Fur shipping ledger of the Cape Smythe Whaling and Trading Company, Barrow, Alaska. Alaska and Polar Regions Department, Rasmuson Library, University of Alaska–Fairbanks.

Brower, Thomas, Sr. 1987. Interview. *Quliaqtuat Iñupiat Nunaŋiññiñ—The Report of the Chipp-Ikpikpuk River and Upper Meade River Oral History Project.* http://www.jukebox .uaf.edu/northslope/Chipp/html2/tobr.html. Retrieved January 2, 2014.

Brown, Bern Will. 2007. *Free Spirits: Portraits from the North.* Ottawa: Novalis.

——. MSS. Bern Will Brown correspondence with C. T. Pedersen. Private collection.

Buck, Anne. 1961. *Victorian Costume and Costume Accessories.* New York: Thomas Nelson and Sons.

Buckman, Caleb. 2015. "Trapping on the Edge of Nowhere." *Alaska Trapper Magazine.* March. Pp. 8–9.

Buist, Pete. 2016. "Muskrats with Three Eyes." *Alaska Trapper Magazine*. April. Pp. 8–9.

Burch, Ernest S., Jr. 1975. *Eskimo Kinsmen: Changing Family Relationships in Northwest Alaska*. American Ethnological Society, Monograph 59. St. Paul: West Publishing.

——. 1998. *The Iñupiaq Eskimo Nations of Northwest Alaska*. Fairbanks: University of Alaska Press.

——. 2012. (Igor Krupnik and Jim Dau, eds.). *Caribou Herds of Northwest Alaska, 1850–2000*. Fairbanks: University of Alaska Press.

——. 2013. (Erica Hill, ed.). *Iñupiaq Ethnohistory: Selected Essays by Ernest S. Burch Jr.* Fairbanks: University of Alaska Press.

Burg, Amos. 1931. "On Mackenzie's Trail to the Polar Sea." *National Geographic Magazine* 60(2): 127–156.

Burn, Christopher R. (ed.). 2012. *Herschel Island Qikitaryuk: A Natural and Cultural History of Yukon's Arctic Island*. Whitehorse: Wildlife Management Advisory Council (North Slope) and University of Calgary Press.

Burnham, George. 1986. *The White Road*. Winnipeg: Interlake Graphics.

Burnham, John B. 1929. *The Rim of Mystery: A Hunter's Wanderings in Unknown Siberian Asia*. New York: G. P. Putnam's Sons.

Burt, William H., and Richard P. Grossenheider. 1976. *A Field Guide to the Mammals of North America North of Mexico*. 3rd ed. Peterson Field Guide Series. Boston: Houghton Mifflin.

Burwash, L. T. [1927]. *Report of Exploration and Investigation along Canada's Arctic Coast Line from the Delta of the Mackenzie River to Hudson Bay, 1925–26*. Ottawa: Department of the Interior, Northwest Territories and Yukon Branch.

——. 1931. *Canada's Western Arctic. Report on Investigations in 1925–26, 1928–29, and 1930*. Ottawa: Department of the Interior, Northwest Territories and Yukon Branch.

Cadzow, Donald A. 1920. *Native Copper Objects of the Copper Eskimo*. Indian Notes and Monographs. New York: Museum of the American Indian, Heye Foundation.

Callan, Georgina O'Hara. 1998. *The Thames and Hudson Dictionary of Fashion and Fashion Designers*. New York: Thames and Hudson.

Cameron, Agnes Deans. 1986. *The New North. An Account of a Woman's 1908 Journey through Canada to the Arctic*. Saskatoon: Western Producer Prairie Books.

Camsell, Charles. 1954. *Son of the North*. Toronto: Ryerson.

Camsell, Charles, and Wyatt Malcolm. 1919. *The Mackenzie River Basin*. Canada Department of Mines Geological Survey Memoir 108. Ottawa: King's Printer.

Carey, Michael. 2002. "Muskrat Johnny." *Fur-Fish-Game* 99(11): 63.

Carpenter, Edmund. 1997. "Arctic Witnesses." In R. Gilberg and H. C. Gulløv (eds.), *Fifty Years of Arctic Research: Anthropological Studies from Greenland to Siberia*. Ethnographical Series 18. Copenhagen: National Museum of Denmark. Pp. 303–310.

Chance, Norman A. 1966. *The Eskimo of North Alaska*. New York: Holt, Rinehart and Winston.

——. 1990. *The Iñupiat and Arctic Alaska: An Ethnography of Development*. Fort Worth: Holt, Rinehart and Winston.

Chapelle, Howard I. [undated]. "Design and Development of Arctic Trading Vessels." *En-*

cyclopedia Arctica, vol. 9. Stefansson Collection, Rauner Special Collections Library, Dartmouth College, Hanover, NH.

Chesemore, David L. 1970. "Notes on the Pelage and Priming Sequence of Arctic Foxes in Northern Alaska." *Journal of Mammology* 51(1): 156–159.

——. 1972. "History and Economic Importance of the White Fox, *Alopex*, Fur Trade in Northern Alaska, 1798–1963." *Canadian Field-Naturalist* 86(3): 259–267.

——. 1983. "Ecology of the Arctic Fox (*Alopex lagopus*) in North America — A Review." In M. W. Fox (ed.), *The Wild Canids: Their Systematics, Behavioral Ecology and Evolution.* New York: Van Nostrand Reinhold. Pp. 143–163.

Clayton, James L. 1966. "The Growth and Economic Significance of the American Fur Trade, 1790–1890." *Aspects of the Fur Trade: Selected Papers of the 1965 North American Fur Trade Conference.* St. Paul: Minnesota Historical Society. Pp. 62–72.

Coates, Kenneth. 1985. *Canada's Colonies: A History of the Yukon and Northwest Territories.* Toronto: James Lorimer.

Cole, Terrence. 1984. "Nome: 'City of Golden Beaches.'" *Alaska Geographic* 11(1).

Collins, Julie. 2015. "Training a Trapline Dog Team." *Fur-Fish-Game* 112(12): 28–31.

Condon, Richard G. 1992. "Natkusiak, ca. 1885–1947." *Arctic* 45(1): 90–92.

——. 1994. "East Meets West: Fort Collinson, the Fur Trade, and the Economic Acculturation of the Northern Copper Inuit, 1928–1939." *Études/Inuit/Studies* 18(1–2): 109–136.

Condon, Richard G., with Julia Ogina and the Holman Elders. 1996. *The Northern Copper Inuit: A History.* Norman: University of Oklahoma Press.

Cook, John A. 1926. *Pursuing the Whale: A Quarter-Century of Whaling in the Arctic.* Boston: Houghton Mifflin.

Copland, A. Dudley. 1985. *Coplalook: Chief Trader, Hudson's Bay Company, 1923–1939.* Winnipeg: Watson and Dwyer.

Crow, Andrew, Anastasia Yarzutkina, and Oksana Koliemets. 2010. "American Traders and Native Peoples of Chukotka in the Early 20th Century." Paper presented at the 2010 International Conference on Russian America, Sitka, Alaska, August 17–22, 2010.

Crowe, Keith J. 1991. *A History of the Original Peoples of Northern Canada*, rev. ed. Montreal: McGill-Queen's.

Csonka, Yvon. 1994. "Intermédiaires au long cours: les relations entre Inuit du Caribou et Inuit du Cuivre au debut du XXe siècle." *Études/Inuit/Studies* 18(1–2): 21–47.

Dalton, Anthony. 2006. *Baychimo: Arctic Ghost Ship.* Victoria, BC: Heritage House.

Dathan, Wendy. 2012. *The Reindeer Botanist: Alf Erling Porsild, 1901–1977.* Calgary: University of Calgary Press.

Demuth, Bathsheba. 2013. "More Things on Heaven and Earth: Modernism and Reindeer in Chukotka and Alaska." In Dolly Jørgensen and Sverker Sörlin (eds.), *Northscapes: History, Technology, and the Making of Northern Environments.* Vancouver: UBC Press. Pp. 174–194.

De Windt, Harry. 1904. *From Paris to New York by Land.* New York: Frederick Warne.

Dickerson, Mark O. 1988. "E. J. (Scotty) Gall." *Arctic* 41(2): 186–187.

Dikov, N. N. 1989. *Istoria Chukotki.* Moscow: Misl.

Diubaldo, Richard J. 1967. "Wrangling over Wrangel Island." *Canadian Historical Review* 48(3): 201–226.

Douglas, William O. 1964. "Banks Island: Eskimo Life on the Polar Sea." *National Geographic Magazine* 125(5): 702–735.

Driggs, John B. MS. Diary, 1894–1901. Private collection.

Dunbar, Moira, and Keith R. Greenaway. 1956. *Arctic Canada from the Air*. Ottawa: Defense Research Board.

Duncan, Kate C. 2000. *1001 Curious Things: Ye Olde Curiosity Shop and Native American Art*. Seattle: University of Washington Press.

Edwardson, Charlie, Sr. 1987. Interview. *Quliaqtuat Iñupiat Nunaŋiññiñ—The Report of the Chipp-Ikpikpuk River and Upper Meade River Oral History Project*. http://www.jukebox.uaf.edu/northslope/Chipp/html2/ched.html. Retrieved January 2, 2014.

Ehrlander, Mary. 2014. "A Winter Circuit of Our Arctic Coast: Hudson Stuck's Literary, Ethnographic and Historical Masterpiece." *Alaska History* 29(2): 21–42.

Eide, Arthur Hansin. 1952. *Drums of Diomede: The Transformation of the Alaskan Eskimo*. Hollywood, CA: House-Warven.

Ellis, Frank H. 1954. "Early Northern Air Mail." *The Beaver* 285(4): 12–15.

Emberley, Julia V. 1997. *The Cultural Politics of Fur*. Ithaca: Cornell University Press.

Ermolaev, A. M., and V. D. Dibner. 2009. (William Barr, tr. and ed.). *Arctic Scientist, Gulag Survivor: The Biography of Mikhail Mikhailovich Ermolaev, 1905–1991*. Calgary: University of Calgary Press.

Ewing, Elizabeth. 1978. *Dress and Undress: A History of Women's Underwear*. London: Bibliophile.

———. 1981. *Fur in Dress*. London: B. T. Batsford.

Ewing, Elizabeth, and Alice Mackrell. 2001. *History of 20th Century Fashion*. New York: Costume and Fashion Press.

Farquharson, Don R. 1976. "Inuit Land Use in the West-Central Canadian Arctic." In Milton M. R. Freeman (ed.), *Inuit Land Use and Occupancy Project*, vol. 1: *Land Use and Occupancy*. Ottawa: Department of Indian and Northern Affairs. Pp. 33–62.

Fay, Francis H., and Robert O. Stephenson. 1989. "Annual, Seasonal, and Habitat-Related Variation in Feeding Habits of the Arctic Fox (*Alopex lagopus*) on St. Lawrence Island, Bering Sea." *Canadian Journal of Zoology* 67:1986–1994.

Ferguson, J. D. 1961. *The Human Ecology and Social and Economic Changes in the Community of Tuktoyaktuk, NWT*. Ottawa: Northern Co-ordination and Research Center, Department of Northern Affairs and National Resources.

Finnerty, Edward W. 1976. *Trappers, Traps, and Trapping*. South Brunswick, NJ: A. S. Barnes.

Finnie, Richard S. 1937. "Trading into the North-west Passage." *The Beaver* 268(3): 46–53.

———. 1940. *Lure of the North*. Philadelphia: David McKay.

———. 1942. *Canada Moves North*. New York: Macmillan.

———. [undated]. "Northern Canadian 'Bush' Flying." In *Encyclopedia Arctica*, vol. 9. Stefansson Collection, Rauner Special Collections Library, Dartmouth College, Hanover, NH.

Fitzhugh, William W., and Valérie Chaussonnet (eds.). 1994. *Anthropology of the North Pacific Rim*. Washington, DC: Smithsonian Institution Press.

Foote, Don Charles. MSS. Don Charles Foote Papers, Alaska and Polar Regions Department Archives, Rasmuson Library, University of Alaska–Fairbanks.

Ford, James A. MS. Alaska Expeditions, 1931–32, Journal. Papers of James A. Ford, box 13, National Anthropological Archives, Smithsonian Institution, Suitland, MD.

Forester, Joseph E., and Anne D. Forester. 1982. *Silver Fox Odyssey: History of the Canadian Silver Fox Industry.* Charlottetown, PEI: Canadian Silver Fox Breeders Association.

Forsyth, James. 1992. *A History of the Peoples of Siberia: Russia's North Asian Colony, 1581–1990.* Cambridge, U.K.: Cambridge University Press.

Fortuine, Robert. 1989. *Chills and Fever: Health and Disease in the Early History of Alaska.* Fairbanks: University of Alaska Press.

Fraser, J. K. 1949. "A Summer Journey down the Mackenzie and along the Western Arctic Coast . . . ." *Arctic Circular* 2(1): 11–13.

Freeman, Milton M. R. (ed.). 1976. *Inuit Land Use and Occupancy Project,* 3 vols. Ottawa: Department of Indian and Northern Affairs.

French, Alice. 1977. *My Name Is Masak.* Winnipeg: Peguis.

Friesen, T. Max. 2013. *When Worlds Collide: Hunter-Gatherer World-System Change in the Nineteenth-Century Canadian Arctic.* Tucson: University of Arizona Press.

Fuchs, Victor R. 1968. *The Economics of the Fur Industry.* New York: AMS Press.

Gapanovich, I. I. 1933. *Rossiya v. Severo-Vostochnoy Asii.* Pekin: Tip. Pekinskoi Russkoi Missii.

Garrott, Robert A., and Lester E. Eberhardt. 1987. "Arctic Fox." In Novak et al. (eds.), *Wild Furbearer Management and Conservation in North America.* Toronto: Ontario Trappers Association, Ontario Ministry of Natural Resources. Pp. 395–406.

Gernsheim, Alison. 1963. *Fashion and Reality, 1840–1914.* London: Faber and Faber.

Gerstell, Richard. 1985. *The Steel Trap in North America.* Harrisburg, PA: Stackpole.

Gibson, Gordon. 2000. *Bull of the Woods.* Vancouver, BC: Douglas and McIntyre.

Gillham, Charles E. 1947. *Raw North.* New York: A. S. Barnes.

Gillingham, D. W. 1955. *Umiak!* London: Museum Press.

Gilmore, R. M. MS. Field notes, 1931. Museum of Vertebrate Zoology, University of California–Berkeley.

Gitlin, Jay, Barbara Berglund, and Adam Arenson (eds.). 2013. *Frontier Cities: Encounters at the Crossroads of Empire.* Philadelphia: University of Pennsylvania Press.

Gleason, Robert J. 1977. *Icebound in the Siberian Arctic: The Story of the Last Cruise of the Fur Schooner Nanuk and the International Search for the Famous Arctic Pilot Carl Ben Eielson.* Anchorage: Alaska Northwest Publishing.

Goddard, Ives. 1984. "Synonymy." In David Damas (ed.), *Handbook of North American Indians,* vol. 5: *Arctic.* Washington, DC: Smithsonian Institution. Pp. 5–7.

———. 1999. *Native Languages and Language Families of North America* (map). Revised and enlarged, with additions and corrections. Lincoln: University of Nebraska Press.

Godsell, Jean. 1959. *I Was No Lady . . . I Followed the Call of the Wild.* Toronto: Ryerson.

Godsell, Philip H. [ca. 1935]. *Arctic Trader: The Account of Twenty Years with the Hudson's Bay Company.* London: Travel Book Club.

Goett, Edward. 1926. "Choose the Right Sawdust: Hardwoods the Source of the Furriers' Best Cleaning Agent." *Fur Trade Review* 53(5): 75–76.

Gordon, George Byron. 1906. "Notes on the Western Eskimo." *Transactions of the Department of Archaeology, Free Museum of Science and Art, University of Pennsylvania* 2(1): 69–101.

———. 1917. *In the Alaskan Wilderness*. Philadelphia: John C. Winston.

Gottschalk, Max. MS. "My Life's Adventure." Typescript. Private collection.

Gray, David. 2005. "Sachs Harbour." In Mark Nuttall (ed.), *Encyclopedia of the Arctic*. New York: Routledge. Pp. 1821–1822.

Gregory, Glenn R. 1995. *Never Too Late to Be a Hero*. Seattle: Peanut Butter Publishing.

———. 1997. *The Trading Post*. Fairbanks, AK: Ulu Books.

Greist, David. 2002. (Elizabeth Cook, ed.). *My Playmates Were Eskimos*. Louisville, KY: Chicago Spectrum.

Greist, Molly. 1968. *Nursing under the North Star*. N.p.: privately printed.

Gruben, Charlie and Persis. [undated, ca. 1980]. "Summer Crossing." In Robert LeMeur (comp.), *True Experiences—Men of the North*. [Tuktoyaktuk, NWT: privately published by Fr. Robert LeMeur OMI].

Gruben, Persis. [undated, ca. 1980]. "My Years in Banks Island, 1929–1939." In Robert LeMeur (comp.), *True Experiences—Men of the North*. [Tuktoyaktuk, NWT: privately published by Fr. Robert LeMeur OMI].

Gubser, Nicholas J. 1965. *The Nunamiut Eskimos: Hunters of Caribou*. New Haven: Yale University Press.

Gumberg, Alexander. MSS. Alexander Gumberg Papers, Wisconsin Historical Society Archives, Madison.

Hall, Edwin S., Jr. 1997. *If Only I Too Had a Map in My Head: A Biography of Simon Paneak*. Typescript. Private collection.

Hall, Edwin S., Jr., S. Craig Gerlach, and Margaret Blackman. 1985. *In the National Interest: A Geographically Based Study of Anaktuvuk Pass Iñupiat Subsistence through Time*, 2 vols. Barrow, AK: North Slope Borough.

Hall, G. Edward, and Martyn E. Obbard. 1987. "Pelt Preparation." In Novak et al. (eds.), *Wild Furbearer Management and Conservation in North America*. Toronto: Ontario Trappers Association, Ontario Ministry of Natural Resources. Pp. 842–861.

Hanable, William S. 1978. "The Wrangel Island Affair." *Explorers Journal* 56(3): 132–135.

Hanbury, David T. 1904. *Sport and Travel in the Northland of Canada*. New York: Macmillan.

Hanssen, Helmer. 1936. *Voyages of a Modern Viking*. London: George Routledge and Sons.

Harding, A. R. [1907]. *Steel Traps*. Columbus, OH: A. R. Harding.

———. 1942 [1915]. *Fur Buyer's Guide*. Columbus, OH: A. R. Harding.

Harding, Christian. 1925. "Experiences in the Arctic." *The Beaver* 256(3): 22–23.

Harkey, Ira. 1974. *Pioneer Bush Pilot: The Story of Noel Wien*. Seattle: University of Washington Press.

Harper, Kenn. 2015. *Arctic Crime and Punishment (In Those Days: Collected Writings on Arctic History, 2)*. Iqaluit, Nunavut: Inhabit Media.

Harrison, Alfred H. 1908. *In Search of a Polar Continent, 1905–1907*. London: Edward Arnold.

———. MSS. Diary. Scott Polar Research Institute, Cambridge, U.K. MS 908/1–2; D and MS 1571/1/1; BJ.

Haugen, Scott. 2000. "Frozen Seashore." *Fur-Fish-Game* 97(2): 24–26.

Heslop, Barbara. 1944. "Arctic Rescue." *The Beaver* 274(1): 8–14.

Hohn, E. O. 1955. "Arctic Schooner Voyage." *The Beaver* 286(3): 24–27.

Holmes, D. A. 1925. "Trading in Eastern Siberia — Part II." *Fur Trade Review* 52(12): 84–88.

Hrdlička, Aleš. 1943. *Alaska Diary, 1926–1931*. Lancaster, PA: Jaques Cattell.

Hudson's Bay Company. 1967. *The Bay Book of Furs*. London: Hudson's Bay Company.

———. [Undated]. *Trapping for Profit*. Winnipeg [?]: Hudson's Bay Company, Raw Fur Department.

Hughes, Charles Campbell. 1960. *An Eskimo Village in the Modern World*. Ithaca: Cornell University Press.

———. 1965. "Under Four Flags: Recent Culture Change among the Eskimos." *Current Anthropology* 6(1): 3–73.

Hunt, L. A. C. O. 1983. (Barbara Hunt, ed.). *Rebels, Rascals and Royalty: The Colourful World of LACO Hunt*. Yellowknife, NWT: Outcrop.

Hunter, Archie. 1983. *Northern Traders: Caribou Hair in the Stew*. Victoria, BC: Sono Nis.

Hutchison, Isobel Wylie. 1934. *North to the Rime-Ringed Sun*. London: Blackie and Son.

———. MSS. Diary, 1933–1934, and papers. Manuscripts Division, National Library of Scotland, Edinburgh, U.K. Acc. nos. 4775, 5509, 8138, and 9713.

Innis, Harold. 1927. *The Fur-Trade of Canada*. Toronto: University of Toronto Library.

———. 1970. *The Fur Trade in Canada: An Introduction to Canadian Economic History*. Toronto: University of Toronto Press.

Isto, Sarah Crawford. 2012. *The Fur Farms of Alaska*. Fairbanks: University of Alaska Press.

Jackson, Sheldon. 1908. *Sixteenth Annual Report on Introduction of Domestic Reindeer into Alaska, 1906*. U.S. Senate, 60th Congress, 1st Session, Document no. 501. Washington, DC: Government Printing Office.

Jenness, Diamond. 1918. "Eskimos of Northern Alaska: A Study of the Effect of Civilization." *Geographical Review* 5(2): 89–101.

———. 1921. "The Cultural Transformation of the Copper Eskimo." *Geographical Review* 11(4): 541–550.

———. 1922. *The Life of the Copper Eskimos*. Report of the Canadian Arctic Expedition, 1913–1918, Southern Party, 12(A). Ottawa: King's Printer.

———. 1928. *The People of the Twilight*. New York: Macmillan.

———. 1957. *Dawn in Arctic Alaska*. Minneapolis: University of Minnesota Press.

———. 1964. *Eskimo Administration: II Canada*. Technical paper no. 14. Montreal: Arctic Institute of North America.

———. 1991. (Stuart E. Jenness, ed.). *Arctic Odyssey: The Diary of Diamond Jenness, Ethnologist with the Canadian Arctic Expedition in Northern Alaska and Canada*. Ottawa: Canadian Museum of Civilization.

Jenness, Diamond, and Stuart E. Jenness. 2008. *Through Darkening Spectacles: Memoirs of Diamond Jenness*. Mercury Series, History Paper 55. Ottawa: Canadian Museum of Civilization.

Jenness, Stuart E. 1995. *Central Arctic Names and Their Origins*. Gloucester, ON: privately printed.

———. 1997a. *Banks Island Names and Their Origins*. Gloucester, ON: privately printed.

———. 1997b. *Victoria Island and Stefansson Island Names and Their Origins*. Gloucester, ON: privately printed.

———. 2004. *The Making of an Explorer: George Hubert Wilkins and the Canadian Arctic Expedition, 1913–1916*. Montreal: McGill-Queen's.

———. 2011. *Stefansson, Dr. Anderson and the Canadian Arctic Expedition, 1913–1918: A Story of Exploration, Science and Sovereignty*. Ottawa: Canadian Museum of Civilization Corporation.

Jones, Edward Darlington. MSS. Edward Darlington Jones letters, May 1929–August 1931. Bancroft Library, University of California–Berkeley. MSS 76/154 P.

Jones, H. G. 1999. "Ada Blackjack and the Wrangel Island Tragedy, 1921–1923." *Terrae Incognitae* 31:91–102.

Jones, J. Walter. 1913. *Fur-Farming in Canada*. Montreal: Commission of Conservation Canada, Committee on Fisheries, Game and Fur-Bearing Animals.

Jones, William Benjamin. 1927. *The Argonauts of Siberia: A Diary of a Prospector*. Philadelphia: Dorrance.

Kakinya, Elijah, and Simon Paneak. 1987. (Knut Bergsland, tr. and ed.). *Nunamiut Unipkaaŋich Nunamiut Stories*. Barrow, AK: North Slope Borough Commission on Iñupiat History, Language and Culture.

Kaplan, Lawrence. 1999. *Inuit or Eskimo: Which Names to Use?* Fairbanks: Alaska Native Language Center. www.uaf.edu/anlc/inuitoreskimo.html.

Keighley, Sydney Augustus. 1989. *Trader, Tripper, Trapper: The Life of a Bay Man*. Winnipeg: Rupert's Land Research Centre.

Kelly, L. V. 1951. "Lady in Distress." *The Beaver* 282(2): 25–29.

Kemp, H. S. M. 1957. *Northern Trader*. London: Jarrolds.

Kilian, Bernhard. 1983. (John R. Bockstoce, ed.). *The Voyage of the Schooner* Polar Bear. *Whaling and Trading in the North Pacific and Arctic, 1913–1914*. New Bedford, MA: Old Dartmouth Historical Society and the Alaska Historical Commission.

Kirillov, N. V. 1912. "Aliaska I eia otnoschenie k Chukotskomu poluostrov." *Izvestiia Imperatorskago Russkago Geograficheskago Obshchestva* 48(1): 295–341.

Kitto, F. H. 1930. *The Northwest Territories, 1930*. Ottawa: Department of the Interior, Northwest Territories and Yukon Branch.

Klengenberg, Christian. 1932. (Tom MacInnes, ed.). *Klengenberg of the Arctic: An Autobiography*. London: Jonathan Cape.

Klengenberg, Patrick. MS. Diary, January to March 1938. Rauner Special Collections Library, Dartmouth College, Hanover, NH. Rauner_Stef_Mss_53.

Klengenberg v. H. Liebes and Company. U.S. District Court, Northern District of California, San Francisco. Admiralty Case Files 1850–1934. RG 21, box 1291, case 18153 (1–5). National Archives and Records Administration, San Bruno, CA.

Klerekoper, Fred G. 1977. *Dogsled Trip from Barrow to Demarcation Point April 1937: Diary of Fred G. Klerekoper*. Barrow, AK: North Slope Borough Commission on History and Culture.

Klingle, Matthew. 2013. "Frontier Ghosts along the Urban Pacific Slope." In Jay Gitlin et al. (eds.), *Frontier Cities: Encounters at the Crossroads of Empire*. Philadelphia: University of Pennsylvania Press. Pp. 121–146.

Koonuk, Hubert, and Ida, Carol Omnik, David Libbey, Edwin S. Hall Jr., and the People of Point Hope. 1987. *Inherited from the Ancestors: The Point Hope Cultural Resource Site Survey*. Brockport, NY: Edwin Hall and Associates.

Koren, John [Johan]. 1909. "Collecting in Northeastern Siberia." *The Warbler* 22–27.

———. 1910. "Collecting on Tchonkotsk [*sic*] Peninsula." *The Warbler* 2–16.

———. MSa. "Log of the Kittiwake, 1 May 1910–9 October 1910." Museum of Comparative Zoology, Harvard University, Cambridge, MA. SMu 1671.42.1.

———. MSb. "Account of the Voyage of the Kittiwake, 1911." Museum of Comparative Zoology, Harvard University, Cambridge, MA. SMu 1671.42.1.

———. MSc. "Journal 17 May 1911–20 October 1913 of Gas Schooner Kittiwake." Museum of Comparative Zoology, Harvard University, Cambridge, MA. SMu 1671.42.1.

Krauss, Michael. 1994. "Crossroads? A Twentieth-Century History of Contacts across the Bering Strait." In William W. Fitzhugh and Valérie Chaussonnet (eds.), *Anthropology of the North Pacific Rim*. Washington, DC: Smithsonian Institution Press. Pp. 365–379.

Krejci, Paul R. 2010. "Skin Drums, Squeeze Boxes, Fiddles and Phonographs: Musical Interaction in the Western Arctic, Late 18th through Early 20th Centuries." PhD diss., University of Alaska–Fairbanks.

Krupnik, Igor I. 1994. "'Siberians' in Alaska: The Siberian Eskimo Contribution to Alaskan Population Recoveries, 1880–1940." *Études/Inuit/Studies* 18(1–2): 49–80.

———. (ed.). 2016. *Early Inuit Studies: Themes and Transitions, 1850s–1980s*. Washington, DC: Smithsonian Institution Scholarly Press.

Krupnik, Igor, and Michael A. Chlenov. 2009. "Distant Lands and Brave Pioneers: Original Thule Migration Revisited." In Bjarne Grønnow (ed.), *On the Track of the Thule Culture from Bering Strait to East Greenland*. Studies in Archaeology and History, vol. 15. Copenhagen: National Museum of Denmark. Pp. 11–23.

———. 2013. *Yupik Transitions: Change and Survival at Bering Strait, 1900–1960*. Fairbanks: University of Alaska Press.

Krupnik, Igor, and Vera Oovi Kaneshiro. 2011. *Neqamikegkaput. Faces We Remember: Leuman M. Waugh's Photography from St. Lawrence Island, Alaska, 1929–1930*. Washington, DC: Smithsonian Institution Arctic Studies Center.

Krypton, Constantine. 1953. *The Northern Sea Route: Its Place in Russian Economic History before 1917*. New York: Research Program on the USSR.

LaDue, Harry J. 1935. *Guide for Trapping and Care of Raw Furs*. St. Peter, MN: Harry J. LaDue.

Lantis, Margaret. 1950. "The Reindeer Industry in Alaska." *Arctic* 3(1): 27–44.

Larsen, Henry A., with Frank R. Sheer and Edvard Omholt-Jensen. 1967. *The Big Ship: An Autobiography of Henry A. Larsen*. Toronto: McClelland and Stewart.

Laut, Agnes C. 1921. *The Fur Trade of America*. New York: Macmillan.

Learmonth, L. A. 1951. "Interrupted Journey." *The Beaver* 282(3): 20–25.

———. 1969. "A Divergent Opinion of the Franklin Investigation." *The Beaver* 299(4): 31–33.

Leffingwell, Ernest de Koven. 1919. *The Canning River Region Northern Alaska*. U.S. Geological Survey, Professional Paper 109. Washington, DC: Government Printing Office.

——. MS. Diary, 1906–1907. Ernest de Koven Leffingwell Papers, folder 12, Rauner Special Collections Library, Dartmouth College, Hanover, NH.

Legg, Herbert. 1962. *Customs Services in Western Canada, 1867–1925*. Creston, BC: Creston Review.

LeMeur, Robert (comp.). [undated, ca. 1980]. *True Experiences—Men of the North*. [Tuktoyaktuk, NWT: privately published by Fr. Robert LeMeur OMI]. Private collection.

Levin, M. G., and L. P. Potapov (eds.). 1964. *The Peoples of Siberia*. Chicago: University of Chicago Press.

Libbey, David. 1983. *Kaktovik Area Cultural Resource Survey*. Barrow, AK: North Slope Borough Planning Department and National Park Service.

Liebes, Arnold. 1917. [Journal of Voyage on Schooner *Herman*, July 10, 1917–November 13, 1917]. Arnold Liebes Collection. California Academy of Sciences, San Francisco.

Lincoln, W. Bruce. 1994. *The Conquest of a Continent: Siberia and the Russians*. New York: Random House.

Links, J. G. 1956. *The Book of Fur*. London: James Barrie.

——. 1962. *How to Look at Furs*. London: Bodley Head.

Long, Ron. 1981. "Fox Trapping in Alaska." In Joe Dart (ed.), *Alaskan's How To Handbook*. Fairbanks: Interior Alaska Trappers Association. Pp. 79–81.

Lowenstein, Tom. 2008. *Ultimate Americans: Point Hope, Alaska, 1826–1909*. Fairbanks: University of Alaska Press.

Lyall, Ernie. 1979. *An Arctic Man: Sixty-five Years in Canada's North*. Edmonton: Hurtig.

Lyman, John. MSS. John Lyman Papers, J. Porter Shaw Library, National Maritime Museum San Francisco.

MacFarlane, John A. 1995a. "Floating Heritage West and North." *Argonauta* (Newsletter of the Canadian Nautical Research Society), January 1995, 9–10.

——. 1995b. "Mariners of the Western Arctic." *Argonauta* (Newsletter of the Canadian Nautical Research Society), April 1995, 11–12.

MacGregor, James. G. 1963. *Edmonton Trader: The Story of John A. McDougal*. Toronto: McClelland and Stewart.

——. 1974. *Paddle Wheels to Bucket-Wheels on the Athabasca*. Toronto: McClelland and Stewart.

Mackiernan, Douglas S. 1964. Interview by Philip F. Purrington regarding the voyage of the whaleship *Fearless*, 1901. Audio recording, June 23, 1964, Index no. 4-A, New Bedford Whaling Museum, New Bedford, MA.

Madsen, Charles, with John Scott Douglas. 1957. *Arctic Trader*. New York: Dodd, Mead.

Maguire, Rochfort. 1988. (John R. Bockstoce, ed.). *The Journal of Rochfort Maguire, 1852–1854: Two Years at Point Barrow, Alaska, Aboard HMS* Plover *in the Search for Sir John Franklin*, 2 vols. London: Hakluyt Society.

Mahoney, Timothy R. 2013. "Locating the Frontier City in Time and Space: Documenting a Passing Phenomenon." In Jay Gitlin et al. (eds.), *Frontier Cities: Encounters at the Crossroads of Empire*. Philadelphia: University of Pennsylvania Press. Pp. 149–164.

Mallory, Enid. 1989. *Coppermine: The Far North of George M. Douglas.* Peterborough, ON: Broadview.

Manning, Thomas H. 1953. "Narrative of an Unsuccessful Attempt to Circumnavigate Banks Island by Canoe in 1952." *Arctic* 6(3): 171–197.

———. 1956. "Narrative of a Second Defence Research Board Expedition to Banks Island, with Notes on the Country and Its History." *Arctic* 9(1 and 2): 3–77.

———. MSS. Thomas H. Manning Papers, Scott Polar Research Institute, University of Cambridge, Cambridge, U.K.

Marchenko, Nataliya. 2012. *Russian Arctic Seas: Navigational Conditions and Accidents.* Berlin: Springer-Verlag.

Masik, August, and Isobel Wylie Hutchison. 1935. *Arctic Nights' Entertainments.* London: Blackie and Son.

Mason, Winfield S. 1910. *The Frozen Northland. Life with the Esquimo in His Own Country.* Cincinnati: Jennings and Graham.

Mawdsley, Evan. 2008. *The Russian Civil War.* New York: Pegasus.

McGhee, Robert. 1974. *Beluga Hunters: An Archaeological Reconstruction of the History and Culture of the Mackenzie Delta Kittegaryumiut.* Newfoundland Social and Economic Studies, 13. St. John's: Memorial University of Newfoundland.

McGrath, Robin. MS. "Stephen Angulalik: The Man with the Million Dollar Smile." Private collection.

Melvin, Leslie. 1982. *I Beat The Arctic.* Anchorage: Alaska Northwest Publishing.

Menovshchikov, G. A. 1964. "The Eskimos." In M. G. Levin and L. P. Potapov (eds.), *The Peoples of Siberia.* Chicago: University of Chicago Press. Pp. 836–850.

Mikkelsen, Ejnar. 1909. *Conquering the Arctic Ice.* London: William Heineman.

Mills, David C. 1926. "The Collection of Furs." *Journal of Home Economics* 18(12): 691–696.

———. 1927a. "The Preparation of Furs." *Journal of Home Economics* 19(1): 16–19.

———. 1927b. "The Manufacture of Fur Garments." *Journal of Home Economics* 19(3): 136–141.

Milne, Jack. 1975. *Trading for Milady's Furs: In the Service of the Hudson's Bay Company, 1923–1943.* Saskatoon: Western Producer Prairie Books.

Morris, Oliver D. 1965. Interview by Irving Reed, Jim Cassidy, and others in Fairbanks, Alaska, October 28, 1965. Oral History Program, Alaska and Polar Regions Department, Rasmuson Library, University of Alaska–Fairbanks. Tanana-Yukon Historical Society tape 97-66-14.

Morrison, William Robert. 1973. "The Mounted Police on Canada's Northern Frontier, 1895–1940." PhD diss., University of Western Ontario–London.

Murdoch, John. 1885. "Arctic Fox." *Report of the International Polar Expedition to Point Barrow, Alaska, in Response to the Resolution of the House of Representatives of December 11, 1884.* Washington, DC: Government Printing Office. Pp. 93–94.

Nagle, Ted, and Jordan Zinovich. 1989. *The Prospector North of Sixty.* Edmonton: Lone Pine.

Nagy, Murielle Ida. 1994. *Yukon North Slope Inuvialuit Oral History.* Occasional Papers in Yukon History no. 1. Whitehorse, YT: Government of the Yukon, Heritage Branch.

——. 1999. *Aulavik Oral History Project on Banks Island, NWT: Final Report*. Inuvialuit Social Development Program. n.p.: Parks Canada—Western District.

Neakok, Warren, Dorcas Neakok, Waldo Bodfish, David Libbey, Edwin S. Hall Jr., and Point Lay Elders. 1985. *To Keep the Past Alive: The Point Lay Cultural Resource Site Survey*. Barrow, AK: North Slope Borough.

Nelson, Richard K. 1969. *Hunters of the Northern Ice*. Chicago: University of Chicago Press.

Newell, Gordon (ed.). 1966. *The H. W. McCurdy Marine History of the Pacific Northwest*. Seattle: Superior.

Noice, Harold. 1924. *With Stefansson in the Arctic*. London: George G. Harrap.

Nome Customs Records Ledger. 1909–1924. MS. University of Washington Libraries, Special Collections, Suzallo Library.

North American Fur Auctions. 1995. *Wild Fur Pelt Handling Manual*. Toronto: North American Fur Auctions.

——. 2009. *Technical Manual*. www.nafa.ca/wild-fur/resources.

Northern Whaling and Trading Company Collection, Archives, University of Alaska–Anchorage.

North Slope Borough. 1980. *Qiñiqtuagaksrat Utuqqanaat Iñuuniaġniŋisiqun: The Traditional Land Use Inventory for the Mid-Beaufort Sea*, vol. 1. Barrow, AK: North Slope Borough, Commission on History and Culture.

Novak, Milan, James A. Baker, Martyn E. Obbard, and Bruce Malloch (eds.). 1987. *Wild Furbearer Management and Conservation in North America*. Toronto: Ontario Trappers Association, Ontario Ministry of Natural Resources.

Nuligak [Bob Cockney]. 1966. (Maurice Metayer, ed.). *I, Nuligak*. Toronto: Peter Martin.

Nuttall, Mark (ed.). 2005. *Encyclopedia of the Arctic*, 3 vols. New York: Routledge.

Obard, Martyn E. 1987. "Fur Grading and Pelt Identification." In Novak et al. (eds.), *Wild Furbearer Management and Conservation in North America*. Toronto: Ontario Trappers Association, Ontario Ministry of Natural Resources. Pp. 717–825.

Okpik, Abraham. 2005. (Louis McComber, ed.). *We Call It Survival: The Life Story of Abraham Okpik*. Life Stories of Northern Leaders, vol. 1. Iqaluit: Nunavut Arctic College.

Olson, Dean F. 1969. *Alaska Reindeer Herdsmen*. Institute of Social, Economic and Government Research no. 18. Fairbanks: University of Alaska.

Orth, Donald J. 1967. *Dictionary of Alaska Place Names*. U.S. Geological Survey, Professional Paper 567. Washington, DC: Government Printing Office.

Owen, Thomas C. 2008. "Chukchi Gold: American Enterprise and Russian Xenophobia in the Northeastern Siberian Company." *Pacific Historical Review* 77(1): 49–85.

Pálsson, Gísli (ed.). 2001. *Writing on Ice: The Ethnographic Notebooks of Vilhjalmur Stefansson*. Hanover, NH: Dartmouth College Press.

Pamperin, Nathan J., Erich H. Follman, and Bill Petersen. 2006. "Interspecific Killing of an Arctic Fox by a Red Fox at Prudhoe Bay, Alaska." *Arctic* 59(4): 361–364.

Parr, Tom. 2012. "Sears Tips to Trappers, Fur Marketing Service." *Fur-Fish-Game* 109(12): 58–59.

———. 2015a. "Montgomery Ward Competed with Sears for Trapping Trade." *Fur-Fish-Game* 112(4): 54.

———. 2015b. "Johnny Muskrat Pocket Knife." *Fur-Fish-Game* 112(8): 55.

Patmore, Percival. MS. Log of the *Baychimo*, 1931. Hudson's Bay Company Archives, Archives of Manitoba, Winnipeg. HBCA RG3/8/5.

Paupanekis, Maxwell. 1972. "The Trapper." In Malvina Bolus (ed.), *People and Pelts: Selected Papers of the Second North America Fur Trade Conference*. Winnipeg: Peguis. Pp. 137–143.

Petersen, Marcus. 1914. *The Fur Traders and Fur Bearing Animals*. Buffalo, NY: Hammond.

———. 1920. *Petersen's Fur Traders Lexicon*. New York: Petersen and Chandless.

Petrone, Penny. 1988. *Northern Voices: Inuit Writing in English*. Toronto: University of Toronto Press.

Phoenix Northern Trading Company. [1921]. *Fur Trading with the Siberian Eskimo: A Few Extracts for the Experiences of Captain C. L. Olsen in Northeastern Siberia*. Tacoma, WA: Phoenix Northern Trading Company.

Pielou, E. C. 1994. *A Naturalist's Guide to the Arctic*. Chicago: University of Chicago Press.

Pinson, Elizabeth Bernhardt. 2004. *Alaska's Daughter: An Eskimo Memoir of the Early Twentieth Century*. Logan: Utah State University Press.

Poland, Henry. 1892. *Fur-Bearing Animals in Nature and Commerce*. London: Gurney and Jackson.

Poncins, Gontran de. 1954. (Bernard Frechtman, tr.), *The Ghost Voyage Out of Eskimo Land*. Garden City: Doubleday.

Portenko, L. A. 1981. *Birds of the Chukchi Peninsula and Wrangel Island*, vol. 1. Washington. DC: Smithsonian Institution.

———. 1989. *Birds of the Chukchi Peninsula and Wrangel Island*, vol. 2. Washington, DC: Smithsonian Institution.

Pratt, Kenneth L., Matt L. Ganley, and Dale C. Slaughter. Forthcoming. "New Perspectives on the Late 19th Century Caribou Crash in Western Alaska." In Igor Krupnik and Aron L. Crowell (eds.), *Arctic Crashes: People and Animals in the Changing Arctic*. Washington, DC: Smithsonian Institution Scholarly Press.

Rainey, Froelich G. 1940. MSS. Field notes, Point Hope, Alaska. Private collection.

Rasmussen, Knud. 1927. *Across Arctic America: Narrative of the Fifth Thule Expedition*. New York: G. P. Putnam's Sons.

Ray, Arthur J. 1987. "The Fur Trade in North America: An Overview from a Historical Geographical Perspective." In Novak et al. (eds.), *Wild Furbearer Management and Conservation in North America*. Toronto: Ontario Trappers Association, Ontario Ministry of Natural Resources. Pp. 21–30.

———. 1990. *The Canadian Fur Trade in the Industrial Age*. Toronto: University of Toronto Press.

Reid, Donald, Daniel Gallant, Dorothy Cooley, and Lee John Meyook. 2012. "Small Carnivores." In Christopher R. Burn (ed.), *Herschel Island Qikitaryuk: A Natural and*

Cultural History of Yukon's Arctic Island. Whitehorse: Wildlife Management Advisory Council (North Slope) and University of Calgary Press. Pp. 118–122.

Richling, Barnett. 2012. *In Twilight and in Dawn: A Biography of Diamond Jenness.* Montreal: McGill-Queen's.

Robinson, J. Lewis. 1944. "The Battle of Fort Ross." *The Beaver* 274(1): 4–7.

Robinson, M. J., and J. L. Robinson. 1946. "Fur Production in the Northwest Territories." *Canadian Geographical Journal* 32(1): 34–48.

Rowley, Graham W. 2007. *Cold Comfort: My Love Affair with the Arctic.* 2nd ed. Montreal: McGill-Queen's.

Royal Canadian Mounted Police, Annual Reports. 1920 onward. Sessional Paper 28, Parliament, Ottawa. https://collections.library.utoronto.ca/islandora/object/govinfo1%3Amounted-police.

Royal Northwest Mounted Police, Annual Reports, 1903–1919, Sessional Paper 28, Parliament, Ottawa. https://collections.library.utoronto.ca/islandora/object/govinfo1%3Amounted-police.

Russell, Frank. 1898. *Explorations in the Far North.* Iowa City: University of Iowa Press.

Ruttle, Terence. 1968. *How to Grade Furs.* Publication 1362. Ottawa: Canada Department of Agriculture.

Sablin, Ivan. 2012. "Transcultural Chukotka: Transfer and Exchange in Northeastern Asia, 1900–1945." *Soviet and Post-Soviet Review* 39(2): 219–248.

Samet, Arthur. 1950. *Pictorial Encyclopedia of Furs.* New York: Arthur Samet.

Saskatchewan, Province of. 1964. *Trappers' Guide.* Regina: Conservation Information Service, Department of Natural Resources Wildlife Branch.

Saul, Norman E. 2006. *Friends or Foes? The United States and Soviet Russia, 1921–1941.* Lawrence: University Press of Kansas.

Schindler, Debra L. 1992. "Russian Hegemony and Indigenous Rights in Chukotka." *Études/Inuit/Studies* 16(1–2): 51–74.

Schneider, William S. 2012. *On Time Delivery: The Dog Team Mail Carriers.* Fairbanks: University of Alaska Press.

Scholander, P. F., Vladimir Walters, Raymond Hock, and Laurence Irving. 1950. "Body Insulation of Some Arctic and Tropical Mammals and Birds." *Biological Bulletin* 99(2): 225–236.

Schrader, Frank Charles, and W. J. Peters. 1904. *A Reconnaissance in Northern Alaska . . . in 1901.* U.S. Geological Survey Professional Paper no. 20. Washington, DC: Government Printing Office.

Schroeder, Gary. 2015. "Buyers Reluctant to Bet on Quick Turn-Around for Prices." *Fur-Fish-Game* 112(1): 50–52.

———. 2016a. "Finding a Buyer for Raccoon and Other Less-Desirable Furs Could Be a Challenge." *Fur-Fish-Game* 113(9): 48–51.

———. 2016b. "With Fur Harvest Down by Half or More Traders Look for Glimmer of a Turn-Around." *Fur-Fish-Game* 113(10): 48–51.

Schweitzer, Peter P., and Evgeniy Golovko. 1995. *Contacts across Bering Strait, 1898–1948.* Anchorage: U.S. National Park Service, Alaska Regional Office.

Scull, E. Marshall. 1914. *Hunting in the Arctic and Alaska.* London: Duckworth.

Seveck, Chester Asakak. 1973. *Longest Reindeer Herder: A True Life Story of an Alaskan Eskimo Covering the Period from 1890 to 1973.* n.p.: Arctic Circle Enterprises.

Shklovsky, I. W. 1916. *In Far North-East Siberia.* London: Macmillan.

Shnirelman, Victor A. 1994. "Hostages of an Authoritarian Regime: The Fate of the 'Numerically-Small Peoples' of the Russian North under Soviet Rule." *Études/Inuit/Studies* 18(1–2): 201–223.

Slezkine, Yuri. 1994. *Arctic Mirrors: Russia and the Small Peoples of the North.* Ithaca: Cornell University Press.

Smith, Gordon W. 2014. (P. Whitney Lackenbauer, ed.). *A Historical and Legal Study of Sovereignty in the Canadian North: Terrestrial Sovereignty, 1870–1939.* Calgary: University of Calgary Press.

Smith, Philip S. 1925. "Explorations in Northwestern Alaska." *Geographical Review* 15(2): 237–254.

Smith, Philip S., and J. B. Mertie Jr. 1930. *Geology and Mineral Resources of Northwestern Alaska.* Geological Survey Bulletin 815. Washington, DC: Government Printing Office. U.S. Department of the Interior.

Solecki, Ralph S. 1950. "New Data on the Inland Eskimo of Northern Alaska." *Journal of the Washington Academy of Sciences* 40(5): 137–157.

Sonnenfeld, Joseph. 1957. "Changes in Subsistence among the Barrow Eskimo." PhD diss., Johns Hopkins University.

——. 1959. "An Arctic Reindeer Industry: Growth and Decline." *Georgraphical Review* 49(1): 76–94.

Spector, Robert. 1998. *Seattle Fur Exchange, 1898–1998.* Seattle: Documentary Book Publishers.

Spencer, Robert F. 1959. *The North Alaskan Eskimo: A Study in Ecology and Society.* Bureau of American Ethnology Bulletin 171. Washington, DC: Government Printing Office. Smithsonian Institution.

Starokadomskiy, L. M. 1976. (William Barr, tr. and ed.). *Charting the Russian Northern Sea Route: The Arctic Ocean Hydrographic Expedition, 1910–1915.* Montreal: Arctic Institute of North America and McGill-Queen's.

Stefansson, Vilhjalmur. MS. Diary, 1906–07. Rauner Special Collections Library, Dartmouth College, Hanover, NH.

——. 1909. "Northern Alaska in Winter." *Bulletin of the American Geographical Society* 41(10): 601–610.

——. 1914. "The Stefánsson-Anderson Arctic Expedition of the American Museum: Preliminary Ethnological Report." *Anthropological Papers of the American Museum of Natural History* 14(1): 1–395.

——. 1921. *My Life with the Eskimo.* New York: Macmillan.

——. 1922. *Hunters of the Great North.* New York: Harcourt, Brace.

——. 1924. *My Life with the Eskimo.* New York: Macmillan.

——. 1926. *The Adventure of Wrangel Island.* London: Jonathan Cape.

——. 1943. *The Friendly Arctic: The Story of Five Years in Polar Regions.* New York: Macmillan.

Stephan, John J. 1994. *The Russian Far East: A History.* Stanford: Stanford University Press.

Stern, Richard O., Edward L. Arobio, Larry L. Naylor, and Wayne C. Thomas. 1980. *Eskimos, Reindeer and Land*. Bulletin 59. Fairbanks: Agricultural Experiment Station, School of Agriculture and Land Resources Management, University of Alaska.

Stuck, Hudson. 1920. *A Winter Circuit of Our Arctic Coast*. New York: Charles Scribner's Sons.

———. MS. 1917–1918. Journal. Episcopal Church Historical Society, Austin, TX.

Sullivan, Hal. 2014. "The 1955–56 F. C. Taylor Catalog Reminds Hal How Much Trapping Has Changed." *Fur-Fish-Game*, 111(8): 42–44.

Sverdrup, Harald U. 1978. (Molly Sverdrup, tr.), *Among the Tundra People*. La Jolla, CA: Scripps Institution of Oceanography.

Swanson, Henry. 1982. *The Unknown Islands: Life and Tales of Henry Swanson*. Unalaska, AK: Unalaska City School.

Swenson, Olaf. 1944. *Northwest of the World: Forty Years Trading and Hunting in Northern Siberia*. New York: Dodd, Mead.

Swithinbank, Charles. MSS. Charles Swithinbank Papers, Scott Polar Research Institute, University of Cambridge, Cambridge, U.K.

Taylor, Russel R. 1946. *The Fur Industry*. Boston: Bellman.

Teien, George C. MS. *Teien's Tales*. University of Washington Libraries, Special Collections, Suzzallo Library, Scandinavian Archives, 0356-001, box 27, folder 10.

Tiulana, Paul 1987. (Vivian Senungetuk, ed.). A *Place for Winter: Paul Tiulana's Story*. Anchorage, AK: Ciri Foundation.

Tolmachoff, I. P. 1949. *Siberian Passage: An Explorer's Search into the Russian Arctic*. New Brunswick, NJ: Rutgers University Press.

Tower, Walter S. 1907. A *History of the American Whale Fishery*. Series in Political Economy and Public Law, 20. Philadelphia: University of Pennsylvania.

Tul'chinskii, K. N. 1907. "Iz puteshestviia k Beringovu prolivu." *Izvestiia Imperatorskago Russkago Geograficheskago Obshchestva* 42(2–3): 521–580.

United States. 1900. *Twelfth Population Census of the United States, 1900*. Alaska. https://archive.org/details/1900_census.

———. 1910. *Thirteenth Population Census of the United States, 1910*. Alaska. https://archive.org/details/1910_census.

———. 1920. *Fourteenth Population Census of the United States, 1920*. Alaska. https://archive.org/details/1920_census.

———. 1930. *Fifteenth Population Census of the United States, 1930*. Alaska. https://archive.org/details/1930_census.

———. 1940. *Sixteenth Population Census of the United States, 1940*. Alaska. https://1940census.archives.gov.

United States Coast and Geodetic Survey. 1926. *United States Coast Pilot, Alaska, Part II, Yakutat Bay to Arctic Ocean*. 2nd ed. Washington, DC: Government Printing Office.

Usher, Peter J. 1965a. *Economic Basis and Resource Use of the Coppermine-Holman Region, N. W. T.* Ottawa: Department of Northern Affairs and National Resources, Northern Co-ordination and Research Centre, NCRC-65–2.

———. 1965b. *Banks Island: An Area Economic Survey*. Ottawa: Department of Northern Affairs and National Resources, Industrial Division.

———. 1971a. *Fur Trade Posts of the Northwest Territories, 1870–1970.* Ottawa: Department of Indian Affairs and Northern Development, Northern Science Research Group.

———. 1971b. *The Bankslanders: Economy and Ecology of a Frontier Trapping Community.* 3 vols. Ottawa: Department of Indian Affairs and Northern Development, Northern Science Research Group.

———. 1971c. "The Canadian Western Arctic: A Century of Change." *Anthropologica*, n.s. 13(1–2): 169–184.

———. 1975. "The Growth and Decay of the Trading and Trapping Frontiers in the Western Canadian Arctic." *Canadian Geographer* 19(4): 308–320.

———. 1976a. "Inuit Land Use in the Western Canadian Arctic." In Milton M. R. Freeman (ed.), *Inuit Land Use and Occupancy Project*, vol. 1: *Land Use and Occupancy.* Ottawa: Department of Indian and Northern Affairs. Pp. 21–32.

———. 1976b. "The Inuk as a Trapper: A Case Study." In Milton M. R. Freeman (ed.), *Inuit Land Use and Occupancy Project*, vol. 2: *Supporting Studies.* Ottawa: Department of Indian and Northern Affairs. Pp. 207–222.

Vakhtin, Nikolai Borisovich. 1992. *Native Peoples of the Russian Far North.* London: Minority Rights Group.

Vanderlip, Washington B., and Homer B. Hulbert. 1903. *In Search of a Siberian Klondike.* New York: The Century Company.

VanStone, James W. 1962. *Point Hope: An Eskimo Village in Transition.* Seattle: University of Washington Press.

Van Valin, William B. 1941. *Eskimoland Speaks.* Caldwell, ID: Caxton.

Vaté, Virginie. 2005. "Anadyr." In Mark Nuttall (ed.), *Encyclopedia of the Arctic.* New York: Routledge. Pp. 86–87.

Vinkovetsky, Ilya. 2011. *Russian America: An Overseas Colony of a Continental Empire, 1804–1867.* Oxford: Oxford University Press.

Vucinich, Alexander. 1960. "Soviet Ethnographic Studies of Cultural Change." *American Anthropologist* 62(5): 867–877.

Vuntut Gwitchin First Nation and Shirleen Smith. 2009. *People of the Lakes: Stories of Our Van Tat Gwich'in Elders. . . .* Edmonton: University of Alberta Press.

Wall, Matthew. 2009. *Caribou Inuit Traders of the Kivalliq Nunavut, Canada.* BAR International Series 1895. Oxford, U.K: Archaeopress.

Washburn, Tahoe Talbot. 1999. *Under Polaris: An Arctic Quest.* Seattle: University of Washington Press.

Watt, Frederick B. 1980. *Great Bear: A Journey Remembered.* Yellowknife: Outcrop.

Waugh, Leuman M. 2011. (Igor Krupnik and Vera Oovi Kaneshiro, eds.). *Faces We Remember. Neqamikegkaput. Leuman M. Waugh's Photography from St. Lawrence Island, Alaska, 1929–1930.* Washington, DC: Smithsonian Institution Scholarly Press, Arctic Studies Center.

Webster, J. Harold, with Edna H. Craven. 1987. *Arctic Adventure.* Ridgetown, ON: G. C. and H. C. Enterprises.

Wegner, Wolfgang, and Evamaria Steinke. 1985. *Der Robin Hood der Beringstrasse . . . Leben des Max Gottschalk.* Würzburg: Arena.

Wendt, George A. 1931. "Radio in the Far North." *The Beaver* 262(1): 187–188.

West, Elliott. 2013. "Grain Kings, Rubber Dreams, and Stock Exchanges: How Transportation and Communication Changed Frontier Cities." In Jay Gitlin et al. (eds.), *Frontier Cities: Encounters at the Crossroads of Empire*. Philadelphia: University of Pennsylvania Press. Pp. 107–120.

Whalley, George. 1962. *The Legend of John Hornby*. Toronto: Macmillan.

White, Patrick. 2004. *Mountie in Mukluks: The Arctic Adventures of Bill White*. Madeira Park, BC: Harbour Publishing.

Whittaker, C. E. 1937. *Arctic Eskimo: A Record of Fifty Years' Experience and Observation among the Eskimo*. London: Seeley, Service.

Wikan, Steinar. 2000. *Johan Koren—feldzoolog og polar-pioner*. Oslo: Chr. Schibsted.

Wilcox, R. Turner. 1951. *The Mode in Furs: The History of Furred Costume of the World from the Earliest Times to the Present*. New York: Charles Scribner's Sons.

Willersley, Rane. 2005. "Fur Trade, History in Russia." In Mark Nuttall (ed.), *Encyclopedia of the Arctic*. New York: Routledge. Pp. 693–695.

Wilmers, Mary-Kay. 2010. *The Eitingons: A Twentieth Century Story*. London: Verso.

Wilson, C. P. 1947. "Nascopie. The Story of a Ship." *The Beaver* 278(3): 3–11.

Wilson, Dean. [n.d.]. *The Alaskan Trapper's Handbook*. Fairbanks, AK [?]: Dean Wilson.

Wolfe, Robert J. 1982. "Alaska's Great Sickness, 1900: An Epidemic of Measles in a Virgin Soil Population." *Proceedings of the American Philosophical Society* 126(2): 91–121.

Wood, Alan. 2011. *Russia's Frozen Frontier: A History of Siberia and the Russian Far East, 1581–1991*. London: Bloomsbury Academic.

Wright, E. W. (ed.). 1967. *Lewis and Dryden's Marine History of the Pacific Northwest*. Seattle: Superior.

Yarzutkina, Anastasia A. 2014. "Trade on the Icy Coasts: The Management of American Traders in the Settlements of Chukotka Native Inhabitants." *Terra Sebius: Acta Musei Sabasiensis* [Romania]. Special issue: Russian Studies from Early Middle Ages to the Present Day. Pp. 361–384.

Zarnke, Randy. 2013. *Alaska Tracks: A Collection of Life Stories as Told by Alaskan Hunters, Fishermen and Trappers*. Fairbanks: Alaska Trappers Association.

Zaslow, Morris. 1971. *The Opening of the Canadian North, 1870–1914*. Toronto: McClelland and Stewart.

———. 1988. *The Northward Expansion of Canada, 1914–1967*. Toronto: McClelland and Stewart.

Zinovich, Jordan. 1992. *Battling the Bay*. Edmonton: Lone Pine.

Znamenski, Andrei A. 1999a. "'Vague Sense of Belonging to the Russian Empire': The Reindeer Chukchi's Status in Nineteenth Century Northeastern Siberia." *Arctic Anthropology* 36(1–2): 19–36.

———. 1999b. *Shamanism and Christianity: Native Encounters with Russian Orthodox Missions in Siberia and Alaska, 1820–1917*. Westport, CT: Greenwood.

ACKNOWLEDGMENTS

First, I must thank my editors Chris Rogers, Susan Laity, and Eliza Childs, and those persons who have commented on the manuscript. Their suggestions have helped to make this a better work: William Barr, John J. Burns, Paul Comstock, Andrew Crow, Craig George, Jay Gitlin, Igor Krupnik, Russell Potter, Thomas G. Smith, Peter Usher, and Judy Valenzuela.

This book is the product of research that began in 1969. It is the result of the generous support and advice that I have received from a large number of persons, many of whom are no longer with us. I am grateful to all of them, and I hope that I have forgotten none of them: Lucy Avakana, Lynne Allen, Douglas D. Anderson, Margaret Asbury, Katherine Arndt, Elsie Backland, John and Kym Backland, Tom Baione, Susan Barr, Louvetta Bertonccini, J. L. ("Larry") Black, Margaret B. Blackman, Lincoln Blassi, Naomi Boneham, Nadine Bonsor, William Boucher, Stephen Bown, Stephen R. Braund, Lawson Brigham, Harry Brower Jr., Thomas Brower Sr., Ernest S. Burch Jr., Bern Will Brown, Christopher Burn, Michael Carey, Kenneth Coates, Terrence Cole, Christina Connett, Kory Cooper, Paul Fenimore Cooper Jr., Maida Counts, Bruce Courson, Andrew Crow, Thomas B. Crowley Sr., Charles A. Dana III, Susan Danforth, Mike Dederer, Gary and Pat Dederer, Bathsheba Demuth, Katherine Donahue, Kim Duthie, Michael Dyer, Mary Ehrlander, Ann Fienup-Riordan, Richard Finnie, William Fitzhugh, Clare Flemming, David and Dinah Frankson, Milton Freeman, E. J. ("Scotty") Gall, Manfred ("Freddy") Garfunkel, Frank H. Goodyear Jr., Archie Gottschalk, David Greist, Bonnie Hahn, Kenneth Hahn, Patrick Hahn, Edwin S. Hall Jr., Edward Harding, V. Heidi Hass, Greg Hayes, Erica Hill, George Hobson, Al Hopson, James A. Houston, Ray Hudson, Charles C. Hughes, David Hull, Father Leonce d'Hurtevant OMI, Harold Huycke, Zephyr Inkpen, Sarah Isto, Kathy Itta, Stuart Jenness, Carl Jewell, Sven Johansson, Norm Kagan, Bernhard ("Ben") Kilian, Jimmy Asetsaq Killigivuk, Jonathan C. H. King, Earl Natsiq Kingik, George ("Blurr") Kingik, Kerm Kingik, Terence Uyuġaluq ("Laurie") Kingik and Sarah Nipiq Kingik, William Kooiman, Luke Koonook Sr. and Angeline Koonook, Michael Krauss, Paul Krejci, Igor Krupnik, Howard Lamar, Chester Lampe, Dennis Landis, Amos Lane, Michael Lapides, Molly Lee, Father Robert LeMeur OMI, Genevieve Lemoine, Sam and

Margaret Lennie, Angsi Long, Dee Longenbaugh, Tom Lowenstein, Ernie Lyall, Nuna Washburn MacDonald, Edna Maclean, Bob and Elizabeth Mackenzie, Ross MacPhee, Thomas Manning, Carolyn Marr, Owen Mason, Leslie McCartney, Holly McElrea, Robin McGrath, Vincent Nageak, Arthur Nagozruk Sr., Murielle Nagy, Bernard Nash Sr., Sammy Nash, Margot Nishimura, Dennis Noble, Kimberly Nusco, Felix Nuvoyaok, Karen Olson, Louise Oliver, George Omnik, Norman Omnik, David Ongley, Katherine Parker, Erica Parmi, Tom Parr, Charlie Pedersen, Teddy Pedersen, Brian Person, Carl Emil Petersen, George W. Porter Sr., George and Effie Porter, Ken Pratt, Mark Procknik, Froelich Rainey, Rosalind Rank, Dorothy Jean Ray, Sharani Robins, Graham and Diana Rowley, James Russell, Neil Safier, Chie Sakakibara, Laura Samuelson, Dorthea Sartain, William Schneider, Mark Seidenberg, L. F. ("Slim") Semmler, Peter and Alma Semotiuk, Chester Seveck, Keith A. Smith, Shirlee Anne Smith, Joseph Sonnenfeld, the staff of the Southworth Library, Grant Spearman, Rosemarie Speranza, Irene Spirer, David and Deirdre Stam, John J. Stephan, Richard O. Stern, Toby Sullivan, Dwight Tevuk, Ben Thylan, John Tichotsky, Ester Kingik Timothy, Leslie Tobias-Olsen, Bob and Sunshine Tuckfield, Lucian W. Turner, Roy Vincent, Erin Wahl, Brian Walsh, Doug Wamsley, Lincoln and Tahoe Washburn, Candy Waugaman, John Whitehead, Nicholas Whitman, Steinar Wikan, Dick Wilson, Jim Wolki, Martin Wolman, Anastasia Yarzutkina, and Randy Zarnke.

INDEX

Page numbers in *italics* refer to illustrations.

222–223, 224, 232, 239, 241; proficiency of, xiv, 147, 216; reputation of, 147, 193, 202, 203

Pedersen, Charlie, 202, 241

Pedersen, May Olive (wife of C. T. Pedersen), *196*, 203

Pedersen, Teddy, 202

Peel River, Canada, 183

Peel's River Post (Fort McPherson), Canada, 87, 95, 183, 184

Penelope (schooner), 88

People of the Twilight (Jenness), 106–107

Perry River, Canada, 197, 199, 240, 278n40

petroleum, 181

Petropavlovsk, Kamchatka, Russia, 118, 119, 120, 121, 122

Phillips, J. W., 110

Phoenix Northern Trading Company, 118–119, 124

Pirktuqana, David, 228

Pitt Point, Alaska, 81

Point Barrow, Alaska, 20–21, 25, 66, 81, 86, 143, 185

Point Belcher, Alaska, 218

Point Franklin, Alaska, 218

Point Hope, Alaska, xiii, 82, 86, 146, 156, 227, 276n10

"pointing," 48

Point Lay, Alaska, 227

Poiret, Paul, 53–54

Pokiak (Alaskan immigrant in Canada), 161–162

Poland, Henry, 53

Polar Bear (schooner), 33, 84–85, 89, 97, 110, 123–124, 273n12

polar bears, 16, 18, 26, 30, 77, 87, 100, 110, 124, 140

Polet, Antonio ("Tony"), 65, 118, 124, 128, 146

Porcupine River, Yukon and Alaska, 95

Porsild, A. E., 157–158

Porter, George, Jr., 198

Porter, George, Sr., xiv, 197, 198

Porter, George W., 197

predators, 19, 30, 228

Pribilof Islands, Alaska, 17

pricing, 34–35, 63

Prince Albert Sound, Canada, 92, 93, 190, 191

Prince Regent Inlet, Canada, 11, 14

Provideniya, Russia, 210

Provideniya Bay, Russia, 118, 121, 125, 140

ptarmigan, 18, 23, 158, 230

Ptarmigan (schooner), 238

Qimniq (wife of Charlie Klengenberg), 7, *168*

Quebec, 17

Queen Maud Gulf, Canada, 176, 190, 191, 197, 201, 239

Quzinga (Eskimo trader), 71

Quwaaren (Yupik trader), 59, 59–60, 67

rabies, 19

Radford, Harry, 176, 179

radio, 37

Rainey, Froelich, 29

Ram (schooner), 71, 119–120, 126

Rampart House, Canada, 169

Rank, Arthur, 106, 271n49

Rank, Ira, xiv, 65, 69, 71, 94, 100, 103, 118, 146, 184, 185, 221, 222, 224, 227

Rank family, 66

Rasmussen, Knud, 135–137, 139, 163–164, 181, 190

ravens, 30

Rawtergin (Chukchi hunter), 122

Read Island, Canada, 201

receiving houses, 39

red fox, 22, 40, 52, 58, 71, 77, 87, 157; color phases of, 16; as predator, 19, 30, 228. *See also* cross fox; silver fox

Reid, Donald, 19

reindeer, 58, 59, 67, 71, 75, 118, 139, 146, 157, 207, 224

retailers, 50

Revillon Frères (furriers), 183, 190

rifles, 51, 71, 74, 75, 80, 82, 86, 176, 229

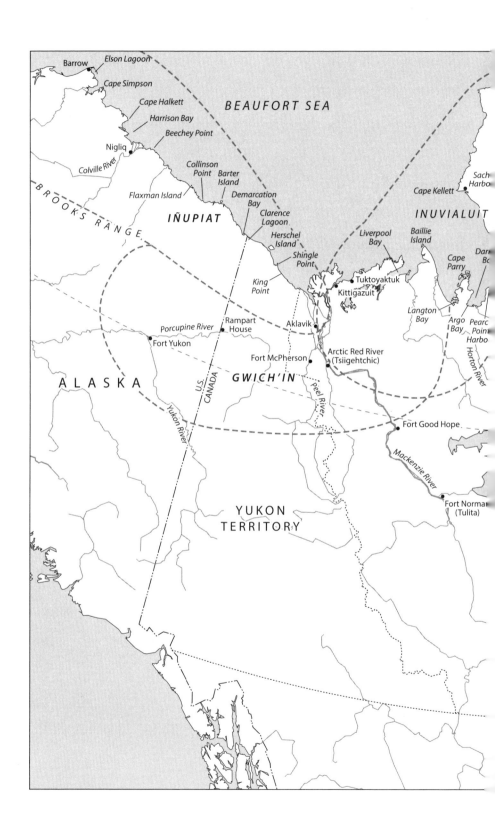